$O_x - 2 \cdot 99$

$2L = 2$

21

John Major

The Making of The Prime Minister

Bruce Anderson

FOURTH ESTATE · *London*

First published in Great Britain in 1991 by
Fourth Estate Limited
289 Westbourne Grove
London W11 2QA

A catalogue record for this book is available from the British Library

ISBN 1-872180-54-X

Designed by Lucienne Roberts, Sans + Baum
Typeset by York House Typographic Ltd, London
Printed in Great Britain by Clays Ltd, Bungay, Suffolk

Contents

Introduction

So Foul and Fair a Day

Just after six o'clock on Tuesday 27 November 1990, John Major's supporters were assembling in the drawing room of No. 11 Downing Street to hear the result of the second ballot for the Tory leadership. The tension was unbearable.

One hundred and twenty-seven hours earlier, John Major had launched his bid for the leadership. Since then, those in No. 11 had been working flat out on his behalf. The campaign had gone well; it had also been great fun. A few hours earlier, everyone in the room had been confident of victory – but now, fun and confidence were both forgotten. There was nothing more to do except wait and worry; everyone was a prey to anxiety. That morning, the figures had looked so encouraging. On the basis of the final, unpublished canvass returns, there was every reason to expect that John Major would win the leadership that evening.

Since then, certainty had drained away. By early evening, only one person in No. 11 Downing Street still thought that a second ballot win was likely. The rest of us had been overcome by end-of-campaign nerves. So, while beginning to realize how little sleep we had had, we were bracing ourselves for a redoubled effort in the two days leading up to the third ballot. Norman Lamont, in charge of the campaign, addressed his troops: 'We are in danger of losing momentum. As soon as the result's announced, let's all move back to Gayfere Street and get stuck into the Hurd vote.'

Statements had been drafted covering every contingency from outright victory to defeat. I handed Norman Lamont the victory one. He brushed it aside with an impatient gesture. 'We won't need that. We're not going to win today.' Drinks were available. Robert Atkins, the Sports Minister, was asked what he would like. 'Whisky,' he replied.

'Anything in it?'

'Yes. More whisky.' He took his drink to the window, and then sought relief from tension by gripping the window frame. He looked as if he was about to wrench the woodwork apart.

A calmer figure joined us, entirely unaffected by nerves, smiling and joking. If it had been anyone else, the rest of us would have found his light-heartedness irritating – but everyone was glad to see John Major looking so relaxed. Indeed, Mr Major had been asleep only an hour earlier; Norman Lamont had had to wake him. John Major was the one person in the room who had no doubts about the result. His team may have lost heart; he had not. He knew that he was on the verge of victory; he expected it that evening.

Suddenly, there was a call for silence. The result was imminent. John and Norma Major had been a few feet apart chatting in different groups. A second later they were standing side by side, clasping hands. A photograph of Cranley Onslow appeared on the television screen. Mr Onslow, as Chairman of the 1922 Committee, was in charge of the leadership election. Then he was speaking. 'Michael Heseltine, 131,' he announced. 'We've won,' yelled one member of the team, who was promptly instructed to shut up. Mr Onslow continued: 'Douglas Hurd, 56 – John Major, 185.' Everybody was yelling. We *had* won.

John Major's vote was two short of the number required for an outright win, but no one in the room believed that the campaign would continue. Indeed, the rejoicing had barely started when Angie Bray, the Major campaign's press officer, asked everyone to be quiet. Michael Heseltine was on television. He had instantly understood the result's significance, and with commendable speed and great dignity he emerged from his house in Chapel Street to address the waiting cameras. He made a brief, magnanimous statement conceding defeat. John Major immediately asked if someone could get Michael on the line. A moment or two later, Douglas Hurd was also on television: also conceding. The leadership contest was over; John Major was about to become Prime Minister.

Within two minutes, Margaret Thatcher arrived. She threw her arms around Norma Major, saying, 'it's everything I've dreamt of for such a long time. The future is assured; the future is assured.' It was a moving scene. Terence Higgins, who was standing beside the two ladies, was not alone in bursting into tears. Most of those present had been staunch supporters of Margaret Thatcher and had hoped that she would win re-election. But during an intense five-day campaign, there had been a transfer of allegiance. All thoughts had been focused on John Major, not on Margaret Thatcher, who had spent the last few days of her premiership clearing up and packing.

Now that she had arrived to join John Major's celebration, the revellers found their emotions torn. At one moment, they might be laughing away, only to catch sight of Margaret Thatcher, and find their eyes watering. Alastair Goodlad, the Deputy Chief Whip, found the right quotation to do justice to the conflict of emotions: 'So foul and fair a day.'

One person did not seem to feel the strain: Margaret Thatcher herself. She was the most composed figure in the room, gaily dismissing any references to her fate. 'Today is today, tomorrow is tomorrow,' she repeated. 'The policies will continue. The party can now have another eleven years.' One man tried to tell her what a heroine she was, but found himself unable to continue, because he started weeping. She treated him with that distant, slightly patronizing sympathy which the stronger sex generally displays towards the weaker sex on such occasions; how could a mere man be expected to keep a stiff upper lip? She was asked whether she would like to address the microphones and cameras banked up in Downing Street – but firmly rejected the suggestion. This was John's evening; she was not going to get in the way. Instead, she started to watch proceedings through the window, pulling back the net curtain in order to have a better view. Inevitably, all the cameras turned their attention to that moment of great pathos; her expression was both eager and sad. Someone told her that she was now on television; she at once stood back and let the curtain drop into place.

In one corner of the room, the Cabinet Secretary, Sir Robin Butler, and one or two others had discussed the next step: the timing of Mrs Thatcher's resignation from the premiership. At that stage, the assumption was that the third ballot would still have to take place, albeit as a formality: there seemed to be no provision in the rules to allow it to be cancelled. The question was whether Margaret Thatcher would have to remain Prime Minister until the Conservative Party had a new leader. However, it was pointed out that when Churchill became Prime Minister, Neville Chamberlain had stayed on as the leader of the Conservative Party – and indeed continued to hold that office until his death in December 1940. So there was a precedent, and if Mrs Thatcher were to resign the following morning, there could be no possible embarrassment to the Palace. The decision to send for John Major would be a formality.

Mrs Thatcher joined the discussion, and swept aside all remaining doubts. Of course she could resign in the morning: it was absolutely clear who was to succeed her – there was no need for any further delay. From the cheerful, almost hearty way in which she talked about 'going to the Palace in the morning', a casual listener, unfamiliar with the technicalities of the British constitution, would never have guessed that she was referring to her final journey as Prime Minister.

Mrs Thatcher and her entourage returned to No. 10. As they reached the foot of the staircase, Cranley Onslow arrived in No. 11. He was immediately surrounded by anxious enquirers. Was there going to be a third ballot. 'No,' he answered firmly, 'I've cancelled it. I'm sure I've broken all the rules, but what does it matter? What's the point of holding a ballot when there's nothing to decide? This is supposed to be the common-sense party.' With that, Mr Onslow stumped off upstairs to have a drink and offer his congratulations to the new leader of the Conservative Party.

The next morning, Mrs Thatcher and Mr Major both paid their visits to the Palace, and John Major returned to No. 10 the youngest Prime Minister of the twentieth century. He was also one of the least experienced and least well known. For some years, political insiders had been aware of his qualities – but until he had become Foreign Secretary, in July 1990, his name had meant nothing to the general public. Now he was his party's choice to succeed Margaret Thatcher, who had become Prime Minister at the General Election which brought him to the Commons as a fledgling backbencher. His rise to power had been almost as dramatic as her fall.

Acknowledgements

It was Jonathon Aitken's idea that I should write this book. Since then, he has monitored its progress with enthusiasm, amusement, and good advice.

Throughout the period of research and writing, I have been immensely fortunate in my adjutants. Claire Gagneux has been a magnificent secretary, researcher – and photographer. This project took much longer than was originally intended: she herself gave up much more time to it than she had ever intended. Her help was utterly indispensable to the entire project.

So was that of my publishers, Fourth Estate, whose tolerance never became entirely exhausted. I am very grateful to Vicky Barnsley, Jane Charteris, Debbie Licorish and Christopher Potter.

David Barbour and Anna Welch also helped with the research.

I am also immensely grateful to Mr and Mrs Major, both of whom found time in overcrowded diaries to cooperate with me. They cannot, however, be held responsible for the book's comments.

Ian Gilmour, Alan Duncan, Tristan Garel-Jones and Patrick Rock read most or all of the typescript. Each of them made valuable suggestions: none of them can be held responsible for any errors or misjudgements.

Alan Duncan's role went far beyond that of proof reader. He found me an office in Westminster – and during the entire six months which I devoted to this book, he gave up a great deal of time and energy to assist me, for which I am immensely grateful.

A large number of politicians, civil servants and friends of John Major also helped me. I would like to record my thanks to the following: Katy Altman, Rt Hon Julian Amery MP, Howard Anderson, James Arbuthnot MP, Jeffrey Archer, Jacques Arnold MP, Rt Hon Kenneth Baker MP, Harry Ball-Wilson, Rt Hon Lord Barber, Nicholas Bennett MP, Conrad Black, Lady Blatch, Angie Bray,

Graham Bright MP, Rt Hon Peter Brooke MP, Peter Brown, Tom and Yvonne Canter, Mrs Judith Chaplin, Rt Hon Alan Clark MP, Rt Hon Kenneth Clarke, QC. MP, Anthony Coombs MP, Michael Crick, Mrs Pat Dessoy, Piers Dixon, Alan Duncan, David Evans MP, Tony Ferri, Simon Fowler, Cecil Franks MP, Tristan Garel-Jones MP, Claire Gibson, Sir Ian Gilmour Bt, MP, Peter Golds, Alastair Goodlad MP, Sir Anthony Grant MP, Rt Hon John Gummer MP, William Hague MP, Dr Keith Hampson MP, Rob Hayward MP, Rt Hon Terence Higgins MP, Rt Hon Michael Howard MP, Bob Hughes MP (Harrow West), Rt Hon Sir Geoffrey Howe QC, MP, Rt Hon David Hunt MP, Rt Hon Douglas Hurd MP, Michael Jack MP, Clive Jones, Rt Hon Tom King MP, Julie Kirkbride, Barbara Kyriakou, Rt Hon Norman Lamont MP, Rt Hon Ian Lang MP, Rt Hon Nigel Lawson MP, Edward Leigh MP, Hon Mark Lennox-Boyd MP, Rt Hon Peter Lilley MP, Miss Jean Lucas, Rt Hon Sir Nicholas Lyell QC, MP, Rt Hon John MacGregor MP, Donald Macintyre, David Maclean MP, Terry Major, Will Manser, John Naples MP, Margaret Marshall, Hon Francis Maude MP, Rt Hon Sir Patrick Mayhew QC, MP, Rt Hon David Mellor QC, MP, Andrew Mitchell MP, Rt Hon Sir Peter Morrison MP, Rt Hon Tony Newton MP, Rt Hon Cecil Parkinson MP, Rt Hon Chris Patten MP, Rt Hon John Patten MP, Bernard Perkins, Michael Portillo MP, Sir Charles Powell KCMG and Lady Powell, William Powell MP, Rt Hon Malcolm Rifkind QC, MP, Rt Hon Richard Ryder MP, Caroline Robb, Patrick Rock, Mrs Gillian Shephard MP, Michael Spicer MP, Derek Stone, Sir Peter Tapsell MP, Rt Hon Norman Tebbit CH, MP, Andrew Thompson, Nicholas True, Andrew Tyrie, Rt Hon Lord Waddington QC, Rt Hon John Wakeham MP, Rt Hon William Waldegrave MP, Stephen Wall LVO, Barbara Wallis, David Wastell, Julie K. White, David Wilshire MP and Sir George Young Bt, MP.

Others wished to remain anonymous. My thanks are also due to the libraries of ITN and the Conservative Research Department, where Charles Forsyth made many efforts on my behalf.

A first book is also a suitable moment to acknowledge long-term intellectual debts. If I have any understanding of British politics, it has benefited immensely from many years' conversations with: Jonathon Aitken, Julian Amery, Peter Bauer, Paul Bew, Robert Blake, Nick Budgen, Alan Clark, Maurice Cowling, Robert Cranborne, Ian Gilmour, Dermot Gleeson, the late Ian Gow, Robin Harris, David Hart, Alexander Hesketh, Norman Lamont, Patrick

Mayhew, John O'Sullivan, Chris Patten, Richard Ryder, the late Peter Utley, John Whittingdale, David Willetts, and Perry Worsthorne. Again, none of them is to be held responsible for any lapses in this – or other – works.

Dedication

To my mother, Netta Anderson; and in memory of my father, James Anderson.

1 The Apotheosis of Margaret Thatcher

Mistress of the Battlefield

In May 1988, at the beginning of the tenth year of her premiership, Margaret Thatcher's position seemed impregnable; she was mistress of the political battlefield. With the exception of the post-Falklands, pre-election year 1982/83, she had never looked more in control of events or of her party, and not since the last months of Michael Foot had the official Opposition posed less of a threat.

The former Alliance parties were in even more of a mess. This was good news for the Conservative Party, which had spent much of the past thirty years worrying about a centrist upsurge. After all, the Tories lost the 1964 election and both 1974 elections not because Labour increased its vote significantly, but because former Tory supporters deserted to the Liberals. In the early to mid-1980s, the Conservatives appeared to have fresh grounds for anxiety about the centre parties, who had an obvious appeal to softer Tory voters alarmed by Thatcherite radicalism. At least during the brief period of Alliance successes, the traditional Conservative slogan, 'a Liberal vote is a wasted vote', had lost its potency.

Not after 1987. By then, gone were the high hopes of breaking the mould of British politics. The only things the would-be mould-breakers had managed to destroy were their own political careers. During the years when the Liberals and the Social Democrats were in partnership, Dr David Owen had been surprisingly good at conceal-ing his contempt not only for David Steel but for almost the entire membership of the Liberal Party. Since 1987, however, he had made up for it. As for the Liberals, they had entered a phase in which they were mainly preoccupied with changing their name every few months, as if they acknowledged their unworthiness to bear the name associated with Gladstone, Asquith, and Lloyd George.

During 1987/88, the Liberals and the SDP faced a stark choice: to form an electoral pact, or a suicide pact. This was not clear to Paddy Ashdown or to his lieutenants. They were behaving as if they had two main political opponents: David Owen, and the voters. For more than two decades, the powerphobic instincts of many Liberal activists had helped to blight their party's prospects. The new Liberal leadership was determined to encourage the full expression of those instincts.

By 1988, then, it appeared inconceivable that the centre parties could improve their position at the next election. Many Tory MPs slept more soundly, facilitating the maintenance of order in the Tory Party. At some stage, most prominent British politicians have found that their most dangerous enemies were not on the benches opposite them, but on the benches behind them. For long periods, this had been true of Margaret Thatcher. Her abhorrence of consensus had always extended to her own party, and so party management had often been a problem for her. She believed in leading from the front; this gave her foes the chance to stab her in the back.

Drying Out the Party

Margaret Thatcher won the leadership in 1975, not because she had won over a majority of Tory MPs to what came to be known as 'Thatcherism', but because they had lost faith in Edward Heath's ability to win elections. She was in an ideological minority in her own Shadow Cabinet.

Few of those in the majority took Thatcherism seriously. They thought it was mere rhetorical persiflage, which their leader employed only because of her inexperience and naïveté. Most of them assumed that if she ever reached No. 10, the realities of power would discipline and mature her. One or two of them, who had taken the measure of her stubbornness, knew that she would refuse to back down, and used to wonder what would happen then; they supposed that they would have to find some way of getting rid of her. Bend, or break; none of them thought that she might actually succeed – and then bend or break them.

From 1975 onwards, with considerable tactical skill, Mrs Thatcher set about gaining control of her own party and sidelining those senior figures who disagreed with her: 'the Wets', as they were later called. In this process, three factors came to her aid. First, the dissident grandees underestimated her, until it was far too late. There are analogies with Stalin, also underestimated by his senior colleagues. The difference is that they paid the price for their misjudgement in the Gulag or the execution chamber; the worst that befell Mrs Thatcher's opponents was deportation to the House of Lords. In 1975, shortly after Mrs Thatcher became Leader of the Party, Rab Butler, patron saint of the Wets, called on Chris Patten, then Director of the Conservative Research Department, and a Wet. 'This . . . ah, Thatcher woman,' said Lord Butler. 'We don't have to take much notice of her, do we?' In those days, many of these whom she later sacked from the Cabinet would have agreed with Lord Butler.

The second factor which helped Mrs Thatcher in her dealing with the Wets was that they were not good rebels. The Wets were wet. Most of them had been brought up in a tradition of party loyalty. Regarding themselves as the real political establishment, they found it impossible to behave like outsiders, scheming for power. To them, *she* was the outsider. It is interesting to speculate what would have happened if the Wets – Carrington, Gilmour, Prior, Pym, Soames, St John Stevas, Walker – had formed a septuple alliance, so that if Mrs Thatcher had tried to get rid of any one of them, all would have resigned. Leaving aside the difficulties with certain members of the group – not all Wets trusted all other Wets – most of them would have found such behaviour alien. The Wets would not – could not – hang together, so they were hanged separately.

There is one other name which might seem to belong with the other seven, and here we come to Margaret Thatcher's third advantage: Willie Whitelaw. The other Wets often made jokes about Willie, mocking his infirmity of purpose, nicknaming him 'Wobblelaw' and mimicking his bumbling manner of speech. They also saw him as their natural leader, exemplifying moderate, one-nation Toryism. By temperament as much as anything, Willie Whitelaw was never a Thatcherite. The word 'ideology' would never have crossed his lips except as a pejorative applied to political opponents. At least in private, over the whisky, he could also be pretty pejorative about Margaret Thatcher. So the other Wets assumed that if push ever came to shove, Willie would be on their side.

They were wrong. Willie was a grumbler, not a plotter. The grumbling was often a safety-valve, an outlet for the stress involved in remaining faithful to a leader with whom he had little rapport. When push did come to shove, Willie Whitelaw sided with Margaret Thatcher. Some of the Wets still blame Willie for his passivity, and now think that they had overestimated him. It could also be argued that they had underestimated him. In two successive radical administrations, Ted Heath's and Margaret Thatcher's, Willie Whitelaw provided the ballast and the bottom. In both cases, his leader was departing from Tory traditions and straining the loyalties of many of the party's supporters. In each case, Willie played an indispensable role in keeping everything together. Neither Mr Heath nor Mrs Thatcher has ever understood how much they owed to him. Had a mild stroke not forced his resignation, Margaret Thatcher might still be Prime Minister. The role of anchor was one for which Willie was suited. Although he is a much cleverer man that the bluff exterior would suggest, he was happier as adjutant than he would have been in supreme command. In a crisis, his instinct is not to act as leader, but to look for a leader.

He did not help the Wets, even though many of them were his friends, while those appointed to replace them were often not his friends. His motives were a complex mixture of caution, chivalry, loyalty, devotion to duty and cowardice. In all this, he enabled Margaret Thatcher to make the transition from the era of Carrington and Soames to the era of Lawson and Tebbit.

This was an era and a new Tory Party in which the rest of the Wets found themselves ill-at-ease. Class and the generation gap played a part in this; the leading Wets could not build up a significant following among the younger backbenchers because they were too grand and too old, though old in experience more than in years. The Wets used to become profoundly irritated by the way in which younger Conservatives, who seemed to think that their party's history began with Mrs Thatcher's election as leader in 1975, derided both the Heath and the Macmillan Governments as part of a post-war drift towards socialism. The Wets were right; many Thatcherites had come to believe in a caricature version of the Macmillan and Heath administrations (though Mr Heath himself seemed happy to collaborate in a rewriting of history than made him out to be an appeasing crypto-socialist). However, ignorance of the past may have worked to the younger set's advantage. The Wets lived too much in the past. They remembered Macmillan well, and many of them had played key roles under Heath. Scarred by the failure of those premierships, they were unable to bring to the glad, confident morning of 1979 the optimism of those who attributed the failures of Macmillan and Heath, not to insuperable problems, but to weakness of character.

In 1979, most Wets had come to believe that the problems of the British economy were insoluble, and that the country could be governed only in condominium with the trade unions. Hence the Wets' dismissive impatience with Margaret Thatcher, who appeared to have no conception of the scale of the difficulties facing her. Perhaps that was just as well. If one is tackling insoluble problems, it is an advantage to know no history. Parsifal succeeded where the greater knights faltered and failed. As Mrs Thatcher set out on her quest, the Wets seemed more and more out of touch, less and less able to come to terms with the new order Mrs Thatcher was creating, in the Tory Party as in the country.

Then there was the problem of Mr Heath, the Wets' ally and albatross; nothing could flourish under his shadow. A sour, bitter figure, consumed by bile and spite, he blighted the Wets' prospects. Throughout the 1980s he was often unwittingly useful to the Tory Whips' office; many a potential rebel against the Government was deterred by the thought of going through the same lobby as Ted Heath.

For all these reasons, and because of Mrs Thatcher's own success, the Wets' influence declined sharply after 1982. Several of the younger MPs who had originally shown Wet inclinations made their peace with Mrs Thatcher and joined the Government.

The Problems of Love-Hatred

The decline of the Wets, however, did not eliminate all Margaret Thatcher's problems with her party. Her style of leadership always precluded an easy life – not that she ever dreamed of seeking one. Rarely has any political leader aroused such strong emotions, among her supporters as among her enemies. There were plenty of Thatcherites who would have died for her; on the other wing of the party, she often provoked an equal intensity of hatred. Even those who were devoted to her could often find her infuriating. 'I love-hate that woman,' said one of her closest advisers and friends, on the day of the 1987 election. 'I can't tell you how much I love-hate that woman.' Every minister who served under Mrs Thatcher would have understood that comment. She always had the defects of her qualities.

Her strength stemmed from her divine discontent. To the final moment of her eleven years, six months, and twenty-four days as Premier, Mrs Thatcher was dissatisfied with the Government. She never really trusted either her colleagues, or the country. She feared that if she eased up on the ministers, they, being mere men, would slump in an armchair with a glass of whisky, agreeing how insoluble everything was. Equally, she suspected that if she let up on the country, it would slip back to its bad old ways; trade union general secretaries with their feet up on the furniture in No. 10 would be sending out for more beer and sandwiches.

At the heart of her vision of government was restlessness, dissatisfaction and an intolerance of compromise. To the end, the establishment embrace never captured her; there was a perennial element of abrasiveness in her dealings with her colleagues. She blamed them whenever she had to make concessions to political reality or give way to *force majeure*. There was always the thinly-disguised criticism that if they had done their job properly, a better solution could have been found. So she rarely achieved stability in her relations with senior colleagues. The case of Geoffrey Howe was the most extraordinary, but over the years she wore out the patience and tolerance of many of her closest colleagues.

From her bruised and battered ministers, tales would filter down to the backbenchers as to how impossible she could be. When everything was going well, this only added to her reputation as the strongest man in the Government. In periods of difficulty, the fact that Margaret Thatcher was so difficult to work for was held against her. A large number of Tory MPs always regarded her with more respect than affection, and more admiration than confidence. There was a widespread hankering after a less relentlessly combative approach. It was held against her that in any air journey with Captain Thatcher, the 'fasten seat-belts' sign would never be switched off. When that point was put to her, she retorted : 'If you fly high, you need your seat-belt on.'[1] Many Tory MPs would have preferred to fly lower, and more safely. There was a recurring complaint that a Government which was constantly increasing spending on health, social security and education could never win credit for doing so; this was blamed, justly, on the Prime Minister's style. A lot of Tory MPs would have like to see more sensitive, more political government, but knew that this would never come about under her.

---

1 *Sunday Telegraph*, 25 March 1990.

Electoral Success and an Economic Miracle

By the summer of 1988, however, many of these political anxieties had been assuaged by that most potential of remedies, electoral success. In those days, Tory MPs would say complacently that as Margaret Thatcher had won three elections, she was entitled to lose a fourth, without for a second believing that she would ever draw on that entitlement. Almost all her parliamentary colleagues were serenely confident that she would achieve a fourth victory. Tory MPs based this assessment not only on their opponents' weaknesses, but on the economy's strength. At that stage, most Tory MPs greatly admired Nigel Lawson.

Mr Lawson's economic recovery began in 1986, swept the conservatives to re-election in 1987, brushed aside 'Black Monday' – as the Stock Exchange *dégringolade* of 26 October 1987 – and culminated in the 1988 Budget, which reduced the top rate of income tax to 40 per cent and the standard rate to 25 per cent. Throughout the post-war years, most economic commentators would have regarded such low rates as unattainable in modern conditions. Mr Lawson proved them wrong, while simultaneously increasing public spending and repaying government debt. By any standards, that was a considerable achievement. One or two monetarist commentators had expressed worries about the economy overheating, but at that stage few Tory MPs took any notice. They were far more relieved that the fears arising from Black Monday – of crash, recession, and even depression – had proved unfounded.

In the summer of 1988, indeed, a substantial majority of Tory MPs broadly accepted the claim that Mrs Thatcher, Sir Geoffrey Howe and Mr Lawson had brought about an economic miracle.[2] They could adduce plenty of evidence in support of this thesis. Inflation seemed more or less under control, as did the public finances. The economy was growing strongly, with the supply side performing particularly well. In 1986 and 1987, while unemployment had been falling rapidly and real wages rising, profitability was high and industrial investment was increasing rapidly.

Ministers were therefore able to argue convincingly that there had been a decisive break with the bottlenecks and rigidities which had characterized so much of post-war British economic history. Ten years previously, Britain had had a high inflation/low growth economy: over-taxed, over-borrowed, and over-manned. Now, everything was transformed. One or two of Mr Lawson's colleagues even

---

2 This author's columns in the *Sunday Telegraph* expressed a similar view.

entertained the possibility that he might have abolished the business cycle. Many Tory supporters could see no reason why Britain should not enjoy a permanent regime of low inflation, steady growth, tax cuts, rising living standards, judicious increases in public spending, *plus* – for any government delivering all that would have an obvious claim on the voters' gratitude – the Conservative Party permanently in power.

Of course, even those Tories who thought that the business cycle might have been abolished were under no illusions about the mid-term cycle. By 1988, the parliamentary mid-term was approaching, with its usual problems of electoral disillusion and by-election losses. The Government was already in trouble over social security and on health, the issue Labour had exploited so effectively during the 1987 election campaign. As a result, John Moore's ministerial career was slipping into terminal decline (something for which John Major must bear some responsibility).

For all that, in the spring and early summer of 1988 it was almost impossible to find a Labour MP with hopes of winning the next election, or a Tory MP who feared losing it. As the summer recess of 1988 approached, the Tory Party's main worry was not the economy, the community charge, or the health service. It was the political health of Neil Kinnock, and the danger that Labour might replace him with an effective leader. At that time it seemed by no means impossible that either – or both – Mr Kinnock or Mr Ashdown might lose the leadership of their parties. The idea that Mrs Thatcher could be unseated would have appeared risible. She was already the longest-serving Premier of the twentieth century. There was apparently no obstacle to prevent her from setting further records.

Yet even the weakness of the Labour Party, which then looked likely to extend her term of office, ultimately worked to her disadvantage. By mid-1988, all the forces which brought her down were already gaining momentum. They fell under three general headings; patronage, policies and personalities.

2 Patronage and Policies

Patronage: the Tinder of Discontent

Many Americans envy the British system of drawing the executive from the ranks of the legislature; it does produce a more battle-hardened breed of ministers. But it is also a built-in source of instability. Trouble arises when too many legislators want jobs in the executive; the difficulty increases in proportion to a government's longevity in power. This is not a new problem, as the case of Peel and Disraeli demonstrates. *Pace* Michael Heseltine, Benjamin Disraeli could still claim to have committed the most spectacular act of revenge by a disgruntled seeker after office. For all that, life was easier for earlier Tory Premiers, right up to the 1950s and early 1960s. At that time, a significant number of backbenchers could still be described as 'Knights of the Shires', who never thought of seeking ministerial office.

Their successors, the esquires of the suburbs, have no such inhibitions. Very often, they think of themselves as professional politicians. As in any other profession, they wish to climb the ladder of advancement. There are 85 ministerial posts in the House of Commons, and though this might seem to be an excessive number under an administration notionally in favour of reducing the role of government, it provides for less than a quarter of the Parliamentary Conservative Party. Some MPs respond to their exclusion from office with good grace; others do not. With every passing year, their resentments increase, in some cases to an intensity of gnawing rancour equally destructive of peace of mind and of loyalty. The number of malcontents increases after every reshuffle. Those who catch the selectors' eye for promotion tend to be promising youngsters who have not yet had time to grow frustrated; those who are dismissed often become instantly frustrated.

On the Tory backbenches there are 75 former ministers, few of whom left office of their own choosing. Most ministers – most prime ministers also – are summoned away from the table with their appetite still unsatisfied. Some sacked ministers subsequently displayed exemplary loyalty to Margaret Thatcher; John Moore and Michael Neubert both helped run her re-election team. Others never forgave her. Margaret Thatcher went out of her way to dispense courtesy and attention to Tory backbenchers. Where her predecessor had been cold and snubbing, Mrs Thatcher was always ready with a little touch of Maggie in the lobbies: enquiries as to a child's exam results, a wife's illness and so on. In earlier years, this had done a great deal to boost her popularity, but as time went on, it could not counteract the malign effects of the patronage problem.

During Mrs Thatcher's last year as Premier, the disgruntled ex-ministers and the frustrated non-ministers numbered at least half the Parliamentary Party. Of itself, this would not have provoked a revolt against the leadership, but it did mean that when things started to go wrong for Margaret Thatcher, the Conservative backbenchers were full of the tinder of discontent. When ministers made mistakes, Tory MPs who thought that they themselves ought to have been ministers did not react charitably. Some backbenchers felt less and less interest in the survival of an administration which had committed the ultimate crime of ignoring their claims.

Given the nature of the modern MP, it may be that the British system places a constraint on the length of premierships. In the long fullness, towards the end of the 1990s, it will be interesting to see how John Major copes with this problem.

Policies: the Bleached Bones of Controversy

The route the former Prime Minister's troops took in their eleven-year march under the banner of Thatcherism is easy to trace; all along it lie the bleached bones of political controversies. The GLC; the social security review of 1985/86; GCHQ; water privatization: in its day, each had seemed to jeopardize the Government's standing. In each case, the danger passed. All those issues are now as irrelevant as last year's food scare.

By 1988, a pattern seemed to have been established. The Government would announce some new proposal which liberal opinion had hitherto regarded as unthinkable and which violated the post-war consensus. Liberal commentators would instantly declare that it would have a catastrophic and irreversible effect on the Government's popularity (as if they cared), while the windier Tory back-benchers would start wittering in protest. The measure would then be guillotined through the House of Commons, with the Tory Whips' office doing everything possible to deter backbench rebels. The Opposition would denounce these tactics as an affront to democracy: every opposition does; every government uses them. There would be trouble in the House of Lords, protests from interest groups, big demonstrations – perhaps violence. By then, even loyal backbenchers and ministers would be wondering aloud – on lobby terms, naturally – whether it was a good idea. Then the bill would finally stagger through to Royal Assent. Six months later, no one would be able to remember what all the fuss had been about.

So as Mrs Thatcher entered her tenth year in office, most Tory backbenchers had become inured to the cycle of radical change leading to criticism and unpopularity but ending in acquiescence. Meanwhile, Labour's behaviour was reinforcing the Tories' complacency.

The adversarial nature of British politics may be the despair of high-minded critics, but the present system cannot function without adversarialism. Any government's business managers can see short-term advantages in having a weak opposition, but wise politicians know that over the longer term, good government needs strong opposition. Legislation will stand up to the rigours of the real world only if it has been forged in the crucible of the Commons. For the first part of the 1987 Parliament, there was no such forging.

After the 1987 election, the Labour Party took the next eighteen months off. The psychological blow of losing that election after their hopes had been raised, plus the prospect of an indefinite extension of their imprisonment in Opposition, hit Labour hard. Also, the Labour Party's practice of electing its Opposition Chief Whip mili-tated against an effective Commons performance. Whenever he was under threat, Derek Foster, the Labour Chief Whip, showed cun-ning in organizing his own re-election; that was the limit of his effectiveness. Under his lack of direction, Labour's whipping effort was miserably inadequate. He could not get his troops to the front line.

Labour's incompetence caused it to miss many opportunities to harass and embarrass the Government, but there was one great uncovenanted benefit. Over-confidence led ministers into error.

Even if it had faced an effective Opposition, the Government might still have introduced the community charge. But there is no doubt that an optimistic assessment, based partly on Labour's weakness, fortified ministers in their decision to press ahead and override the political risks.

A Charge Too Far

In early 1991, the community charge ended in retreat and fiasco. This does not mean that the decision to introduce it was unjustified. There was a good case for the community charge. Something had to be done about local government in Britain, much of which had been in a mess for many years. The public which it was supposed to serve took little interest in its proceedings; at many local government elections, the turn-out lost its deposit. The minority which could be bothered to vote did so almost exclusively on national issues.

Out of apathy, malignity. The purpose of local government is to provide efficient services and enhance civic pride, but in many cities, the Labour councillors who were almost permanently in power held efficiency and civil pride in equal contempt. They divided their time between trying to run their own foreign policy, pouring scorn on the values and way of life of their respectable residents, and squandering money. All this did great damage. The class warriors were helping to create an underclass, for a version of Gresham's Law came to operate in many cities: the bad drove out the good. The type of local authority which behaved as if its aim was to own every house in the borough while employing every inhabitant would end up with acres of empty, decaying properties; thousands of demoralized council tenants who had been virtually encouraged to run up large rent arrears; and high unemployment, as penal rates drove businesses to the suburbs, where they were joined by anyone else who could find the means of escape. Naturally, all this was accompanied by vandalism and crime, which breed on demoralization. So bad local government was not just wasting money: it was wasting people, blighting lives.

In seeking to rectify this and produce decent local government, it was no use starting with structures: that had been tried, and had failed. Without democratic participation, and thereby accountability, no structure will work. The key to accountability, as the American colonists had realized, is a link between taxation and representation, without which democratic government cannot flourish. In the mid-1980s, there was a tripartite system of local government finance consisting of the rate support grant, the domestic rate, and the business rate. All three elements were seriously flawed.

The domestic rate was an inequity founded on a fiction. Any property tax is inequitable, for the bills have to be met out of income, and many property owners – particularly pensioners – have low incomes. In theory, of course, the rateable value of a property was based on it potential rental income. But that is where fiction enters the equation, for the market in rental property had been destroyed. When domestic rates were first introduced around the beginning of the century, local authorities supplied water, gas and electricity; it did not seem unreasonable to pay for property services with a property tax. Today, most local authority services are personal. Above all, however, the domestic rating system might have been designed to produce representation without taxation. By 1987, there were 35 million voters, but only 18 million ratepayers. In some inner-city authorities, only a quarter of those eligible to vote paid rates. That was no basis for accountability.

At least the domestic ratepayer had a vote; the business ratepayer was defenceless. Every time a left-wing local authority put up the rates by 50 or 60 per cent, businesses were deterred, driven out or destroyed, and jobs lost in the inner-city areas which most needed them.

Then there was the third leg of the tripod: the rate support grant. The RSG was at least as complicated as the Schleswig-Holstein question, which had been understood only by three professors, one of whom was dead, another mad, while the third had forgotten. Indeed, the rate support grant may had been absolutely beyond the comprehension of the human intellect, for it was calculated on a basis of rateable value plus sixty-eight different criteria of need, each one of which gave scope for endless uncertainty and haggling. In 1987, some local authority treasurers were still negotiating with the Department of the Environment over their RSGs for 1985/86.

To all that must be added the various measures which the Conservative Government had taken to curb local authority spending, all of them more or less admitted to be short-term alternatives to a fundamental reform based on accountability. Each of these palliatives, sired by expediency out of ad hoc – there seemed to be about one a year – had its own mind-breaking complexity.

In short, we had a system which was without rationale, unfair, destructive of the quality of life in our cities, and almost as incomprehensible to the experts who had to administer it as to the electors who could not be bothered to vote in it. Naturally, previous attempts had been made to reform local government finance. In 1976, Sir Frank Layfield produced his report. This had been expected to come up with a solution; it did not do so. Layfield's analysis of the difficulties involved in any change was always more persuasive than his arguments in favour of it. In a cautious, tepid manner, the report endorsed a system of local income tax. It also provided all the evidence necessary for the argument that as the problem of local government finance was insoluble, we might as well stick with the present system.

That was the conclusion generally drawn from Layfield, and it was one which may wise, cynical Tories shared. They took the view that the ratepaying beast was used to its burdens, and that as long as no one foolishly stirred it by by ill-advised pledges to remove them, it would continue to plod on at a level of grumbling well below the threshold of electoral danger. The problems of introducing a new tax had been well summarized by Louis XIV, who said that whenever he made an appointment, he created one ungrateful man and twelve disappointed ones. In any tax change in which the same amount of revenue has to be raised, there will be losers as well as gainers. The gainers' thanks take the form of 'about bloody time'; the losers are not so polite. The infamous Scottish rate revaluation of 1985, for instance, did not increase the Government's takings: for every person paying more, someone was paying less. No one would have thought that from the Scots ratepayers' reaction.

None of this would not have surprised Michael Heseltine, Mrs Thatcher's original Environment Secretary. In 1979, his hope was that after the Tories' first Budget, there would be banner headlines: 'Taxes Down!' Somewhere in column nine of page four, meanwhile, it would be announced that the domestic rate was to stay. Most reasonable men would have agreed with Mr Heseltine; there a sensible government would have left it. Mrs Thatcher is not a reasonable man; hers was never a sensible government. She was determined to get rid of the domestic rate, and regularly committed her party to doing so.

Her motives in this were not necessarily altruism towards the inner cities. She objected as much to them being Labour-run as she did to them being badly run: she would not have acknowledged the distinction. Above all, she felt acutely the unfairness of the rates; she was always attuned to the grievances of her middle-class supporters. Mrs Thatcher never accepted that the problem of the rates was insoluble. When it came to supposedly insoluble problems, her instinct was to take a bludgeon to the ministers and officials who had diagnosed them as such. Even so, she might not have acted were it not for Scotland.

Over time, property values change, so if a tax is to be based on property, that property ought to be regularly revalued. The English legislation recommended a revaluation every five years or so, but did not make it obligatory – much to ministers' relief. The latest revaluation for domestic rates had been in 1973, and had the rating system survived, it might have been the last one; no sane government would have agreed to the turmoil involved in a further revaluation. Things were different in Scotland; they generally are, due to the separate legal system. No doubt to flaunt the difference, some brute or blackguard of a parliamentary draftsman had included in the relevant Scottish legislation a provision that there *had* to be a revaluation every five years. The then Scottish Secretary, George Younger, complied. This was foolish of him. It would have been wiser to amend the provision, on any old pretext; better to endure a few weeks' parliamentary embarrassment than the agonies of a revaluation. If Michael Heseltine had been Scottish Secretary, there would have been no revaluation.

There was one, however, and an immediate revolt by the upwardly-revalued, a lot of them Tory supporters enraged that Scotland had been treated in this way when England was exempt. It was no use pointing out to such persons that a separate legal system, of which they were generally proud, did entail separate laws – and that the rate burden had been redistributed, not increased. Such arguments were brushed aside. Many Scottish Tories thought the whole thing was an English plot – and anyway what was Maggie doing adding to their bills, when she had promised to abolish the rates? Widespread fury among Scottish ratepayers was the largest single factor in the loss of eleven Scottish Tory seats in 1987.

Even before the election, Malcolm Rifkind, by then Scottish Secretary had sounded the alarm, and Mrs Thatcher was aware of the urgent need to placate the Scots. Meanwhile, William Waldegrave, who was then chairing the DoE committee examining local government finance, had devised the community charge. In that first, tentative phase, it was thought of as a possible burden-reducing supplement to the domestic rate, not as a substitute for it. Margaret Thatcher had no use for tentative supplements. In her attempts to avert disaster in Scotland, she wanted a firm proposal which would honour her pledge to abolish the domestic rate. The result was the community charge.

An Appalling Way to Introduce Change

The new charge was introduced to meet a political deadline, with the principle being enunciated before the details had been thought through. Its acceptance by the Government was due less to its own merits than to the defects of the alternative proposals. If a property tax, a local income or sales tax, and one hundred per cent funding by central government were all ruled out, the community charge was the only remaining option. So a new tax was produced in haste to meet a political deadline which took no account of administrative requirements. This was an appalling way to bring about such a major change. However, it was probably the only way and the only circumstances in which local government finance would ever have been reformed.

Once launched on the process of change, the Government decided to recast all three elements of the previous system. First, the domestic rate was replaced by the community charge. In future, all adults would make a flat-rate contribution, set by the local authority, with rebates available for the less well-off. However, as at least half of local authority spending would continue to be funded by central government partly out of income-tax receipts, there would still be an element of progressive taxation.

Second, the business rate was in effect nationalized. It became uniform throughout the entire country, and future increases would be limited to the rate of inflation. This *was* an altruistic move by the Government, for it meant that the impact of business rates was redistributed in favour of the inner cities at the expense of the shires and suburbs.

Third, the rate support grant was simplified. In future, to make it easier for all those involved to understand the system, only six criteria of need would be used instead of the previous sixty-eight.

But the authors of the community charge could not find a way of eliminating precepting. Under our present system of multi-tiered local government, higher-level authorities pass on certain charges to the rate- or chargepayers of lower-level authorities by sending them a bill, known as a precept. As long as precepting continued, the good housekeeping efforts of lower-tier authorities could be sabotaged by their seniors' extravagance; this made it harder to achieve accountability. Even with precepting, however, the overall result of the Government's reform was a much simpler system which seemed to have considerable advantages over the muddle it replaced. However, there were difficulties in converting the theoretical gains into practical benefits, especially political benefits.

The first problem concerned fairness. From the beginning, perhaps the most potent argument against the community charge was that under it, a Duke would pay the same as a dustman. The fact that the Duke also paid the same as the dustman for water, electricity and gas was ignored: they had not previously been charged for at progressive rates. The fairness controversy was exacerbated by the rate at which the new charge was levied, which came as an unpleasant surprise to the Government. Local authorities, especially Labour ones, took full advantage of the muddied waters of the changeover to increase their spending, and their revenue. In order to meet the increased spending which accompanied the introduction of the community charge, it would have been necessary to increase rate bills by 35 per cent. As the local authorities had calculated, the high community charges were blamed not on them – as an equivalent rate increase would have been – but on the Government.

When the community charge was first mooted, the Government had been accused of redistributing income to Tory-voting ratepayers at the expense of non-Tory-voting non-ratepayers. If this had been the calculation, it went badly awry.

It Seemed a Good Idea at the Time

Throughout the north of England, especially in the small towns, one can find terrace after terrace of owner-occupier houses, which had had a low rateable value with bills of no more that £150 to £200 per annum. There were many such cases in the Ribble Valley constituency. Some of these households now found themselves paying three times as much in community charge. As they were the swing voters in a score or so of marginal constituencies, their protests had a considerable impact on Tory MPs.

From the beginning, a significant number of Tory backbenchers were unhappy about the community charge; some were genuinely worried about fairness, others merely about votes. One of them was Michael Heseltine, an asset to any rebellion, who could claim that he had been against the whole idea from the start, and who had indeed scotched various embryonic proposals for a community charge during his time as Environment Secretary. There was also Sir George Young, one of the most high-minded of Tory MPs and therefore particularly good at pressing the charge of unfairness, as well as Colonel Michael Mates, a skilful organizer, and Sir Rhodes Boyson, who warned of political dangers with the authority of impeccable populist credentials.

Colonel Mates devised a variant of the community charge based on 'banding', whereby the less well-off would gain at the expense of the better-off. Sir Rhodes wanted central government to take over responsibility for all spending on education; this would have cut the charge bills by about half, and so drawn its sting. Under Mrs Thatcher, ministers refused to accept either scheme. They took the view that banding would undermine the principle on which the charge was based; while the Treasury was horrified at the loss of revenue implicit in the Boyson scheme. To Nigel Lawson, it seemed to justify all his worst fears; opposition to the community charge had not been confined to the backbenches.

From the beginning, Mr Lawson and many Treasury officials were unhappy about the whole idea. Lawson the politician thought it foolhardy, while Lawson the Chancellor – with the support of his officials – correctly foresaw one consequence of the new charge: constant pressure on the Treasury to find cash to mitigate its effects. In 1989, Mr Lawson did what he could to resist calls for additional funding, taking a tougher line even than Mrs Thatcher. At one stage during the negotiations with Chris Patten, then Environment Secretary, Mrs Thatcher sought to modify Mr Lawson's intransigence by saying, with prescient if unconscious dramatic irony, 'We do still want to be here in five years' time.' But Mr Lawson's hand could be forced only as far as £300 million, a wholly inadequate figure. 'Haven't got it', he would keep on repeating, 'Haven't got it, haven't got it'. Since then, there have been several further raids on the Treasury, culminating in the March 1991 Budget, and its switch of £4.7 billion from local central government by means of a 2.5 per cent increase in VAT.

In sum, the electoral and financial consequences of the community charge were much more serious than those who favoured it's introduction had foreseen. This was due to the Government's economic difficulties. Around 1988, it was widely assumed that by the time the first community charge bills came through letter boxes, there would have been further cuts in the standard rate of tax. The resurgence of inflation put paid to that, as well as greatly increasing mortgage-payers' burdens. In many households, the increase in mortgage costs was far more of a problem than the community charge – but the charge became a focal point for discontent.

If by the spring of 1991 interest rates had been around 8.5 per cent while the standard rate of income tax had just been reduced to 20p, the community charge would have survived, as would Margaret Thatcher. Inflation did for them both. By 1989/90, assisted by inflation, the new charge was adding to the Tory Party's problems in the opinion polls – and to Tory MPs' difficulties on the doorstep. In the local elections of May 1990, the unpopularity of the community charge was to some extent disguised by good Tory results in London, and by Party Chairman Kenneth Baker's skill in highlighting them: his three-borough trick. By then, even Margaret Thatcher had come to doubt the wisdom of introducing the charge; a majority of Tory MPs agreed with that assessment.

In the early 1970s, as the new Northern Ireland Office was set up in Northern Ireland, one of its officials, a classicist, devised a coat of arms and a Latin motto, now sadly lost. But the motto's translation does survive, and would also have served for the community charge: 'It seemed a good idea at the time.'

Policies II: the History and Geography of Europe

Nothing in Britain's history had prepared us for membership of the EEC. The very fact that we could describe it as 'joining Europe' illustrates the difficulty: we do not even accept that we have the same geographical status as the rest of the Community.

We certainly have a different history. Within living memory, apart from the irrelevant exception of Ireland, all the other member states have had their government overthrown in a coup, have been invaded by their neighbours, or have invaded their neighbours. Many of their boundaries are the creation of recent peace treaties, while their institutions are the product of revolution; in certain cases, several revolutions. On the continent, a constitution is some-thing written on paper, and therefore easy to tear up. Whatever the arguments for or against a written constitution in Britain, an unwrit-ten constitution could only have emerged from long centuries of political stability. Our institutions – at any rate in England – were last reshaped by revolution in 1689, and by war in 1066. We have reasons to be grateful to the Channel.

Equally, again due to this deep-rooted stability, in English politics at least, public expressions of nationalism amount to little more than the Union flag draped over a table at a Tory public meeting in the village hall. The modern Tory Party consists of both John Bull nationalists and economic liberals; the combination, healthy for both groups, has created a formidable political force. Because of this, English nationalism cannot be exploited by radicals or reactionaries. It is harnessed to conservatism, to buttressing the establishment and the institutions of the state. No one need feel threatened by English nationalism; outside the fantasy world of the millenarian left, hardly anyone does.

On the continent, as one would expect of societies at an earlier stage in political evolution, nationalism is much more potent and much less controllable. Nationalists and economic liberals only rarely co-exist, which often means that the nationalist ticket is available to inadequately house-trained politicians such as M. le Pen.

If we define a 'real country' as a fusion of state and nation capable of playing a significant role in world affairs, then apart from Britain, there are only two real countries in the EEC: France and Spain.[1] Italy is still no more than a geographical expression, neither state nor nation. Denmark, Portugal, Holland and Greece are all ex-coun-tries; the rest are never-were countries except, of course, for Ger-many. It is now becoming a country again with consequences that are unforeseeable – above all by the German bien-pensantry – but which are bound to be interesting.

Most of our EEC partners have good reason to distrust their neigh-bours, their institutions, or themselves. It is understandable that they should seek a supra-national security. The British have no such incentive. Our suspicions are aroused, not by our own national institutions, but by any suggestion of a European super-state, with its overtones of Philip II, Louis XIV, Napoleon and Hitler.

Because of this divergence, for the past twenty years, Britain's

1 Even Spain's credentials could be ques-tioned. Rarely if ever has a country's political elite drawn its concept of national indentity so exclusively from the future, and so little from the past.

relationship with the European Community has been mired in intellectual incoherence. Many of those who were strongly in favour of British involvement in the EEC practised systematic intellectual dishonesty, giving the electorate a false account of the implications of British membership. Mr Heath's successful application for membership was presented to the public in terms of economic self-interest plus jingoism; this would be a chance to brace those foreigners up a bit with some much-needed leadership. Allegations from the anti-Europeans that Britain would be committing itself to a progressive loss of sovereignty and, ultimately, to Euro-federalism were dismissed with scorn. If any company promoter had issued such a misleading prospectus, he would have ended up in goal.

The persons involved in those economies with the truth, however, were not necessarily congenital liars. They had concluded, first, that there was no alternative to British membership of the EEC and, second, that it would be too risky to seek the British people's agreement to membership on the basis of an honest account of its consequences; the voters might say no. So the Euro-minded custodians of the public interest convinced themselves that, on this occasion, there was a higher morality in deceit. Self-righteousness and Euro-enthusiasm often go together.

Two powerful influences inspired some of our politicians to disregard geography, defy history and economize with the truth. The first was war. Many members of the political generation responsible for British entry had fought in the last war. Their foremost political priority was to work for peace and to ensure that no third, final catastrophe overwhelmed our civilization. It is easy to understand how the wartime generation reached this conclusion. We Europeans had a wonderful heritage of painting and poetry, of churches and cuisine – and of political philosophy. We were unrivalled for our insights as to how man ought to live; we were also, it appeared, incapable of living together. In 1945, in the ruins of old Europe, there did seem powerful grounds for believing that only European union could save European culture.

The second, reinforcing influence was economic decline. In the 1960s and 1970s, when the temporary soldiers of 1945 became ministers, they found themselves wrestling with seemingly intractable economic problems, while Britain was outperformed by the member states of the EEC. Real countries or not, they had real economies. The British ministers, despairing of a domestically generated economic recovery, concluded that the only way to match the EEC's dynamism was to join the EEC.

To all this must be added the influence of post-imperialism, and of Dean Acheson. His comment that Britain had lost an empire but not yet found a role was widely resented, but even more widely influential. A large section of the political elite accepted his diagnosis: Europe was their cure.

Margaret Thatcher's Europe

It was not Margaret Thatcher's cure. The focus of her concern was narrower; she always instinctively distrusted the politics of grandiloquence. While never a little Englander, she always believed that Britain's problems could be solved only by the British. To seek to pass our responsibility for our destiny over to foreigners would be as ineffective as it was immoral.

Mrs Thatcher distrusted broad-brush economics. She would have been suspicious of these who argued that merely by joining the EEC, we could become as successful as the rest of the EEC. If our problems were caused by an over-large public sector, over-mighty trade unions, low productivity and profitability, and the lack of an enterprise culture, these were matters we had to sort our for ourselves, whether or not we joined the EEC. Equally, if the EEC budget were so organized that Britain would be penalized for its success as a global trading nation and for the relative efficiency of its agriculture, there would inevitably be a large financial downside to British membership; the benefits were harder to quantify.

Mrs Thatcher was never more than a lukewarm European, attracted by the idea of free trade, but unmoved by the European ideal. Indeed, at one moment during the 1975 referendum campaign, she hinted at an ambivalent attitude towards continued British membership – but that impression was quickly contradicted. Then, as later, it would have been impossible for the leader of the Tory party to be opposed to membership of the EEC. Such a stance would have outraged too many powerful interests in industry, in the City – and on the Tory benches. The Tory Euro-enthusiasts might have been a minority, but they were an indispensable minority, and they would have been prepared to split the party.

Margaret Thatcher therefore had to make the best of British membership, and seems to have managed to convince herself that the free-trade advantages outweighed the defects. During the first years of her premiership, she did fight a series of battles with the rest of the Community over the size of the British contribution to the EEC budget. At the time, this issue seemed to be disrupting not only Britain's membership of the EEC, but the entire Community, and some of the resentments from that period have lingered on to poison Britain's relationship with Brussels. After Mrs Thatcher reduced one of her early Euro-summits to rubble, Sir Ian Gilmour, then the deputy Foreign Secretary, commented wearily: 'She will insist on treating heads of government as if they were members of her Cabinet.'

Paradoxically, the contributions row also helped to consolidate the UK's membership of the EEC. First of all, the issue itself had to be resolved: no British government could long have tolerated such a drain on the public purse. Second, the argument was about details, not fundamentals: about the size of our membership contribution, not the principle of a membership contribution. Third, as the Community was largely paralysed by the budget row, there was no opportunity for the Commission to alienate Britain by any federalizing proposals. With every passing year, the British economy became more integrated with the EEC, so that the withdrawal option became less and less plausible.

By the mid-1980s, Margaret Thatcher herself seemed to have established a *modus vivendi* with the Community, though she never for a moment fell under its spell. Her relations with other Community leaders improved. She and Giscard had loathed one another, and her dealings with Helmut Schmidt were equally fraught. With Helmut Kohl, there was a considerable improvement, though their personalities were too different to allow much rapport. Curiously enough, she and President Mitterrand found *entente* easier; it helped that M. Mitterrand, who has a good eye, was fascinated by Margaret Thatcher the woman. '*Cette femme Thatcher,*' he told Roland Dumas on his appointment as France's Euro-Minister, '*Elle a les yeux de Caligule, mais elle a la bouche de Marilyn Monroe.*'

In 1984, the British budget issue was resolved. In 1988, at Brussels, Mrs Thatcher accepted a deal on the Common Agricultural Policy, after a discussion that was to have fateful consequences for Geoffrey Howe. Increasingly, British ministers were able to boast about what good Europeans we were becoming: how much better we were than most of the rest at complying with the judgments of the European Court *et al.*

There was a positive development. In Article 8 of the Treaty of Rome, signed in 1957, the European Community had committed itself to achieving a 'single market' – one in which there would be no intra-EEC trade barriers – within 12 years. For years, that commitment gathered dust. Then in 1985 Lord Cockfield arrived in Brussels.

The Arthurian Legend, the Single Market and Jacques Delors

Arthur Cockfield – 'the Arthurian legend' – had no track record as a Euro-enthusiast. During the British contribution dispute, he at one stage advocated withholding Britain's payments. But in Brussels, he took up the cause of the single market with all the zealotry of a convert. He brought to this his formidable powers of intellect, application and persistence, buttressed by an apparent indifference to harmonious personal relations. In his willingness to trample on the feelings of others to secure an objective, Arthur Cockfield exceeded Margaret Thatcher. It often seemed that the aspect of his job he most enjoyed was the opportunity it gave him to travel around Europe rubbing governments' faces in unpleasant truths.

Lord Cockfield; quickly decided that a single market could not be achieved in a Europe of different currencies and tax regimes. To him a single market need a single economy, which in turn meant a single state. Margaret Thatcher, horrified by this, quickly lost faith in Lord Cockfield, she thought he had gone native. But this did not prevent her from endorsing the Single Act: the 1986 legislation which was accepted by all member states and created the framework for the single market. She did this because her enthusiasm for the extension of free trade under the Single Act and single market outweighed her doubts about its federalist aspects.

The Single Act significantly increased the role of majority voting in the EEC's decision making process, thus diminishing the national governments' power of veto. It had clear federalist implications. But this was hardly a new development. The EEC had been theoretically committed to federalism ever since its inception, and the Treaty of Rome itself is full of federalist sentiments. In 1985/86, Mrs Thatcher took the same view adopted over the years by many British politicians in their dealings with the Community: that it was safe to sign the Single Act, because its federalist passages were no more than grandiose vagueness; the foreigners did not mean what they said.

Some foreigners, however, did mean it – especially Jacques Delors, President of the European Commission since 1985. M Delors, a French social democrat steeped in *dirigisme* and mercantilism, was not a noted enthusiast for markets. He accepted the single market in its Cockfield version because it provided a powerful impetus towards federalism. He also devised two ways of supplementing that impetus. The first was the 'social charter', an attempt to palliate the capitalist rigour of the single market by introducing a social democratic framework of workers' rights throughout the Community. This won the support, not only of left-wing politicians in all the EEC countries, but of a large number of German interest groups. Throughout Germany, there was considerable anxiety about 'social dumping'. By this was meant the ability of poorer member states to undercut German firms, both by paying lower wages and by avoiding many of the burdensome social costs and obligations imposed on German industry. The Germans chose to ignore the argument that so-called 'social dumping' is a poor country's only hope of competing with its prosperous rivals.

In Margaret Thatcher's eyes, the social charter not only undermined the single market: it threatened to restore to British trade unions, via Brussels, the powers and privileges which she had gone to such trouble to remove. She hated the whole idea.

EMU and ERM

The real threat, however, came less from the social charter – which was still in a vague, embryonic form – but from economic and monetary union (EMU). The EEC had always been in favour of EMU; the Werner Report, published in 1970, had envisaged its completion by 1980 at the latest. By the mid-1980s, cynical observers had come to expect that EMU would happen on the day all pigs were supplied with wings. Then came M. Delors.

Fortified by Lord Cockfield's arguments, Jacques Delors pushed ahead with specific proposals for EMU, and in 1989 the Delors Report was published, setting out proposals for a three-stage transition to EMU. Stage I was anodyne, but Mrs Thatcher was not alone in absolutely opposing stages II and III: they found little support anywhere in Britain.

Mrs Thatcher faced two difficulties in her campaign against M. Delors. The first was that she could not follow her strongest instincts, which would have been to denounce the whole notion of EMU. She was not able to do that because for years her Government had officially been committed to EMU. She could not suddenly announce that she had never believed in it, and had only pretended to do so because she had assumed that the foreigners did not mean it either. Now someone was trying to fit wings on the pigs, and we were confronted by the consequences of two decades of hypocrisy and intellectual incoherence.

The Prime Minister's second difficulty concerned the exchange rate mechanism (ERM) of the European monetary system (EMS).[2] The purpose of the ERM is to secure a large measure of exchange rate stability among its member countries. As their currencies are in effect aligned to the Deutschmark, this should force all participants in the ERM to exercise a German level of monetary discipline and counter-inflationary zeal – though in France and Italy, the ERM's rigours were abated during the 1980s by the survival of exchange control and restrictions on capital movements.

From 1979 onwards, three groups of Tories were attracted by the idea of joining the ERM: the Europhiles, the pragmatists and the pessimists. The Europhiles were as eager as ever to sign up for anything with 'European' in its title. The pragmatists argued that if counter-inflation was the Government's goal, why not deploy the state-of-the-art anti-inflationary weapon: the Bundesbank? The pessimists, confronted by apparently endemic inflation, feared that no British government would have the political will to deal with it. The only solution was to call on outsiders to do the job for us. Ironically, among the pessimists' ranks in the late 1970s was Nicholas Ridley.

None of this had any weight with Margaret Thatcher. Unlike the Europhiles, she disliked entanglement in and surrender to EEC institutions, especially on anything as central as monetary policy. She also disagreed with the pragmatists' assessment, for Margaret Thatcher, though a monetarist, was also a politician who wanted to win elections. As such, within a framework of tight monetary policy, she wanted to retain control of domestic interest rates. In the early and mid-1980s, the case for doing so was so reinforced by the fact

---

2 Technically, Britain has belonged to the EMS since its creation in March 1979 – but until we joined the ERM, our membership of EMS was on a par with French membership of NATO.

that the money markets regarded sterling as a petro-currency, so that movements in the oil price tended to have a divergent effect on the pound and the Deutschmark.

Margaret Thatcher's greatest disapproval, however, was reserved for the pessimists. She refused to accept their conclusion that she and her Government could not be trusted to deal with inflation. She found the thought of relying on foreigners to discharge such a basic duty of government repugnant. In her view, she was a counter-inflationist or she was nothing.

Though Mrs Thatcher may have opposed the ERM, she was unable to say so in public. Her freedom of manoeuvre was restricted both by pressure from Cabinet colleagues and by her own past statements. From the mid-1980s onwards, largely in order to pacify Mr Lawson and Sir Geoffrey Howe, she had stated that Britain would join the ERM 'when the time was right'. It quickly became apparent, however, that the 'time was right' formula was not a policy: it was an attempt to use sticking-plaster to cover an abyss. Mrs Thatcher would reiterate the commitment through gritted teeth, her lack of enthusiasm manifest in every gesture, and then dwell in loving detail on the preconditions that would have to be met before we could join. In their statements, Sir Geoffrey Howe and Mr Lawson would be fulsome in their enthusiasm for the ERM. With every utterance, it was clear that for her the time would never be right, while for them it had long been right. The situation was risible. The Government had no policy.

During the last phase of Margaret Thatcher's premiership, it became increasingly hard to disentangle European issues from questions of personality – and in particular, from Mrs Thatcher's relationship with Mr Lawson and Sir Geoffrey Howe. This of course greatly added to the unease on the Tory backbenches.

The Fat Boy and a Diet of Brussels

Tory MPs' unhappiness was increased by the 1989 Euro-election campaign, which was abominably mishandled. The Tory Party's problem was to combat mid-term apathy and discontent among its own supporters, many of whom saw the Euro-election as a good opportunity to give the Government a much-deserved kick in the pants. So of course would Opposition supporters. The turn-out was bound to be low – in the event, 37 per cent – so the Tories' task was to persuade its hard core to vote. Given that objective, the campaign was a lamentable failure.

In any well-run Tory election campaign, one essential ingredient is fear. Waverers have to be frightened at the thought of what will happen if the other lot get in. So someone in the Tory Party has to play the role of the Fat Boy in *The Pickwick Papers*: 'I wants to make your flesh creep.' In the Euro-campaign, this would always have been a stiff task, for two reasons. First, the irrelevance of the European Parliament: many Tory supporters could see no point in voting for the second chamber of Strasbourg town council. Second, hard-line Tories tend to be Euro-sceptics; as they are not convinced that there ought to be a European Parliament, they are reluctant to acknowledge its legitimacy at the ballot-box. Among better-informed Tories, those doubts were only reinforced by the Party's Euro-MPs and candidates. A majority of them were Christian Democrats at best, with only a marginal interest in British conservatism and nil loyalty to Margaret Thatcher.

So the Fat Boy would have had his work cut out. He was not even deployed. Instead the Tories ran a specious campaign, whose fatuity is best summarized by the poster advertisement: 'Stay at home on June 15th and you'll live on a diet of Brussels.' That type of clever-clogs gimmickry may win plaudits at advertising agents' conventions but it has no purchase on real voters in the real world. The Tories' failure in the Euro-campaign was seized on by the party's Euro-enthusiasts as evidence that the PM's curmudgeonly attitude to Europe was electorally damaging. This was also Neil Kinnock's conclusion. After the Euro-election, the leader of the Opposition, by then in the habit of taking his opinions from the opinion polls, decided that Labour could win votes by seeming more pro-European than the Tories. The Euro-election offers no evidence in support of that view. It was a typical mid-term result, with an 8.5 per cent swing against the Government – moderate by by-election standards – and a local government by-election turn-out. The Government's failure was due to its general unpopularity and to a wretched campaign, denying the Tories the advantage they might otherwise have derived from superior local organization.

Mrs Thatcher herself took little part in the election: she was too busy running the country. In her absence, Tim Bell played a major role. Tim Bell is a lively fellow, but he is an advertising man, not a politician. So the true lesson of the Tories' Euro-campaign was not that the PM's line on Europe was unpopular, but that advertising men should not be allowed to run election campaigns. The back-room boys should stay in the back room.

The Euro-campaign added to Mrs Thatcher's problems on Europe. Most Tory MPs have no strong feelings about the EEC, so many of them also seek the guidance of the opinion polls. When Mrs Thatcher's rating were high, her handbagging approach was popular on the Tory benches. When her aggressive style seemed to be damaging the party's standing, Tory MPs were inclined to give credence to the Europhiles' claim that many of our problems in Europe were created by her refusal to be diplomatic. At all times, a majority of Tory MPs, equally opposed to withdrawal and federalism, simply wanted to maximize the advantages of membership and minimize its disadvantages. Few of them understood the formidable obstacles in the way of that deceptively common-sense policy or the well-nigh impossibility of adopting an *à la carte* approach to the EEC.

That failure of understanding worked against Mrs Thatcher. In 1989, with a Euro-election lost, trouble on the ERM, no policy on EMU, Mr Lawson resigning and Sir Geoffrey Howe moving into internal exile within the Government, the fault-line on Europe was more and more apparent. This seemed to threaten not only the loss of the next election, but a breach which would wreck the Tories' prospects for years to come. Commentators were already drawing parallels with the split over the Corn Laws; that had kept the Tories out of power for twenty years.

Two years previously, no one would have dreamt that Mrs Thatcher would ever encounter political trouble over foreign affairs. Especially by comparison to Neil Kinnock, her mastery was self-evident. Now Europe, the scene of some of her earliest triumphs, had returned to haunt her.

3 Heseltine, Howe and Lawson

Nonentities and Galley-slaves?

Throughout Margaret Thatcher's premiership, her Cabinets were often characterized as a collection of timorous nonentities working in galley-slave conditions. The reality was more complex. Certainly, Margaret Thatcher was a dominant Prime Minister, and also a domineering one. More ruthlessly than any previous peacetime Premier, she used the power of her office to control the Government. But she did not always get her own way. It was possible for strong ministers to stand up to her, and she respected those who did so, though that was not always apparent from her immediate reaction.

Equally, the Cabinet as a whole could thwart her. It did so over public spending in the early 1980s, and throughout her premiership it inhibited her on Europe. Not even Margaret Thatcher could succeed in substituting Prime Ministerial fiat for Cabinet government. However, even if she could occasionally be restrained, her ministers never found her a comfortable colleague. She used her control over the Cabinet agenda to impose her views; she also used her power to hire and fire. On specific issues, she would interfere, override, insist, veto; sometimes she would shout and insult and bully. At times, almost all her ministers found her behaviour hard to take. Here again, she was the victim of her success, for a long period in office creates twin problems in the relationship between ministers and Prime Ministers.

The first is the danger that they will get on one another's nerves. The process of working together for long periods in conditions of great stress can bind people together; it can also magnify petty irritations into fully-blown grievances. That was the effect that Margaret Thatcher often had on her colleagues. The second danger is that over time, strong ministers will develop their own agenda, and find it more and more irritating to have to defer to the PM. Margaret

Thatcher's style of government was bound to maximize that irritation.

Michael Heseltine, Geoffrey Howe and Nigel Lawson are three very different men, but in each case, both factors were at work. By the end of her premiership, despite their differing opinions and their divergent temperaments, they had made common cause: to do her down.

Michael Heseltine

It was the most dramatic resignation in British political history. He swept straight from the Cabinet room to the TV cameras, then strode across Whitehall – the television crews bustling along behind – to prepare for a press conference at which he would make plain his distaste for the way Margaret Thatcher ran her Government. Michael Heseltine had blasted a hole in that Government's side, at a moment when it was already in trouble. There seemed to be parallels with the resignations of Nye Bevan and Joe Chamberlain (in 1903); both had been a prelude to electoral defeat and a long period in opposition for the parties concerned.

Leaving aside the manner, there was nothing fundamentally surprising about Michael Heseltine's decision to resign. He is not to be compared with Nigel Lawson or Geoffrey Howe; he had never been a close associate of Mrs Thatcher's. She inherited him. He then made it impossible for her to dispense with him; she never chose him. Ted Heath had given Mr Heseltine a Shadow Cabinet post, but when Mrs Thatcher drew up her first Shadow Cabinet, she would have demoted him had he not been due to make a second reading speech within a few hours. So he survived, but not necessarily for long. At that time, a demotion for Mr Heseltine would not have aroused controversy: he had only been a junior minister in the Heath Government, and had no irresistible claim to a Shadow Cabinet post.

He quickly staked such a claim. In October 1975, Harold Wilson was still the heavyweight champion of British politics. Despite its small Commons majority, the Labour Government was very much in charge; the Tories, under their inexperienced female leader, seemed a long way from power. So the Tory Party met at Blackpool in an uncertain mood; morale was in short supply. Michael Heseltine set out to provide some. He turned what ought to have been a routine speech on industry into a masterpiece of demagoguery, which won him instant fame and made him virtually the second most popular figure in the Tory Party. From then on, it became an annual performance, part of the build-up towards the leader's speech on Friday afternoon.

There were those who affected to despise his performance, regarding it as meretricious; there were some who were just plain jealous. But most sensible Tories, without themselves succumbing to Mr Heseltine's oratory, saw its value as part of the rich tapestry of party conference week. Noel Picarda, humorist and erstwhile Tory candidate, used to perform an impromptu cabaret at party conferences. This included a sketch of two elderly peers leaving the rostrum after one of Michael's Nuremberg performances, one saying to the other: 'You can shay what you like about that fella Hesheltine, or brilliantine, or whatever it is you call him. He can't half find the party's clitoris.'

He may have delighted the representatives, and perhaps especially the ladies; this did not allay Mrs Thatcher's suspicions. She saw him as a flashy, unreliable character and an unreconstructed Heathian corporatist. Even if she could not sack him, she was determined to keep him away from the key economic departments, and in Opposition she quickly reshuffled him from Industry to Environment. Mr Heseltine did not like her either; if the pair of them had been dogs, they would have crossed the street to fight one another. But he would have forgiven her anything if only she had made him Secretary of State for Industry.

Michael Heseltine would have been the most interventionist Industry Secretary of all time. This would not necessarily have involved legislation, or even increased expenditure. In the departments he ran, he used to pride himself that whenever he proposed a spending increase he would invariably offer to finance it with an equivalent cut in some other programme. He did have better grounds for insisting that he was neither a corporatist nor a PSBR Wet than for his later claim not to be a federalist.

By intervention, Michael Heseltine meant personal intervention. His methods would have owed far more to Lord Beaverbrook than to Tony Benn, or to Mussolini; one could envisage Mr Heseltine setting off at the head of a convoy of lorries in a piratical swoop on some underused resources. Michael Heseltine has great confidence in his own persuasiveness in face-to-face encounters. He would have arranged meetings with industrialists and relied on the force of his personality to sweep everyone along. It is easy to imagine the sort of conversation that would have taken place between Mr Heseltine and, say, Lord Weinstock. 'Arnold, what do you want? An Earldom? Senior steward of the Jockey Club; be a member of White's? I'll fix it, I'll fix the lot. In return, I want you to set up the following three industries by the end of next week . . . '

Mrs Thatcher was wrong to lump Michael Heseltine in with Ian Gilmour and Jim Prior – but she never displayed any interest in differentiating between varieties of intervention. She continued to employ Michael Heseltine for the same reason that Lyndon Johnson continued to employ J. Edgar Hoover, though she would have used different language: 'Better to have him inside the tent pissing out, than outside the tent pissing in.'

The PM was determined to limit Mr Heseltine's influence: that meant keeping him away from the DTI. So six years of Tory Government elapsed. Margaret Thatcher appointed four Industry Secretaries, none of them Michael Heseltine. It was clear to the meanest intelligence that however long she served as Premier, and however many Industry Secretaries she ran through, she would never turn to Michael Heseltine.

Then came Westland. Even at the time, it was hard to understand how the affairs of a small West Country helicopter company could have led to one Cabinet minister walking out and another being forced from office; to the Law Offices almost resigning, with the Attorney-General threatening to send the police into No. 10 – and finally, to a crisis which threatened the Prime Minister herself.

In retrospect, Westland becomes even more incomprehensible. At the time George Younger put it well. Everyone involved, he said, 'had got overcooked'. Michael Heseltine became more overcooked than anyone; it is hard not to bracket his behaviour over Westland with the Mace incident.[1] Michael Heseltine may have marched out of the Cabinet; he had no intention of marching out of history. Like General MacArthur, he intended to be back, at least as a Cabinet minister, and preferably as Prime Minister. So he set about planning his return. From 9 January 1986, when he resigned, until 28 November 1990, the day he returned to the Cabinet, Michael Heseltine was running for office: an electoral gestation-cycle even longer than the one inflicted on American politicians.

There were other comparisons with America. Michael Heseltine, a

---

1 In 1976, Mr Heseltine picked up the Mace in the House of Commons during a debate on the Shipbuilding Bill. He had been incensed by some chicanery on the part of the Labour Whip's office. Though he did not actually swing it round his head, his behaviour did give currency to the nickname 'Tarzan'.

self-made multi-millionaire, was able to finance his operations. Neither the expenditure nor the staff was significant by US standards; in Britain, they were unprecedented. His almost five-year campaign cannot have cost him less than £1 million and much of this was spent in the party's interests. For Mr Heseltine made himself a slave to the rubber-chicken circuit. Night after night, all over the country, whenever a Tory organization or a Tory MP wanted him to speak, he would be there. He used to say that the worst part of it all was facing a group of twenty or thirty who blithely expected him to be able to perform for them in Little Piggleton parish hall exactly as he would have performed for 4,000 people in the Winter Gardens, Blackpool.

Michael Heseltine did not go through all that out of masochism, or even in a desire to surpass Jeffrey Archer. Little Piggleton was part of his strategy. He knew that he had to project himself to Conservative MPs as someone who could win elections. It would require a popularity crisis, if not indeed an election defeat, to unseat Margaret Thatcher. In such circumstances, he would have an advantage: he could not be held responsible for the Government's predicament. That and his election-winning gifts might help him to override whatever doubts his fellow MPs would have.

In all this, Mr Heseltine had one major problem: Margaret Thatcher. Not least among her reasons for wanting to go on and on was her desire to eliminate any prospect of Michael Heseltine succeeding her. If she had won an election in 1991 or 1992, he would have been approaching his sixtieth birthday. Realistically, with every passing year his prospects would diminish. So he had to hope that she failed. While doing so, he had to pretend to be loyal, especially around election times. If he were to jeopardize the party's chances at the polls, he would never be forgiven. Indeed, any overt act of treason – even one that did not alarm the voters – would infuriate many of the backbenchers whose votes he needed. So Mr Heseltine had a ticklish task; no wonder he pounded the motorways in search of speaking engagements. Could anyone prepared to spend his Friday evenings in the Little Piggletons possibly be a traitor to his party?

In a conversation with Michael Heseltine during the run-up to the 1987 election, I said that Mrs Thatcher would not only win that election, but the one after it as well. Mr Heseltine reacted as if I had stuck a red-hot needle into him. 'No,' he cried, 'she couldn't. The party would never stand for it, the party would never stand for it!' He was proved right. In the early phase of the 1987 Parliament, however, that did not seem likely. In those days, he would cheerfully proclaim that he was destined for obscurity. He never believed it.

The Big H Mob

As that Parliament advanced, his belief that he had a future was buoyed up by a psephological calculation. It seemed increasingly unlikely that the Tories under Mrs Thatcher could improve on their 1987 performance – only 42.3 per cent of the vote. That had translated into a 100-seat majority merely because the Opposition was divided. Since then, Neil Kinnock had won back a large slice of the centre vote, and Paddy Ashdown seemed determined to help him hang on to it. The best the Tories could hope for was a small overall majority, in which case the party would be looking for a leader capable of inspiring a revival; who better than Mr Heseltine? This would apply *a fortiori* if there were a hung Parliament, and therefore the certainty of an early second election. Moreover, Mr Heseltine could always hope that when Tory MPs came to appreciate the weakness of the Government's position, he would not have not wait until the election.

Michael Heseltine had always been good at winning the loyalty, respect and liking of those around him. That was true, for instance, of Norman Lamont, one of his Ministers of State at Defence. Mr Lamont's views on Europe and on the economy were not Michael Heseltine's, but he enjoyed working with Michael, and developed an abiding regard for him. That was typical of most ministers who had worked for Mr Heseltine. But his associates usually spice their affection with an ironic appreciation of his foibles. While he was Environment Secretary, publicity was given to a notorious criminal known as 'Big H'. The nickname was promptly applied to the Secretary of State. 'Il Duce' is also current in Heseltine circles.

Initially, however, Il Duce had seemed reluctant to exercise his charm on the Tory Parliamentary Party. 'Ted and Margaret hadn't any friends, and that didn't stop them,' he would point out. 'So why should it bother me?' His natural inclination was to sling the party on to the back of a camel and gallop into the sunset, but this was tempered by advice from less Rudolph Valentino-like characters. As soon as Mr Heseltine resigned, he gathered around him a small group of MPs who from then on acted as his staff officers. They encouraged him to cultivate the troops, and organized a succession of lunch and drinks parties at which Tory MPs were wooed.

These staff officers were able backbenchers who for one reason or another had never been made ministers. First there was Dr Keith Hampson, loyal to Mr Heseltine over many years. Dr Hampson had been a rising young man in the Heath era, and never lived that down. He could not bring himself to make sufficient rhetorical concessions to placate the new proprietress. Nor did his being such an effective PPS help him as much as it might have done had his boss been anyone but Michael Heseltine. He also had an unfortunate court case. A prosecution which should never have been brought deservedly failed, but messy incidents do not help to win promotion.

Then there was Michael Mates, who had been a Colonel on the General Staff. While working as Willie Whitelaw's PPS – a role for which his burly, ursuline physique ideally suited him – he fell out with Airey Neave, then Mrs Thatcher's Chief of Staff. A secretary in Mrs Thatcher's office resigned, and Col Mates became *persona non grata*.

Messrs Hampson and Mates were the core of the team. Dr Hampson was a first-class researcher and speech-writer. Mr Heseltine also recruited Julian Haviland, late of ITN and *The Times*, to help with drafting. Peter Tapsell also became a Heseltine associate; they had known each other since Oxford. In 1979, Michael Heseltine knew whom he wanted as his Parliamentary Secretaries, but realized also that there was no point in asking for them: herself would never agree. His choices were Peter Tapsell and Kenneth Baker.

Such are the vicissitudes of politics – but Peter Tapsell would almost certainly have been too grand to accept. Grandness, indeed, is Sir Peter's weakness. He has the port and carriage of a senior minister – in the Far East, he is widely thought to be the Chancellor, or the Foreign Secretary, or both – but he was never prepared to make the little sacrifices necessary to smooth his path to office. Along with Jonathan Aitken , Richard Body and Peter Horden, he forms a little group of outstandingly able senior Tory backbenchers who have never held office (Mr Aitken still has time); sadly, however, Peter Tapsell wanted office much more than any of the others.

He also ensured his exclusion from it. In opposition days, Mrs Thatcher, who regarded him as unsound, had been persuaded to overcome her reservations and make him a junior Treasury spokesman. Some of Peter Tapsell's friends went to considerable efforts in that persuasion process. Alas, Peter found juniority irksome; within a few months, for no particular reason, he resigned. Over the next few days, Mrs Thatcher greeted his advocates with a hard look and a 'so there!' expression. Having thrown away political capital on a lost cause, they felt badly let down. 'You have torpedoed your political career,' Norman Lamont told him, while restraining himself from adding, 'and done mine no good either.'

To be fair to Peter Tapsell, he realized that he would be unable to serve in a Thatcher Government: the disparity of hers was too great. Equally, however, in those days, Peter Tapsell thought that he had no need for pettifogging accommodations: great events would sweep him to his deserts. As the years passed, he came to pin his hopes on that personification of a great event, Michael Heseltine. Others also joined the team. There was Sir Neil MacFarlane, who had never forgiven Mrs Thatcher for firing him as Sports Minister. Finally, there was William Powell. Mr Powell, a former Chairman of Cambridge University Conservative Association (CUCA), has the temperament of a Whip, and is a perceptive observer of his colleagues. An MP since 1983, he would sooner or later have been given office, but after 1987 he grew pessimistic about Mrs Thatcher's electoral prospects, and switched his allegiance to Michael Heseltine. No one in the Heseltine camp had as much knowledge of the parliamentary party.

Big H Turns to Modern History

But Mr Heseltine did not spend all his time plotting or speaking. He also wrote books, with the help of Dr Hampson and Mr Haviland. Two appeared[2]: a third, on Japan, is now postponed *sine die*. They are at least as good as most efforts by opposition politicians. They also skilfully avoided personalities.

When the first work appeared, low persons in search of sensationalism rushed to the index to look up 'Thatcher, Margaret' and 'Westland'. There was no mention of Westland, and all the references to Mrs Thatcher were respectful banalities. In the second book, the PM was tongue-in-cheeked. Mr Heseltine informed us that 'Margaret Thatcher proclaimed Britain's European destiny in her speech at Bruges'. If there was any passage in the Bruges speech which could, to the literal-minded ignoramus, convey such an interpretation, she meant it as little as Michael Heseltine believed it.

---

2 *Where There's a Will* (1987) and *The Challenge of Europe: Can Britain Win?* (1990).

The key to the books' approach to contemporary events is to be found in the introduction to the first one. Mr Heseltine quotes Raleigh: 'Whosoever in writing a modern history shall follow truth too near the heels, it may haply strike out his teeth.' However, the books are evidence against a charge frequently made against Mr Heseltine: that of opportunism. Especially on Europe, commitment takes precedence over calculation. He makes no attempt to temper his enthusiasm for the EEC to the doubts of the majority of Tory backbenchers. Admittedly, and most unconvincingly – usually after setting out paragraphs of lucid, pro-federalist arguments – he does deny that he is a federalist. But the average backbencher knows all about the duck test (if it walks like a duck, and quacks like a duck, it is a duck). Mr Heseltine quacks like a federalist.

Once out of office, most senior ministers gradually diminish in stature. New faces fill the gaps round the Cabinet table; new names emerge into stardom. As time presses, ex-ministers suffer the ex-factor; their achievements belong to the past. Finally, the day comes when there is nothing left except elder statesmanship. Michael Heseltine postponed that fate. By 1989 it seemed certain that whatever Mrs Thatcher might think, he would come second or first in the ballot to replace her; second place would guarantee his return to the Cabinet. But his hopes were set on victory; increasingly, he did not think he would have long to wait.

Geoffrey Howe

Sir Geoffrey Howe has had a seminal influence on modern Conservatism. For the last quarter of a century, the dominant strand in Conservative Party thinking has been economic and social liberalism, now endorsed by John Major. Sir Geoffrey is entitled to as much credit as anyone for propagating those ideas from the 1950s onwards.

Post-war Conservative economic thought was not just a matter of the transition from Keynesianism to monetarism. It is possible to distinguish three phases: defensive, exploratory and triumphalist. The defensiveness was the product of defeat. After the Tories' crushing losses in 1945, most of the rising men in the party decided that it could recover only by identifying itself with the aspirations of ordinary people and becoming the party of welfare and mass prosperity. In future, Tories would have to base their thinking on Keynes and Beveridge. Hence the era of Butler and Macmillan, in which the

Tory Party not only won three elections but created the social conditions for future, even more radical, successes. From the 1950s onwards, the gradual transformation of British society made the Labour Party's electoral task progressively harder, and ultimately enabled Margaret Thatcher to lead her *petit-bourgeois* revolution. So in their defensive operations, Butler and Macmillan laid the demographic foundations for the triumphalist phase: Thatcherism. They might have been as reluctant to claim the credit as the Thatcherites were to admit a debt of gratitude.

Thatcherism also had intellectual foundations. Here again, there was insufficient attention to debts of gratitude. Thatcherism did not come into being overnight in 1974 when Keith Joseph realized that hitherto he had not been a real Conservative. Over many years, the Institute of Economic Affairs had done much of the preparatory work; so had Sir Geoffrey Howe and the Bow Group. Geoffrey Howe was one of the founders of the Bow Group in 1951 and remained its intellectual patron. In its great days, up until the end of the 1960s, the group was a conduit, bringing bright youngsters into politics and popularizing *inter alia* practical free market economics.

As they were too young to bear the scars of the 1945 defeat, Bow Groupers were happy to espouse notions such as deregulation and the rolling back of the state. They also supported the social and penological reforms of the 1960s: legalizing homosexual behaviour, abolishing the death penalty, *et al*. In some cases, their equivalents of Keynes and Beveridge were Wolfenden and Roy Jenkins.

The Bow Group was much less Etonian and aristocratic than any such Tory organization would have been before the war. So it can claim not only to be the progenitor of economic and social liberalism, but the precursor of classlessness. It was an intellectual pathfinder in the second phase of post-war Tory evolution, when the party moved from defence to attack. Many of the measures which Mrs Thatcher later enacted were first aired by Bow Groupers, and by Geoffrey Howe.

From the beginning, it was clear that Sir Geoffrey would play a leading role in any Thatcher government. From the beginning also, there were tensions between the two. This was partly due to temperamental incompatibility. Their working relationship would have resembled another episode in the saga of hostility between Celt and Saxon – except that Sir Geoffrey, the Welshman, played the Anglo-Saxon, and Mrs Thatcher, though English, the Celt.

Like all Celts, Margaret Thatcher is impatient with the constraints of reality. As PM, in private meetings, she used words as a stimulus and a spur, to open up new and exciting possibilities, but also to goad her duller-witted colleagues into action. She generally classed Sir Geoffrey with the dull-wits. His virtues are patience, thoroughness and doggedness. Over the years, that tortoise saw off many a hare. As much as any official, he believes that politics is the pleasure principle, administration the reality principle. No proposal that has been scrutinized by him would have unforeseen pitfalls.

But the former PM would get fed up with all that pedantic harping on pitfalls, and his way of speaking used to irritate her. Sir Geoffrey's slow, drab delivery did not enliven his subject-matter. He never learned the knack of putting his most important point in the first half of his first sentence. With Mrs Thatcher, this was essential: no one could be sure that there would be a second half, let alone a second sentence.

She was not good at controlling her irritation. Early on in their long partnership, Mrs Thatcher had fallen into the habit of being rude to Geoffrey Howe; the rudeness continued until his final Cabinet meeting. Those who witnessed such scenes for the first time were often shaken, and concluded that if this partnership were a marriage, it would quickly end in divorce – or murder. When neither occurred, it was generally assumed that this was one of those relationships incomprehensible to outsiders, but which fulfils a need in each of the two participants. She would shout at him – perhaps it was as well there was no crockery around; he would merely blink and then resume his suede-shoed exposition. Over time, others around them got used to the rudeness, though a senior ambassador was heard to complain that it was embarrassing as well as interesting to have the PM draw him on one side so that she could rubbish the Foreign Secretary.

However, all this was storing up trouble. Over the years, there was a steady, corrosive accumulation of mutual resentment and even loathing: they came to set one another's teeth on edge. This is no way to run a government; business between a Prime Minister and one of her most senior colleagues ought not to be conducted as a Punch and Judy show, even if Judy had the truncheon.

As early as Opposition days, Mrs Thatcher used to wonder aloud about replacing Sir Geoffrey, then Shadow Chancellor, with Sir Keith Joseph or even, possibly, with Roy Jenkins.[3] But the former was a political impossibility, the latter a fantasy. There was no

3 Hugo Young, *One of Us*, 1989, p.141. The conversation Mr Young describes must have taken place very late at night.

alternative to Sir Geoffrey, as Mrs Thatcher knew in her heart. Even so, there was always an element of *faute de mieux* in Mrs Thatcher's attitude to Sir Geoffrey – more *faute* than *mieux*.

An Ailment of Middle Life

Around 1978, Woodrow Wyatt, a confidant of Margaret Thatcher, noticed that she had stopped saying, 'What shall I do about Geoffrey?' and replaced it with, 'What shall I do about Geoffrey's wife and that ridiculous job of hers?' Mr Wyatt, as he then was, concluded that Mrs Thatcher would be worried about Elspeth Howe's Deputy Chairmanship of the Equal Opportunities Commission only if she had finally decided to make Sir Geoffrey her Chancellor. In the event, Lady Howe resigned from the EOC without making a fuss. She would find other ways of causing trouble.

Even if the Prime Minister had been civil to Sir Geoffrey, it is unlikely that she and Lady Howe would have become friends. The two ladies were also temperamentally incompatible. In middle life, Elspeth Howe discovered feminism, which, like most juvenile ailments, is more serious in older people. Equally, like most feminists, Lady Howe seemed to reserve an especial resentment for Margaret Thatcher, no doubt because the PM had advanced her own career and therefore opened new frontiers for women without help from any of the gloomy, litigious frumps in the feminist organizations.

Over the years, Lady Howe's antagonism grew, which was hardly surprising. Any woman of spirit would have resented the Prime Minister's treatment of her husband. So if and when Sir Geoffrey's thoughts turned to revenge, there would be no discouragement from his wife. She would always have been prepared to play Lady Macbeth. For most of his career, Geoffrey seemed an ideal Duncan.

Commonwealth Leaders, Europe and Sundry Other Vulgarities

Needless to say, there were also policy disagreements between the Prime Minister and Sir Geoffrey, especially when he became Foreign Secretary. It was Sir Geoffrey's misfortune to inherit the Foreign Office just as Mrs Thatcher was switching her own attention to foreign affairs. When in the 1983 post-election reshuffle she broke the news to Francis Pym that he was to be replaced by Sir Geoffrey, Mrs Thatcher said, 'Francis, I want a new Foreign Secretary.'[4] It

---

4 F Pym, *The Politics of Consent*, 1984, p. xi.

would have been more accurate if she had announced: 'I want to be my own Foreign Secretary.'

Subsequently, she and Sir Geoffrey disagreed over South Africa. She had little time for the Commonwealth or most of its leaders. Bernard Ingham was once asked if she respected any of the other Commonwealth heads of government. 'No-o,' replied Bernard, 'except perhaps for one or two from the little West Indian islands.' Bob Hawke and Rajiv Gandhi once kept her waiting for a dinner meeting because they could not be bothered to break off a drink and gossip, and as for Brian Mulroney of Canada, an oily, posturing, whining cant-monger, that he had the nerve to call himself a Conservative only made matters worse. Apropos of the wretched Mulroney, someone once ventured a vulgarism in Margaret Thatcher's presence. Quoting another acute observation of Dean Acheson's, in which he described something-or-other as 'just like Canadian foreign policy: all piss and wind', the Prime Minister laughed in agreement.

To her, Commonwealth conferences meant being lectured on human rights and democracy in South Africa by dictators who had no intention of introducing either in their own countries, and on the need for economic sanctions by leaders of the front-line states whose own beggared economies were absolutely dependent on trade with South Africa. Rightly convinced that capitalism and apartheid were incompatible, she was profoundly opposed to sanctions.

It would be wrong to bracket Sir Geoffrey Howe with Kenneth Kaunda, but unlike his Prime Minister, Sir Geoffrey did have benevolent feelings about the Commonwealth, seeing it as an idealistic venture, however flawed in practice. He would have favoured closer co-operation with Commonwealth leaders, and more concessions on sanctions. He also had sentimental memories of Africa. Geoffrey Howe spent part of his national service as a subaltern in Kenya, an experience he greatly enjoyed. But despite the emotions it aroused, South Africa was a peripheral policy question on which disagreements could be contained at a level well below rupture; Europe was a different matter.

At certain stages in their dealings with the EEC, Sir Geoffrey and Mrs Thatcher made a surprisingly good partnership; whenever a hard cop/soft cop routine was called for, the UK had one to hand: 'the violin and the chain-saw' as one diplomat described it. The only trouble was that the PM often wanted to use the chain-saw on her Foreign Secretary.

As we have seen, Margaret Thatcher could just about reconcile herself to a Common Market, but was constantly suspicious of the encroachments of the European Community, and abhorred federalism. Geoffrey Howe had always been a Euro-enthusiast. Like many such, he is inclined to express – or conceal – his ultimate goals in a burble of vague metaphor. We are told of the merits of trains without destinations, as if anyone would ever take a train which did not have a destination. However, despite the cloudy imagery, there was no infirmity of purpose. When it came to Europe, he was on for the ride – and quite happy to ride against his own Prime Minister. Like almost all of those who share his faith, Sir Geoffrey is self-righteous and intolerant in matters of Euro-dogma, and dismissive of those who disagree with him.

Inevitably, he and the PM disagreed strongly over the ERM; she was even more hostile to him than she was to Mr Lawson. The PM thought that he was trying to work against her over the ERM. Nigel Lawson had convinced himself of the merits of the ERM as a counter-inflationary weapon. Although Mrs Thatcher rejected that argument, she was prepared to take it seriously. She did not extend such tolerance to Sir Geoffrey's advocacy of the ERM, which she thought stemmed from Euro-fanaticism.

Sir Geoffrey thought that the Prime Minister's views on Europe were naïve, purblind, self-indulgent and contrary to the national interest. Increasingly, he saw his task as Foreign Secretary as mitigating his Prime Minister's shortcomings. This – to be fair, more than the loss of Chevening, the Foreign Secretary's country house – helps explain his attitude to losing the Foreign Office. As long as he was Foreign Secretary, Sir Geoffrey was able to sublimate his resentments in the task of thwarting her on Europe; thereafter, there was no such outlet.

Aristotle and Winnie-the-Pooh

At all stages, however, policy disagreements between Mrs Thatcher and Sir Geoffrey were exacerbated by what she saw as his chronic indecision. It may be that their different working styles – and her rudeness – added to this problem, but throughout Sir Geoffrey's period as Chancellor and as Foreign Secretary, the complaints about his indecisiveness grew, especially in No. 10. He was said to run the Treasury like a seminar. When he reached the Foreign Office, officials were initially awed by the amount of briefing he worked through. But when, having broken all records for the consumption of paper, he requested still more, they began to suspect a displacement activity: briefing as a substitute for action. Most of the officials who dealt with him liked and respected Geoffrey Howe; many of them also came to despair at his refusal to make up his mind. He was also unable to delegate.

The liking and respect helps to explain why the FO loyally covered up his indecisiveness as long as he was at its head. One official who worked closely with Geoffrey Howe later described him as 'a mixture of Aristotle and Winnie-the-Pooh'. But after Sir Geoffrey's departure, and especially once Douglas Hurd became Foreign Secretary – Mr Major was there for too short a period for officials to take his measure – the stories began to emerge. Diplomats and junior ministers could not conceal their delight at having a Foreign Secretary who would actually take decisions.

Charles Powell Goes Native

In No. 10, the liking and respect were less in evidence. Increasingly, Mrs Thatcher began any meeting with Geoffrey Howe in a mood of pre-emptive exasperation. She had always been prone to regard the Foreign Office with suspicion. Her sulphurous relations with Sir Geoffrey further poisoned her dealing with the FO, and also brought Charles Powell[5] into the controversy.

Mr (now Sir Charles) Powell became the Prime Minister's Foreign Affairs Private Secretary in 1984. Extraordinarily enough in view of what came later, the PM did not immediately take to Mr Powell. She had liked his predecessor, John Coles, and found it hard to get used to the new man. But that was a very brief phase. The two quickly developed a close working relationship, and indeed a friendship, in which Charles was assisted by his ebullient Italian wife Carla (known as Monte Carla, the most active Italian volcano).

When Charles was first appointed to No. 10, the Foreign Office was worried about how the PM would react to Carla. The two ladies were to meet at a drinks party, and it was suggested to Charles that Carla should dress in a sober manner. Carla responded to this advice by wearing an outrageously exotic creation. As soon as she arrived,

---

5 See Biographical appendix

Margaret Thatcher gazed wide-eyed at the dress, and then darted over to talk to its owner. Shortly afterwards, the pair of them disappeared. Someone wondered what had happened; where was the PM, and what had she done to Carla?

They were finally tracked down to the flat, and the PM's bedroom. The wardrobe doors were open. The bed was covered in dresses. Carla was saying 'what this needs is . . . and I know just where we can find it.' Thereafter, she was not only Charles's wife, but a gentlewoman of the bedchamber.

In their early days in No. 10, the Powells only had one telephone line. Charles once arrived home to find Carla gassing away to one of her girlfriends about hairdressers and dressmakers. Charles signalled that she should move the conversation to a close; he was expecting an important 'phone call, Carla took no notice. Finally, Charles interrupted her: she covered the mouthpiece with her hand. 'Carla, would you please get off the line? I think the PM may be trying to reach me.' 'But Charles, darling, this is the Prime Minister.' The Westland affair, in which Mr Powell's name was widely mentioned over the leaked Solicitor General's letter, strengthened the bonds between the Powells and the PM. That they were both under attack drew them closer together.

Mr Powell was ideally suited to the role of Thatcher aide. His capacity for work and ability to master detail rivals that of his mistress, and he developed an unerring ability to predict her attitude to events. In turn, she came to rely on him more and more, so that his term of office in No. 10 was indefinitely extended. Through gritted teeth, the Foreign Office offered Mr Powell a number of desirable embassies, including Madrid, in an attempt to entice him away from No. 10: there were those in the FO who would have preferred to make him Consul-General in Ulan Bator. But the offers came to nothing. Mrs Thatcher was not prepared to lose him. As the years passed, he became in effect her National Security Adviser. Indeed, during the Howe years at the FO, Charles Powell sometimes found himself taking the decisions Sir Geoffrey would not take – acting therefore not merely as National Security Adviser, but as Foreign Secretary. This fanned Sir Geoffrey's resentments; he blamed the situation on Mr Powell's arrogance and the PM's high-handedness.

Geoffrey Howe's version of events gained credence in some quarters, for only a few insiders were aware of the indecisiveness factor, and he has many friends. Throughout the last phase of her premiership, Mrs Thatcher's treatment of Sir Geoffrey added to the unease in certain sections of the Tory benches. At one stage, Willie Whitelaw was heard advising Sir Geoffrey to give Mrs Thatcher an ultimatum: either Mr Powell must go, or he would. Sir Geoffrey would have been as unwise to issue such a threat as Lord Whitelaw himself would have been unlikely to do so.

Mr Powell's role naturally aroused resentment. Incited by Sir Geoffrey Howe, many of the most senior officials in the FO believed that his job was to keep the PM under control, not to abet her. This was especially true of the Permanent Secretary, Sir Patrick Wright, a traditionalist figure addicted to Buggins' turn and the rulebook. Mr Powell was accused of committing the worst sin in the diplomatic calendar: going native – and in a posting where the natives were particularly dangerous: 10 Downing Street.

The FO's grievances were exacerbated by a standard Whitehall procedure. Prime Ministers rarely send their colleagues rude minutes. If a PM wants to express discontent with a minister's action, the practice is for a No. 10 private secretary to write to the minister's private secretary; such minutes are circulated to relevant Whitehall departments.

Charles Powell often had occasion to write to Geoffrey Howe's private secretaries. Mr Powell, a master draftsman, would express himself clearly and sharply; Whitehall colleagues not in the firing-line would chuckle while Sir Geoffrey smarted. None of this was Mr Powell's fault. If his minutes were stinging, they reflected his boss's anger; he was merely an instrument of her wrath. Indeed, Charles Powell often reduced the voltage from the electric-chair intensity of the PM's feelings to a mere jolt at domestic current level.

There was nothing improper in Mr Powell's behaviour. Certainly he was neither reluctant to wield power, not to protect his own turf. Other Downing Street aides learned that even accidental incursions into Powell territory encountered minefields, barbed wire, sirens, searchlights, dogs, machine-guns – and hot pursuit. Ultimately, however, he did his job the way he did because that was how Margaret Thatcher wanted it done; his power was an extension of her will.

Given the manner in which Mrs Thatcher ran her premiership, it was almost inevitable that she would have found a Charles Powell figure; one of the wisest of the current crop of senior ambassadors once observed that if Charles did not exist, it would have been necessary to invent him. With him at the PM's side the Government worked more effectively. Moreover, once Geoffrey Howe had ceased to be Foreign Secretary, the complaints about Charles Powell ceased. His relations with John Major and Douglas Hurd ran smoothly – because Mrs Thatcher's did. When Mrs Thatcher resigned, he instantly transferred his loyalty and his energy to the new PM, just as Talleyrand and Fouché had from Napoleon to the Bourbons. Charles Powell, although an infinitely more amiable figure, has some of the qualities of Talleyrand, and of Fouché. There was no sign that Mr Major's confidence in Sir Charles fell short of Mrs Thatcher's.

Though he greatly admires Charles Powell, Sir Robin Butler, the Head of the Civil Service, intends that Charles's successor, Stephen Wall, should discharge his duties in a more orthodox fashion; the Foreign Office concurs. It remains to be seen whether this will be possible. It may turn out that Charles Powell's role was a function of the realities of modern government.

The PM did not actually move Sir Geoffrey from the FO until July 1989, after his behaviour during the run-up to the Madrid Summit had removed any last-minute doubts. But she took the decision in principle almost eighteen months earlier during the EEC Summit in Brussels, after a classic case of Howe indecisiveness. At issue was the future of the Common Agricultural Policy, which had been threatening to wreck the EEC's budget. The negotiations had arrived at a compromise which preserved the CAP, but in a modified, less expensive version, thus avoiding a financial crisis. So Margaret Thatcher faced a dilemma. On the one hand, she disliked the whole idea of the CAP, and was uneasy about any deal which enabled it to survive. On the other hand, there was a strong case to be made that the Brussels package was the best deal Britain could get.

What should she do, she asked Sir Geoffrey? Answer came there none. David Williamson, the British Secretary-General of the Commission, was summoned to join the discussion. He, Charles Powell and Sir David Hannay, the then British Ambassador to the EEC, all helped Mrs Thatcher to make up her mind to accept the terms on offer; Geoffrey Howe played no useful part in the meeting, and at one stage actually left the room for a time.

Mrs Thatcher, then at the height of her own political power, decided that he would have to be replaced. She had no inkling that by the time she did so, events would have moved against her – part of a process that eventually allowed him to have his revenge.

Nigel Lawson

Sir Geoffrey Howe's role in Mrs Thatcher's downfall had dramatic irony; Nigel Lawson's had pathos. He was the disciple she loved: the Lucifer among her angels. Geoffrey Howe earned his position by determination and long service: Nigel Lawson won his by brilliance. In Opposition, Mr Lawson formed part of her praetorian guard, contributing to party thinking while roughing up Labour Treasury ministers in the House. He could also be pretty rough with his own colleagues, which pained Willie Whitelaw and other senior figures. In an attempt to make him more amenable, Nigel was sentenced to a stint in the Whips' office; the attempt failed.

Despite the Whips' efforts, a number of Mr Lawson's colleagues disliked him. When those around him were talking nonsense, he could not be bothered to conceal his contempt, and so made enemies – usually among the inadequate; but some backbenchers are inadequate. Furthermore even those who liked him often distrusted his political judgement. They regarded him as a formidable warhead, with an inadequate guidance system. Some thought that if he became a senior minister, his great abilities would merely serve to get him into greater trouble. Ultimately, they may have been proved right.

In those days, however, Margaret Thatcher regarded Nigel Lawson with affection and admiration. She enjoyed robust interchanges of ideas with him, and had already marked him down as a key figure in the Thatcherite generation who would inherit the earth once the Wets had been driven into extinction.

The Rise of a Monetarist

In 1979, she made him Financial Secretary to the Treasury, one of the three or four most important posts outside the Cabinet. As such, he played a major part in devising the medium-term financial strategy (MTFS), the Treasury's attempts to use monetary targets to bring down inflation. At that time, there was no doubting his monetarist credentials. In September 1981, he joined the Cabinet as Secretary of State for Energy, where he made his most important single contribution to Mrs Thatcher's success. Convinced that sooner or later there would be a miners' strike, he encouraged the power stations to build up their coal stocks. That coal was an indispensable weapon in the defeat of Arthur Scargill.

After the 1983 election, Mr Lawson had his reward. As the generality of commentators – and many Tory MPs – still underestimated both his achievements over the previous four years and the Prime Minister's determination to Thatcherize her Government, his appointment as Chancellor was greeted with surprise and, in some quarters, dismay.

Within a few weeks, there was a public expenditure crisis over a trifling sum, which gave an impression of panic, and ushered in the era of banana-skins. Most of his backbench colleagues regarded Mr Lawson's first two years in the Treasury as unsuccessful and they were also unhappy years for the Government as a whole. By the summer of 1985 there was widespread discontent among Tory MPs, and a desire to shed ministerial blood. Had Mr Lawson been required to run for re-election to the Chancellorship in a ballot of his parliamentary colleagues, it would not have been worth his while to stand.

However, it was Leon Brittan who fell victim to the mood and was demoted from the Home Office. Mr Lawson survived, and then had almost three years of apparently unblemished success. An election-winning recovery; a good performance during that election which suggested that he was a politician after all; the 1988 Budget – all endeared him to this colleagues, as did his obvious mastery of his job. It was as if Nigel Lawson had been preparing all his life to be Chancellor. He brought to the task all Denis Healey's arrogance and intellect, plus a greater grasp of the technicalities. Mr Lawson loved dancing on the high notes of economic policy; he relished the cut and thrust of debate with his officials and the Treasury liked having him in charge. A Government in which the Chancellor is not in command of his brief is like a car without oil; by 1988, Nigel Lawson's Treasury appeared to be in Rolls-Royce order.

His influence on government went far beyond the Treasury. Those who served with him in Cabinet testify to a power of mind displayed across the whole range of business – and also to a ceaselessly inventive radical intelligence. Mr Lawson constantly came up with new ideas for the Government's programme. His colleagues give him much credit for the Thatcher Goverment's success in regenerating itself in office and avoiding the intellectual exhaustion that had overcome previous administrations.

Any Chancellor who does as well as Nigel seemed to be doing is bound to be discussed as a possible Premier. He was; and by the spring of 1988 a significant number of his parliamentary colleagues took the prospect seriously. By then, however, for him as for her, it was all going wrong.

Nigel Lawson's Budget speeches were always great set-piece occasions; he enjoyed mastering the House as he displayed his mastery of his subject-matter. The 1988 Budget was his most triumphant performance, but even by the time he delivered the speech, his troubles had begun. He and the Prime Minister had fallen out.

A week before the Budget, Mrs Thatcher actually criticized her own Chancellor at Prime Minister's questions. She told the House that it was wrong for the Government to risk inflation by trying to manipulate interest rates in pursuit of an illusory exchange-rate stability. Thus she made public a disagreement between her and the Chancellor over the fundamentals of economic policy, a disagreement that rumbled on, unresolved, until it finally provoked Mr Lawson's resignation nineteen months later. It was to leave the Government divided, its policy in ruins, and the Prime Minister's authority undermined. Eventually, it was to lead to her resignation also. The paradox – and the pathos – is that these twin paladins of monetarism, the two greatest articulators of Thatcherism, had fallen out – over monetarism.

At the core of monetarism is a common-sense proposition: that money is a commodity as well as a means of exchange and a measure of value. Changes in the supply of money relative to the supply of other goods therefore alter its value. So if money is to perform its function as a measure of value and a means of exchange, and inflation or deflation are to be avoided, increases in the supply of money must be firmly controlled.

In order to do that, however, it is necessary to be able to measure effective monetary growth: no simple task in a modern economy where the mere printing of banknotes or minting of coins represent an almost irrelevantly small percentage of the money supply. From 1979 onwards, Mr Lawson addressed himself to this problem. The Government used – that is, targeted – a series of indicators, and in Mr Lawson's view, none of them worked. The rate of increase in the chosen monetary measure bore no relation to the rate of increase in inflation.

It seemed that Professor Charles Goodhart had been right when he argued – 'Goodhart's Law' – that the act of targeting a monetary indicator destroyed its value. His explanation was that an indicator which had seemed a reliable guide to the real world when it was allowed to adjust freely would no longer be so when its movements were subject to the constraints of government policy. In other words, those attempting to measure the money supply had the same problem as the anthropologist attempting to measure an Eskimo woman's sex-life. As soon as a thermometer is introduced into a sensitive region, that which is being measured changes.

But Nigel Lawson did conclude that there was one reliable method of controlling the money supply: the exchange rate. Here, a determining influence on his thinking was the inflationary surge of 1979-81. That was brought under control, not by a successful targeting of sterling M3 – then the favoured indicator – but by the foreign exchanges; the rise of the pound to $2.40 supplied the necessary squeeze.

Exchange-rate Monetarism

Mr Lawson went even further. In 1985 the pound had depreciated rapidly against the dollar, and in 1986 the same thing had happened against the Deutchsmark. Mr Lawson believed that such violent movements, unjustified by economic fundamentals, made life unnecessarily difficult for business. Just as it was the Chancellor's task to deliver a stable and predictable counter-inflation policy, so Mr Lawson came to regard it as his duty to ensure exchange-rate stability also. He decided that rather than relying on a single monetary indicator, or even on a basket of indicators, he should trust the markets' judgement. After all, movements in the value of the currency reflect the markets' assessment of domestic monetary conditions and of the prospects for inflation: so why not steer by the exchange rate?

On this point, Sir Alan Walters has questioned Mr Lawson's motives, accusing him of being carried away by the pleasure of grandstanding at meetings of international finance ministers and of succumbing to *folie de grandeur*. There was more to Mr Lawson's policy than Sir Alan's *ad hominem* criticisms would suggest. First, it was based on his experience of trying to run monetary policy. Second, there could obviously be no possibility of stable exchange rates if inflation rates were significantly divergent. By the mid-1980s, however, all the major industrial nations were at least in theory committed to counter-inflation. If they were to honour that commitment by pursuing sound monetary policies, there would be no reason not to have relatively stable currency markets.

Mr Lawson never argued that exchange-rate stability was an alternative to an effective domestic monetary policy. In his view, the two were mutually reinforcing. Only a tight monetary policy could achieve exchange-rate stability, which would then act as a permanent discipline to maintain the tight policy. This was the background to his enthusiasm for the European Exchange Rate Mechanism (ERM) – not as an alternative to counter-inflation, but as a ratification of it. Indeed, he wanted to take the pound into the ERM in November 1985 at DM3.75.

Those who subsequently accused Mr Lawson of monetary incontinence and of a permissive attitude to inflation have never explained why in that case he wanted to join the ERM at so high a DM parity. Had the UK done so, the inflation of 1988/90 could not have occurred. In all probability, neither could the election-winning recovery of 1986/87: joining the ERM at that rate might indeed have been analogous to rejoining the Gold Standard in 1925. In his desire to take the UK into the ERM at that level against the DM, Mr Lawson could not have been playing fast and loose with inflation. It is far more likely that he would have been playing fast and loose with deflation.

The ERM was not Mr Lawson's only counter-inflationary instrument. He also wanted to abolish or at least curtail mortgage-interest tax relief. By giving the housing market a much-needed cold shower, this would have struck at the psychology of inflation. Mrs Thatcher, however, would have none of it. Opposed as she is to all other forms of borrowing, she will not hear a word of criticism against mortgage-holders.

This argument over mortgage-interest tax relief highlighted the fundamental difference between Nigel Lawson and Margaret Thatcher. He is an intellectual, guided by the light of pure reason, ready to follow his arguments wherever they may lead him whatever the short-term consequences. He is convinced that in the longer run, economic truth and electoral advantage would converge. She is a creature of prejudice and political calculation. Whatever the arguments against mortgage-interest tax relief, she was certain that its removal would cause a revolt among her own bedrock middle-class supporters.

It was not only on mortgages, however, that Mrs Thatcher blocked Mr Lawson. She did not accept his historical analysis. She believed that her Government had conquered inflation by applying monetarism, and that this was the only way to keep it under control. She was extremely suspicious of any moves towards fixed exchange rates, for she was convinced that this would be an attempt to buck the markets: one of her principles was that markets cannot be bucked. So she rejected Mr Lawson's entire monetary and exchange-rate policy, horse, foot and guns.

Although she had made a reluctant commitment in principle to join the ERM she showed no sign of ever honouring it. In this distrust of the ERM, her views were reinforced by those of Professor Sir Alan Walters, whom she often consulted on economic policy. Throughout the mid-1980s, while commuting between Washington and 10 Downing Street, Sir Alan advanced three main arguments against British membership of the ERM.[5]

1 That on examination, the record of the ERM countries in dealing with inflation was not as successful as its proponents claimed.

2 That fixed exchange rates did not work. There might be a case for having a single European currency, but it was impossible to try to compel different currencies to behave as if they were one currency.

3 That if Britain were to join the ERM we would find ourselves forced into interest rate levels which had a perverse relationship to the needs of domestic monetary policy (this point did not seem to be contradicted by the UK's initial experience of ERM membership).

The Prime Minister agreed with Sir Alan and refused to allow the Chancellor to take Britain into the ERM. This was intensely galling for Mr Lawson. He found himself in the job he had always wanted, but forbidden to do that job in his chosen way.

Mr Lawson was and is a proud and imperious man, with infinite resources of intellectual self-confidence. he was convinced of the correctness of his chosen strategy – convinced that it, and only it, could deliver the Government's monetary objectives. Like Geoffrey Howe on Europe, Mr Lawson believed that he was right. As the PM's

---

5 Alan Walter's views are summarised in his book *Sterling in Danger* (1990). Counter-arguments can be found in Samuel Brittan's columns in the *Financial Times*. Nigel Lawson's memoirs, to be published after the election, will also deal with the subject, and are unlikely to express agreement with Professor Walters.

opposition was due to prejudice, he considered himself entitled to circumvent it. That is what he tried to do.

It was the boldest experiment in economic policy in British history. Never before had a Chancellor sought to override the Prime Minister's veto and proceed regardless. Only a Chancellor of Mr Lawson's intellectual power, seniority in office and self-confidence-cum-arrogance would have made the attempt. Mr Lawson decided that Britain would achieve exchange-rate stability and join the ERM by stealth. From early 1987 until early 1988, he sought to stabilize the pound at around DM3.00.

He was unfortunate in his timing. The British economy had forged ahead after 1981 for social and cultural reasons as much as economic ones. The recovery could not have occurred without the financial deregulation that took place between 1979 and 1981. In turn, this had a more dramatic effect than had been expected because the British people were ready to borrow on an unprecedented scale. Traditional attitudes to indebtedness had been transformed for a complex of reasons. Two stand out: the spread of consumerism via television advertising, and the decline of Puritanism. There was an analogy between the permissive borrowing of the 1980s and the permissive sex of the 1960s. In 1980, the average British family had borrowed – relative to income – half as much as the average American family. By the late 1980s, the British family had borrowed slightly more than its American counterpart. That enormous increase made possible the entrenchment of Thatcherism. The spread of home-ownership, the erosion of trade-union attitudes and other aspects of embourgeoisement were all facilitated by borrowing. Borrowing enabled the British economy to grow rapidly. It also confounded economic forecasters' predictions of a down-turn. Those took insufficient account of the cultural stimulus, leading to an increased propensity to borrow, which was undeterred by high real interest rates.

As Nigel Lawson later put it, all this was 'too much of a good thing'. By 1987, as so often in the post-war years, economic growth was encountering supply-side constraints, with the inevitable result of inflation and balance-of-payments problems. The economy could not cope with the volume of increased borrowing. All the domestic indicators suggested, therefore, that monetary policy ought to be tightened – and Mr Lawson did indeed increase interest rates after the 1987 election.

Then came Black Monday. Although the Chancellor himself was less alarmed at the prospects for the world economy than almost anyone else in the Treasury, he followed the example of the rest of the developed economies and relaxed monetary policy. However, Black Monday had no discernible dampening effect on the British economy, nor even a corrective one: the overheating continued, abetted by the monetary stimulus.

On top of that, Mr Lawson was intervening to prevent the pound rising above his DM target. He did this partly by instructing the Bank of England to sell sterling, and partly by keeping down interest rates. Both methods injected liquidity into the system at a time when domestic monetary conditions were already too lax.

At that stage, the markets were over-impressed by arguments that the German economy was moving into sclerosis, and Nigel Lawson was right to conclude that once the pound moved above DM3.00, it was overvalued. In retrospect, however, an overvalued pound would have been a lesser evil than an overheating money supply. Moreover, by targeting the pound/DM rate, Mr Lawson was falling foul of Goodhart's Law. No longer able to move freely, the exchange rate was neither a good guide to domestic monetary conditions, nor was it able to provide a corrective. In the longer term, a pound/DM rate of 3.10-3.20 might have proved unsustainable. In the short term, it could have acted as a braking mechanism – just as an overvalued pound had in 1979-81. The year 1987/88 was a bad one for exchange-rate monetarists; it would have been better to let policy be determined by domestic monetary conditions.

Mr Lawson could, of course, argue that had we been in the ERM, it would not have been necessary to loosen domestic policy in order to maintain parity. He might also claim that had we joined the ERM in 1985, the problems of adjustment would have been solved by 1988. Those may be good arguments in favour of ERM membership; they do not justify a covert attempt to implement a partial strategy, which was likely to incur all the disadvantages and few of the benefits of ERM membership.

Mr Lawson knew what he wanted to do, was refused permission to proceed, and then tried to do it anyway. Mrs Thatcher knew what she wanted to do, but failed to ensure that her Chancellor followed her instructions.

Pull Premier, Pull Chancellor

Either the Thatcher strategy or the Lawson strategy might have been successful. The pull-Prime Minister-pull-Chancellor compromise had no chance of success. The Prime Minister should either have submitted to Mr Lawson's judgement, or ensured that he had submitted to hers, or found herself a new Chancellor.

This was the second occasion on which a Cabinet minister had publicly defied her for a time, the first being Michael Heseltine over Westland: both ended in tears. However unpopular her bossy-boots reputation may have been, she chose the wrong moments not to live up to it. Perhaps she should have watched 'Spitting Image' more often to remind herself how she was supposed to treat Cabinet ministers.

Supporters of the Prime Minister point out, of course, that though she was aware of the unresolved intellectual disagreements, she was not informed about Mr Lawson's pound/DM operations until Sir Alan Walters told her and warned her of the consequences for monetary policy. It was that warning which led to the PM firing her shot across Mr Lawson's bows on the eve of the 1988 Budget.

One or two of Mr Lawson's colleagues, aware of his defiance of the PM over the exchange rate, suspected that the Budget itself contained another surreptitious attempt by Mr Lawson to implement his strategy and sabotage the Prime Minister's. They thought he was trying to undermine the community charge. Before the Budget, Nicholas Ridley asked Mr Lawson if he would go easy on any plans to reduce the top rates of income tax. Mr Ridley feared that this would only heighten criticism of the community charge on grounds of unfairness. So when Mr Lawson scrapped the three existing upper bands, at 40, 50 and 60 per cent, and replaced them with a single higher rate, the suspicion arose that he was trying to deter the PM and Mr Ridley from pressing ahead with the new charge.

That overstates Mr Lawson's Machiavellianism. The community charge *did* influence his thinking on the Budget – in the opposite direction. He had been powerfully attracted to the idea of abolishing all upper rates of tax, thus providing additional incentives and enabling large savings on administrative costs. In view of the community charge, he felt that this option was not open to him.

The Prime Minister did not hold the tax cuts against him. Her grievance was inflation. From 1988 on, inflation was mounting, and Margaret Thatcher was appalled. She *hates* inflation, and could not bear the thought that after nine years of Tory Government, it was returning. This time, there was no one to blame but her Chancellor. Sir Alan and she believed that by trying to buck the markets rather than control the money supply, Mr Lawson had been the guilty man. Nigel Lawson scornfully rejected this charge. He thought that the responsibility for inflation lay with those who had rejected his counter-inflation strategy. He also objected to the way in which Mrs Thatcher preferred the opinion of a part-time adviser, Sir Alan Walters, to that of her Chancellor.

Paradoxically, there was one respect in which the return of inflation made it easier for the Prime Minister and the Chancellor to bury their differences. In the short run, they both agreed on what needed to be done to curb it: interest-rate increases. Equally, the ERM issue seemed less pressing, for once inflation began to accelerate, the option of immediate membership disappeared.

Even so, throughout the period from March 1988 to October 1989, the PM's relationship with her Chancellor remained unstable. There were three reasons for this: first, the ERM issue was still unresolved – which meant that the Government had no coherent long-term policy. The markets were aware of this, and at regular intervals claimed to be unsettled by it. Second, Mrs Thatcher's and Mr Lawson's temperaments were too similar to permit a *rapprochement*. Both were stubborn and stiff-necked; each was convinced of his or her own rightness and the other's error. They could neither forget the history of their quarrel, nor forgo opportunities to reopen it and justify their actions. All this made the markets still more uneasy. Third, although she did not seriously consider removing him, Mrs Thatcher had lost confidence in Mr Lawson, and transferred it to Professor Walters.[6]

Her respect for Alan Walters dates from the framing of the 1981 Budget – the Valley Forge of Thatcherism, and the most influential Budget since Lloyd George. In 1981 Professor Walters had stiffened the PM in her determination to cut public spending and increase taxes. She believed that the 1981 Budget had laid the foundations for the economic successes of the 1980s, and she drew a lesson from the experience: when in difficulties, consult Alan Walters.

---

6 On one occasion, she did wonder about the possibility of making Nicholas Ridley Chancellor, but she knew that this was not a realistic suggestion.

Sir Alan's position was further strengthened because Nicholas Ridley agreed with him. Mr Ridley, a Thatcherite even before Margaret Thatcher herself, had always given the Prime Minister his absolute loyalty. This and his unwavering commitment to their common cause had made Nick Ridley the PM's closest confidant: the minister most likely to be invited round to No. 10 for a late-night whisky and an unguarded conversation.

In 1987 and 1988, Mr Ridley grew uneasy about Nigel Lawson's abandonment of monetary targets. He told Mr Lawson so, but was unable to change his mind. He also told the Prime Minister, with whom his views had more influence.

Ceasefire

In late 1988, her anxieties increasing, Mrs Thatcher decided to formalize Sir Alan's role and bring him back to No. 10 as her economic adviser. Nigel Lawson protested. He told her that Sir Alan's arrival would only confirm the markets' suspicions of divided counsel. He expressed doubts as to whether Sir Alan, an eminent academic used to a public role, could attain the anonymity desirable in an adviser, and he warned that Sir Alan's arrival would give mischief-makers the opportunity to invent splits. Mrs Thatcher went ahead with the Walters appointment. Trouble ensued; increasingly 10 Downing St and the Treasury put the worst possible construction on the other's actions. Reports reached the Treasury that Sir Alan had been expressing anti-Lawson sentiments at City lunches, and this was seen as part of a plot. No doubt Alan Walters had made such remarks, but these were indiscretions, not a conspiracy. The Professor had not realized the speed with which the proceedings of a private lunch could become public, sometimes in an exaggerated form.

Bernard Ingham, meanwhile, blamed the Treasury for encouraging anti-Walters comments in the *Financial Times*. Again, there was no conspiracy: it was simply a matter of officials and ministers failing to break the habit of telling *FT* journalists what they thought, on lobby terms. The *FT*'s main economic commentator, Sam Brittan, was a partisan of the ERM who felt antagonistic to Alan Walters – but these were his own views. Mr Brittan has never been anyone else's mouthpiece.

Throughout 1988 and 1989, mutual friends of the Prime Minister and the Chancellor tried to make peace. They failed. Even though each retained a regard for the other, there was no peace treaty between them, only a number of ceasefires.

4 'Events, My Dear, Events'

From a Non-event to a Reshuffle

Harold Macmillan was onced asked what aspect of the premiership caused him the greatest difficulty. 'Events, my dear, events,' he replied. During 1989 and 1990, Margaret Thatcher could have given the same answer. For the first time since her early months in No. 10, she no longer seemed to be in control of events.

The tenth anniversary of Margaret Thatcher becoming Prime Minister fell on 4 May 1989. Over the previous few weeks, when any of her staff raised the question of a celebration, she had quickly stopped the discussion, insisting that for her it would be a normal working day. She knew that jubilees are for monarchs, not for embattled democratic politicians. As it happened, 4 May was not a normal day, for on it, a by-election was held, leading to a Labour gain from the Conservatives in the Vale of Glamorgan. Over the previous year, the by-election tide had been running against the Government. The Labour Party had almost won Kensington, and but for the two former Alliance parties' insistence on cutting each other's throat, the Tories would have lost both Epping Forest and Richmond.

Even so, the Glamorgan result was an unpleasant tenth-birthday present for the PM – and it was quickly followed by defeat in the Euro-election. The timing of that defeat was also unfortunate; there was a danger that the loss of prestige would undermine Mrs Thatcher's standing at the Madrid EEC summit.

Before that summit, however, Geoffrey Howe and Nigel Lawson had already sought to weaken their Prime Minister's position. On the morning of Sunday 25 June 1989, when Mrs Thatcher was in No. 10 making her final preparations before leaving for Madrid, Sir Geoffrey and Mr Lawson asked to see her. A tense meeting ensued. Yet again, the ERM was the issue. The Foreign Secretary and the Chancellor, by then convinced that for her the 'right time' would occur simultaneously with the Greek Kalends, were also worried that if there were a row at Madrid, she might harden her opposition.

They therefore threatened to resign unless she replaced 'when the time was right' with a timetable for British membership. As Mr Lawson was to discover later in the year, Margaret Thatcher does not warm to ultimata – but nor could she lightly contemplate parting with her Chancellor and her Foreign Secretary. The shock in the markets and on the Tory benches would have been too great.

The tone of the meeting was frigid. Throughout, the PM bristled with hostility, although she did agree to consider the arguments the two ministers had advanced. But as the meeting ended it was not clear who had won. Afterwards, the PM's initial reaction was defiant. She scornfully rejected a draft statement which had been jointly prepared by the Foreign Office and the Treasury. Charles Powell had to work through the night in his bedroom in the Ritz Hotel, Madrid, to produce an alternative. The Powell version went some way to satisfying the Howe-Lawson demands by setting out criteria for judging when the time would be right: the so-called 'Madrid conditions'. These were:

1 That the British rate of inflation should be significantly lower, and much nearer to the average of the ERM countries.

2 The abolition of restrictions on the movement of capital within ERM countries.

3 Significant progress towards the completion of the Single Market.

4 Free competition in financial services throughout the EEC.

5 A strengthening of competition policy throughout the EEC.

Afterwards, Downing Street spokesmen insisted that Mrs Thatcher retained her freedom of manoeuvre. They argued that as policy had been to join when the time was right, and the Madrid conditions merely spelt out a few footnotes amplifying that general statement, nothing had changed. It was not clear whether they were being disingenuous, or whether they were deceiving themselves: Madrid marked a fundamental change.

By shifting her ground and defining conditions, Mrs Thatcher made it easier for the weight of pro-ERM sentiment in Whitehall, the City, the Tory benches and the Cabinet to exert its momentum against her. From Madrid onwards, it was no longer a question of whether Britain would join the ERM, but when. It was also no longer a question of whether Mrs Thatcher would have a new Foreign Secretary, but when. Sir Geoffrey had sealed his fate.

The July 1989 reshuffle was expected to include a number of changes at senior level. John Major had been widely tipped for promotion within the Cabinet, while it was assumed that Chris Patten would join the Cabinet. There was obviously a case for moving Nick Ridley away from the Department of the Enviroment; he was too acerbic to reassure the Green lobby or soothe community charge anxieties.

Equally, the Cabinet careers of John Moore and Paul Channon had come to an end. Mr Moore's political death had already occurred, and a ratification of that by his removal from office was overdue. Mr Channon, a thoroughly decent man and potentially a good minister, had suffered a series of cruel misfortunes. He was in no way to blame for them, but like Napoleon, Margaret Thatcher preferred lucky generals.

All these moves were widely predicted. Some months earlier, there had also been speculation that Sir Geoffrey Howe might move either to be Leader of the House or to the Home Office: it seemed unlikely that Mrs Thatcher would wish to fight the 1991 or 1992 Election with the same Chancellor *and* the same Foreign Secretary whom she had appointed in 1983. But in the run-up to the reshuffle, there was no expectation of any changes at the top of the Cabinet. The Howe/Lawson ultimatum was not public knowledge, while over Hong Kong and the killings in Tiananmen Square, the PM had for once seemed in harmony with the Foreign Secretary. Moreover, Bernard Ingham remained silent on this occasion, perhaps deterred by the complaints his previous briefings had aroused. In view of the subsequent row over Sir Geoffrey, those who had criticized the Downing Street Press Secretary might reflect that at least the Ingham method lessens the shock.

The reshuffling of Sir Geoffrey did come as a shock. At around 8 a.m. on the morning of Monday 24 July 1989, Andrew Turnbull, Mrs Thatcher's principal private secretary, telephoned Stephen Wall, then Sir Geoffrey Howe's private secretary, with a request that his boss should call on the PM.

'But you're not thinking of moving him, are you?' replied Mr Wall.

'Just ask the Foreign Secretary to come over here,' said Mr Turnbull.

To his dismay and anger, Sir Geoffrey was told that he had to move, and was offered the Leadership of the House. Mrs Thatcher told him that she could, of course, have offered him the Home Office, but she knew that he did not want to be Home Secretary. The PM also added that she had no wish to move Douglas Hurd, in whom she every confidence. Sir Geoffrey confirmed that he had no wish to be Home Secretary. As for the leadership of the House, characteristically – though in this case pardonably – he took time to make up his mind, thus delaying the rest of the reshuffle.

The decision to reshuffle Sir Geoffrey was widely unpopular on the Conservative benches, as was demonstrated by the cheers which greeted his entry to the Chamber later that week. The MPs cheering were of course unaware of the background to the reshuffle. But in their indignation, Sir Geoffrey and his friends then undermined his position. It appeared that in the course of the negotiations over his new post, there had been an unseemly wrangle over country houses and Cabinet *placement*. Given the vicissitudes of politics, ministers should guard against becoming too attached to the prerogatives of office – but Chevening, the Foreign Secretary's country residence, is a beautiful house, and both the Howes were most upset that their tenancy had been terminated so brutally. They were foolish to broadcast the fact, thus allowing their feelings to take precedence over their dignity. Equally, the summary decision to deprive Mr and Mrs Lawson of Dorneywood, another country residence, so that it could be reallocated to the Howes also made Sir Geoffrey seem selfish. It may be that Sir Geoffrey resented Mr Lawson's failure to come to his aid.

In order to make trouble, the Howe camp leaked the fact that Sir Geoffrey had been offered the Home Secretaryship, Douglas Hurd's job. On a basis of pure supposition, the press reported that Mr Hurd was upset, while a lot of Tory MPs felt that he, too, had been treated badly. This was not so. Apart from the arguments for giving Sir Geoffrey the Home Office, there was a strong case to be made that in view of his seniority, Sir Geoffrey was entitled to that post if he wanted it. One person who did not dispute that assessment was Mr Hurd himself.

Mr Hurd is a man of admirable self-control and laconic grace: stoicism comes easily to him. It is hard to gauge his innermost feelings, for he would not allow their ruffles to appear in public. But in the course of dinner that week he not only disclaimed any injured feelings, but insisted that the Prime Minister was absolutely entitled to act as she had, and that he would have been quite happy to move to be Leader of the House. There seems no reason to doubt his sincerity.

If Mr Hurd had felt resentments, they were less likely to concern Geoffrey Howe being offered the Home Office than John Major being given the Foreign Office. Just like Nigel Lawson and the Treasury, that was a job for which Douglas Hurd had been preparing all his life; his qualifications were much more obvious than John Major's. Mr Hurd was then fifty-nine, Mr Major forty-six. Clearly the PM had taken the view that she did not want Douglas Hurd as her Foreign Secretary, probably because she regarded him as exclusively influenced by FO orthodoxy. It was obviously her intention that John Major would stay at the Foreign Office until the General Election. By that time, though Mr Hurd could still be a candidate, other claimants to the FO would surely have emerged. It must have seemed to Douglas Hurd that his best chance of getting the job he most wanted had gone.

He showed not a flicker of resentment. Over the first few days of John Major's Foreign Secretaryship, press articles appeared asserting that it was preposterous to make this callow youth who knew nothing about abroad Foreign Secretary. Unwisely, Mr Major allowed this to upset him. Douglas Hurd dropped him a note telling him that he would turn out to be a first-class Foreign Secretary and to take no notice of the carpers. Admirable advice, admirably done.

Sir Geoffrey was less serene. There was also trouble over his appointment as 'Deputy Prime Minister'; Bernard Ingham was accused of belittling the job in his lobby briefings. This was not Mr Ingham's fault: he had a problem with Buckingham Palace. The Palace is sniffy about deputy premiers. Its position is governed by a memorandum of 1951, which states that the office of Deputy Prime Minister is unknown to the British Constitution and will remain so until there is legislation to the contrary. Indeed, the Palace will not countenance the words 'Deputy Prime Minister' appearing on any official document. Mr Ingham had to brief the press in line with the Palace's reservations. He also pointed out that given modern communications, there was no question of the Deputy PM being in charge while Mrs Thatcher was abroad: she could and would remain in control. He did say that Sir Geoffrey would take over pro tem were the PM to become incapacitated.

One could argue that the Palace was being unnecessarily restrictive. One of the glories of the British Constitution is its capacity to evolve in response to new circumstances. The premiership itself existed long before its status was defined by legislation. Lord St John of Fawsley (Norman St John-Stevas) brought the authority of the editor of Bagehot to the defence of the Palace, arguing that a deputy premiership would fetter the Crown's prerogative to appoint Prime Ministers. But as Lord St John himself acknowledged, the methods by which modern political parties elect their leader already circumscribes the royal prerogative. Nor is it clear that the Palace would ever wish to be placed in the position of having to make an unguided choice of premier.

One point was clear. It was not for Bernard Ingham to decide that the Palace had got the Constitution wrong; his press briefing was constrained accordingly. In the overheated atmosphere of that week, however, it was taken as yet another snub to poor Geoffrey, and another piece of mean-spiritedness by Mrs Thatcher, unable even to let him have the deputy premiership without pouring scorn on it. That view was as influential as it was unfair.

The Commons was about to break up for the summer recess – so there was no time for No. 10 to correct mistaken impressions about the reshuffle. Many Tory MPs left Westminster in an unhappy mood, worried about the economy, convinced that the reshuffle had been botched, wondering even whether the PM's powers of judgement had not declined. There were mutterings that perhaps it would have been better is she had quit on her tenth anniversary. There also began to be talk about a challenge to her leadership.

The Tory Leadership

Traditionally, the grandees of the Tory Party chose its leaders. Lord Kilmuir's memoirs[1] describe what happened in 1957, after Sir Anthony Eden's resignation. One by one, the Cabinet were summoned to 'Bobbety' Salisbury's office, to be asked by Lord Salisbury, who had difficulty pronouncing his 'r's, 'Well, which is it, Wab or Hawold?' (Butler or Macmillan). For years, this system worked well. But any election method whose proceedings were so mysterious inevitably gave rise to myths: in this case, the myth of the men in dark suits.

In newspaper articles over the years it has been asserted that these figures – senior Cabinet ministers in both Houses, the Chairman of the 1922 Committee, the Chief Whip, other grandees – were ruth-

---

1 *Political Adventure: The Memoirs of the Earl of Kilmuir* (1964), p. 285.

less in their scrutiny of the current leader's performance. Any sign of loss of grip, and a delegation would arrive to inform him that he would find a bottle of whisky and a revolver in the library. According to some of the more hyperbolic accounts, Tory leaders enjoyed approximately the same security of tenure as Catherine the Great's lovers.

This is nonsense, as the record demonstrates. Balfour was replaced only after losing three elections and his appetite for the job. Baldwin survived election defeats, as did Churchill, who was allowed to carry on into extreme old age. Eden went because his health was broken, and Macmillan because he feared that his health was broken.

A couple of days after telling his son Maurice and his son-in-law Julian Amery that he would fight the next election, Macmillan changed his mind. This was due to pressure, not from the men in suits, but from his bladder; he was advised, wrongly, that he might have a malignant prostate. There is no evidence that his doctor had been nobbled by the 1922 Committee.

Alec Douglas-Home did resign quickly after the 1964 defeat – but he himself had decided that he was the wrong man for the job. Indeed, Willie Whitelaw, then an apprentice dark suit, tried to persuade Sir Alec to carry on. Convinced that Wilson would win the next election – as he did the following year – Mr Whitelaw would have preferred Sir Alec to be the losing Tory leader, so that his successor could start with a clean sheet.

In modern times, before the introduction of elections, there were two successful revolts against the Tory leadership. The victims were Sir Stafford Northcote in the early 1880s, and Lloyd George and his coalition in 1922. In each case, it was not the dark suits who led the revolt, but the young Turks. In 1922, almost all the grandees tried to save Lloyd George. When they failed, F.E. Smith complained that the cabin boys had taken over the ship.

So there is no truth in the notion that past Tory leaders hardly dared stroll down a House of Commons corridor for fear of bumping into the Chairman of the '22. Nor is it hard to understand why Tory leaders had so little to fear from the dark suits. By definition, the men in suits were generally cautious, small 'c' conservatives who had long outlived the fires of youth. They were also likely to be friendly with the leader, a friendship which might well go back to boyhood. Self-esteem as well as sentiment would make them reluctant to conclude that he should go – because if his day was over, so probably was theirs.

The dark suits would almost always prefer the tried to the untested, the known to the unknown. Immune alike to the impatience of younger men and the pressure from marginal constituencies, they would have a strong prejudice in favour of the status quo. If the dark suits had still been in charge in 1975, Ted Heath would have survived – and had he fallen under a bus, his successor would not have been Margaret Thatcher. By the autumn of 1990, she might have found the dark suits more of a problem – but her position would have been no more insecure under suit rule than under MP power. The dark suits, however, lost power after 1963. It is unlikely that the introduction of democracy could have been long delayed, but the controversy over the nomination of Lord Home to succeed Mr Macmillan brought the old system to a rapid end.

Lord Home, Mr Macleod and the Magic Circle

Lord Home's appointment came as a surprise to many, not least within the Conservative Party. Alec Home has many qualities, including a considerable intellect. In other circumstances he would have made an excellent Prime Minister, and might indeed have led his party to re-election; he almost did. But in 1963, he was not the right man to take on Harold Wilson. In an age of satire but not irony, as Christopher Booker has described it, Lord Home's very qualities made him ill-suited to the temper of the times. So much the worse for the times, to prefer Harold Wilson to Alec Home – but the Tory Party must win elections before it can reform manners and morals. The way in which Lord Home became leader of the party damaged his electoral chances, as did the refusal of Iain Macleod and Enoch Powell to serve in his Cabinet.

As a result of widespread dissatisfaction with the choice of Lord Home, the traditional system of electing Tory leaders was discredited even before Iain Macleod wrote his famous article.[2] In some respects, however, Mr Macleod's arguments were as mischievous and misleading as the book he was reviewing. In his references to the 'magic circle' and the number of Old Etonians who had been involved in the selection of Lord Home, Macleod missed the point. Events turned out as they did in October 1963 not because of an Etonian plot, but because Harold Macmillan was determined to prevent Rab Butler becoming Prime Minister. Indeed, as Macleod

---

2 'The Tory Leadership', *Spectator*, 17 January 1964. This was a review of Randolph Churchill's *Fight for the Tory Leadership*.

mentions, since 1959 Macmillan had advanced the Cabinet careers of Maudling, Heath and Macleod himself in the hope that one of them would emerge as a possible successor. None of them had been to Eton.

It was only when none of those three succeeded in establishing a pre-eminent claim that Macmillan turned first to Hailsham, then to Home. Throughout, Macmillan's overriding, obsessive priority was to stop Butler. Macleod attributes this to Macmillan's view 'that Butler had not in him the steel that makes a Prime Minister, nor the inspiration that a leader needs to pull his party through a fierce general election'. The inadequacy of that explanation is made plain by the reference to inspiration, hardly Lord Home's attribute. The causes of Macmillan's antipathy to Butler had more to do with psychology than with psephology.

In the 1930s when Macmillan's marriage was a shell and his political ambitions looked unlikely ever to be realized, Butler was the coming man in the Conservative Party. He remained so until the end of appeasement and the fall of Chamberlain; he had been a staunch supporter of both, but survived to serve new causes and new masters.

Macmillan later seemed to rise above earlier miseries to serenity. He appeared to forgive many of his former enemies, including appeasers, and even ennobled Boothby, his wife's lover. He and Butler were largely in agreement on social and economic issues. Moreover, he unexpectedly defeated Butler for the premiership in 1957; such a victory often eases magnanimity. Not in this case: it was as if Macmillan had allowed himself one outlet for all the frustrations and bitterness of his 1930s: revenge against Butler. The degree of his antagonism to Butler was irrational: that made him unscrupu-lous. By ruthlessly excluding from the consultation process anyone who would have disagreed with him, he proved that the traditional method of selecting a Tory leader could be manipulated. He chose as his adjutants men who were neither as clever nor as sharp as he – and unlike them, he knew what he wanted. A master of the arts of flattery, cajolery and beguilement, he deployed them to the full to achieve it. At the time, William Rees-Mogg found an apt description of the events of 1963: 'The Consevatives have ceased to be gentle-men without becoming democrats.'[3]

Macmillan succeeded: the Queen sent for Lord Home on the basis of misleading advice. But that was not the fault of the dark-suits system: it had been subverted, and replaced with Mr Macleod's magic circle –

---

3 Quoted in Anthony Howard: *RAB: The Life of R. A. Butler* (1987), p. 323.

more correctly Macmillan's bewitched circle. Macleod's mistake was to pay too much attention to Eton, and too little to Harold Macmillan. The Eton connection may have made the Prime Minister's task easier; it did not explain his motives. Rab Butler nearly went to Eton;[4] even if he had done so, Macmillan would still have wanted to stop him becoming Premier.

The Dark Suits Lose Power

After the 1964 election, the Tory Party turned its attention to a new method of choosing its leader. The result was the 'Douglas-Home rules'. In future, although the views of the National Union – representing the party's membership – and of Tory peers would be made known, the decision would be left to members of the House of Commons.

Leaders of the Tory Party would be subject to annual re-election, to take place when Parliament reassembled in November. It was made easy to challenge an incumbent leader: an alternative candidate only required one proposer and one seconder, whose names were to be kept secret. The 1922 Committee had the task of conducting any election. There was also a provision for a two-stage electoral process. The first leg was in effect a referendum on the existing leader. In order to win outright on the first ballot, a candidate was required to win more than half the votes of those entitled to vote, *and* his majority over his nearest rival had to be at least 15 per cent of the total number of Tory MPs. Though nothing was made explicit, the implication was clear: a sitting leader unable to win outright on the first ballot ought to consider his or her position.

That impression was strengthened by a further provision allowing new candidates to enter the contest at the second-ballot stage. This opened the way for a stalking-horse challenge in the first ballot, in which a candidate with no prospect of winning could test party opinion. If the leader was unable to win outright, senior frontbenchers could then enter the contest.

In the second ballot, a simple majority of the electorate would suffice. If no candidate achieved that, there would be a third and final round. In this exhaustive ballot, MPs would also be required to express a second preference; the candidates at the bottom of the poll

---

4 Ibid., p.11.

would be eliminated in ascending order and their votes redistributed until someone attained an overall majority.

It is a sophisticated system, and has at times been criticized for being unfair, but there is a logic to the two-stage process. After Sir Anthony Meyer's challenge in 1989, the rules were altered slightly, in that the names of the proposer and seconder are now made public. There is no significant backbench pressure, however, to change the Douglas-Home rules.[5]

Mr Heath, their first beneficiary in 1965, was also their first victim in 1975. Mrs Thatcher's margin of victory over Willie Whitelaw in that second ballot led to a widespread assumption, which subsequently proved to be invalid. It was believed that any candidate who had the courage to challenge an incumbent in the first ballot and succeeded in taking the contest on to the second stage would gain such a moral momentum as to be unstoppable. The subtleties of the two-ballot system would therefore fall victim to the Tory Party's sense of fair play.

It is true that Mrs Thatcher's boldness in taking on Ted Heath won her admirers, and that Willie Whitelaw's personality was not such as to enable him to woo those admirers away. In 1975, after two election defeats, the Tory Party was in a febrile mood. It is still a moot point as to what would have happened if Mr Heath had stood down, or if Mr Whitelaw had challenged him in the first ballot. In either case, Mrs Thatcher's majority would have been reduced, as indeed it might have been if Mr Whitelaw had been given a clear run against her (some other Wets still blame Jim Prior for splitting the Whitelaw vote). In all probability, however, she would still have won.

No one seems to have given serious thought to challenging Mr Heath until he had lost two elections. Perhaps because her leadership style was even more combative, Mrs Thatcher did not enjoy a similar indulgence. In 1981, after declaring that the Government was heading straight for the rocks (so it seemed to many at the time), Sir Ian Gilmour thought about a leadership contest. He decided against it partly because Chris Patten was hostile to the whole idea. Meanwhile, Geoffrey Rippon also took soundings, and there were suggestions later that Peter Walker would have run if he had obtained one hundred firm pledges of support. At the time, there was no sign of his attempting to procure them, although it would have been hard for him to do so while serving in Mrs Thatcher's Cabinet.

---

5 Although they make no provision for a tie.

The Stalking-ass

Thereafter, the idea of a leadership challenge died, until 1989. Then the rumours started. Throughout the summer months, there would be talk that a challenge was inevitable, followed by reports that the challenger in question had thought better of it. Various names were mentioned: Ian Gilmour; John Biffen, a former Leader of the Commons; Sir Barney Hayhoe, who had been a Minister of State; Richard Shepherd, a clever backbencher generally thought of as a right-winger but who had developed an intense dislike of what he saw as the Prime Minister's illiberal manner of running the Government – and, of course, Michael Heseltine. It generally assumed that anyone who did run would be acting as Mr Heseltine's stalking-horse.

Within the Heseltine camp, Michael Mates was in favour of a smash-and-grab raid on the premiership. The galloping colonel was moving towards his middle fifties and had never held office. Keith Hampson and William Powell took a more cautious line, and were worried about the risks of a premature challenge. Their view carried the day with Mr Heseltine.

Another name was also mentioned. Perhaps it was inevitable that the least plausible and most preposterous of the possible challengers would also prove the most persistent. Sir Anthony Meyer regards himself as a Tory of the old school. By this, he seems to understand that if he ever ran into trouble in his constituency, the Tory Party should rally round, with the Party Chairman treating him to oysters and champagne. If the party should call on him for loyalty, he would recognize no obligations. Sir Anthony has written a book[6] to justify his actions. There is no sign of any ghost-writing. It is a product worthy of its author: one of the most fatuous and feather-headed books on politics that has ever appeared. At one point, Sir Anthony opines: 'Mr Heath . . . has . . . a generosity of spirit of which Mrs Thatcher is quite incapable.'[7] If you believe that, to quote the Iron Duke of Wellington, you will believe anything. Anyone who fears that the social changes in the modern Conservative Party may have gone too far could reassure himself by reading Sir Anthony's book.

Long before 1989, most of Sir Anthony's colleagues had written him off as a bleating, hand-wringing ninny: Keith Joseph after a lobotomy. But in the summer of 1989, he elbowed his way into history, and his Warholian quarter of an hour of fame. As other more sensible men hung back from challenging Mrs Thatcher and

6 *Stand up and be Counted* (1990).

7 Ibid, p. 63.

searched for a stalking-horse to take their place, Sir Anthony volunteered for the role: as a stalking-ass. By late October, Anthony Meyer had almost certainly decided to challenge Margaret Thatcher. The events of 26 October removed any lingering doubts.

The Fall of Lucifer

Nigel Lawson had never reconciled himself to Alan Walters's presence in No. 10. In that frame of mind, the Chancellor was quick to take offence, and on Wednesday 18 October he seemed to have been given cause. Bernard Ingham, with the PM in Kuala Lumpur for the Commonwealth Conference, was informed that the *Financial Times* had carried a story about Sir Alan Walters writing an article reaffirming his opposition to British membership of the ERM, and describing the ERM as half-baked. But when the full text of the article was faxed to Kuala Lumpur, the Prime Minister's staff relaxed. Sir Alan's piece had been written two years previously for an obscure American journal, and its publication had already been postponed twice. So the PM's economic adviser had been guilty of nothing more than an oversight. Mrs Thatcher dismissed the matter from her mind and got on with the job of sorting out the Commonwealth.

That was not the end of the matter. In the first place, a large number of Tory MPs were angry. They had not grasped the point about the time-lag: they thought that having the PM's economic adviser quarrelling in print with the Chancellor was no way to run a government. It was bad luck for the Prime Minister – in her last months as PM she had a run of bad luck – that she was in Malaysia when the story broke. Had she been in London, she would have apologized to Mr Lawson before he had had time to brood. Equally, if Professor Walters had been in London, rather than in Washington, he might even have concluded that in view of the furore, his position was untenable: Alan Walters is a proud man. But both Sir Alan and Mrs Thatcher were thousands of miles away, and the more Nigel Lawson considered the matter, the more determined he became that something had to be done. So on the Friday, two days after the *FT* article had appeared, while Mrs Thatcher and other Commonwealth leaders were enjoying a retreat on the island of Langkawi, Nigel Lawson went to see the PM's Parliamentary Private Secretary, Mark Lennox-Boyd.

Mr Lawson's purpose was to convey a blunt message. He thought he had made clear to Mr Lennox-Boyd that he found the situation intolerable, and that unless the PM dispensed with Sir Alan's services, he would have to consider his own position. But there was an error in transmission – or reception. Mark Lennox-Boyd formed the impression that Nigel Lawson was fed up; he did not realize that there was any question of the Chancellor resigning. That was the key to the next few days' events. Mr Lawson believed that he had made his views plain, and assumed that the PM would be informed of them; he had not, so she was not. Mark Lennox-Boyd told her office that Mr Lawson was annoyed – which neither surprised nor worried them. As far as they were concerned, the matter could be forgotten. No doubt someone would have had a word in Sir Alan's ear and expressed the hope that there were no more articles in the pipeline. But on the basis of Mr Lennox-Boyd's report, the PM and her entourage were not aware of any need for further action.

One could speculate indefinitely as to who was at fault: Mr Lawson, or Mr Lennox-Boyd. This author would be inclined to place more of the blame on Nigel Lawson. Mark Lennox-Boyd is neither an insouciant character nor a bad listener. On the other hand, Nigel Lawson can at certain moments become curiously inarticulate, especially when in the grip of strong feelings, as on this occasion. By definition, Mark Lennox-Boyd should not have let Nigel Lawson leave the room until he was certain that he understood precisely what was on the Chancellor's mind – but it is conceivable that, even on such a vital matter, Mr Lawson failed to make himself clear. From that misunderstanding a crisis burgeoned.

On the following Tuesday, while Mrs Thatcher was flying back to London, Mr Lawson had a tough time in the Commons. John Smith found the whole affair a rich source of mockery, and the Tory benches as well as his own laughed with him at the Chancellor's expense. Nigel Lawson does not enjoy such treatment. He underlined his annoyance in a television interview, in which he called on the Prime Minister to silence Sir Alan.

On Wednesday, after her return, Mr Lawson saw Mrs Thatcher, but did not mention Sir Alan: another crucial misunderstanding. The PM assumed from his silence that he also regarded the matter as closed. Mr Lawson, on the other hand, saw no reason to speak. He had made his point; it was now up to her to take a decision, and he felt that it would be ungallant to press her when she had got off a plane at 4.00 a.m. and, no doubt, had some catching up to do.

Moreover, Mr Lawson knew that she would not enjoy getting rid of Sir Alan. A proud man himself, he had no wish to gloat over her injured pride. Thus his silence made the misunderstanding terminal.

He did ask to see her early the next morning; as he thought, to hear her decision. Unaware that there was a decision to take, she also wanted to see him – to discuss a point for Prime Minister's questions that afternoon. So when they met, she thought that the agenda was PM's questions: nothing else. She was astonished, therefore, when Mr Lawson asked her whether she was going to sack Sir Alan; her first reaction was to assume that something of which she was still unaware had happened overnight. Mr Lawson, meanwhile, thought he was being conciliatory: he made it clear that he would be quite satisfied if Sir Alan quit No. 10 by the end of the year.

After ten minutes, Mr Lawson still had not grasped the PM's absolute unpreparedness for this exchange; she had not understood how determined he was. So when the conversation ended with Mr Lawson rising and announcing that as she was not going to sack Sir Alan, he must consider his position, this came as a complete shock to Mrs Thatcher.

If Mr Lennox-Boyd had understood what Mr Lawson was trying to say – or if, indeed, the Chancellor had used the Chief Whip as a conduit, the outcome would almost certainly have been different. Although Nigel Lawson's standing with the party had declined since July 1988, it would still have been inconceivable for the PM to retain her adviser and lose her Chancellor. But the choice was presented directly to her, as an ultimatum. From the beginning, she was convinced that after Madrid, whatever the political costs, she could not yield to a second ultimatum from Mr Lawson. It is just about possible that Mr Lawson could have remained in office had Peter Lilley, the Financial Secretary to the Treasury, been told earlier what was happening. Mr Lilley, a friend of Professor Walters, would immediately have contacted him; Sir Alan would then almost certainly have resigned, as he was to do after Mr Lawson's departure. But Mr Lilley did not know until too late. On that Thursday, Mr Lawson had been due to fly to Germany for talks with Herr Waigel, the Finance Minister. Mrs Thatcher who was still hoping that he would calm down, assumed that he had set off as planned. In fact, the Chancellor went back to No. 11, and summoned his Deputy, Norman Lamont. Throughout the rest of the morning, Mr Lamont tried to persuade Mr Lawson not to resign – but the Chancellor was as immovable as the Premier. At no stage had Nigel Lawson been bluffing. Having staked out a position, he was not prepared to lose all credibility by abandoning it. At 2.20p.m., Mr Lawson returned to No. 10 with his letter of resignation – which was not made public until around five o'clock.

Mrs Thatcher then went to the House. During her statement on the Commonwealth Conference, she declared with some vehemence that it would be very difficult to blackmail the British Government 'or me in particular'. Hardly anyone else picked up the irony.

When Mr Lawson's resignation was announced many of the Prime Minister's closest supporters and friends were filled with foreboding. It was not only their fear that a government deprived of Nigel's intellect and influence would be seriously weakened. They found it desperately worrying that such a paladin of Thatcherism was no longer willing to remain in her Cabinet; this seemed to justify not only the criticisms of her leadership style, but also the anxieties that her powers were waning. Norman Lamont feared that this was the beginning of the end for her; he was not alone.

Not everyone who shared Mr Lamont's assessment shared his dismay. Hopes rose in the Heseltine camp. On his way to the Lords to listen to the Queen's Speech, Mr Lamont found himself walking alongside Peter Tapsell. 'In a month's time, you and I will both be serving in a Heseltine Cabinet,' said Sir Peter.

Another Reshuffle

In the post-Lawson reshuffle, the PM and her advisers did what they could in damage limitation. John Major, the obvious choice, became Chancellor. Douglas Hurd, also the obvious choice, became Foreign Secretary, though the PM briefly considered giving that job to Tom King. David Waddington, then Chief Whip, became Home Secretary, the post he had always wanted. The PM was also pleased that, at last, she was able to send a right-winger to the Home Office; Mr Waddington was the first hanger to hold the job since Reggie Maudling. Thus far, it had been a good reshuffle. If it were possible to strengthen a government which had just lost Nigel Lawson, those appointments were the way to do it. There were still two problems: who should be Chief Whip, and how to placate Geoffrey Howe. Sir

Geoffrey was cross that he had not been consulted about Cabinet changes.

It was not easy to find a suitable Chief Whip. In their time, John Major and Peter Brooke had been thought of as likely Chief Whips, and indeed Mr Major once almost got the job. By then, both were already Cabinet ministers, and therefore too senior. Two other good candidates, Francis Maude and Michael Portillo, were regarded as too young for the job. Then there was John Cope, who as Deputy Chief Whip had stood in for John Wakeham after the Brighton bomb. But during that time he had managed in some unspecified way to forfeit the Prime Minister's confidence.

Among Mr Waddington's Whips' office team, there were at least two possible Chief Whips: Alastair Goodlad and Tristan Garel-Jones. But Mr Goodlad, incomprehensibly sacked from a parliamentary secretaryship in 1987, had only just been recalled to the Government; in those days, the Prime Minister hardly knew him. Also, Mr Goodlad was junior to Mr Garel-Jones.

The final three candidates for the post of Chief Whip was Tristan Garel-Jones, David Hunt and Richard Ryder. Tristan had served in the Whips' office for seven-and-a-half years, with distinction. Margaret Thatcher would have been surprised to be told so, but Mr Garel-Jones was someone to whom she owed a great deal. However, during those years he had made a lot of enemies, especially on the right of the party. The Chief Whip has to be a unifier; had Mr Garel-Jones been appointed, there would have been trouble from the right. David Hunt, a former Deputy Chief Whip, he had spent only four months as the Minister of State dealing with the community charge, so everyone was reluctant to move him. Richard Ryder was also thought to be slightly too junior. David Waddington, the outgoing Chief Whip, recommended Tristan Garel-Jones. But the PM was lukewarm; Tristan was not from her wing of the party, and what would her friends think?

Then the Geoffrey Howe problem erupted. Sir Geoffrey grew crosser still when he learned that Charles Powell had been in the meeting at which the senior Cabinet posts were discussed. His anger was reinforced by his wife. Lady Howe arrived at his office in the Commons, and marched up and down loudly proclaiming her fury at this snub to her husband. Sir Geoffrey went to see the Prime Minister, inflamed with grievance. She meanwhile was losing interest in the question of who should be Chief Whip; she was also – for once

– aware of the need to soothe Geoffrey Howe's feelings. So when Sir Geoffrey offered a plausible candidate, his suggestion was accepted.

His choice was Tim Renton. Mr Renton was a senior Minister of State, and though on the left of the party, a man with few, if any, enemies. He had one drawback: from time immemorial every Tory Chief Whip had previously served as a junior Whip: not Mr Renton. But he seemed to have a Whip's personality. Tim Renton was duly appointed. He was the wrong choice. This was nothing to do with the lack of previous experience, nor indeed with the way he performed his duties. Mr Renton's problem was that he did not enjoy the Prime Minister's full confidence.

The Chief Whip's job is to inform the prime Minister about the state of opinion within the Parliamentary Party and to ensure that the Government's legislative programme is carried through the Commons. But a good Chief Whip can also advise the PM how to display a surer political touch both in dealings with backbenchers and in handling government business. In order for that to be possible, the Prime Minister must value and indeed seek out the Chief Whip's judgement.

Tim Renton was not a Thatcherite and had never been one of her circle. The Geoffrey Howe connection may have helped him get the job; it did not endear him to her. John Major, who did not regard the Howe connection as a source of strength, had asked Mark Lennox-Boyd if the PM was aware of it. He was right to be doubtful. It may have been more her fault than Tim Renton's, but Mr Renton was unable to develop a close relationship with her. Throughout, he put his energy and loyalty at her disposal. But their official dealings never warmed into intimacy.

For that to happen, the chemistry had to be right and Tim Renton never crossed the chemistry threshold; he probably never could have. At a juncture when the PM needed a Chief Whip's guidance more than ever, she appointed the wrong man to give her such guidance. She ought to have known that – but she was an erratic picker of ministers. The choice of Tim Renton was a further sign that the neglect of politics was becoming endemic in No. 10. If she had accepted David Waddington's advice and appointed Tristan Garel-Jones, she would still have been Prime Minister today.

The reshuffle was completed and the focus of the action switched, as if to give the audience some comic relief. Exit tragic hero Lawson; enter Meyer the weaver.

The Blur Candidate

Sir Anthony Meyer found an apt description of his own leadership challenge: 'Looking back on it, it was all a blur.'[7] The most important event in his campaign was a negative one: the decision of the tabloid press to hold back a sex-scandal story for fear that publication would be blamed on Bernard Ingham. But in Thatcher HQ, there was no complacency about the Meyer challenge. Those around her under-stood that his was not time to take the Parliamentary Party for granted.

Officially, her campaign was run by George Younger, formerly Secretary of State for Scotland and for Defence, who had resigned from the Government that July after ten years' consecutive service in the Cabinet, something achieved by very few politicians this century. He was about to become Chairman of the Royal Bank of Scotland, and had announced that he would not contest his seat at the next election. George Younger was a good choice. Affable, courteous, popular, a moderate, old-school, reassuring character, he was ideally suited to appeal to wavering backbenchers. But 'Gentleman George' was only the public part of Mrs Thatcher's campaign. Behind the scenes, her supporters ran a Whips' office operation.

Initially, this was co-ordinated by Mark Lennox-Boyd as PPS. But he had also recruited the assistance of three of the most politically astute men in the House of Commons: Tristan Garel-Jones, Richard Ryder and the late Ian Gow.

Ian Gow had been Mrs Thatcher's PPS from 1979 until 1983; he had been the *sans pareil* of PPSs. Devoted to Margaret Thatcher and a steadfast Thatcherite, he was also immensely popular in the Tory Parliamentary Party. Though he had subsequently resigned from the Government over the Anglo-Irish Agreement, his adoration for Margaret Thatcher was undiminished. When Mark Lennox-Boyd asked him to help with her campaign he initially tried to decline on the grounds of incompetence; he was certain that the Prime Minister could find better men than he. Mr Lennox-Boyd told him that this was no time for false modesty. Mr Gow insisted that the modesty was genuine, but added that if they wee so foolish as to think they needed

---

7 *Stand Up and be Counted*, p. 165.

his services, then of course every second of his time and every ounce of energy were Margaret Thatcher's to command.

It was Ian who brought in Richard Ryder: a characteristically shrewd idea. Mr Ryder, a long-headed, thoughtful fellow, was a recent graduate of the Whips' office, and knew the Parliamentary Party well.

Nobody could have rivalled Tristan Garel-Jones's knowledge of the Parliamentary Party. Mr Garel-Jones knew *everything*. He was as well-informed about most of his colleagues as their wives or bank managers: in a number of cases, rather better. His position was mildly complicated by the fact that he was Deputy Chief Whip. Unlike the 1922 Committee which, as umpire, has to remain neutral in any contest, the Whips' office has an ambivalent role in leadership elections. Whips are members of the Government appointed by the Prime Minister, so they ought to show loyalty to her. But equally, the Whips can do their job only if they retain the confidence of all sections of the Party, including the Prime Minister's critics. In previous years, it had been customary for the Chief Whip and his Deputy to propose and second the Prime Minister in her annual re-election – but in those years, there had been no question of a challenge. In 1975, during the Heath/Thatcher contest, the Whips' office had remained neutral, something for which Ted Heath never forgave Humphrey Atkins, the then Chief Whip – but then Mr Heath never forgave a lot of people.

In November 1989, Tim Renton, still trying to master the arcana of his office, was nervous about overt participation by the Whips. So a characteristically Byzantine formula was devised to cover Mr Garel-Jones's involvement. In this, Tristan was determined to protect the Whips' office's reputation for neutrality. The solution he came up with may seem tortuous – a Chinese Wall without the wall – but it was sustained by his own sense of honour. First, he would stand down from the office for the duration of the campaign. Second, he would continue to perform his duties as normal. Third, his involvement in the Thatcher camp would be kept secret. Finally, the Whips' office itself would neither take any part in the campaign, nor be informed about its progress.

Indeed, the Thatcher camp decided to keep its existence largely secret. There was no complacency: they knew that they were in arms against the sea of discontent on the backbenches, not against the hapless Meyer. Indeed, Mark Lennox-Boyd's instinct was to run a high-profile campaign, but Richard Ryder dissuaded him. Mr Ryder thought the party would take the view that after ten years in power, Mrs Thatcher should not have to go to the trouble of breaking a butterfly upon a wheel. So if her supporters were seen to campaign vigorously against Sir Anthony, her authority would be compromised. The Thatcher team therefore decided to campaign unseen, with a peripatetic HQ. Tristan Garel-Jones found an unused office in the bowels of the Commons, and meetings were also held at his house in Catherine Place, Westminster, and at Mr Lennox-Boyd's house in Pimlico. Shana Hole, then Lord McAlpine's secretary, who had also worked in No. 10, helped organize the office. As ever, she combined efficiency and charm.

All this activity was successfully concealed from the Tory Parliamentary Party. Richard Ryder himself is temperamentally inclined to secrecy; he was trained by a master of covert operations, Airey Neave, who ran Mrs Thatcher's campaign against Ted Heath. Mr Neave had tried to solve the problem that confronts any leadership candidate: that a certain number of his or her parliamentary colleagues are liars. This is not just because they are congenital scoundrels; there is an element of self-preservation involved. It is a brave backbencher who announces that he does not support the leader of his party. Equally, many backbenchers think that a little reinsurance might be prudent: no harm in sidling up to the challenger's people – in secret of course – and whispering a message of support. At the end of the day, the ballot is secret.

So Mr Neave knew that he could not rely on his canvass returns. He decided, therefore, that the best form of canvassing was not to let the MP in question know that he was being canvassed. Under this 'run silent' technique – the phrase comes from submarine warfare – canvassers would simply hang around the tearoom, falling into casual conversations – sometimes eavesdropping – without declaring their own allegiance. They might even act as *agents provocateurs*. In 1975, Mr Neave's canvassers had not been aware of each other's identity; he took the view that it was worth the time they wasted in canvassing one another to make sure they behaved naturally.

In 1989, Messrs Gow, Ryder and Garel-Jones followed the Neave formula. 'Run silent' canvassing works best if those undertaking it are untypical supporters of their candidates, and Tristan Garel-Jones came up with a perfect example of an un-Thatcherite Thatcher supporter: Sir George Young. Despite a tendency to worry about social problems, George Young is a thoroughly decent fellow. He had served as a Parliamentary Secretary between 1979 and 1986 and was to have been rewarded with the Ministry of Overseas Development. Then another name had to be accommodated in the reshuffle. There was a piece too many for the jigsaw, and instead of being promoted, George Young was sacked. It was one of the most unfair ministerial dismissals of the Thatcher years. Sir George had grounds to feel aggrieved; it is not in his nature to give way to such feelings. Though he would never bang on about loyalty, it is at the core of his moral code.

During that 1989 campaign, Margaret Thatcher came to recognize his qualities. Over the ensuing months, Tristan Garel-Jones made it his business to remind her of them, regularly. When Tristan ran such a campaign, it was usually successful, and in July 1990, Sir George was recalled to the Government as number three in the Whips' office. Anyone who thinks that such a calculation might have been at the back of his mind in November 1989 does not know George Young.

James Arbuthnot, a member of the 1987 intake with good contacts among his fellow '87ers, was also involved in the 'run silent' exercises, while Michael Jopling, a former Chief Whip, also helped in the Thatcher campaign. All in all, about twenty backbenchers worked to re-elect Margaret Thatcher. They generated a considerable quantity of intelligence which was collated by the unofficial Whips' office. For every single MP, a sheet of paper was stored in a ring-file, on which all contacts with him or her were logged. On this basis, regular assessments were made. Some MPs would have been amused, or horrified, at the amount of information on them that the three wise men had assembled. Other MPs who grumbled about being taken for granted did not realize that they had been canvassed several times already. In many cases, the person to whom they were grumbling was their latest canvasser. As in 1975, the canvassers themselves were not aware of one another's identity – so Ian, Richard and Tristan sometimes received two different reports of the same conversation in which two Thatcher canvassers had been probing one another.

Mr Garel-Jones had a small list of untouchables; characters so perverse and unreliable that he thought them not worth bothering about. In compiling this, he may sometimes have relied too much on Whips' office enmities. Tristan Garel-Jones disliked Nicholas

Winterton, and had criticized him for irregular attendance at House of Common's votes. Mr Winterton featured on Tristan's little list, but he voted for Margaret Thatcher.

The Whips' Office has to prepare for every contingency. So despite their loyalty to Mrs Thatcher, the Whips did consider the remote possibility that she might either fail to win outright on the first ballot, or win by such a small margin as to be irreparably damaged. In that eventuality, the plan was to run Douglas Hurd as a 'Party unity' candidate, and to mobilize a broad coalition of support behind him in order to stop Michael Heseltine. To emphasize the unity aspect, his proposer and seconder were to come from opposite wings of the party; Alan Clark, a right-winger, and Nick Scott, a Wet. John Major and Chris Patten would also have given Mr Hurd their enthusiastic backing. The Hurd option was not required in November 1989. It was to be revived in November 1990.

Contingency planning apart, however, a Thatcher victory was never in doubt; the only question was the majority. Here, there were some key margins. It would obviously be of great psychological value if Mrs Thatcher could obtain 326 votes – an overall majority of Members of the Commons. Once she fell below that figure, 300 was the next barrier. It would be a blow to her position if she could not achieve 300 votes against Anthony Meyer. By the end of the campaign, Messrs Garel-Jones, Gow and Ryder were confident that they had 300 votes; indeed their predictions were almost identical with the end result: Thatcher, 314; Meyer, 33; abstentions, 24; 3 MPs were unable to vote. Most of the press took the view that this was a satisfactory outcome for Margaret Thatcher. Her campaign team knew better, and acted accordingly.

The Killers in the Bushes

Shortly after the result, Willie Whitelaw and Alec Home met at a dinner in the Farmers' Club, and discussed the leadership election. They agreed that a combined total of sixty adverse votes and abstentions was a bad result, and that the Prime Minister ought to be worried.

As the weeks passed, Mr Garel-Jones's anxieties mounted. He knew that if sixty of Margaret Thatcher's colleagues were not prepared to support her against Anthony Meyer, there was a lot more discontent which a serious challenger could mobilize. Tristan finally suggested a talk with the PM. This proposal was enthusiastically seconded by Mr Lennox-Boyd, and the three of them went round to the flat in No. 10 for a drink on the evening of Sunday, 16 April.

Bernard Ingham, who had been keen on the idea, contributed little to the evening, and nothing critical of the PM – to the surprise and annoyance of Mr Lennox-Boyd. Mr Ingham took the view that as he was technically a civil servant, he ought not to participate in the discussion. Tristan Garel-Jones made up for him. He told Mrs Thatcher that as well as the sixty who had voted against or abstained, there were another 100 malcontents lurking in the bushes. If she did not take action, he told her, repeating the point: 'All those people will come back and kill you. They will indulge in the daylight assassination of a Prime Minister.' Mr Garel-Jones listed key policy areas: Europe (especially the ERM), the community charge and the economy. The word 'tone', though never used, was implicit throughout. Margaret Thatcher listened attentively, thanked the three for their trouble, and promised to think hard about the points they had made. This was as positive a response as they could have hoped for: it was not followed up by action.

That was partly due to the difficulty of taking action. As Michael Heseltine has since discovered, there is no easy way to reform the community charge. As long as inflation remained high, there was no question of reducing interest rates, or – it then seemed – of joining the ERM. So the Prime Minister was boxed in by events, especially by inflation. She was also the prisoner of her emphatic style, especially on Europe. On all policy issues, she had generally taken such a decided attitude that it was not easy for her to adjust her position. Equally, there was a limit to the concessions she was prepared to make, especially to the Europeans.

There was a further, structural problem in Mrs Thatcher's Downing Street. Over the years, the political wing of her office had shrunk in status and importance, as the official side came to predominate. In this, the PM was partly a victim of her previous successes. It is not easy for any adviser to tell a Prime Minister who had won three elections and been in office for more than a decade that she ought to pay more attention to politics.

Personalities also played a part. In the first place, the officials were so formidable. There was no one in the political wing of No. 10 to rival Charles Powell and Bernard Ingham. Bernard Ingham was an outstanding Press Secretary, but he did the job for too long. By the end, he had decided who his friends and enemies in the media were, and had lost flexibility; he was too ready to dismiss criticism of the PM as merely the product of malice. Charles Powell used to encourage her ambitions to stay in office; he could always cite leaders who had served for even longer. Others in No. 10 felt that Mr Powell, with no direct experience of party politics, was too impatient of its constraints. It is possible that, just like Margaret Thatcher, Mr Powell's attention was so taken up with global events that he neglected the vital backyard: Westminster.

Then again, Westminster was not officially Mr Powell's responsibility. Mrs Thatcher had a small political staff in No. 10, but it did not always function effectively. None of Ian Gow's successors as PPS enjoyed Ian's authority, and not all of them were good choices.

Originally, Ian Gow's replacement was to have been Michael Spicer, but when he travelled with Margaret Thatcher during the 1983 election they did not strike up a rapport. So a different PPS had to be found in a hurry. Incomprehensibly, the choice fell on Michael Alison, who was about to be sacked as Minister of State at the Home Office. Mr Alison is an upright, honourable man – but far too diffident and stiff a personality to be a good PPS. Having done the job badly for an entire Parliament, he was succeeded by Archie Hamilton, who had impeccable Thatcherite credentials, but lacked an easy, insinuating manner.

Mr Hamilton, the younger son of a peer, is six feet six inches tall and served in the Coldstream Guards: not necessarily a figure to whom the average modern Tory backbencher would pour out his anxieties. A PPS needs to have patience, which will be tested to the uttermost by fools, knaves, whingers and bores. Archie Hamilton never gave the impression that his stock of patience was inexhaustible. He did pass on some critical comments to the PM, and once brought in Tristan Garel-Jones to give her a thorough briefing on the state of party opinion – but he did not particularly enjoy the job. After only 13 months, he moved on to be a Minister of State, and was followed by Mark Lennox-Boyd.

Mr Alison, Mr Hamilton and Mr Lennox-Boyd were all Old Etonians, as was Mrs Thatcher's final PPS, Peter Morrison; Ian Gow was a Wykehamist. The PPS is paid a small allowance by the party – but not nearly enough to compensate for the loss of a minister's salary. So Messrs Hamilton, Lennox-Boyd and Morrison were chosen partly because they are well-off: all of them gave up ministerial jobs to become the PPS; each of them could afford to do without the ministerial income. That is a consideration which weighted with Mrs Thatcher.

Mark Lennox-Boyd had much more of a PPS's personality than Mr Hamilton or Mr Alison. He took trouble with the backbenchers, and faithfully reported their anxieties to No. 10. He also wrote the PM some forthright notes, and arranged for her to see Willie Whitelaw. Lord Whitelaw may have retired, but his antennae had not: in 1989/ 90, he was getting worried, and began to say that the Prime Minister should have stood down after ten years. Over her last year as PM, Mrs Thatcher had two or three meetings with Lord Whitelaw. But Lord Whitelaw had no specific advice to give Mrs Thatcher. Equally, Mr Lennox-Boyd's warnings were not taken seriously by some of the Downing Street officials, who thought him inclined to panic, and discounted his reports of unrest on the backbenches. No. 10 was getting out of touch.

As well as a PPS, the Prime Minister also had a political secretary. Between 1979 and 1983, this was Richard Ryder. On becoming an MP he was succeeded by Stephen Sherbourne. Mr Sherbourne, a donnish figure whose own political views had been Wet-of-centre, is a man of great political shrewdness; always calm, whatever the pressure: one of the safest pair of hands in the business. A product of the Conservative Research Department, he had held a number of important back-room posts over the years – but the list of appointments that he has turned down is even more impressive. For Mr Sherbourne has one character defect, which he has never managed to bring under control. Every so often, he gives way to an urge to escape from politics. This happened in December 1987; he has still not been recaptured.

His replacement was John Whittingdale, also an alumnus of CRD, aged only twenty-nine. But in a succession of senior posts both at the Research Department an as an adviser to ministers Mr Whittingdale had already set a number of records for youthful advancement. He, Jock Colville and J.C.C. Davidson were the youngest men this century to be appointed to such an important job in No. 10. But John Whittingdale never enjoyed Davidson's influence – any more than Margaret Thatcher resembled Bonar Law or Baldwin. When Mr Sherbourne handed over to Mr Whittingdale, he told him to remember that the Prime Minister was not always right, and that it would sometimes be his job to tell her she was wrong. This was easier advice to give than to execute.

From 1987 onwards, she took less and less notice of political danger-signs. Mr Whittingdale was no more successful than anyone else in reining her back; he can hardly be blamed for that. It was hard for someone of his age to succeed when PPSs, the party machinery and Cabinet ministers had failed.

Those around Mrs Thatcher – and the PM herself – had experienced previous bouts of unpopularity: she had always recovered from them. They expected her to do the same again; so did she. Her confidence was undiminished. She often expressed the view that it was virtually impossible to dislodge a sitting Prime Minister. Once or twice, she even talked as if she did not care. After the Meyer contest, she told Mr Lennox-Boyd: 'I've done it: I've earned my place in history. I didn't give a damn what happened.' So despite the efforts of Mr Garel-Jones and Mr Lennox-Boyd, there was no change of direction. Most of the time, Mrs Thatcher would have drawn no distinction between a change of direction and a loss of direction. She had never been a trimmer, and had no intention of becoming one. Margaret Thatcher was determined not only to stay in office, but in power.

Increasingly, others doubted her ability to achieve this. Nothing seemed to be going right for the Government. Despite interest rates that were causing great pain to mortgage-holders – and therefore to a lot of Tory voters – inflation was still rising. It had taken much longer than ministers had expected to make the economy slow down. Although that was an indication of the success of Thatcherite economic policies, it was an unwelcome one. It meant that the recession was behind schedule; could there be a sufficient recovery in time for the election?

Since the war, no British government has lost office without first losing its power while still nominally in office. In 1951, 1964, 1970, February 1974 and 1979 the incumbent Government had already forfeited its authority before it was defeated at the polls. By early 1990, as never before under Margaret Thatcher, it was an open question as to whether this might be happening again. In response, Labour gained ground. By March, it was regularly recording a lead of twenty per cent in the opinion polls, and on 22 March, it won Mid-Staffordshire, a safe Tory seat. Labour has rarely found it easy to win safe Tory seats; they generally fall to the Liberals. The Mid-Staffs result was the Labour Party's best post-war by-election performance; perhaps Mr Kinnock's image-builders had made him electable.

On the day after Mid-Staffs, I interviewed Mrs Thatcher, and asked whether the question of her leadership of the party could be resolved in good time for the election. 'I do not quite see what there is to resolve,' she replied. Others did.

The Lion and the Ox-wagons

It was clear that the defeat of Anthony Meyer had settled nothing. Mr Garel-Jones's 100 dissidents were no happier, and Michael Heseltine was beginning to stir. Like a lion planning a raid on an ox-wagon circle, he was padding towards his target. The beleaguered garrison inside No. 10 had more and more reports of his leonine features being spotted at the very edge of the bush. As the local elections approached, he was poised and ready to spring.

Everything would depend on those local elections, due on 3 May. In local government, elections are run on a four-year cycle, so the seats to come up in 1990 had last been contested in 1986, a bad year for the Tories because of Westland. Further substantial Tory losses would have had disturbing implications for the Government. But in the first year of the community charge, and given the Government's generally low standing, heavy losses were likely; there was even talk that the Tories might lose 600 seats. Had that happened, it was widely assumed that Michael Heseltine would launch a challenge. The mechanics of this would have been difficult: Mrs Thatcher was not due to face re-election until November, and it would have been unwise of Mr Heseltine to subject the party – and himself – to a six-month campaign. It is possible that a dark-suits delegation might have called on the PM and asked her to stand down; it is hardly likely that she would have agreed to do so.

Whatever the mechanics, many Tory MPs thought that a disastrous local election result could finish her. On the night, however, it seemed that disaster had been avoided; the Government benefited from all the pessimistic expectations. Instead of 600, a 'mere' 200 seats had been lost, counterbalanced by gains in London. Outside London, it was still a bad result for the Tories, but Michael Heseltine went back into the bush, and the PM was safe – until November.

Her other troubles continued. The previous October, Kenneth Baker's slogan for the Blackpool Party Conference had been: 'The

Right Team for Britain'. It turned out to be one of the most unfortunate political slogans ever devised. Before the end of that month, Nigel Lawson had left the team. He was only the first to go.

Ministerial life is a gruelling affair, and it is hardly surprising that after long years in office, some politicians grow tired and decide to quit at the moment of *their* choosing, not the PM's or the electorate's. In the summer of 1989, both George Younger and David Young made voluntary departures from the Cabinet. Then at the New Year of 1990, Norman Fowler announced that he was resigning, partly to spend more time with his family. Mr Fowler had wanted to be Chairman of the Party, possibly because it might have helped him to his greatest ambition in politics: the Home Secretaryship. But Mrs Thatcher had picked Kenneth Baker as Party Chairman, and she had just appointed a new Home Secretary. So Mr Fowler decided on an amicable departure.

The next to leave was Peter Walker, another of the handful of politicians to have served for ten consecutive years in Cabinet. In Mr Walker's case, the surprise was that he had stayed so long. In 1970, at the age of thirty-eight, he had been Secretary of State for the Environment, and widely thought of as a future PM. By 1990, at the age of fifty-eight, he was Secretary of State for Wales, and that would have been his last job. So he also went off to spend more time with his family; he has young children.

There was nothing sinister in either of these departures, but it added to an impression of disarray, which was to be confirmed by the Nicholas Ridley affair. It is still not clear how Mr Ridley came to give the interview in the *Spectator* which led inevitably to his resignation. Perhaps he thought that the interviewer, Dominic Lawson – Nigel's son – would have protected him from himself. Mr Lawson, who is confident that the bits he published were 'on the record', can be acquitted of sharp practice. Mr Ridley cannot be acquitted of negligence. At no stage did he clarify in his own mind the basis on which the interview was being conducted; he behaved as if he did not care what appeared in the magazine. His departmental press officers were uneasy about the whole affair; they suggested that if he did give the interview; he should do it in the DoE. It is hard not to believe that Nick Ridley had a subconscious ministerial death-wish.

There might be two explanations for this. In the first place, when Nigel Lawson resigned, Mr Ridley had been bitterly disappointed not to succeed him. He also had spent much of his life preparing for the job of Chancellor. More recently, he had been right about the consequences of shadowing the DM – and from the beginning he had disapproved of this new-fangled exchange-rate monetarism, and held fast to the monetarist orthodoxy of early Thatcherism. Mr Ridley thought that he had earned the Chancellorship. It was denied him because it would have been politically impossible to appoint him. That is a consideration which has never weighed much with Mr Ridley; he is a walking political impossibility. But to be refused the Treasury on what seemed to him frivolous and unjust grounds was hard. He may from then on have become semi-detached.

Second, he was becoming more and more worried about Europe, and the prospect of the UK joining the ERM. He was also concerned lest, in the midst of her other difficulties, the PM should be losing the stomach for a fight. So he may have been trying to help her. The interview was to have the opposite effect.

Mrs Thatcher always regarded herself as the best politician in her Government. She never ceased to be amazed at the things her ministers said and did, and the trouble they landed themselves – and her – in. Over Nick Ridley, there was no such detachment. She was desperately upset. From the beginning, however, her head ruled her heart. She, those around her, and finally – once he returned to England from Budapest – Nick Ridley himself, could see no alternative to resignation.

Ironically, Mr Ridley's departure from the Government made it easier for Britain to join the ERM. Until then, the matter had been in the hands of a Cabinet sub-committee consisting of the PM, Mr Hurd, Mr Major, and Mr Ridley: in other words, a 2-2 division. With Mr Ridley's departure, that became 2 against 1, and Margaret Thatcher was losing her will to resist; even she could sometimes bow to the inevitable.

With the Ridley interview, the Government had suffered another self-inflicted wound. Some Tory backbenchers were wondering whether governments could develop death wishes. Whenever Mrs Thatcher and her team seemed to be approaching calmer waters, something would go wrong. The Government was behaving like a patient whose will to live had gone and who would not rally, whatever the doctors did.

Yet over the few weeks after Mr Ridley's departure, the Government's position did improve a little – for no obvious reason. At the end of July, one or two polls showed the Labour lead down to single figures – that had been Party Chairman Kenneth Baker's target for the end of the year. Then came the Iraqi invasion of Kuwait.

In early August, some Tory MPs were rediscovering the pleasures of cautious optimism. They would remind one that a government without Nicky Ridley was no worse off electorally. Within two or three months, the rate of inflation and interest rates would surely be coming down, while the war, with a Kuwait factor seemingly reminiscent of the Falklands factor, would carry the Government through the interim of unpopularity until there was good economic news. Perhaps the Old Girl's luck had not failed her after all.

This mood barely survived until the first political frost of autumn. In the first place, there was little analogy between Kuwait and the Falklands. The Kuwait issue could not be dramatized in such starkly patriotic terms, and the direction of any war would be in American hands. Even by September, doubts were emerging as to whether there would be a war at all. If fighting should start, there were fears that it might prove messy, protracted and bloody. If so, how would public opinion respond? Could we rely on the Falklands response of pride in our troops and, for the fallen, stoicism?

Meanwhile the problems of the economy were looking equally messy, protracted and bloody. The UK seemed back in the days of stagflation – stagnation plus inflation – something that should not have been possible after eleven years of Thatcherism. Despite inflation, the Government did decide to join the ERM. But the predicted benefits, economic and political, were slow to appear (too slow for Mrs Thatcher's prospects for re-election). A one per cent cut in interest rates was welcome; less welcome were the forecasts that ERM membership would make it harder to achieve further cuts. At least on the Government side, those who favoured ERM membership had always insisted that it would not be a soft option; they were proved right. Neither the interest rate nor the opinion poll rate moved significantly in the Tories' favour.

A Dead Parrot Bites Back . . .

The Tory Party arrived at Bournemouth for its annual conference in an anxious mood, seeking reassurance. None was at hand.

Being Chairman of the Conservative Party is one of the hardest jobs in British politics, because of the burden of expectations. The Chairman generally owes his appointment to a reputation as a communicator: many in the party expect him to work miracles, instantly. But as Angus Maude once put it, when describing the difficulties he experienced as minister in charge of presenting the Government's case: 'If one of my Cabinet colleagues drops a catch, it's no use me picking up the ball and appealing for a wicket.'

In 1989, the party had appointed a Director of Communications, one Brendan Bruce. This was Peter Morrison's idea, and Margaret Thatcher took much persuading as to his merits. He was hired as the Party's answer to Peter Mandelson, at approximately twice Mr Mandelson's salary. Even though not experienced in politics, he was supposed to be an expert in the black arts of advertising. By the end, however he seemed to have become little more than Kenneth Baker's press officer. (When Chris Patten became Party Chairman, one of his first acts was to dispense with Mr Bruce's services.)

Kenneth Baker cannot be blamed for Brendan Bruce, whom he inherited. There were other mistakes, however Mr Baker brought energy to the job of Party Chairman; no chairman has ever put in more hours. Under his direction, in the middle of a Parliament, Central Office was working at almost a general election pace. But much of this effort was unproductive. Private polling was being conducted at five-minute intervals, partly under the guidance of Dick Wirthlin, who had been one of Reagan's pollsters, but who did not have the same grasp of British politics, and whose services were expensive. A mid-term anti-Labour campaign was launched: 'Summer Heat on Labour'. The Labour Party remained unscorched, unlike the Tory Party's finances.

Overall, there was too much activity and too little strategy – which is not to say that it would have been easy to devise a strategy, but the attempt ought to have been made. Its absence was notable at the Bournemouth conference: the flattest conference many Tories could remember. There was on high point: Margaret Thatcher's speech. No one listening to her would have thought this was a stricken leader of an embattled party. Indeed, her touch was lighter than in previous years. Even in her sixteenth and final conference speech as leader, she was still improving her technique, especially when it came to telling jokes. One of them misfired. In the language of 'Monty Python', she had mocked the Liberals, accusing them of being the 'dead parrot' party. The audience enjoyed it – but along the coast at Eastbourne, the parrot was coming back to life.

Mrs Thatcher had several times expressed her concern that the Eastbourne Tories should choose a worthy successor to her murdered friend Ian Gow. They failed. The candidate, Richard Hickmet, and his Central Office advisers fought a bad campaign, with crude literature which managed to outrage the sensibilities of Eastbourne and so squander the Ian Gow factor. To win the sympathy vote, a party has to come across as sympathetic. The loss of Eastbourne, as grievous as it was unexpected, shook Tory MPs. They had already had a bellyful of bad news, and they knew there was more to come. As an Hibernian parliamentarian once put it, 'Ireland's cup of troubles is running over, and it is not yet full.'

Changes of mood among MPs are easier to sense than to quantify, but after Bournemouth and Eastbourne I detected a sharp decline in the Tory Party's morale. A number of Thatcher loyalists, who had spent the last few months stiffening their colleagues' resolve, now began, privately, to despair. In the *Sunday Telegraph*, I had written many articles exhorting Tory backbenchers to remain steady under fire, and insisting that as long as the party remained united, there was still time to recover and win. During those months, several Tory MPs had invited me to visit their patch and go round a few doorsteps with them: then I would understand how bad things were. I had been unmoved, endlessly citing statistics about previous mid-terms, and previous recoveries.

Post-Bournemouth, I began to think I should have spent more time away from London and to lose hope in the possibility of a Tory victory. I suspect that a lot of Tory MPs who had hitherto been loyal to the Prime Minister thought similarly; they could not go through any more political pain barriers.

. . . So Does a Dead Sheep

Throughout the year the leadership question had been discussed. There was a general view that the day of the stalking-horse was over. If there were to be another candidate it had to be a proper one. That meant Michael Heseltine, though there had also been some talk of Geoffrey Howe.

As a candidate, however, Sir Geoffrey's time was up, something he himself recognized. But he could still play a role. A man whose political life had been spent avoiding drama and who had seemed to shrink with horror from the more Thespian aspects of his profession, at last reached for the limelight and the star billing. The owlish figure of Geoffrey Howe moved centre stage.

It was never likely that Sir Geoffrey would have had a happy time in his new post. The Leader of the House should be in charge of co-ordinating the Government's policies; it is a wide-ranging political role, especially when it is linked to the Deputy Prime Ministership. But for all the grandeur of his title, the Leader of the House can do his job effectively only if he has the Prime Minister's confidence. Geoffrey Howe did not enjoy the PM's confidence, and therefore was a cipher. Even if he had been heaped with dignities and country houses, she would still not have been interested in what he had to say. At least as Foreign Secretary, he had had a department to run and an endless supply of ambassadorial telegrams to read. But the Leader of the House's entire official life depends on his contacts with the PM. On a good day, Sir Geoffrey would be treated with cold civility.

Here, the PM was to blame, and not only for her rudeness. The decision to make Geoffrey Howe the Leader of the House was a crass misjudgement. She should have known that as she could not – and would not – get on with him, the appointment was bound to fail. Sir Geoffrey should not have been given a choice of posts; it ought to have been the Home Secretaryship, or nothing. No one could claim that the Home Secretaryship, one of the three great offices of state, was a demeaning offer. Only three politicians this century – Sir John Simon, Rab Butler and James Callaghan – have occupied all three great offices: the Treasury, the FO, the Home Office. Both Simon and Butler only had the FO briefly – in Butler's case, it was the unhappiest period in his ministerial career – while Callaghan was a rotten Chancellor. Sir Geoffrey could therefore have been the first politician to play a major innings in each of the three.

As Home Secretary, he would still have had a department to run. He might have refused to accept it, but he could not claim to have been insulted by the offer, and had he resigned, would not have won great sympathy. Not that Sir Geoffrey is by temperament a resigner. His instincts are to hang on; the hard slog, not the grand gesture. Had he been offered the Home Office, and only the Home Office, the probability is that he would have accepted it, and that he would be Home Secretary today – serving under Margaret Thatcher. However, in order to appoint Sir Geoffrey to the right post, Mrs Thatcher

would have had to take him seriously – instead of regarding him as a
Geoffrey was unhappy with the Prime Minister's insistence in pressing ahead with that piece of legislation, despite its rejection by the
House of Lords. He took the view that it was hard to ask a jury to
convict unless both Houses of Parliament had been persuaded of the
merits of the Bill. The Prime Minister was impatient alike with the
House of Lords, Sir Geoffrey's arguments, and Sir Geoffrey.

As usual, Sir Geoffrey was clearly annoyed at being denied the
consideration due to him as Leader of the House and Deputy Prime
Minister. On this occasion, however, some observers thought that he
was even more put out than usual, and might have been on the point
of resigning. This was Tristan Garel-Jones's view. Sir Geoffrey
himself denies this, describing the whole affair as 'a characteristic
incident that had been part of life in a Thatcher government for 100
years'. He concedes that 'people who had not previously been
concerned with our long-standing relationship might have misinterpreted what was going on' – but insists that nothing unusual took
place, and that there was no question of his resigning.

Mr Garel-Jones, a shrewd observer, is well acquainted with the
background to the Thatcher/Howe relationship. Nor are his anxieties necessarily proved groundless by Sir Geoffrey's denials. It is
bumbling old encumbrance who would put up with almost anything.
In his biography of Rab Butler, Anthony Howard describes how
Macmillan came to regard Butler as an old trout that could be tickled
at will. In the case of Mrs Thatcher vis-à-vis Sir Geoffrey, the
contempt was less well-concealed.

Others were less sure that Sir Geoffrey could be written off. In 1990,
as the months passed and Margaret Thatcher's position deteriorated, Sir Geoffrey's mood came to be a source of anxiety among
some of the more politically-aware members of the administration.
In July 1990, there was trouble over the War Crimes Bill. Sir
possible that Geoffrey Howe himself had not realized just how fed
up he had become. Tim Renton – who knows Sir Geoffrey well –
believes that he spent two days persuading him not to resign.
Anyway, Mr Garel-Jones concluded that if Sir Geoffrey had reached
that point over War Crimes, it would not be long before he did resign
over something else. So Tristan went with No. 10 to express the view
that Sir Geoffrey should be tempted out of politics by some irresistible offer, to render his resignation uncontroversial. It is unlikely,

however, that Sir Geoffrey would have succumbed, even is some such inducement had been found.

Paradoxically, the previous few months had seen the emergence of a pragmatic compromise on Europe, on which most of the party could unite. It consisted of the 3 'E's – the hard ecu, the ERM and enlargement. The hard ecu, a British response to the Delors Plan, seemed to offer a free-market, non-dirigiste approach to economic and monetary union (EMU). Although the timing of UK entry came as a surprise, by then the heat had gone out of the ERM issue. Enlargement involved expanding the Community to bring in both the EFTA countries and – as soon as their circumstances allowed – the emergent democracies of Eastern Europe. Given that the 3 'E's offered something for everyone, there seemed no reason for Tories to quarrel among themselves about Europe. For once, however, it was Sir Geoffrey who seemed set on provoking a dispute.

During both the party conference and the Rome EEC summit, he made a number of statements highlighting the philosophical differences between himself and the PM. It was as if he were determined to ensure that the Government would appear divided on Europe. On the *Sunday Telegraph*, Perry Worsthorne and I agreed that this could not continue. Whatever the costs of sacking Sir Geoffrey Howe, the cost of retaining him in office was greater. With Sir Geoffrey in Cabinet, the Government could not unite on Europe – and it would be unthinkable to fight an election campaign with the Premier and her Deputy constantly contradicting one another: shades of Messrs Foot and Healey on nuclear weapons in Labour's 1983 campaign. The *Sunday Telegraph* intended to run a piece in the issue of 4 November 1990 calling for Sir Geoffrey's dismissal. It is unlikely that Margaret Thatcher would have taken any notice of us – but Sir Geoffrey himself had decided to act. On Thursday 1 November, he resigned.

Especially coming from Geoffrey Howe, his resignation letter was not the work of an afternoon. He had first begun to discuss resignation a week earlier, and from then on he and his political aides were working on a draft. The PM was unaware of this – but in the course of the week, she unwittingly took action to seal his decision.

The Rome summit seemed to have worked to Mrs Thatcher's advantage, in that although it ended in fiasco, the blame for this fell on the Italian hosts, and not on her. The Italians seem to have reacted angrily to some British press reports predicting that they would run the summit incompetently; in their annoyance, they were even more incompetent than usual.[9]

On the Tuesday, Mrs Thatcher made a statement to the Commons: there was nothing in her text to alarm the Foreign Office, or Sir Geoffrey Howe. The problems arose in her answer to questions. Then, unscripted, her real feelings broke through. In particular, she was dismissive of her own Government's hard ecu, saying: 'In my view, it would not become widely used throughout the Community.'[10] At that moment, as one sketch-writer put it, Chancellor John Major – responsible for the hard ecu negotiations – looked as if he had just swallowed a toad. If his own Prime Minister failed to take the proposal seriously, the rest of the Community was hardly likely to do so.

This was Mrs Thatcher at her worst – and best. However difficult it made life for her colleagues, there was something admirable in her heroic refusal to mellow into the orthodoxies of government, even after eleven years as Prime Minister. But Sir Geoffrey found it intolerable. He was due to be interviewed by David Frost that Sunday. Europe was bound to come up, and Sir Geoffrey knew that he would be unable to restrain himself from saying what he thought: a further reason to expedite his resignation.

At the Cabinet meeting two weeks earlier, Mrs Thatcher had assailed Sir Geoffrey. She had blamed him – unfairly – for the delay in a Parliamentary Pensions Bill, which would also provide what would effectively amount to a redundancy payment for Ministers leaving office. She said that she had just seen Patrick Nicholls, who had resigned as a Parliamentary Secretary following a drink-driving case. Mr Nicholls had not received a pay-off: if the Bill had been ready for the last session, he would have done. It was all Sir Geoffrey's fault.

In fact, it had been the Treasury's fault. With its customary niggardly attitude towards anything involving increased public expenditure, the Treasury had been objecting that the Bill's provisions would be too expensive: hence the delay. But Sir Geoffrey did not respond to the PM's criticisms. He maintained as dignified a silence as was possible under her verbal barrage.

Two days after the hard ecu statement, Cabinet met again; it was to be Sir Geoffrey's final Cabinet. Unconscious of the significance of the occasion, Mrs Thatcher rose to it, and ensured that their working relationship should end on an appropriate note. Even by her stan-

---

9 There is an irony here. The comment that the Italian Presidency resembled a ride in a bus driven by the Marx brothers came originally, not from a British source, but from a senior Spanish diplomat at the EEC.

10 *Hansard*, 3 October 1990, col. 878.

dards, she was rude to him – ruder than several of those present could ever remember her being.

This time, trouble arose because a number of bills for the new session were still not ready. Lord Belstead, then Leader of the Lords, said that there was hardly any legislation available for the Upper House to consider; he was almost at the point of having to give their Lordships an additional recess. Hearing this, the PM flew at Sir Geoffrey, asking him angrily what he had been doing and why there were no bills. Part of the responsibility for this lay with the individual ministers who were still drafting their legislation – Messrs Parkinson, Patten and Rifkind had all missed deadlines. None of them moved to join Sir Geoffrey in the firing-line.

Inasmuch as he could still think about anything as she belaboured him, Geoffrey Howe might have recalled the previous discussion and seen a grim irony in the thought that he too was about to become a victim of the Treasury's dilatoriness. Perhaps this redoubled his determination to ensure that the PM would also be out of office before the Pensions Bill became law. As another member of the Cabinet described the scene: 'Talk about going on and on. It was as if she was hitting him round the head: boom, boom, boom. And he just sat there, soaking it all up.'

But after sitting there, he went back to his office, summoned his staff, completed his letter, asked for an appointment with the PM, and at it, resigned. The last act had begun.

5 The Fall of Margaret Thatcher Act I

Conspiracy or Cock-up?

The fall of Margaret Thatcher was the most extraordinary event in the history of British democratic politics. That it should have created shock waves was only natural; had it not been for the Gulf War, the effect would have been even greater. Like many of her closest supporters, Margaret Thatcher herself had come to believe that her position was invulnerable, however unpopular she might be at times. She herself has adapted to the loss of office with dignity and self-restraint, but some of her friends have given way to feelings of bitterness.

The human mind is naturally reluctant to attribute great events to small causes. Thus it is with many of Mrs Thatcher's supporters. From the beginning, they rejected the simple explanation: that her position had become imperilled because there seemed a grave risk of the party losing the next election; her fate was then sealed by a poor campaign. To many Thatcherites, it was aesthetically more satisfying to believe that she had been the victim of a conspiracy – hatcheted down by those who owed her not only loyalty, but their political careers.

As soon as she lost the leadership, a 'stab in the back' theory began to develop. There were obvious analogies with the original stab in the back myth, about the surrender of the German armies in November 1918 when the German front line was still on foreign soil, its armies apparently undefeated. Margaret Thatcher had won three elections; those most prone to believe in a conspiracy believed that she could also have won a fourth. She had also secured the votes of a majority of Tory MPs, coming tantalizingly, unbearably close to an outright win. Add to that the special dimension she brought to the leadership – her gift for turning politics into passion – and it is easy to understand why many of her partisans, as much Thatcher addicts as Thatcher supporters, felt acute withdrawal symptoms. In that mood, they were looking for someone to blame, some focal point for their resentments. In this, they were abetted by some mischief-making journalists, who affected a loyalty to the fallen Margaret Thatcher which they had never displayed while she was in office.

The fact that during a key phase in the supposed conspiracy, John Major was having surgery, and then convalescing in Huntingdon, only added to the eagerness with which the conspiracy theorists searched for a murder weapon with his fingerprints on it. As John O'Sullivan, an early devotee of the conspiracy school who subsequently changed his mind, put it: 'After all, in any good detective story, at the moment when the killing takes place the murderer always appears to have been conducting a symphony concert in front of an audience of 1,500.'

The conspiracy theory has only one problem: an entire lack of evidence. A conspiracy is not to be confused with 'what if' conversations, or with a pessimistic view of Margaret Thatcher's prospects. For there to have been a conspiracy, it is necessary that either Mr Major himself or a group of his close supporters should have worked to undermine Margaret Thatcher's support in the first ballot. That is the opposite of the truth. Almost everyone who was later prominent in the Major campaign not only voted for Margaret Thatcher in the first ballot, but gave her their full support. Of the thirty or so most prominent members of the Major team, only three did not support Margaret Thatcher in the first ballot. Rob Hayward had no animus against Mrs Thatcher; he had simply become convinced that she was an electoral liability. David Mellor, though a Minister of State, had developed an intense dislike of the Prime Minister, and had been in contact with Mr Heseltine. Mr Mellor's views were widely known at Westminster; he had never made much attempt to conceal them. Robert Atkins, a junior minister, also disliked the PM; he had not concealed his views either.

Since Mrs Thatcher's fall, Norman Lamont has been a principal target of smears, sneers and innuendo, all of which are as untrue as they are unfair. Mr Lamont was a pessimist, not a conspirator. Since Nigel Lawson's resignation, he had taken a gloomy view of the Government's prospects, and he never thought that Margaret Thatcher's campaign was going well. That did not prevent him from working on her behalf. Andrew Mitchell, later a Major supporter, confided to Norman Lamont that he had doubts about supporting Margaret Thatcher; Mr Mitchell also asked Mr Lamont not to pass that on to the Thatcher camp. Mr Lamont not only argued hard –

and successfully – to convert Mr Mitchell; he informed the Thatcher team so that they could make additional efforts at persuasion. He also reported on others he regarded as wobbly and asked his PPS, William Hague, to check up on some doubtful northern MPs.

After the first ballot, everything changed. Many Majorites became convinced that Margaret Thatcher should now step aside. But this was not a conspiracy; it was an exercise of political judgement. It was also more consistent with the rules of the leadership election than Mrs Thatcher's initial behaviour. As we have seen, the implications, though unstated, are clear: an incumbent leader who does not win on the first ballot should consider his or her position. Of course, having fallen inches short after all those years of service to party and country, Margaret Thatcher cannot be blamed for trying to carry on. Nor can others be blamed for concluding that she ought not to.

There was no conspiracy. It is true, however, that – with the best of motives – the most senior member of Margaret Thatcher's Government let her down, and that a largely unknown figure played the crucial role in making John Major Prime Minister.

Put Up or Shut Up

After Sir Geoffrey's resignation, Michael Heseltine, aroused by outrage and opportunity, wrote an open letter to his constituency chairman. In it he stopped short of announcing a leadership challenge: about a millimetre short. He then set off on a trip to the Middle East in the expectation that on his return, an irresistible momentum would sweep him from Heathrow to Downing Street. On his return, all that he found was an angry constituency chairman, who felt that before being given a walk-on part in Mr Heseltine's coup, he should have been consulted. That weekend's publicity seemed to go against Mr Heseltine.

But this was not a general election; it was a contest in front of an electorate of 372. Mr Heseltine's minor embarrassments in Henley were irrelevant; they did not enhance Mrs Thatcher's standing among Tory MPs. What they did enhance was her self-confience, and that of Kenneth Baker, the Party Chairman. This was danger-ous, for there was nothing to justify increased self-confidence. That mood of over-optimism produced tactical blunders. The first was to try to exploit Mr Heseltine's difficulties, and counter-attack. The aim was to inflict lasting discredit on him. He would either be forced into a contest which he would lose, or, by refusing to stand even after all his plotting, would reveal the weakness of his position.*

Throughout the week Ken Baker, Bernard Ingham and others told him, in effect, to put up or shut up. That was doubly foolish. Offered a choice between a suicidal attack and a humiliating retreat, Mr Heseltine would choose suicide, every time. He may have been a plotter; he was still a lion, not a jackal. Any notion that he would just slink away was based on a misreading of his character. To be fair to Mr Baker, he was convinced that Michael Heseltine was bound to run. However – at least until Geoffrey Howe's resignation – others still thought that a contest could be avoided, and that Mr Baker and Mr Ingham were making a leadership election more likely. Nothing in the mood of the Tory Parliamentary Party justified their behaviour. As soon as the House returned that Wednesday, Michael Mates, Keith Hampson and William Powell were patrolling the corridors, the bars, the lobbies, the tearoom – listening, noting, persuading, assessing: calculating. *Their* soundings were encouraging.

Mr Baker conducted no such exercise. Nor did he consult those best able to assess the mood of the Parliamentary Party. None of them was feeling over-confident. Tristan Garel-Jones had by then left the Whips' office to become a Minister of State at the Foreign Office – but he was still one of the two most acute assessors of mood of the party: the other being John Major. Though he kept his feelings to himself, Mr Garel-Jones was worried. Nothing had been done to placate the Garel-Jones hundred; the danger he had foreseen was now imminent.

During that week, Mr Major told me that he did not like the smell of the Parliamentary Party. This was also the view of Richard Ryder, Francis Maude, and David Davis: three excellent judges, all Thatcherites and thus well placed to see trouble from erstwhile loyalists. Conservative Central Office was not so well placed, and neither was No. 10. In the July reshuffle Mark Lennox-Boyd had moved on to become a Minister in the Foreign Office; his replacement as PPS was Peter Morrison.

Politics run in Mr Morrison's bloodline. In the 1950s and early 1960s, his father, John Morrison, now Lord Margadale, had been a formidable Chairman of the 1922 Committee. Peter Morrison himself had been a Whip or Minister since 1979, as well as Deputy Chairman of the Conservative Party, so although he was only forty-

---

* Others were also considering their positions. Around this time, two Cabinet Ministers – separately – approached Norman Tebbit to enquire whether he would support them, should Margaret Thatcher lose the leadership. Mr Tebbit will not reveal their names, but does state that neither of them was among the eventual leadership contestants.

six, he had had great experience of government. However, early promotion has one drawback: it can lead to premature retirement. By 1990, it was clear that Mr Morrison would not be made a Cabinet minister; after eleven years, he could not carry on as a junior minister. The Prime Minister was very fond of him, however, and would have been reluctant to sack him from the Government. A solution was found: to appoint him her PPS. For Mr Morrison also, a ministerial salary is not a consideration. But Peter Morrison was a bad choice as PPS.

He found it hard to reach those parts of the party where her influence needed to be reinforced. In his devotion to Margaret Thatcher, Mr Morrison rivalled Ian Gow. Unlike Ian, he had no understanding of those who did not share his feelings. If the courtiers on the steps of the throne are to understand the limitations of power, they must strive to retain a degree of detachment; Mr Morrison was all attachment. He therefore found it impossible to persuade any MP who was not already a convinced supporter of the Prime Minister's. Nor did he see any need to seek the counsel of others who might have been more sceptical. Here the death of Ian Gow put the Prime Minister at a grievous disadvantage. Ian had been murdered by the IRA on 30 July. Had he lived, he would undoubtedly have given No. 10 a more rounded picture of opinion within the Parliamentary Party than Mr Morrison was able to supply.

Peter Morrison also had his own enemies on the Tory benches. In the early 1980s, he had been the Pairing Whip, whose job is to oversee pairing arrangements – by which a Government and an Opposition member agree that both of them will be absent from a division, to their mutual convenience, but leaving the Government's majority unaffected. The Pairing Whip has to strike a balance, ensuring that the Government has the necessary votes but also giving his colleagues the occasional night off. Mr Morrison was held to err on the side of caution, and in a self-righteous manner. Sometimes a refusal is more palatable if expressed in a sympathetic tone; Mr Morrison's colleagues complained that he was inclined to deliver pompous lectures. In 1990, some resentments from that era still lingered.

Mr Morrison was neither equipped to sense danger, nor to avert danger. No. 10 proceeded to a further misjudgement. Just as the aim of putting pressure on Mr Heseltine was to end the uncertainty, so the decision was taken that if there had to be a contest, it should take place as quickly as possible. Nominations for the first ballot would close on Thursday 15 November. Should there be a ballot, it would be held on Tuesday 20 November – despite the fact that Mrs Thatcher was due to be in Paris from Sunday 18 until the lunchtime of Wednesday 21 November.

During both the 1983 and 1987 General Elections, Mrs Thatcher had paid brief visits to summit conferences. With an electorate of 36 million, 99.9 per cent of whom would follow the campaign only on television, this may even have worked to her advantage. With an electorate of 372, most of whom expect some flesh-pressing, and many of them fearing that the PM was becoming too remote from domestic politics, a foreign trip was a mistake. Paris was not worth one vote. However, Margaret Thatcher had taken a conscious decision to play the Prime Minister. She felt that she ought not to, allow a party election to interfere with the conduct of her duties, and that she should not have to do so. She held it beneath the dignity of her office to have to go cadging for votes. That attitude is commendable; she should still have deputed the cadging to competent persons.

The Worm Turns

The decision on the timing of the ballot had been taken before Sir Geoffrey Howe made his resignation speech. Twelve days had elapsed between the resignation and the speech; he had used them well. As an intellectual critique, it was inferior to Mr Lawson's effort a year previously; as a political criticism, it could not have been surpassed.

The word devastating has become a cliché which litters political reporting, as if devastation were an hourly occurrence at Westminster. But on that Tuesday, 13 November, Geoffrey Howe really was devastating. It was not only the most effective speech of his career; it was one of the most influential parliamentary performances of the century. Margaret Thatcher might have survived a lesser speech. Sir Geoffrey rose to his feet at 4.19 p.m. His tone was light and witty, avoiding any suggestion of bitterness or self-pity. Over the previous few days, both the Prime Minister and Mr Baker had sought to play down the gravity of his resignation by attributing it purely to questions of style. As Sir Geoffrey put it ' . . . if some of my former colleagues are to be believed, I must be the first minister in history who has resigned because he was in full agreement with Government policy'.[1] This was greeted with loud laughter, on the Tory as well as the Labour benches.

---

1 *Hansard*, 13 November, col. 461.

Sir Geoffrey went on to link Margaret Thatcher's obstinacy over the ERM to the Government's failure to control inflation. He repeated the claim Nigel Lawson had made a year previously, in his resignation speech, that the rise in inflation was directly linked to the delay in joining the ERM. In another passage which also had the Tory benches laughing, Sir Geoffrey bracketed the PM's dismissal of the hard ecu and her recent foray into cricketing parlance during the Lord Mayor's banquet speech, when she said, 'The bowling's going to get hit all round the ground. That's my style.'[2] Though Sir Geoffrey's cricketing reference was no less implausible, the effect was all he could have desired: 'It was . . . tragic . . . to hear my Rt Hon Friend dismissing, with such personalized incredulity, the very idea that the hard ecu proposal might find growing favour among the peoples of Europe . . . How on earth are the Chancellor and the Governor of the Bank of England, commending the hard ecu as they strive to, to be taken as serious participants in the debate against that kind of background noise? I believe that both the Chancellor and the Governor are cricketing enthusiasts so I hope there is no monopoly of cricketing metaphors. It is rather like sending your opening batsmen to the crease only for them to find, the moment the first balls are bowled, that their bats have been broken by the team captain.'[3]

Sir Geoffrey referred to his own 'commitment to government by persuasion', but went on: 'I realize now that the task has become futile, trying to stretch the meaning of words beyond what was credible, and trying to pretend that there was a common policy when every step forward risked being subverted by some casual comment or impulsive answer.'[4] He found the only appropriate conclusion to such a speech: 'I have done what I believe to be right for my party and my country. The time has come for others to consider their own response to the tragic conflict of loyalties with which I myself have wrestled for perhaps too long.'[5] Sir Geoffrey has subsequently insisted that this was not intended to probe the consciences of other pro-Europeans in the Cabinet, and not to incite Michael Heseltine. But whatever his intentions, to most of his hearers the words had one plain meaning. He had issued an invitation Michael Heseltine could not refuse.

When Sir Geoffrey sat down, at around 4.36, Margaret Thatcher was in grave danger. In the speech, he had repaid her for the maltreatment of a decade and a half. As Confucius ought to have written: 'never turn your back on a turning worm'.

---

2 *Times*, 13 November 1990.

3 *Hansard*, col. 464.

4 Ibid.

5 Ibid.

Those to whom Margaret Thatcher was a Messiah were unmoved by Sir Geoffrey's departure, as they had been by previous resignations, and would have been by the fate of almost any Cabinet minister. It was the fashion among some of those most slavishly devoted to her to deride most of her ministers; they were abetted in this by the tabloids. The PM herself did not do enough to discourage this behaviour, largely because it reflected her own attitudes at certain moments. But most Tory MPs were not Messianic Thatcherites, and were alarmed by her inability to establish a stable relationship with senior colleagues. If a secret poll had been taken of the Tory Parliamentary Party after Sir Geoffrey's speech, there would have been a majority assent to the proposition: 'There is something deeply wrong with Mrs Thatcher's style of government; it may be time for her to go.'

The First Ballot

The Stalking Lion

Though both the Heseltine camp and Sir Geoffrey insist that there was no collaboration, Michael Heseltine and his team had been hoping that the Howe speech would make an impact. The outcome exceeded all their expectations. Battle was joined. On Wednesday 14 November, Mr Heseltine announced his candidacy. He was proposed by Sir Neil Macfarlane and seconded by Sir Peter Tapsell. Margaret Thatcher – proposed by Douglas Hurd and seconded by John Major – responded with equal confidence.

In September, Mark Lennox-Boyd had given Peter Morrison all the files from the Thatcher/Meyer election: a valuable legacy. This time, there could be no question of a low-key campaign, and no need for secrecy. In that respect at least, Peter Morrison's task should have been easier. He did not capitalize on his advantages.

George Younger was recalled to the colours. He obeyed the summons reluctantly. This was not because he had become disloyal; by then he was more banker than politician. As Chairman of the Royal Bank, he felt he could not just throw up his duties, which lay in Edinburgh. He was also due to be shooting in Scotland on the Saturday. So he was not able to spend much time in London, or to give the 1990 leadership election anything like the time and energy he had devoted to the Meyer contest. Moreover, he was not as powerful a voice in 1990 as he had been in 1989. Though he was still as popular with his fellow backbenchers, they knew that his thoughts were no longer on the House of Commons: he had become a yesterday's man, unable to reassure MPs about today's anxieties. Indeed, his main value to Mrs Thatcher was negative. If he had not been on the team, questions might have been raised as to why Gentleman George no longer supported her. That would have involved time-wasting explanations, denials and fuss. So it was important to have his name on the letterhead, as non-executive Chairman of the Thatcher campaign.

But there was no one to fill the executive role. John Moore agreed to help, but he was in America for the first few days of the campaign, and even if he had been in Westminster, his support would not have been worth much. Although a former Cabinet minister, Mr Moore had never been a parliamentary heavyweight. He, too, was quitting the Commons at the next election. Those who are retiring from the House find themselves at a disadvantage in winning over colleagues whose main aim is to ensure their own survival.

It was also announced that Michael Jopling, a former Chief Whip and Agriculture Minister, would help to organize Mrs Thatcher's campaign. This seemed a better choice: Mr Jopling was a more substantial Commons figure. He had adjusted to life on the back-benches more successfully than most ex-Cabinet ministers do. In his case, the claim TV producers make for any MP they entice on to a current-affairs programme has validity; he is a weighty, respected, senior figure. He did not seem prepared to pull that weight for Margaret Thatcher, however. There was one problem about having Mr Jopling organize her campaign: no one had asked him in advance. When it was announced in the media that he would be involved, he was furious, but concluded that the best course was to keep quiet and do nothing. He was overheard saying in the lobbies that Douglas Hurd would make a good PM. To most MPs, unaware of the background, Mr Jopling sounded like a semi-detached member of a campaign run by a leadership which had become semi-detached from the Parliamentary Party.

However, though Messrs Younger, Jopling and Moore may not have made much impression, the Thatcher team was not short of big-name support. Gerry Neale, in charge of media operations, had no difficulty in fielding Cabinet ministers on all the current-affairs programmes that wanted them. One or two ministers were surprised by a lack of co-ordination. Cecil Parkinson said that he found himself 'flying solo': he would telephone Thatcher HQ to tell them he had been invited to appear on such-and-such a programme, and Mr Neale would say, 'Thank you for letting us know.' Before doing an interview with Brian Walden, Mr Parkinson thought he had better consult Mrs Thatcher herself. He wished her all the best for Paris, and went on: 'If Walden says, "Have you spoken to her recently?" – would it be helpful for me to say: "Within the last hour, and she is in good heart."?'

'Of course,' Mrs Thatcher replied.

But even if there was a haphazard quality to the media operation, this did not matter; the media campaign was not important. It was vital that there were plenty of Thatcher spokesmen on television – she might otherwise have been accused of not taking the election seriously. But what the spokesmen said mattered little; they were not going to convert any of the 372 electors.

Mrs Thatcher herself gave a couple of rather flat newspaper interviews, but decided to turn down TV bids. This may have been a mistake. The previous year, after Nigel Lawson resigned, she had been interviewed by Brian Walden, a friend and her favourite interviewer. For the first time in his career he had given her a rough time, and indeed got the better of her. She had still not altogether forgiven Mr Walden for that performance, and decided not to risk the same thing happening again.

Had she known she was in desperate trouble, she might have discarded resentment, and caution. Margaret Thatcher determined to fight her way out of adversity is a formidable interviewee. The onrush of personality, the face ablaze with conviction, those flashing eyes: the acme of femininity, with a punch like Joe Louis – it might just have persuaded a few wavering Tory MPs that there was only one Margaret Thatcher, and there could only be one Prime Minister.

Margaret Thatcher did not realize how vulnerable her position was. She was not aware that her campaign was faltering in the crucial battle-zone: the Commons. This was nothing to do with the media, or with the big names. In 1990 as in 1989, the key elements in the campaign ought to have been the canvassing effort in the House and the unofficial whipping operation. The latter went badly wrong.

Ian Gow, of course, was dead. Richard Ryder did once drop into Lord McAlpine's house in Great College Street, Thatcher HQ for this campaign. He brought Tristan Garel-Jones with him; they were on their way to dine with Alan Clark in Wilton's. But Mr Morrison does not like or trust Mr Garel-Jones. Worse still, Tristan's name had actually been recorded as doubtful. Shana Hole, once again borrowed from Alistair McAlpine, had the presence of mind to walk smartly out of the room with the piece of paper on which that monstrous inaccuracy had been perpetrated: even so, the meeting did not go well. Mr Garel-Jones, though unaware that he was not regarded as a reliable Thatcher supporter, could sense tension. Subsequently, he telephoned with a couple of suggestions. He was politely informed by Mark Lennox-Boyd that his help was not required. Richard Ryder was told by Mr Morrison not to bring Tristan along again; Mr Ryder complied – he himself did not return either.

Mr Lennox-Boyd gave some help, but apart from Mr Morrison the two main campaigners were Michael Neubert and Gerry Neale. Michael Neubert was a former Whip, and Gerry Neale had been involved in the previous campaign because he had recently been George Younger's PPS. Mr Neale and Mr Neubert are good fellows – but as operators, they themselves would not claim to be in the same class as Messrs Garel-Jones, Gow and Ryder.

As far as many MPs were concerned, the public face of the Thatcher canvass consisted of Norman Tebbit and George Gardiner. The latter, a right-winger, is one of the PM's longest-serving, most loyal and least well-rewarded supporters. But neither he nor Mr Tebbit was the right choice to win round worried middle-of-the-road backbenchers. On this occasion, their efforts were inadequately supplemented by a 'run silent' operation. George Young was now a Whip, and unable to help. Others felt that their efforts were not being properly directed and that the intelligence they fed back to Great College Street was not being acted on. Some of them, feeling leaderless, relaxed their efforts. When the Thatcher campaign files were handed over to Francis Maude for use in John Major's campaign, they were found to contain many blank pages: there had not been a complete canvass.

At the beginning of the leadership campaign, ITV's 'Parliament' programme decided to try to work out the result. It started with several advantages – in particular, a first-class production team, headed by the editor, Howard Anderson (no relation), and his deputy, Julie Kirkbride. Unlike the majority of television journalists, they understand the Tory Party. Mr Anderson and Miss Kirkbride worked through the list of Tory backbenchers, using their knowledge to make assessments. They also ran the list past five or six friendly MPs, cross-checking and collating. One of the programme's presenters, Sue Cameron, is also Mrs Keith Hampson – but a Chinese Wall that would satisfy any City regulatory authority insulated Miss Cameron from information that Dr Hampson might have found interesting.

As a result of their efforts, the 'Parliament' programme concluded that the result would be: Thatcher 192 votes, Heseltine 140 – the rest abstainers, or those whom the programme felt unable to identify. Though both Mrs Thatcher's and Mr Heseltine's votes were underestimated, Mr Anderson and Miss Kirkbride were spot on with the margin of victory: 52 votes. So their canvassing exercise was much more successful than Mr Morrison's. That a television programme could perform more efficiently than the Thatcher campaign is conclusive evidence of that campaign's incompetence.

The Party and the Country

Not only had the canvassing on MPs been neglected; no attempt been made to mobilize the party in the country on Mrs Thatcher's behalf. On Fridays, Tory MPs return to the bosoms of their constituency associations. Even in a secret ballot, a couple of days steady presssure can achieve results: over the next weekend, it was to help John Major to become Prime Minister.

Until she lost the leadership, there were few spontaneous outbreaks of pro-Thatcher sentiment. But a good campaign need not rely on anything so fickle as spontaneity. As ever, had the choice been left to Tory activists in the constituencies, the existing leader would have been confirmed in office. In the short time available – another consequence of the abbreviated campaign – it might have been difficult to organize large-scale constituency pressure; the attempt was not ever made.

As if to complete the depletion of Mrs Thatcher's campaigning resources, in November 1990 the Whips' office remained strictly neutral. On the Tuesday morning, at the Department of the Environment 'morning prayers' meeting – when ministers and political advisers meet without officials – Tim Boswell, the DoE Whip, reported the Whips' office assessment: that Margaret Thatcher would win by about two to one. He went on to add that a certain number of colleagues were bound to be lying, so the figure was not absolutely reliable. It was clear that the Whips had done nothing to identify, let alone deter, the liars. Against Anthony Meyer, the Sri Lankan Third XI of leadership contestants, Margaret Thatcher had fielded her strongest side. Against Michael Heseltine, she deployed her own Third XI.

As her campaign failed to get into its stride, many of Mrs Thatcher's supporters grew worried. At weekends, the Tory Party's political market-makers spend a lot of time on the phone to one another. During Saturday and Sunday 17/18 November, the telephone traffic was especially heavy, and full of anxiety. Again and again, the same point was repeated: that whatever Peter Morrison was saying about the figures, it did not *feel* right. By that weekend, Norman Tebbit was also worried.

Mr Morrison, however, expressed serene confidence – and he was in charge. Over the previous few days, John Whittingdale had voiced his doubts. Every time he did so, Mr Morrison replied with a complacent smile, and promised to remind Mr Whittingdale about their conservation in a few days' time. To all enquirers, Mr Morrison's response was equally confident. He would tap his jacket pocket, repeating, 'It's all in here, it's all in here.' By 'all' he meant around 238 votes for Margaret Thatcher. He also thought that up to eighty backbenchers would abstain.

There was, however, an irony. As regards the figure of 238, Mr Morrison would often add blithely 'but of course 15 per cent of them are liars.' He never sounded as if he believed this – still less that he was proposing to take any corrective measures. He would conclude by saying that he thought the PM could be guaranteed 220 votes.

Two hundred and thirty-eight minus 15 per cent is 202: in his insouciance, Mr Morrison had arrived close to the truth. On Sunday afternoon, buoyed up by Peter Morrison's forecasts, she went to Paris. Jeffrey Archer, who spoke to her before she set off, described her mood as 'anxious, but not worried'.

When the result of the ballot was announced, many people were surprised by the small number of abstainers. There is one possible explanation for this. In 1975, the Heath camp's over-confidence undoubtedly encouraged some MPs to vote for Margaret Thatcher:

they could not bear the thought of Mr Heath being triumphantly re-elected. Airey Neave, aware of this, encouraged such reactions by persistently understating Mrs Thatcher's support. It is at least likely that Mr Morrison's over-confidence led some anti-Thatcher MPs to decide that an abstention would not be good enough: they had to vote against her. If so, that would be the sole influence Mrs Thatcher's campaign had on the outcome of the ballot.

A Treacle Shower?

Once in Paris, the PM threw herself into summiteering with her usual zest. On Monday evening, there was a bizarre incident. Margaret Thatcher's relationship with Herr Kohl, the German Chancellor, had never been easy. In terms of ability to grasp detail, Helmut Kohl may not match Margaret Thatcher, but he is considerably better than Ronald Reagan. However, Mrs Thatcher never extended the same tolerance to his broad-brush approach as she had to the former President. She also made insufficient allowances for the nature of German politics. Although Herr Kohl always won a higher percentage of the popular vote than she had,[6] the German system of proportional representation meant that he was obliged to form a coalition with the Free Democrats. That gave Hans-Dietrich Genscher, a slippery Euro-fanatic of whom Margaret Thatcher did not approve, a lifetime freehold on the German foreign ministry.

But Helmut Kohl had never given up hope of establishing a friendship with Mrs Thatcher. On Monday 19 November, they were due to dine at the British Embassy in Paris. As always on such occasions, Mrs Thatcher had in mind a business-like agenda – the GATT round, Iraq and Kuwait, EMU, *et al*. Old King Kohl had other ideas. A bluff, burly fellow, he exuded elephantine friendliness. Through the interpreter, he told her that he had come to cheer her up: on such occasions, friends should share their troubles; this was not an evening for a formal agenda. At the best of times, Margaret Thatcher has no taste for *Gemütlichkeit* – especially as she probably suspected an element of *Schadenfreude*. So there was she, wanting to talk business – she would find in that all the distraction she needed from domestic problems – confronted by Herr Kohl, looking more than ever like the tuba player in an oompah band, determined to wallow in sentiment. She was determined not to allow herself to be given a treacle shower.

---

6 The British electoral system is the envy of many European politicians. Poul Schluter, the Danish Prime Minister, once said to Mrs Thatcher: 'Margaret, what I wouldn't give for even twelve months of the power you enjoy under your voting system.' 'Ten years is better, Poul,' she replied.

That was to be her last ever Euro-disagreement, at least as Prime Minister. As was only fitting, she had her way, and the discussion moved firmly towards business.

A Sleaze Shower

Back in London, meanwhile, there had been some distinctly unsentimental business. The *Sun* newspaper had decided to come to Mrs Thatcher's aid, and did so characteristically by running an assault on the characters of Michael Heseltine, Keith Hampson and Michael Mates. That was the *Sun* at its worst.

The *Sun* has good points. Its leaders are sometimes the best in any daily paper – a remarkable achievement given the constraints of space and vocabulary. The leaders are, of course, overshadowed by its coverage of other matters. This is not universally offensive. The *Sun*'s brawling, triumphant bawdiness is a distinctive English voice, with echoes of Chaucer, Shakespeare and Fielding. But the *Sun* also contains a great deal of sleaze, and here many Tories' attitude is hypocricital. Moralizing backbenchers who will talk as if a late-night discussion programme on Channel Four with viewing figures in the low tens of thousands threatens the country with the decadence that overwhelmed the Roman Empire, avert their gaze from the *Sun*, with its millions of readers and staunch support for the Tory Party. Some sensitive Tories have a bad conscience about all this, and tend to associate the *Sun* with what they regard as the less attractive features of Thatcherism. Rupert Murdoch, the *Sun*'s proprietor, is not a popular figure on the high-minded, traditional wing of the Tory Party.

So the *Sun's* attack on the Heseltine camp angered a lot of Tory MPs. There were even – entirely unjustified – suspicions that Bernard Ingham might have been involved. As an essay in character-assassination, the *Sun* piece was ineffective: a fricassée of stale gossip. Ineffective nastiness is doubly counter-productive: there is no point in a hatchet-job that leaves its intended victims unscathed, surrounded by friends offering sympathy. 'Disgusting' was how one Cabinet minister friendly to Mrs Thatcher described the article; he spoke for many. In a few cases, that feeling of disgust might even have confirmed a decision to vote against the PM. The *Sun* was no help to her, and did no damage to Mr Heseltine.

An Attack of Nerves

On the Tuesday, those in Paris with Margaret Thatcher noticed that her mood had changed. Suddenly she became nervous, and appeared gripped by foreboding. But Peter Morrison showed no sign of nerves. Indeed, he insisted on coming to Paris in order to man the telephone links to London; he wanted to be the first to tell her the good news.

Just before 6.30, two groups assembled, one in Mrs Thatcher's bedroom in the British Embassy in Paris, the other in her office in the Commons. In the bedroom, apart from Mrs Thatcher, there were: Sir Ewen Fergusson, the British Ambassador to France; Peter Morrison; Charles Powell; and Bernard Ingham. In London, Norman Tebbit, Tim Bell, Gordon Reece and John Whittingdale were preparing to celebrate with a glass of champagne. Charles Powell stayed on the line to Mrs Thatcher's office, while Peter Morrison prepared to talk to the Chief Whip on a line that had been specially installed for the evening. Ian Twinn, a scrutineer, broke away from the count to rush to Mrs Thatcher's office with the result, so – characteristically – Mr Powell heard first, about a minute before Mr Morrison. He could not bring himself to break the news.

In order to win outright, Margaret Thatcher would have had to achieve two targets. First, at least 187 votes – 50 per cent of the Parliamentary Party plus one. Second, to beat Michael Heseltine by at least 56 votes – 15 per cent of the Parliamentary Party. The actual figures were:

Margaret Thatcher	204
Michael Heseltine	152
Abstentions	16

Mrs Thatcher had fallen short of outright victory by 4 votes. A swing of just two MPs from Michael Heseltine to her was all that would have been needed.

When she was told, her initial response was typically stoical. There was no display of emotion, just a little toss of the head and the jaw set tighter. But one of those present who knew her best was convinced that then and there, she realized it was all over. There followed a moment of farce, while those in the bedroom tried to work out the percentages involved. Probably because everyone was in a state of shock, no one seemed to be sure how the voting system worked, or on what basis to calculate the 15 per cent. Different theories were offered, and the problem was compounded by the fact that no one was very good at calculating percentages. But London confirmed the bad news.

Peter Morrison at least remained clear-headed, and pressed Mrs Thatcher to issue an immediate statement in the Embassy forecourt. So she came bouncing out of the building, preceded by Bernard Ingham, who pushed all aside, marched up to a startled John Sargeant of the BBC, who had been about to make a routine report, and said: 'Very pleased that I got more than half the Parliamentary Party vote and disappointed that it is not quite enough to win on the first ballot, so I confirm it is my intention to let my name go forward for the second ballot.'

This was more or less the statement which had been drafted by her campaign team for use in such a contingency, and 'It is my intention' contained a deliberate ambiguity. Although it sounded firm, it also allowed the possibility that the intention might be modified after she had consulted others. There had been no consultation, not even of Douglas Hurd, her proposer, who was with her in the Paris Embassy. Later, some of Mrs Thatcher's Cabinet colleagues were critical of her decision to press ahead without consulting anyone and thereby trying to bounce her Cabinet colleagues. This was unfair. She was right not to consult or hesitate. Any sign of public wavering would have been fatal. In mortal peril, she was surely entitled to essay one more flourish of her banners, one last blast on the trumpet, one final attempt to rally her fading forces.

After the bold show of defiance in front of the Embassy, she went back inside and agonized. She talked to Denis Thatcher, who was characteristically pithy, supportive and disparaging about the Parliamentary Conservative Party. She also spoke to Tim Renton, who was not discouraging, and to Kenneth Baker, who urged her to fight on. Then she went to change for a banquet at Versailles. In the opinion of one observer she was 'outwardly chirpy, inwardly deeply miserable'.

Charles Powell, who did not feel in a banqueting mood, gave up his place at Versailles to Peter Morrison. Mr Powell had work to do: the Labour Party had moved a motion of no confidence in the Government, due to be debated on Thursday. So while a cheerless group put on its bravest face and set off to Versailles, Mr Powell dictated a first draft of the Prime Minister's speech. Later, Charles Powell and Bernard Ingham conferred, and tried to work out what was best for Mrs Thatcher: both were pessimistic about her chances. Mr Powell remembers being asked by a garden girl – a No. 10 secretary – what would happen now, and replying, 'I'm afraid that's it.'

Mr Powell was up early to prepare for the final session of the summit. Tristan Garel-Jones telephoned him to give a pessimistic account of the state of party feeling, and to inform him about the meeting that had taken place in his house the previous evening. The pessimism was reinforced by a conversation Mr Powell had with Peter Lilley, whom he asked to help with the PM's speech. Mr Lilley replied gloomily that there was no point: it was all over; the Prime Minister was not going to win.

So ended Margaret Thatcher's final summit – as Premier, at any rate. She had earned the right to conclude her Prime Ministerial involvement with international affairs in a grand finale – but democratic politics rarely allows grand finales. Winston Churchill did not return to Potsdam. Margaret Thatcher had a miserable journey back from Paris.

The Second Ballot

Tooth Trouble

One morning in June 1990, John Major woke up and realized that there was something the matter with his teeth. He was informed that the problem was an impacted wisdom tooth which would need an operation, followed by ten days' convalescence. It is not easy for Chancellors to clear a week out of their schedule (Mr Major always intended to curtail his convalescence). After consulting his diary, John Major decided to have the operation over the weekend of 17 and 18 November, and to take the following week off. From June to November, in addition to the usual stresses of being Chancellor, he had to take penicillin and painkillers for the tooth; British politicians need stamina.

Mr Major was due to go into the east London hospital on Friday 16 November. Before the tooth problem arose, he had agreed to speak at a dinner on that Friday in the Reform Club, organized by Tim Smith and his Beaconsfield Conservatives to raise money for Lynda Chalker's marginal constituency of Wallasey. Jeffrey Archer, an old friend of Mr Major's, was to take his place.

Towards the end of the week before the operation, Mr Archer telephoned Mr Major and suggested that in view of the political crisis, he postpone the surgery. John Major, saying that others had been making the same point, firmly refused. This was not just because he was fed up having a troublesome tooth and wanted to get the operation over with. He thought that a postponement would send all the wrong signals. 'People would assume that I was waiting around like a vulture hoping to pick up some bones,' he told Mr Archer. 'I will not tolerate people thinking that of me. I expect Margaret to win: I am not seconding her in the hope that she will lose.' Saying that he would be out of hospital on the Sunday, he invited Jeffrey Archer to spend Monday with him at home; neither doubted that there would be plenty to discuss. It is fascinating to speculate what might have happened if the operation had proved more complicated than expected, putting John Major completely out of action for a few days – but the surgery went smoothly. Mr Major left hospital on the Sunday and went home to rest.

On Monday morning, Jeffrey Archer arrived chez the Majors at about 10.30. The telephone had already started ringing, but Mr Major had decided to take very few calls; he had no wish to fuel speculation. So Norma fielded the phone, and deflected most callers with the excuse that John was asleep. When Jeffrey Archer arrived, the Majors had only one newspaper, the *Daily Telegraph*, which they took at home. So Jeffrey set out for the rest, but could not find a *Times*. All the other papers were suggesting that if Mrs Thatcher did not win in the first ballot, Douglas Hurd would be a strong candidate. Then Mr Major's private office rang from the Treasury, to say that there was a favourable mention of him in *The Times*. John Major asked them to fax the article, but the middle page of the fax did not arrive. So Jeffrey Archer set out for a second time, and returned with a *Times*.

The later morning was given over largely to gossip and a discussion of England's prospects in the forthcoming Ashes series. Then they sat down to lunch, which Norma Major had prepared, choosing a menu that required a minimum of chewing. Over the main course, moussaka, Jeffrey raised the question of the hour: what if the PM did so badly in the first ballot that she could not continue? John Major claimed to be not altogether certain that he was the right man to lead the party. He thought that the wisest course of action would be for the Whips to take a sounding as to which of Douglas Hurd or himself would have the better chance of stopping Michael Heseltine. He would be happy to fall in with whatever advice the Whips gave. At this, Norma Major interjected: 'You do realize you're talking about becoming Prime Minister?' John Major and Jeffrey Archer both smiled.

Over the previous few days, one or two of Douglas Hurd's friends had raised the same topic with him. Mr Hurd had shown an equal reluctance to thrust himself forward. He was also aware that over the previous year, John Major had emerged as a serious candidate for the Leadership: 'Couldn't John Major do this?' he said on one occasion. At this stage, neither Mr Hurd nor Mr Major were thinking seriously about a Leadership bid. Despite their doubts about the Thatcher campaign, they both assumed that she would win. Inasmuch as they did give any thought to contingency planning, both instinctively favoured a brokered solution which would relieve them of the need to campaign against one another.

In view of John Major's teeth, Norma Major had made some jelly for pudding. 'Why do I only get jelly when I'm ill?' enquired Mr Major, and had two helpings. The conversation switched away from the leadership election; both men assumed that Margaret Thatcher would remain in office. They moved on to the problems the party would face between then and the election. John Major also said that he wanted to make a philosophical speech. This would contain no figures: there would be no reference to interest rates, the ERM or the mortgage rate – or any of the other topics which preoccupied him as Chancellor. He wanted to set out a clear vision of the party's future and – a recurrent preoccupation – define an agenda for Toryism in the 1990s.

At 5.30 p.m., Jeffrey Archer left Huntingdon to fulfil yet another speaking engagement, this time at Sussex University. As the Majors waved him goodbye, John Major still thought that his role in the leadership campaign would consist solely of seconding Margaret Thatcher in the first ballot. A little over twenty-four hours later, he instantly agreed to second her in the second ballot also.

The Men in Suits

As they digested the implications of the first ballot result, the Thatcher camp realized that they would have to mount an entirely different operation in any second ballot campaign. That meant fresh personnel, and a new Chief of Staff. Mrs Thatcher and Mr Tebbit both concluded that the obvious person to take charge was John Wakeham. Mr Wakeham, a shrewd, laconic, safe-pair-of-hands character, had been Chief Whip for a whole Parliament and Leader of the House for two years. He knew his parliamentary colleagues well. They liked and trusted him; he was the right choice as campaign manager.

But John Wakeham also had his own agenda. Though the men in dark suits have no formal role these days, the party's elder statesmen still regard themselves as, in effect, its trustees. John Wakeham was absolutely loyal to Margaret Thatcher; he was equally loyal to the Conservative Party. When he started work on the Tuesday evening, it was on the assumption that the party's interests and Margaret Thatcher's interests were identical. Over the next twenty-four hours, he gradually redefined Mrs Thatcher's interests. He seized immediately on one crucial point: the absolute importance of the Cabinet. As he said at the time, a Prime Minister can be removed from office in only two ways: by a vote of no confidence in the House of Commons, or by losing the confidence of the Cabinet. If Mrs Thatcher still enjoyed the Cabinet's backing, she could proceed with confidence. If not, she would have to think again. Mr Wakeham asked John MacGregor, Geoffrey Howe's successor as Leader of the House, to ascertain the position by canvassing his Cabinet colleagues.

Mr MacGregor began that operation on Tuesday night. He asked his colleagues two questions: did they support Mrs Thatcher, and did they think she could win. Of the twenty-two members of the Cabinet, he excluded Mrs Thatcher herself, obviously, and also Messrs Hurd and Major, who were deemed to have expressed their views by proposing and seconding her. Other colleagues, aware that Mr Hurd and Mr Major had not really been in a position to exercise a free choice, suspected that their public loyalty did not reflect their private views.

Although Mr MacGregor spoke to the two Cabinet ministers in the Upper House – Lord Mackay, the Lord Chancellor; and Lord Belstead, the Leader of the House of Lords – their views were also discounted by their colleagues. It was assumed – correctly – that they would support the Prime Minister, but that this judgement would be based on reflex loyalty, not on any appreciation of the state of feeling in the Commons.

The Death Warrant

So the crucial factor was the attitude of the seventeen uncommitted Cabinet ministers. By the time he concluded his soundings – mid-morning on Wednesday – Mr MacGregor had a death warrant for Margaret Thatcher. The verdict was 12-5 against her. Only Kenneth Baker, Peter Brooke, David Hunt, Cecil Parkinson and John Wakeham thought she could carry on and win by a decent margin. All the rest thought she should stand down. Two of them – Messrs Clarke and Patten – now declared that they no longer supported her. The other ten – Messrs Gummer, Howard, King, Lamont, Lilley, MacGregor himself, Newton, Rifkind, Waddington and Waldegrave – did still support her. Most of them indeed declared that should she run, they would stand by her to the end. But all of them thought that she would either lose or just scrape home by a margin that would render victory instantly hollow.

Almost all of the PM's dozen opponents had reached their decision only after great agonizing. In a majority of cases, their personal loyalty was not in doubt. Indeed, the pro-Thatcher five's judgement was more open to question than that of the twelve antis. The five included David Hunt, who had been in Japan since the previous Thursday, and was therefore unaware of the mood in Westminster after the first ballot. Most of his colleagues thought that had he been in London, he would have voted with the majority. There was also Peter Brooke, the Northern Ireland Secretary, who was almost as out of touch: he had been spending most of his time in Northern Ireland. Cecil Parkinson, utterly loyal to Margaret Thatcher, refused to accept that her and the party's interests could ever diverge.

When Kenneth Baker became Party Chairman, he had decided that never at any stage should a glimmer of daylight appear between him and Margaret Thatcher. That remained his policy until the end; some of his Cabinet colleagues believed he had become so obsessed by the need to earn her trust that he had lost sight of the wider interests which a Party Chairman should safeguard.

John Wakeham seemed equally determined to retain Mrs Thatcher's confidence. But his role was more complex, and more ambiguous. Throughout the twenty-six crucial hours after the first ballot, Mr Wakeham had one overriding aim – to safeguard the party's interests – and three subsidiary objectives. First, to ensure that if Margaret Thatcher decided to contest the second ballot, she should do so on the basis of the most accurate possible information as to the state of feeling in the party. Second, that if she were to fight on, she would win. Third, that if she were to leave office, she should do so in the most dignified manner possible.

Towards the end of Wednesday morning, Mr MacGregor called on Mr Wakeham at the Department of Energy. That was an interesting departure from Whitehall protocol; Mr MacGregor, as Lord President of the Council and Leader of the House, ranked higher in Cabinet precedence than Mr Wakeham. Normally, the lower-ranking minister goes to the office of the higher-ranking one. But Mr MacGregor is not a man to stand on his dignity: for the purpose of this exercise, Mr Wakeham was the senior partner. On the basis of his canvass, Mr MacGregor already knew that Margaret Thatcher's premiership was at an end. Reluctantly John Wakeham found himself forced to come to the same conclusion. They now had the task of convincing her.

For John Wakeham, this was a particularly difficult problem. The PM was on her way back from Paris, expecting him to take charge of her re-election campaign. He was in the awkward position of a doctor, called in to treat a patient eager for recovery, who discovers that the condition is beyond treatment. Nor would Margaret Thatcher be the easiest of patient to convince that all hope was gone. Mr Wakeham's position was made harder because of his personal attachment to the PM. He was not only a senior colleague, but a good friend. They had been drawn especially close after the Brighton bomb outrage of October 1984, in which Mr Wakeham's first wife Roberta was killed. He later remarried, and his bride was Alison Ward, another family friend of the Thatcher's; she had been Margaret Thatcher's secretary and confidante for many years.

Now it seemed that John Wakeham might have to ease his old friend out of No. 10. He proceeded to act in a straightforward manner, executed with great subtlety. He knew that if she was finished, there was only one person who could convince her that her time was up: Margaret Thatcher. She had to hear for herself the true state of party opinion; only then might she accept that the obstacles were insuperable. However, Mr Wakeham did not rule out the possibility that by her own endeavours, she might dramatically transform the battlefield. She had conquered insuperable obstacles before. So as well as trying to inform her of the strength of the forces ranged against her, John Wakeham also began to organize a Thatcher second ballot campaign. He wasted no time with the 3rd XI, but instantly contacted Messrs Garel-Jones and Ryder. Both agreed to help, but both expressed grave doubts about her chances of winning. Mr Ryder said that he would only agree on condition that he could see Mrs Thatcher and inform her of the obstacles in her path to re-election.

The Men in Suits Come to Lunch

There was no time for either Mr Wakeham or Mr MacGregor to begin this process before a larger meeting began in No. 10. By then, the whole Tory Party was talking about the men in suits: now they had come to lunch with the Prime Minister. When she arrived back in No. 10, Norman Tebbit was already waiting for her. He was shortly joined by Messrs Wakeham and MacGregor, plus John Moore from her campaign team, Kenneth Baker, Cranley Onslow and Tim Renton. Peter Morrison was also present, as were John Whittingdale and Andrew Turnbull, her principal private secretary.

Kenneth Baker led off the discussion. He told her that only she could defeat Michael Heseltine, but that she must campaign more positively, with a stress on party unity. By that, he was signalling that there should be no more silly attacks on Michael Heseltine. Mr Baker suggested that there should be a new campaign team, led by Douglas Hurd and John Major. He believed that she had lost votes during the campaign: next time, it should be possible to reverse that.

John Wakeham sounded supportive, but this was more a matter of tone than substance. He told her to disregard talk of the humiliation involved in a second ballot, or in the risk of defeat. She was perfectly entitled to fight on, and if she won, the party would soon put all this behind them. Anyway, assuming there were a humiliation factor, it would have applied if she had been defeated at any stage, or had withdrawn.

The latter argument was dubious. Clearly a first ballot defeat would have been humiliating, as would a second round defeat, or even a victory by a greatly reduced margin. To withdraw after leading the first ballot by fifty votes could not be so regarded. While appearing to support her, Mr Wakeham was introducing the concept of humiliation, and deftly steering her towards an honourable alternative.

Then John MacGregor spoke. Over the next few days, he was to be widely criticized, especially by Cabinet colleagues, who could not understand why he had failed to inform her about the results of the

Cabinet canvass; some of the critics felt he could have delivered the *coup de grâce* there and then. Mr MacGregor thought differently. A warm and sensitive man, he knew what a blow it would be to Mrs Thatcher's pride to learn that her own Cabinet had turned against her. Though he was not looking forward to telling her, he knew that he had to, but was determined to do so in private. He felt strongly that to announce his figures in front of others would indeed have been a humiliation. However, he tried to signal a negative message. He said that the Cabinet was supportive, but uneasy, putting the stress on uneasy. There were also signs of flakiness among the junior ministers; some Cabinet colleagues could not or would not speak for their ministerial team. He concluded by advising her to see the Cabinet herself, one by one.

Kenneth Baker then reinforced John MacGregor's message by informing her that some of her own best supporters were saying that she could not win. He cited John Gummer, Michael Howard, Norman Lamont and Peter Lilley. The PM's reaction to all this was uncharacteristic, and therefore significant. A Margaret Thatcher full of confidence and fight would instantly have flown at Mr MacGregor for more details. 'What d'you mean, uneasy? Who's uneasy? Tell me their names,' she would have insisted – 'and who are these flaky junior ministers?'

Even the strongest can quail in the face of terrible news. At least subconsciously, Margaret Thatcher did pick up Mr MacGregor's signals. She did not demand further and better particulars, because she was aware of what she was being told, and did not want to confront it. Margaret Thatcher shrinking from a confrontation; John Wakeham's tactic was beginning to work. As for the Cabinet, her only comment was to wonder when she could make time to see them. She had to make a statement in the House on the Euro-summit, have her weekly audience with the Queen, and then prepare for the next day's debate. As ever in these hectic few days, events were crowding in on judgement.

The lunch-time discussion continued. Tim Renton told her that he had had a number of calls saying that she should stand down; there was also some desire for a wider choice of candidate. Last night, he would have said that there were twelve possible defectors from among her first ballot supporters; that morning, he put the figure at around twenty-five. However, he added the caveat that he did not guarantee these figures; the Whips' office had been well out with its estimate of 230. He was also sure that some defectors could be won back; the election was too close to call.

Mr Renton also reported Wilie Whitelaw's views. Lord Whitelaw was alarmed, both about the risk of humiliation, and at the thought of a low margin of victory in the second ballot. He had not wished to join them at lunch, and did not want to be a man in a suit. If she called him in, he would advise her as a friend.

Cranley Onslow expressed sympathy for her, saying that it did seem an absurd electoral system. He added that he was worried about the confusion over the unreliability of the first ballot estimates. He was thus implying that Mrs Thatcher's campaign had been mishandled. This would have been stated more forcefully, and not only by Mr Onslow, if Peter Morrison had not been at the lunch. Mr Onslow said that the '22 Executive was full of frustration and rage at the mess the party had got itself into. There was some desire for a wider choice of candidate, but also for party unity. There was no feeling that she should stand down – nor that Michael Heseltine should become leader. He turned to policy issues. The problem was not Europe, but the community charge. Mrs Thatcher interjected to point out that she could not pull rabbits out of a hat in a few days. Kenneth Baker agreed, but insisted that something must be done.

John Wakeham brought the discussion back to the campaign. She could win. Some backbenchers were unimpressed by Michael Heseltine's appeal. But to win, she would need to bring in the Cabinet. Yet again, an upbeat tone was accompanied by a downbeat content and yet again, Mr Wakeham brought her back to the question of the Cabinet. John MacGregor then added a further note of pessimism. He mentioned that though both Alan Clark and Michael Alison supported her, neither thought she could win. They feared that a large number of ministers would desert her. Mr MacGregor concluded that if she were to fight on, the decisive factor would not be policies, but commitment. He did not say whose commitment he had in mind.

Norman Tebbit agreed as to the unimportance of policy, except for the community charge. He thought she ought to ask one question: if she were not the Cabinet's candidate, who was? Again, the Cabinet question was pushed to the forefront – and Ken Baker kept it there, by adding that it was essential for the Cabinet to be seen to rally to her. It was agreed that she should see the Cabinet one by one. At this stage, Mrs Thatcher was under the illusion that she would be seeing the individual ministers to ask for their support, not for their views. John Wakeham and John MacGregor knew that the ministers would have their own agenda.

The lunch was drawing to an end. John MacGregor repeated the point that many of her own good supporters were now wobbly. Kenneth Baker made his earlier coded message explicit, and urged her not to indulge in personal attacks on Michael Heseltine. He declared that the campaign would be won or lost in the tearoom or in the lobbies. Finally, John MacGregor reassured her that the campaign would not be a demeaning process.

By then, Margaret Thatcher may well have felt both in need of reassurance, and beyond it. She seemed slightly on auto-pilot. While listening intently, she maintained a demeanour of brisk authority. But the usual edge was missing. When the men in suits lunch broke up, everything had gone according to John Wakeham's plan. If Margaret Thatcher had hoped that the picture might seem brighter in London than it had in Paris, she had been disabused.

As she left No. 10 for the House, however, Mrs Thatcher looked cheerful. Bernard Ingham told her that the press would expect her to say something, so she did: 'I fight on, I fight to win.'

Eyes on Their Boots

Mrs Thatcher then moved to the Commons, to deliver her statement on the Paris summit. Here, there was no falling away from her normal magisterial assurance. It was as if there had been no ballot and no Michael Heseltine. Some of the Cabinet ministers who were present oscillated between admiration and horror. Kenneth Clarke, rock-hard in his conviction that she should go, listened to the statement with his eyes fixed firmly on his boots, lest the TV cameras light on him looking incredulous. He could not believe what he was hearing. She was ploughing on, apparently blithe in her indifference to everything that had happened. She sounded just like her normal Prime Ministerial self; he could only conclude that she intended to remain Prime Minister. He caught a Cabinet colleague's eye; they both grimaced.

When the statement was over and the ministers had dispersed to privacy, there were loud lamentations – and imprecations – about the wimpishness of the men in suits, and in particular of Kenneth Baker and John MacGregor. What was the point, they asked themselves, of Mr MacGregor's canvassing exercise if he had not had the guts to give her the message? This reaction was as unfair as it was understandable. Mr Baker may have sounded as if he were encouraging her to run, but he had not given her a false account of party opinion. Far from contradicting Messrs MacGregor and Wakeham's subliminal pessimism, he had reinforced it. As for John MacGregor, the charge of cowardice against him was unfounded. At most, he was guilty of squeamishness, good manners and decency and he had made the necessary point.

Most of his colleagues did not know that. Nominations for the second ballot were to close at midday tomorrow, and for all they knew the only choice would be Margaret Thatcher or Michael Heseltine, which in many MPs' eyes was no choice; a victory by either would lead to disunity, and electoral defeat. Gloom led to anger. At this stage, Kenneth Clarke decided that he could no longer serve under her. If she did not resign, he would. Chris Patten actively considered resignation, though he had not made his final decision by the time she made hers. He would have supported her in the second ballot campaign, so it must be doubtful whether he could have stayed in Cabinet. In this mood of growing resentment, one or two ministers had lost all sympathy with her. They believed that she was irredeemably obstinate while some of their senior colleagues were irredeemably cowardly. Frustration was turning to fury, and the MacGregor canvass returns were leaked to *The Times*.

In fact, Mr Wakeham's plan was on schedule. The men in suits may have lost control of the party; they had not lost their power over it. In an emergency, older Tory traditions were asserting themselves. From their celestial – or infernal – Carlton or White's, the previous generations of men in suits had every reason to compliment their successors.

Confused, of Watford, and No Turning Back

While Mrs Thatcher and her entourage were digesting the result in Paris, in London all was confusion. The confusion started with the declaration of the result of the first ballot: many expectant Tory MPs had crammed in to Committee Room 12, but Cranley Onslow, the Chairman of the 1922 Committee, gave out the figures in Room 10, where the majority of the press had gathered. When the news of this reached Room 12, there was a widespread outbreak of irritation and pomposity; then again, persons in a state of delayed shock often concern themselves with trifling matters while the world is turning upside down.

Initially, a number of MPs who were later to come to a very different conclusion thought that Mrs Thatcher could go on and win. William Powell took part in a radio programme covering the result; his immediate reaction was that the leadership election was over, and that Mrs Thatcher had won; he assumed that Mr Heseltine would have to concede. Tristan Garel-Jones, who heard the result in the Foreign Office, also heard Mr Powell, and assumed that he was acting on instructions, and that the contest was now over. Norman Lamont, who was in the Treasury, also thought that Mrs Thatcher would now win. Others, however, concluded straight away that Mrs Thatcher's position had been rendered untenable. Chris Patten was one of these. As soon as he had heard the result, he telephoned Tristan Garel-Jones and expressed his view vigorously, saying that if ever there was a time when the men in suits were needed, this was it. Tristan was not initially convinced; when the conversation ended, Mr Patten's first comment was 'confused, of Watford' (Mr Garel-Jones's constituency). But Chris had suggested that there be a meeting later that night to discuss matters, and Tristan agreed. Tristan also felt that he ought to get over to the Commons as fast as possible.

Like Mr Lamont and Mr Powell, he changed his mind as soon as he reached the House of Commons. Though the Tory backbenchers seemed to have dissolved into a state of primal chaos, a mood was crystallizing – against the Prime Minister. Ministers, Whips and other notables were buttonholed by a stream of backbenchers, all insisting that Margaret Thatcher was finished. One point was repeated endlessly and became the dissidents' refrain: 'How can I ask my electorate to vote for her when 168 of her own colleagues would not do so?'

Mr Garel-Jones ran into five or six Thatcherites, who all said the same thing: 'That's it, then.' A number of junior ministers, pre-viously loyal to the Prime Minister, had now concluded that she could not win. Large number of PPSs were all reporting the same message. A number of Tory MPs were also insisting that though they had supported Margaret Thatcher in the first round, they would not do so again. To a certain extent, this was disinformation. There is no doubt that among those loudly proclaiming that they had supported the PM on the first ballot were some of the MPs who had misled Mr Morrison into believing that the PM had her majority. However, this was not just a matter of Heseltinis coming out of the closet. There were genuine defections. Rob Hayward, the Tory MP for Kingswood, lists psephology among his recreations in *Who's Who* and is generally recognized as the best number-cruncher in the Tory Party. He predicted the result of the Meyer election with 100 per cent accuracy, and his colleagues have come to rely on his forecasts.

On that Tuesday evening, Mr Hayward drew up a list of thirty-seven backbenchers who he thought might defect from Mrs Thatcher to Mr Heseltine in a second ballot. The news of the Hayward list spread rapidly. Large numbers of MPs sought him out, and eagerly demanded details, which he supplied. The Hayward list was a major factor in convincing several senior figures that Mrs Thatcher could not win.

Over the past few days, events had moved rapidly enough; now the pace accelerated dramatically. When the House of Commons is in the grip of excitement, the mood of MPs can change with the rapidity of a chemical reaction. So it was that Tuesday evening; everywhere in the lobbies, bars and dining rooms, excited Conservative MPs were conferring. One element was missing in all this. Whether because Margaret Thatcher's closest supporters were in shock, in Paris, or arguing among themselves at the 'No Turning Back' group, there was no sign off at a Thatcherite counter-attack in those crucial early hours. It would have been possible to circulate quite widely among Tory MPs and form the impression that the PM had no supporters left.

However, some of Mrs Thatcher's closest supporters were planning a counter-attack. In a committee-room off Westminister Hall, a number of members of the 'No Turning Back' group assembled to discuss their position. The NTB, as it had come to be known, consisted of Thatcherites most of whom had been elected to the Commons in 1983. Its members included Michael Brown, Chris Chope, Michael Fallon, Michael Forsyth, Neil Hamilton, Alan Howarth, Edward Leigh, Peter Lilley, David Maclean and Francis Maude – as well as Angela Rumbold (elected in 1982) and Michael Portillo (1984). The NTB had come to regard itself as Mrs Thatcher's praetorian guard. The PM seemed to share this view: she was known to look favourably on the group, and a number of its members had already joined the Government. Now, however, the NTB was split.

Peter Lilley and Francis Maude both argued that Mrs Thatcher could not survive; Alan Howarth gave lukewarm support to that view. All of the rest disagreed, some of them vehemently. As Peter Lilley spoke, Neil Hamilton grew angrier and angrier, and subjected Mr Lilley to a barrage of sarcasm and heckling. The atmosphere quickly deteriorated, and Francis Maude finally stalked out, saying that he had had enough. In fact, the NTB reconvened in Mr Maude's room later that evening, and in one form or another, was in almost permanent session for the next twenty-four hours.

The Owls

That evening, the Strangers' Dining Room in the House of Commons was full of agitated diners. The few Labour groups looked on with amusement as Tories swapped the latest intelligence. There was much more table-hopping than on any normal evening in the Harcourt Room, though it tended to by-pass one table at which Sir Ian Gilmour, Sir Charles Morrison and Sir Dennis Walters were dining. The wettest of the Wets were not having an impromptu celebration: they had arranged to meet before the ballot result was known. Their enjoyment of dinner would not be diminished, however, by the thought that the fifteen-year Thatcherite usurpation might shortly be at an end.

At a neighbouring table, I was dining with Alan Clark, Jonathan Aitken and Nicholas Budgen. Jonathan and I, impressed by the PM's determination to fight on, assumed that she would win, though both of us found grounds for anxiety in Nick Budgen's behaviour. Mr Budgen is one of the ablest and most interesting parliamentarians of the present day, but there is one respect in which he stands supreme. No one in Parliament is a more skilful advocate of lost causes: no cause is definitively lost until Mr Budgen has come to its defence. Mr Budgen had been a persistent critic of Mr Lawson's economic policy and of Mrs Thatcher's Northern Ireland policy. He found the PM's triumphalist style distasteful and over the previous few months had seemed more and more out of sympathy with the Government as a whole.

Yet on Tuesday evening, Mr Budgen declared his unswerving loyalty to Mrs Thatcher. I thought of *Zuleika Dobson*, in which the arrival of two black owls on the battlements of Tankerton Hall heralded the death of the Duke of Dorset and the extinction of his line. I was sure that Mr Budgen's pledge of loyalty would have the same effect on Mrs Thatcher's prospects as the owls did on His Grace of Dorset.

Alan Clark needed no owls to guide him. He was never an orthodox Thatcherite: his admiration for the PM was based on patriotism, not on economics. But in his devotion to her, he rivalled Ian Gow. None the less, over dinner on that Tuesday evening, Mr Clark was emphatic that Mrs Thatcher was finished. 'We'll all have to be loyal,' he would repeat. 'We must ride with her until the end. But it is a death ride. She cannot win – and we're going to have Michael Heseltine as Prime Minister, closely followed by Neil Kinnock.'

During the meal, there was some desultory discussion of alternatives to Mrs Thatcher. It was then that Alan Clark first floated an idea which he was to mention on several occasions over the next twenty-four hours: that Tom King, his Secretary of State, should be a candidate. Mr Clark argued that Mr King could unite the party, while his bluff, straightforward manner would go down well with the public. Mr Clark's companions were unpersuaded. Over the next twenty-four hours, that was to be the general reaction to his proposal. It was also Tom King's: he considered the idea of standing only to dismiss it. There is an irony. Mr King found a quick way of repaying Mr Clark. Tom King had never been happy with Alan Clark's role in the MoD, or the way in which Mrs Thatcher had seemed to value his opinions on defence policy more than those of the Secretary of State. So as soon as Mrs Thatcher departed, Mr King struck, and added a new war aim to the Gulf agenda. Thereafter, though Saddam Hussein was always the more important military target, in some MoD circles Alan Clark ran him close.

Drinks with Tristan

In the course of dinner, Mr Clark learned that Tristan Garel-Jones had invited a few colleagues to discuss forthcoming developments; they would meet after the ten o'clock vote, at the Garel-Jones residence in Catherine Place, near Victoria. The Catherine Place gathering has passed into mythology, but when it was first mooted, it did not sound like an unusual occurrence. It seemed the most natural thing in the world that some colleagues would go off to Tristan's after the vote. Catherine Place is within easy popping-round distance of the Commons, especially if ministerial cars are available, and Tristan Garel-Jones is an admirable host who enjoys nothing more than talking politics late into the night. Since 1979, the 'Blue Chip' group of MPs (see p.241) have held their monthly dinners at his house, which has also been the rendezvous for innumerable ad hoc discussions. On this occasion, there was plenty to discuss. It was the situation which was extraordinary – not the Catherine Place meeting.

The meeting was important, but as a catalyst, not a conspiracy. It did clarify the minds of some of those present, and confirmed them in their pessimism about Margaret Thatcher's chances: they all swapped stories about defecting junior ministers and PPSs awash with gloom. But even without Mr Garel-Jones's intervention, those involved would have talked to one another. Catherine Place was only the best-organized[7] and most publicized of a score of such meetings.

Subsequently, Mr Garel-Jones claimed that he assembled his guests by accident. His sincerity is not in question, but Mr Garel-Jones's accidents are not as other men's accidents. He may have thought he was merely sweeping up a few chums for a noggin or two; he ended up with a dozen men, most of whom were to be key players over the next few days, including Norman Lamont, who became John Major's Chief of Staff, and John Patten, Douglas Hurd's de facto Chief of Staff. There was only one non-minister among Mr Garel-Jones's guests: Tim Yeo, Douglas Hurd's PPS. He became a minister two weeks later. At the nucleus of the Catherine Place meeting were three of Mr Garel-Jones's fellow Blue Chips and closest political associates: William Waldegrave, Chris Patten – both Cabinet Ministers – and John Patten, a Minister of State pushing at the Cabinet door (the two Pattens are not related). Also present were Norman Lamont, Tony Newton and Malcolm Rifkind, three more of the younger members of the Cabinet. Messrs Newton and Rifkind are at the wetter end of the Tory Party. Mr Lamont, though a social liberal, is a hard-line dry on economic policy. All three are thoughtful men, whose views would carry weight.

Mr Lamont had suggested that another Cabinet Minister be invited: Peter Lilley. Only the second member of the 1983 intake to reach Cabinet, he is a rock-ribbed Thatcherite on the economy. But though Tristan Garel-Jones was in favour of hearing Mr Lilley's

---

7 A report in the *Economist* of 9 March 1991 cast doubt on the quality of Mr Garel-Jones's hospitality '. . . though one minister had been told to come for coffee, nothing was offered to them as they sat about in their overcoats'. This is inaccurate. Although no coffee was offered, a number of those present did take off their coats and served themselves from a liberally-supplied drinks table.

views, others including Chris Patten felt that his presence would be unhelpful. Had he attended, they would have been proved wrong. Although a Thatcher loyalist, Mr Lilley was rapidly concluding that she ought to stand aside.The other participants were: Douglas Hogg, also a Blue Chip, Richard Ryder, who also arrived late, Tim Yeo, Alan Howarth and Alan Clark.

Mr Garel-Jones had invited Francis Maude and Michael Portillo, two of the brightest young Ministers of State. But Mr Maude had already attended one bruising meeting, and did not feel he could face another. Mr Portillo would not have wished to attend any gathering that could subsequently be labelled a conspiracy. He was interested only in preserving Mrs Thatcher's position, not in a free-ranging discussion. His presence would have made some difference to the tone of the meeting, for Michael Portillo was a die-hard Thatcher supporter who was utterly opposed to her resigning. Mr Maude, on the other hand, though a Thatcher loyalist, had been convinced that her cause was lost. There was one final invitee, who also declined: Graham Bright, John Major's PPS. Mr Major, had already asked him not to attend.

At Catherine Place, it quickly emerged that most of those present, having despaired of Margaret Thatcher's chances, were primarily interested in stopping Michael Heseltine. There were two exceptions, however. Chris Patten has always liked Mr Heseltine; he felt he could live with a Heseltine premiership. The other Heseltine admirer – despite their different views on Europe and on the economy – was Norman Lamont, who had worked for Michael Heseltine. At Catherine Place, he insisted that Michael would be a perfectly acceptable Prime Minister. But no one at Catherine Place gave Mr Heseltine their first preference. Alan Clark yet again advanced Tom King's name, and yet again found no takers. He was to persist with this one-man campaign for much of the next twenty-four hours, without success. He discovered that a large number of colleagues who were sure of little else *were* convinced that Mr King would not become leader of the Conservative Party.

During the course of the evening, there had been much discussion in anti-Heseltine circles of the need for a unity candidate to stop Michael. A lot of people were thinking back to 1975 when Mrs Thatcher had not only benefited from the momentum of her first ballot result: the Wet vote had been split between Jim Prior and Willie Whitelaw. (There had been two other candidates as well.) It was assumed that the only hope of stopping Michael Heseltine would be to have one, unity candidate. A number of those at Catherine Place held this view, and argued that the Whips or other eminent persons should take soundings and then decide who that candidate should be. Equally, almost everyone at Catherine Place was aware that Messrs Hurd and Major were reluctant to stand against one another, so there was some discussion of a unity candidature. However, no one was able to suggest any means of arriving at this.

Tristan Garel-Jones's instincts were against a unity candidate, partly because he regarded the whole idea as impractical. There was no agreed procedure for any sounding operation, which would either have to be conducted as a full-scale primary election – for which there was no time – or by the men in suits, in which case it would lack legitimacy. No one was able to rebut these objections, and the idea of a unity candidate made no headway during the Catherine Place meeting. That was of great significance; a single 'Stop Heseltine' challenger could have emerged only if he had commanded the instant support of almost all the Catherine Place mafia. There was no such support – but nor did any other definite conclusion emerge from the meeting. By the end of the evening, very few of those present had declared their allegiance. The two Pattens had announced for Hurd, while Norman Lamont had committed himself to Major, and Alan Clark was still promoting Tom King; the rest had not yet shown their hands.

Mr Garel-Jones was coming round to the news that there ought to be three candidates. A few days earlier, he had also briefly considered a fourth nominee, but then decided against it. Since he arrived in the House of Commons, one of the main aims of Tristan Garel-Jones's political life has been to advance the career of Chris Patten. As the 1980s wore on, Mr Garel-Jones developed an equal, if slightly less idolatrous, regard for John Major. Tristan Garel-Jones had begun to look forward, not to a dream ticket, but to a dream ballot. Some time in the early 1990s, on Margaret Thatcher's retirement, the Tory Party would be faced with a wonderful choice, while he himself was confronted with a most difficult, embarrassing and yet pleasurable dilemma: John Major, or Chris Patten. That moment would be the climax of Mr Garel-Jones's career, and the fulfilment of all his ambitions. Two of his closest friends would have the chance to run for the premiership, and one would attain it. Mr Garel-Jones never intended to devote the rest of his life to politics: it would not have been surprising if, shortly after Mr Major or Mr Patten became

Premier, he had murmured 'Nunc Dimittis' and retired to Spain, his work done.

Now, everything had ceased to run to plan. Mr Major was a candidate, certainly – but Mr Garel-Jones knew that it was too early for Chris. If a strong move to draft Chris had emerged from the Catherine Place meeting, he would have given it every encouragement. But, as Mr Garel-Jones had expected, there was no pro-Patten move. Mr Patten himself recognized that the vacancy had come too soon: he had spent only sixteen months in Cabinet, and most of that was wrestling with the community charge. The next day, he took a few soundings: of Cabinet colleagues, his PPS Jeremy Hanley, and his political adviser Patrick Rock. They all confirmed his view that he could not mount anything more than a challenge for third place.

Tristan, meanwhile, was coming round to the view that he ought to support Douglas Hurd. His motives in doing so were inevitably questioned, and even caused domestic dissention. On the following evening, there was yet another political meeting at Catherine Place, this time between Mr and Mrs Tristan Garel-Jones. Catali Garel-Jones kept Tristan awake until 3 a.m.; she could not understand his refusal to back their dear friend John.

The majority of Mr Garel-Jones's colleagues thought they understood perfectly well. Tristan was running Douglas, aged sixty, to keep Chris's options open. Not for the first time, however, the easy, cynical explanation is also incorrect. Mr Garel-Jones knew from the very beginning that Douglas Hurd stood little chance. Even by the time of the Catherine Place meeting, Tristan was almost convinced certain that if Mrs Thatcher stood down, Mr Major would win. There was only one chance – albeit slim – of making Douglas Hurd Prime Minister, and that was to persuade John Major not to run. If Tristan really had been a duplicitous conspirator, he might have tried to engineer that. Instead, he did everything to ensure that both Mr Hurd and Mr Major would stand.

Though they were not close friends Mr Garel-Jones liked and admired Douglas Hurd. Above all, however, he supported Mr Hurd because he felt bound to him. As long ago as 1986, during the Westland troubles, Tristan had told Douglas that should Mrs Thatcher be forced out, he was the obvious man to succeed her. Then in late 1989, Tristan Garel-Jones was involved in the contingency planning for a Hurd succession. Now that he was trying to ensure that Mr Hurd ran, in order to stop Mr Heseltine and, in effect, to ensure John Major's succession, he also felt that as he had helped to wind the clock, he ought to be there to hear it strike. After playing some part in creating the Hurd campaign, he thought it was his duty to see that it was properly run. He also wanted to ensure that Mr Hurd was not humiliated. So Tristan Garel-Jones joined the Hurdites. In one of the several, always amicable, telephone conversations he held with Mr Hurd during the leadership contest, John Major showed the extent to which he held Tristan Garel-Jones's defection against him. 'Give Tristan a hug for me,' he said to Mr Hurd.

The Catherine Place meeting reached only one conclusion: that those present should inform the Whips of their feeling that Margaret Thatcher should resign. Some believed that she now had no chance of defeating Mr Heseltine in the second ballot. Others – this was Mr Garel-Jones's view – thought that she could scrape home, but by such a small majority as to give her no hope of reuniting the party. All of them now wanted her to stand aside and give her senior colleagues their freedom of action.

Chris Patten and others had been angered by her Paris statement; they felt that she was exploiting the loyalty of Messrs Hurd and Major, and denying them their opportunity. Those who were most concerned to stop Mr Heseltine found it no pleasurable irony that the main obstacle to doing so now appeared to be Margaret Thatcher.

Alan Clark

Even if there had been a formal agenda at Catherine Place, Alan Clark's presence would have disrupted it. At that stage, Mr Clark was not thinking clearly. He had grasped one point as quickly as anyone: that Margaret Thatcher was finished. But his capacity for cool judgement was undermined because two of his strongest passions were in play: a love of Margaret Thatcher, and a love of politicking. He was neither able to reason calmly, nor to resist the lure of speculation. Over the next twenty-four hours, Mr Clark was the busiest man in the Conservative Party. He was always present wherever the overturned ant-hill was at its most frantic – and whenever groups of ministers were having a crucial conversation. During those hours, up and down the Commons' ministerial corridor, Mr Clark knocked on all the most interesting doors. On that Wednesday, 23

November, when two or three were gathered together, Mr Clark was among them.

As well as patrolling the corridors, Mr Clark also managed to appear on almost every television channel, extolling Margaret Thatcher while directing a stinging irony against Michael Heseltine and the other rebels. Though too late to help Margaret Thatcher, this may have encouraged the counter-attack against Mr Heseltine of which John Major was to be the ultimate beneficiary. Mr Clark, one of the most articulate members of the Government, is a natural television performer – which no doubt explains the Ministry of Defence's decision to prohibit his appearance during the Gulf War.

All this activity led to Mr Clark being widely distrusted. As was observed, he did not seem to be clear whether he was working for the CIA or the KGB. During those first few hours of confusion, both Major and Hurd supporters formed the impression that he was firmly in the Hurd camp. This was mistaken. The confusion arose because though Mr Clark was clear-sighted about Mrs Thatcher's fate, he had not yet focused his mind on the succession – as his attempts to promote Tom King demonstrated. In particular, he had not taken account of political developments since his involvement in the previous year's leadership speculation. Mr Clark had concluded – probably accurately – that Douglas Hurd could no longer beat Michael Heseltine. But he had not registered the rise of John Major. At Catherine Place he was still talking in terms of Mr Major receiving only thirty-five or forty votes, and assumed that any Major would be no more than a marker for the future.

Mr Clark's overriding goal was to stop Michael Heseltine. If Mr Heseltine could not be stopped, then Mr Clark would have been quite content to take part in Thatcher's last stand, and fall at her side, fighting to the end. It took him a couple of days to realize that this would not be necessary, and that a candidate had emerged who could indeed thwart Mr Heseltine.

The Catherine Place meeting ended with all those present returning to the House to speak to the Chief Whip. Characteristically, Mr Garel-Jones also passed on their views to Mrs Thatcher's entourage, via Charles Powell.

6 The Fall of Margaret Thatcher Act II

An Interrupted Convalescence

John Major, meanwhile, was convalescing in Huntingdon, and try-ing to minimize his contacts with London. His operation provided a good excuse: throughout Monday and Tuesday, most of those who telephoned were told that he was asleep, or not really able to talk, or some such. In fact he would have been perfectly able to talk on the phone. His overriding concern was to do nothing that could be construed as disloyalty. Although he was worried about the state of opinion in the party, until the first ballot he still thought and hoped that Mrs Thatcher would win. His personal ambitions were for the longer term; in the short run, his principal objective was to stabilize the Thatcher Government, not to replace Margaret Thatcher.

He did take some calls, mainly from close associates and friends: Robert Atkins, Graham Bright, Norman Lamont. They all agreed that they did not trust the Thatcher campaign's figures. But Mr Major urged them to say nothing that might give the impression that he was preparing to stand; it would have been a false impression. Mr Major was dismayed by the first ballot result; despite being away from Westminster, he realized straight away that it created a new situation. Chris Patten telephoned him early on, partly to exchange views, partly to sound out his intentions, and partly to dissuade him from seconding Mrs Thatcher's nomination in the second ballot. Mr Patten found him pessimistic about her prospects, extremely cau-tious about his own position – and unmovable in his intention to back her as long as she wanted his backing. Mr Patten told him that he was proposing to organize a meeting; Mr Major was wary about that, too, and indicated that Mr Bright should not attend.

Graham Bright is good at keeping his own counsel; although a burly, jolly fellow, he is surprisingly skilful at remaining impassive. After the first ballot, his ability to do so was put to the test. A stream of MPs came up to Mr Bright to register their support for Mr Major. Some of them pressed Graham Bright to urge his boss to tell her to go, to refuse to second her nomination – to stand against her if necessary. As this went on, Graham Bright had three objectives: to remain polite to everyone; to remember the names of supporters, should that information become relevant – and to squash any suggestion that Mr Major had any other objectives than Margaret Thatcher's re-election. Throughout the Wednesday, the speculation mounted. Wherever Mr Bright went in the Commons, he was cornered by MPs. Some asked what John Major intended to do, others assured him of their support for Mr Major – some did both. By lunchtime, about eighty Major supporters had spoken to Mr Bright – an impressive total, considering that Mr Major's friends had done no canvassing, and that he himself was not a candidate.

John Major was now in the grip of conflicting emotions. His heart was with Margaret Thatcher, to whom he felt immense loyalty and gratitude. It was she who had given him his promotions and opportunities. If he was now in a position to succeed her, that was due to her patronage as well as to his own ability. Mr Major believed that Margaret Thatcher deserved better of her party and of her country than to be driven out of office in these circumstances. He found it difficult to comprehend that her premiership could be coming to an end – and yet his head told him that she was in desperate trouble.

Mr Major, one of the best Chief Whips the Conservative Party never had quickly understood the implications of the first ballot result, and his judgement was reinforced by conversations with other colleagues. He knew that the PM could not win a decisive victory in the second ballot. He also knew that if she stood aside, he would almost certainly find himself a candidate for the premiership. In politics, when events are moving so rapidly that the normal navigational aids cease to function, some MPs fall back on the compass of ambition; others steer by principle – John Major chose the latter course.

During Wednesday, he firmly rejected any suggestions that he break with Margaret Thatcher; to act in that way would have been alien to his nature. He made it clear that if she decided to stand, he would be with her. In less romantic, melodramatic terms, he would have been content to be a cavalryman in Alan Clark's death ride. Several of those who spoke to him suggested that he advise her to stand down. Among them was this writer; by then, largely by talking to Thatcherite MPs, I had become convinced that she could not win. 'If I am asked for my advice. I will give it,' Mr Major replied, 'I always tell her the truth.' He was never asked for that advice. By the time he might have expected to speak to her, advice was no longer relevant: she had decided to go.

By Wednesday lunchtime, some of Mr Major's friends in Westminster – especially Graham Bright, Norman Lamont, and Gillian Shephard – had already discounted Mrs Thatcher's prospects, and were eager for a Major campaign to begin. As the afternoon wore on, they wee affected by the general gloom arising from the supposed failure of the men-in-suits lunch and the apparent impasse. Towards evening, Mr Bright was insisting to all enquirers that as the PM was going to stand again, there was no question of a Major campaign. After that, in Gill Shephard's words, 'all activity ceased'.

The Tearoom and the Palace

As Margaret Thatcher was leaving the Chamber after her successful statement, Michael Portillo and David Evans intercepted her behind the Speaker's Chair. Loyal Thatcherites, they wanted her to come to the tearoom, where MPs would naturally gather after a major statement – especially that afternoon. But Peter Morrison, who thought she deserved some minutes to herself, said that she had no time; she had to see the Cabinet (in fact, her weekly audience with the Queen was a more pressing engagement). Stung, David Evans caught Mrs Thatcher's attention: 'Prime Minister, if you haven't got time to come to the tearoom, I think you may find that in future, you will have more time than you expect.'

Taken aback, Mrs Thatcher replied, 'Should I come to the tearoom?'

'Yes, Prime Minister,' insisted Mr Evans.

She then rallied, and said smilingly: 'The Cabinet can wait. Let's go to the tearoom.' Norman Tebbit, who had overheard the exchange, escorted her.

On the way, John MacGregor managed to get in a private word with her, and communicated the results of his canvass. She received the information calmly, listening intently, outwardly unmoved. It had to be a brief visit to the tearoom; and it was not wholly successful. As Mr Tebbit put it 'some of them couldn't meet her eye'. There was no marked rallying to her. Cecil Parkinson, though, was jaunty. He told her that all her friends thought that the Cabinet was full of 'wobblers', who might be saying at the moment that she should not stand because they thought she would be defeated, but in the end they would back her.

Mrs Thatcher was soon to test Cabinet opinion for herself, but first, she rushed into her own Commons office to complete the formal preparations for her second ballot campaign. She spoke to John Wakeham, who confirmed that he was organizing the campaign, and she also contacted Douglas Hurd and John Major, who both agreed to sign her nomination papers.

That done, the PM made a trip to the Palace. We can speculate in vain as to what was said at that meeting. Over the eleven and a half years of Margaret Thatcher's premiership, there were endless newspaper reports to the effect that the Queen and her Prime Minister did not get on. It is certainly true that when it comes to Prime Ministers, the Queen's judgement is not infallible: she liked Harold Wilson. But we do not yet know anything about her relationship with Margaret Thatcher. For eleven and a half years, I asked almost everyone who worked closely with Margaret Thatcher what the true state of affairs was between Monarch and Premier. Naturally, one took the elementary precaution of waiting to pose the question until the gossip was flowing and the glasses had been filled. But I always got the same answer: that Mrs Thatcher *never* discussed her dealings with the Monarch. It seems improbable that Her Majesty was any less discreet. All the supposed reports turn out to be nothing more than recycled rumour.

However, two scraps of evidence are on record, both of which contradict the rumours. It was often noted that when she encountered the Queen, Margaret Thatcher curtseyed lower than anyone else in the room. That was expressive of more than her known reverence for the institution of the Monarchy. As for Her Majesty's attitude, within a few days of the PM's retirement, the Queen conferred on her the Order of Merit – the intellectuals' Garter – a decoration in the sovereign's personal gift, and a signal mark of favour.

Whatever her reverence for the Queen, it is hard not to believe that Mrs Thatcher would gladly have cancelled that evening's audience; she had other preoccupations. It was to be the last of her regular audiences with the Queen.

The Headmistress's Study

Afterwards, she returned to the Commons, girt for battle. John Wakeham and Peter Morrison had arranged for her to see the Cabinet one by one, from about six o'clock onwards. The choice of venue and the method of meeting were both significant: both part of the Wakeham plan. Of Mrs Thatcher even more than most premiers it can be said that wherever she is, there is the head of the table. All the same, Downing Street is her territory; the House of Commons is nearer to a neutral zone. If the ministers had had to get into their cars and drive to No. 10, the ambience would have been subtly different. Instead, they met her in the PM's room in the Commons, near the ministerial corridor where many of them had been meeting and talking all afternoon. It was already a charged atmosphere, not conducive to the calm assertion of Prime Ministerial authority. At times, as a crowd gathered outside her office, the excitement rose; excitement is contagious, and emboldening. It is unlikely that the result would have been different even if the meetings had taken place in No. 10, but the ground would have been slightly more favourable to a Prime Ministerial counter-attack.

She certainly tried to counter-attack. At about 5.30, before she had begun her Cabinet interviews, she spotted Francis Maude in her outer office, and invited him in. Overnight, Mr Maude had agonized – but despite pressure from his fellow NTBers, was convinced that Margaret Thatcher would not beat Michael Heseltine. He too did not believe that those around her would tell her the truth, so he decided that he should: a mission worthy of Meshach, Shadrach or Abednego. He told her that if she did decide to fight on, he would clear his diary for the next seven days and work on her behalf. He also said that he did not think she could win. Their talk lasted for about ten or fifteen minutes, and Mrs Thatcher remained unruffled and good-natured. Asked if he had made a dent in her confidence, Mr Maude replied, 'No. She had made a dent in mine.'

The next character scheduled to see her, the first of the Cabinet ministers, was a harder man to dent. Although he had served on her front bench in Opposition, and in Government since 1979, Kenneth Clarke's loyalty was of a cooler variety than Mr Maude's. But though he had never been one of Margaret Thatcher's intimates, Ken Clarke liked and admired Margaret Thatcher. She had stood by him during difficult phases in his ministerial career; he felt that, if possible, he ought to reciprocate.

Throughout the first ballot, Mr Clarke did support Mrs Thatcher. Like many others, he started to get alarmed over the weekend, and stopped believing in the Thatcher camp's predictions. On the Monday and Tuesday, he had a number of 'what if' conversations with John Wakeham and others. Ken Clarke felt strongly that for her to finish ahead in the first ballot, but by an inadequate margin, was the nightmare scenario. After the result, he thought that the priority was for her to return from Paris with dignity, so that the men in suits could fulfil their role. On Tuesday evening, in TV interviews, Mr Clarke insisted that she had won – but he was doing so merely to create a smokescreen, behind which the PM and the men in suits could arrange an honourable withdrawal. He was defending the Prime Minister, in the confident expectation that it would all be over by the Wednesday afternoon.

On the Wednesday morning, Mr McGregor spoke to him as part of the Cabinet canvass. Ken Clarke gave his opinion in a vehement manner: that was it; she had had it. In response, Mr MacGregor was guarded, but Mr Clarke was able to confirm what he knew anyway on the basis of other conversations: that others shared his view. By the afternoon, Mr Clarke was becoming exasperated; where were the men in suits? He expressed this exasperation when Peter Morrison rang him up to ask for his support in Mrs Thatcher's second ballot campaign. In robust terms, he told Mr Morrison not only that he would not support Mrs Thatcher, but that he thought it would be madness for her to run again. She would lose votes in droves, and Michael Heseltine would then be able to hijack the party. Ken Clarke was not against Mr Heseltine per se, but he did think that it would be impossible for the party to unite behind him.

Mr Clarke went to the Chamber. After Mrs Thatcher's statement, he spoke to Norman Lamont and Chris Patten behind the Speaker's Chair; they were all convinced that something had to be done. Mr Clarke was due to see the Prime Minister at 6.00. He felt that in bringing Ministers together in a crowded House of Commons corridor, the Thatcher team excelled their own high standards of incompetence. The atmosphere was confused and overheated; the little knots of excited ministers were often joined by passing MPs, who mainly seemed to be Thatcher deserters. PPSs reported the latest soundings, which invariably consisted of more bad news for the Prime Minister. The opportunity all this gave the anti-Thatcherites to reinforce one another in their determination to speak their minds and tell her to go was more damaging to the PM's chances than any conspiracy would have been.

Then Mr Clarke entered her office. She tried to rally him – 'Come on, Ken. Come on, Ken,' she repeated. Mrs Thatcher conceded that the first ballot campaign had been a shambles, but assured him that this time there would be a proper effort. Mr Clarke was unmoved. He told her that the best she could hope for in a second ballot was a Charge of the Light Brigade, and quoted 'C'est magnifique, mais ce n'est pas la guerre.' If she stood again, she would go down to defeat. She must accept that this was the end.

Mrs Thatcher accused him of defeatism. He agreed – but pointed out that he was being defeatist because she was facing defeat. He told her that he did not so much object to her being defeated as the effect such an outcome would have in breaking up the party and undermining the authority of government. He also pressed her to release Douglas Hurd and John Major from their pledges to support her, a point to which she did reply.

Ken Clarke did not enjoy his session with Margaret Thatcher. He felt strongly that she should not have been put in this humiliating position of being told to her face to go by her Cabinet colleagues. He blamed the men in suits for evading their responsibilities. But he felt even more strongly that if they had shirked their duty, he would not shirk his. He hardened his heart, and spoke his mind.

As Mr Clarke left her office, five or six of his colleagues pounced on him. What was it like; had he stuck to his guns; what had she said; what mood was she in – for all the world like small boys crowding round the first victim to emerge from the headmaster's study. Mr Clarke concealed the disagreeable nature of the task he had performed behind a jaunty manner; that manner gave courage to potential fainthearts.

Mrs Thatcher was to see fifteen Cabinet ministers in the course of the consultation exercise. If the aim had been to enable her to stay in office, Ken Clarke was the worst choice to be the first man in. None of his colleagues could have equalled his capacity to undermine her confidence and to stiffen the resistance of the other eleven critics. However, he owed his position in the batting order to accident, not design. The arrangements for Cabinet ministers to see the PM were made by Peter Morrison, who remained loyal to the end and beyond.

Mr Clarke's name was near the top of the alphabetical order, and he was available at six o'clock; that was that.

Ken Clarke had succeeded where Francis Maude had failed; he had smashed a breach in the walls. Over the next two hours his colleagues completed the job of finishing off the garrison. That was a surprisingly easy task, for Margaret Thatcher's resistance ebbed quickly. There was little more talk of defeatism. She repeated the pledge that the second ballot campaign would be properly run, but the colleagues repeated to her their belief that she could not win. The pain and humiliation that all this caused Margaret Thatcher can only be guessed at. She was not prepared to relive the experience for this author, and who can blame her? I suspect that even in her own memoirs, she will be restrained when describing her feelings. To have to sit there while her own chosen colleagues destroyed her premiership was an ordeal which even her enemies might have wished to spare her. Politics is the cruelest profession; it was as if all Margaret Thatcher's victories and achievements had only increased her vulnerability.

Throughout these meetings, however, she tried to conceal that vulnerability. She was determined to maintain her dignity and her poise. She might no longer be able to command; she would not stoop to plead, or to reproach. But the hurt showed. At 5.30 she had been gay and brisk with Francis Maude. By 7.00, when Malcolm Rikfind saw her, she was clearly very depressed. She advanced her standard argument: that she had never lost an election, and still commanded the support of the Parliamentary Party – but by then, she was only going through the motions; she could no longer summon the conviction to reinforce her points. Mr Rifkind described her as looking 'listless, sad, and woebegone'. Michael Howard saw her shortly after Mr Rifkind; he described her as looking 'like a wounded bird'. Mr Howard's session with her helped convince the PM that all hope had gone. A staunch Thatcher loyalist, his initial response to the first ballot result had been to call on Michael Heseltine to withdraw. But as the hours passed, his opinion began gradually to change, for though Mr Howard is an amiable and charming fellow, he is also stubborn and tenacious, especially where basic loyalties are concerned. However, the pressure of his colleagues' opinions finally wore down his resistance, though he was not to form a settled view until well into Wednesday morning.

Michael Howard admires, indeed loves, Margaret Thatcher. He also owes her a great deal; he was the first member of the 1983 intake of MPs to reach the Cabinet, chosen in large measure because of his dry, free-market views. Now Mr Howard found himself having to tell the PM to go. He started by assuring her that if she did decide to carry on he would back her to the hilt, campaign for her and fight until the end. 'I wish to God I didn't have to say this,' he continued. 'I don't think you're going to win. I fear there is a danger that the margin against you could be quite big.' He then went into detail, identifying three insoluble problems. The first was that normally dependable characters with marginal constituencies were declaring that they could no longer hope to sell her on the doorsteps. Second, a large number of MPs were saying that though they had regarded themselves as obliged to vote for her in the first ballot, they did not feel bound to do so in a subsequent ballot. Third, all this was creating an anti-Thatcher momentum. Lots of MPs wanted to end up on the winning side; as more of their colleagues began to declare for Michael Heseltine, making it less and less likely that Mrs Thatcher could win, they too were tempted to desert her.

Michael Howard concluded by telling her that he thought John Major could beat Michael Heseltine. Mr Howard felt that by taking on himself the responsibility of advising the PM to leave office, he was also incurring the responsibility of helping to prevent a Heseltine succession.

By this stage, those around Mrs Thatcher noticed that she was becoming calmer, but that there was an increasingly remote quality to her composure. She had now almost stopped arguing with the Cabinet ministers. She merely listened patiently and intently, making very few comments. There were occasional moments of humour. As Chris Patten left her office, around 7.00, he tried to exploit the headmaster's study ambience and introduce a note of light relief by making a flagellatory gesture towards his own backside. In reality, the flagellation had fallen on Margaret Thatcher.

One of the last ministers to see her was William Waldegrave, who had only joined the Cabinet in the post-Howe reshuffle. So he was ready to feel especially shamefaced at advising her to go – but she put him at his ease. Her parting words to him were: 'Bless you, William.' David Waddington also saw her towards the end. He had formed the impression that she had already decided to go, when she confirmed it by saying: 'Do you know the most unfair thing about all of this? I've now got to go back to No. 10 and sit up all night writing my speech for tomorrow.'

Throughout her meetings with ministers, she shed not a single tear. Others did. Most of the ministers found it an immense strain; few were far from tears, and several found it difficult to control their voices. Michael Howard was almost overcome by emotion; John Gummer was weeping as he left her room. It was natural that those closest to her, such as Michael Howard, should feel the worst strain. That was also true of Mr Gummer who, though not an ideological Thatcherite, had come to feel great affection for her. He had not had an altogether happy time as Party Chairman, and was not promoted to the Cabinet at the end of his stint. But Mrs Thatcher had promised him that she would not forget his claims – and nor had she. In the July 1989 reshuffle, John Gummer joined the Cabinet. In any normal circumstances, he would have been determined to repay her with the uttermost loyalty. On this occasion, he was convinced that her cause was beyond help.

Like Messrs Gummer and Howard, Peter Lilley also owed a great debt to her patronage. He, too, was a member of the 1983 intake who had been favoured and given accelerated promotion because of his Thatcherite views. Messrs Gummer, Howard and Lilley all hated telling Margaret Thatcher that she should stand aside. So did Norman Lamont, whose rise to the Cabinet had been slower, but who, nevertheless, greatly admired Margaret Thatcher. All four men found their interviews with her one of the most unpleasant experiences they had ever undergone, and they knew that their defection must be equally painful for her. Throughout the 1980s, she had been Thatcherizing the Cabinet. They were the beneficiaries: the Thatcherite elect. Now they were helping to bring her premiership to an end; it was as if the Old Guard had advised Napoleon to give up generalship. All four men felt for her; all marvelled at her restraint, and at the entire absence of any hint of '*Et tu, Brute*'. Although those involved did not realise it at the time, these four interviews helped to lay the foundations of the Major campaign. All four men had committed themselves to perform one last service for Margaret Thatcher: to stop Michael Heseltine.

A Thatcherite Counter-attack?

There were one or two moments of relief for Mrs Thatcher. Cecil Parkinson offered his support, as did Peter Brooke, although he did add that because he was spending so much time in Ulster, he was not in touch with the backbenchers. Mr Brooke turned up in white tie. He apologized for his excessively formal dress, but did say that there had been a time in his life when he had thought that no important business could be transacted unless one was wearing white tie: Mr Brooke had been President of the Oxford Union. She laughed; but that was merely an interlude among all the blows.

There was also a brief Thatcherite counter-attack. By coincidence, the No Turning Back group had been due to meet that night for one of their monthly dinners, which were held in the offices of the Institute of Economic Affairs, in Lord North Street. Throughout the evening, the NTB tried to act as a Thatcherite redoubt, while drawing their curtains to frustrate the film crews and photographers.

Before their dinner, several NTBers also attended a meeting of the 92 group, the memberships overlap. This takes its name from 92 Cheyne Walk, the address of Major (later Sir) Patrick Wall, one of the group's founders. The 92 started life as a small dining club during Heath Era. In those days, its aim was to keep the Tory Party Tory. Since then, its membership has expanded, and it now meets in the Commons. The members of the 92 are Thatcherite loyalists, though of a more sedate, less ideological disposition than the NTB.

By about seven o'clock, David Maclean, with the honed antennae one would expect of a former Whip, had realized what was happening on the Ministerial corridor: he feared that Mrs Thatcher might be about to resign. So he rushed into the 92 meeting, and told the group's Chairman, George Gardiner, of his fears. Mr Gardiner suggested that the group might put out a statement supporting her, which would appear in the morning papers. 'Tomorrow night will be too late, George,' said Mr Maclean. 'We've got to move now.' George Gardiner pointed out that there would be no one to type a statement. '**** the typing, George,' replied David Maclean. 'Let's go and see her.' So David Maclean and George Gardiner set off for her office, accompanied by David Evans, Michael Portillo and John Townend, who had all heard the exchange. On arrival, they found their way barred by Peter Morrison, who told them that they could not see her. Mr Portillo was not disposed to argue. He told Mr Morrison that unless he got out of the way, he would knock him down. Mr Morrison yielded.

They found Mrs Thatcher with Norman Tebbit. At last, she had given way to tears. It was apparent from her demeanour that she had also lost hope. Deeply moved, the five men expressed their support and their hope that she would carry on. She thanked them, and as they left, asked Mr Portillo to stay behind. He told her that if she were to use all the instruments of her Prime Ministerial power, she could win the second ballot, but he left her office fearing that he had failed – and determined to make another attempt.

A Phone Call to Huntingdon

At about 8.15, Margaret Thatcher slipped out of her office, and was driven to No. 10 to talk to Denis Thatcher. Just before she left the Commons, Norman Tebbit urged her to sleep on her decision, telling her that she owed it to herself to do so. She agreed, but Mr Tebbit – and she herself – knew that her mind would not change: it was all over.

When Mrs Thatcher's party returned to No. 10, Peter Morrison had a duty to perform. At around 8.30 he telephoned John Major in Huntingdon, to alert him to the possibility that Mrs Thatcher might stand down. Mr Major took the news gravely. His first reaction was sorrow for Margaret Thatcher, and sadness that her premiership should have ended in this way. He felt that she had deserved a more dignified finale. He asked Mr Morrison to pass on his very best wishes, and to reassure her of his support.

Now it was time to begin to consider his own position. His deliberations were regularly interrupted by the telephone; Norman Lamont and Graham Bright reported on the latest developments in Westminster – as did Robert Atkins, Kenneth Clarke and David Mellor, who also tried to persuade him not to sign Mrs Thatcher's nomination papers. He refused; nor did he let his friends know what Peter Morrison had said. At 10.30, Mr Morrison phoned back; it was now probable that Mrs Thatcher would resign. Mr Major told him that he was very sorry, and again asked him to tell the Prime Minister how much he felt for her. Norma Major was moved and upset by the news, but not by any consequences for John Major; all her thoughts were with Margaret Thatcher, whom she liked and admired. Mrs Major could readily imagine Mrs Thatcher's feelings at that moment, and found it hard to think of anything else.

The question Norma Major had asked on Monday: 'Do you realize you're talking about becoming Prime Minister?' was no longer a joke, or a fantasy. However, Mr Major was determined to test the mood in London before he took a decision as to whether to run, though he could not help being impressed by the judgement and urgings of characters such as Norman Lamont and Graham Bright – neither of them prone to reckless enthusiasm – who were both talking as if a Major premiership was a realistic possibility.

Norma Major, who had been reminding him for the past three days – with steadily diminishing impact – that he was meant to be a convalescent, then said: 'I suppose you'll have to go to London tomorrow?'

'I suppose I will,' replied John.

'Well, don't wear yourself out. I'll be down as soon as possible.'

They then discussed the mechanics of household organization, and Norma announced, squashing John's protests, that she would drive him to London, even though she would have to turn straight round and go back to Huntingdon.

One point that did occur to him, then and later, was how much he would regret giving up the Chancellorship, a job he had always wanted and was greatly enjoying. He had presided over only one Budget, in difficult circumstances – and had been looking forward to the opportunities a Chancellor would enjoy in an easier economic climate. Mr Major knew that a minister can rarely determine the timing of his career moves. He can do no more than take the opportunities as they become available. That applies *a fortiori* to the premiership. Determined to concentrate on thinking through the practical questions that would have to be resolved over the next few days, he was still not allowing himself to be carried away by dreams of No. 10.

He was tired, and decided to make it an early night. Without yielding to Norma's anxieties, he was conscious of the need to conserve his strength for the next few days. But he did not spend long agonizing, either then or during the leadership campaign. He was always able to stand back from the drama and consider his own prospects in a detached manner, with a Chief Whip's perspective.

In his entire life, John Major can remember only two sleepless nights. The first is supposed to have happened when, as a small boy, he was refused permission to have a Dalmatian puppy; his parents

Top
Tom Major's handiwork:
Gwen was the model

Bottom
260 Longfellow Road

Top
John Major aged eight

Bottom
The Major Family

Top
Foreign Secretary:
Mrs Thatcher with John Major
as Foreign Secretary,
at Chequers

Bottom
Chancellor of the Exchequer

Above
Wisden and Trivial Pursuit –
The Majors at Home

Top
The Bunker in Session 1
David Wilshire, Robert Hughes,
Andrew Mitchell, Gill Shephard,
Rob Hayward

Bottom
The Bunker in Session 2
Bruce Anderson, Alan Duncan,
Francis Maude, David Davis

Top
Richard Ryder and David Mellor

Middle
Alan Duncan's Drawing Room
Robert Hughes, Iain Sproat,
Angie Bray, David MacLean,
Claire Gibson, Alison Ramage

Bottom
Alison Ramage, Ian Lang,
John Gummer

Top
Francis Maude and Cecil Parkinson

Bottom
The Majorettes

Top
Gordon Reece and Norman Lamont

Bottom
William Hague

Top
Michael Jack, Norman Lamont,
Terence Higgins, Robert Hughes,
John Major, Ian Lang

Middle
Campaigning Takes Its Toll
Cecil Franks and Julia White

Bottom
John Major, John Gummer,
Robert Atkins, David Cardigan,
Andrew Mitchell

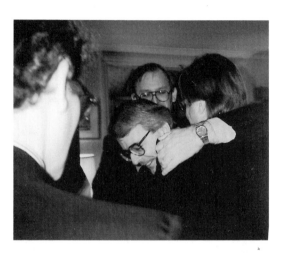

Top
"These Chelsea Supporters"
David Mellor greets John Major

Bottom
The Victory Speech

Above
Spreading the Good News

Top
Norma and John

Bottom
Norma Major and Robert Hughes

Top
Michael Howard and John Major

Bottom
Celebrations

Above
Rivals reconciled

Top
Mrs Thatcher congratulates her successor

Bottom
The War Leader

Above
No 10

did not feel that the Major household could cope with a full-grown Dalmatian. But it must be open to question whether he really had had a sleepless night, or merely convinced himself that he had not slept and reproached his parents with the fact at breakfast: little boys do not have sleepless nights. The second occasion is wholly credible. Late one night when he was Chief Secretary, tiredness overcame him when he had still not mastered his brief for the next day's meetings. He realized that there was no point in working on – but he also found that sleep evaded him. He could neither absorb the material properly, nor switch his mind off and go to sleep. On that Wednesday night, he had no such difficulty. He banished all thoughts of No. 10 and slept soundly.

No Unity Candidate

Before he saw Mrs Thatcher, Chris Patten hosted a meeting in his own Commons office. Though it was a smaller gathering and a different cast, this was effectively a continuation of the Catherine Place meeting. The other participants were: Ken Clarke, David Davis, Tristan Garel-Jones, Alastair Goodlad, Rob Hayward and Richard Ryder. Mr Patten had initially consulted Mr Hayward in his role as psephologist; the others arrived one by one. The discussion then focused on the question of a unity candidate.

At this point, Richard Ryder played a decisive role. He expressed the strongest opposition to the idea of a single candidate. First of all, he pointed out that the idea was completely impractical; there was no way of establishing who that candidate ought to be, and nominations for the second ballot had to be submitted by twelve noon the next day. But that was not Mr Ryder's conclusive argument. He declared that any one anti-Heseltine nominee, enjoying overwhelming Cabinet support, could easily be seen as the establishment candidate seeking to frustrate the people's choice. This would apply *a fortiori* were the nominee to be Douglas Hurd. Michael Heseltine would undoubtedly try to claim that this was a Cabinet versus backbenchers election; with the Tory Party in a volatile mood, this might even carry him to victory.

The others were all persuaded by Mr Ryder's arguments. At this stage, the group moved down the corridor to John Wakeham's office: they wanted to inform him of their views, and to find out what Mrs Thatcher was thinking. Mr Wakeham, however, remained delphic. He and David Waddington were now almost convinced that she would stand down, but they did not communicate their views to the younger Cabinet ministers, who were in a state of uncertainty. The atmosphere in the ministerial corridor became increasingly frantic. None of the ministers could see a way out for her except resignation. But none of them was confident that she would respond in that way. In a career built on courage and boldness, she had often defied augury; nor had she ever previously given the impression of willingly submitting her judgement to that of her Cabinet ministers. Some of her colleagues feared that nothing would deter her from a last stand: 'Come the three corners of the Party in arms and we shall shock them.' As the evening wore on, the arguments and the speculations grew more heated, with little help from post-prandial refreshment; the situation was stimulant enough.

Various possibilities were discussed. As Defence Secretary, Tom King was obviously weary about a change of Premier on the eve of a war, so he floated the idea of a lame-duck premiership: Mrs Thatcher would announce that she would retire at the end of the Gulf War. Kenneth Baker supported him, but Mr King and Mr Baker found no supporters: everyone else felt that the leadership issue had to be resolved there and then. Kenneth Clarke, meanwhile, had been busy since his interview with Mrs Thatcher. First, he had given some thought to the question of whether he himself should stand, and had dismissed the idea; he did not feel he could mount a serious challenge. He might have reconsidered his position if Mrs Thatcher had still been a candidate, and neither Mr Hurd nor Mr Major had been against her.

Meanwhile, a rumour was sweeping the corridor that Douglas and John were reluctant to stand against one another. The question of a joint candidacy was revived, with the suggestion that each of the two should nominate a group of friends, and that after taking soundings, the two groups should meet and agree on a single name. Fortified by Mr Ryder's arguments, Ken Clarke thought this was a daft idea, and Messrs Lamont, Lilley, Patten and Rifkind joined him in insisting that both men should stand. Alastair Goodland, the Deputy Chief Whip, was hovering around the corridor – entirely appropriate behaviour for a senior Whip. After establishing that Norman Lamont was in touch with John Major, and would dissuade him from agreeing to any joint candidacy, Mr Clarke and Mr Goodlad fished Douglas Hurd out of a dinner.

Mr Hurd was in favour of the idea of soundings: it was in character that he should be. The idea of grave and reverend signores meeting to resolve the matter would instinctively appeal to Mr Hurd, who had no taste for the drama or the vulgarity of a contest. Where at that moment the Tory Party could have laid its hands on either gravity or reverence would have been another matter.

Ambition played no part in Mr Hurd's calculations. Indeed, he saw an entirely opposite attraction in a brokered solution. Still not certain that he wanted to run, Douglas Hurd was fairly sure that the soundings would come out in favour of Mr Major; he could then bow out gracefully. Mr Clarke and Mr Goodlad bluntly told him that there was no question of soundings. For a start, there was no time: nominations had to be in by twelve noon. They reassured Mr Hurd that the contest would be conducted in as friendly a manner as possible. With that reassurance, still reluctantly, Mr Hurd agreed that if Margaret Thatcher stood aside he would be a candidate.

Kenneth Clarke then reverted to trying to stop Mrs Thatcher running. He and one or two others contacted Mr Major and urged him not to sign her nomination form. Mr Major replied with a refusal that was as polite as it was absolute. Mr Clarke was – as he later described it – 'unreasonably suspicious that everything was being strung out'. If Mrs Thatcher were determined to stand, she might hope that by pointing a pistol at the party's head, and offering them the choice between her or Michael Heseltine, she could secure re-election. It was clear that Tory MPs wanted a wider choice – but less clear how they would actually vote if only the narrower choice were available. Mr Clarke decided that Mrs Thatcher's position should be further weakened. He suggested to John Wakeham that there should be a Cabinet meeting that night. Mr Wakeham – who knew a lot that Mr Clarke did not know – refused to consider the idea. Kenneth Clarke then made it clear that he would raise the leadership issue at the next morning's Cabinet.

As the evening wore on, some Cabinet ministers discussed whether they should try to force the Prime Minister's hand by threatening to resign if she did not stand down. Chris Patten, Malcolm Rifkind and Kenneth Clarke went furthest down this road, and it was characteristic of Kenneth Clarke that he was the first over the top. By the end of the evening, Mr Patten and Mr Rifkind had not made up their minds. They were determined not to support her in a second ballot, and in such circumstances, it is questionable whether they could have remained in the Cabinet. But though they were considering resigning, they had not come to a decision. Mr Clarke had: if she were to stand, he would resign. John Wakeham was left in no doubt of that, for onward transmission to No. 10. But Mr Wakeham knew that there was no need to transmit any more bad news to No. 10.

The evening was now breaking up. One or two other colleagues had taken up Mr Clarke's call for a Cabinet meeting that night. Mr Wakeham told them not to be so silly, and to go home to bed. They took his advice. Suddenly, the excitement evaporated, leaving only weariness. The ministers went off in search of their equally sleepy drivers, and so one of the most extraordinary days in the history of the House of Commons ended with a straggle of cars leaving New Palace Yard.

From the Cabinet to the Cabinet Room

Over in No. 10, the lights were still burning in the Cabinet Room. Margaret Thatcher was spending her last hours as leader of the Conservative Party as she had spent the past fifteen and three-quarter years: displaying her stamina. She had started her day in Paris, finished off the summit, flown to London, addressed the Commons and answered questions; she had seen the Queen. No doubt sundry other matters had also required her attention, such as a war in the offing. Now she had another speech to write. A typical day, in other words – except for the two hours she had spent being destroyed by her Cabinet.

After her talk with Denis Thatcher, she was quickly downstairs, to begin a long speech-writing session. A large speech-writing team had already assembled, consisting of: Andrew Dunlop from the No. 10 policy unit; John Gummer; Robin Harris, also from the policy unit; Dominic Morris, one of the No. 10 private secretaries; Charles Powell;[4] Andrew Turnbull; John Whittingdale. Norman Tebbit joined them at various stages; he was also doing television interviews and keeping in contact with the Commons.

The question of the leadership was not discussed, though it was apparent to everyone there that she had decided to go. The fact that a speech could be drafted in such circumstances was a tribute to the PM's powers of self-control. It was not an entirely typical speech-writing session, however. Even after fifteen years as Leader of the Opposition and PM, Margaret Thatcher still brought a ferocious intensity to the final stages of drafting a speech; it was part of the process of psyching herself up for a big occasion. By the end, there was less blood-sacrifice of speech-writers than in earlier years, but as those around her had the scars to prove, no Prime Ministerial speech was truly complete until she had tossed and gored several persons. That night, everything was more tranquil.

The politicians and political advisers round the table – all devoted to her – were conscious of a great sadness and a feeling of helplessness; several of them were on the verge of giving way to grief or bitterness, or both. The example of her peremptory briskness restrained them. Finally the speech was finished. A muted group said their good-nights, still unable to believe that this was the last time they would work on a Prime Ministerial speech with Margaret Thatcher.

Meanwhile Michael Portillo had been making a last, desperate attempt to rally Thatcherite forces for a counter-attack. At about nine o'clock he, Michael Forsyth and Michael Fallon left the NTB meeting in Lord North Street and drove to No. 10. They were told that the PM was unable to see them: she was too busy with her speech. Mr Forsyth then wrote her a letter, which was given to John Whittingdale.

During a coffee break, Mr Whittingdale told the PM about the visit. 'Oh, I'd have seen them,' she replied, 'I'll always see my friends.' John Whittingdale then suggested that he invite them back, and she agreed; he contacted Mr Portillo. By midnight, the three Michaels had returned, along with Neil Hamilton and Ian Twinn. There was a brief emotional meeting with the PM; they pledged their support, and urged her to flight on. She listened and thanked them; they knew they had not changed her mind.

Then, Andrew Turnbull drew Mrs Thatcher on one side; he had prepared a checklist of the steps that had to be taken if she were going to resign. He tried to convey the information in a matter-of-fact tone, as if this was just part of the normal day's work; she responded in an equally business-like fashion. Shortly after 1 a.m., the Prime Minister got into the lift, and went upstairs to the flat.

At 6.30 a.m. two men arrived at the gates of Downing Street. A doubtful police officer phoned through to No. 10 and was connected to Charles Powell already back on duty; Mr Powell was always at his desk before 7 a.m. 'Got two chaps here claiming to be Tory MPs: they'd like to talk to someone in the PM's office; their names are Brown and Leigh.'

'If their names are Brown and Leigh,' Charles replied, 'they might well be Tory MPs; you'd better let them in.'

Mr Powell had a brief word with them. They had come to persuade her not to resign. He told them that the PM could not see them then; she was still dressing. They were shown into the ground-floor waiting room, given a cup of coffee, and promised that she would be informed of their presence. If the message ever reached Margaret Thatcher, it was either instantly submerged amid all her other preoccupations, or else she could not face seeing them. Her mind was made up. It may be that she wanted to conserve her strength for her remaining duties, and not to risk becoming emotional in response to the pleas of her supporters. So the two MPs waited, and waited. The Downing Street waiting room is adequately comfortable. There is usually an *Economist* of recent vintage, and it also contains a curious selection of books which Cabinet ministers have donated to the No. 10 library over the years. But it is not designed for long-stay residents. Even though the MPs were brought the occasional cup of coffee, they still felt like displaced persons in a transit camp. The hours passed: no summons came. They were still in the waiting room when the Cabinet meeting started, at 9 a.m. Then John Whittingdale came and told them what they had already realized: that Margaret Thatcher was informing the Cabinet of her decision to resign.

Rather than expose them to the world's television cameras lined up in front of No. 10, Mr Whittingdale led them through the Cabinet Office. The two were beyond consolation; tears were streaming down Michael Brown's face.

The Cabinet meeting had been brought forward for the convenience of those attending Elizabeth Douglas-Home's memorial service in Westminster Abbey. Before a normal Cabinet meeting, the ministers who are waiting for the PM to arrive gather in the middle of the Cabinet ante-room for a jovial exchange of news and pleasantries. On that Thursday, they waited in dead silence, standing around the walls, and leaving a great gap in the middle of the room.

The PM arrived and walked into the Cabinet room. Still in dead silence, her colleagues trooped in after her. She sat down, and began to read her resignation statement. Then her voice wavered. Her lips quivered; there were tears in her eyes; she came to a halt. The Lord Chancellor, James Mackay, who sat next to the PM, put an arm round her shoulder and said gently, 'Let me read it, Prime Minister.'

'Yes, Margaret,' said Cecil Parkinson, 'let the Lord Chancellor read it.'

'No,' she replied emphatically, stiffening in her seat, sitting bolt upright, and visibly controlling her features. The Lord Chancellor withdrew his supporting arm. She picked up her text, started again, and read it through without a tremor. By then, several of her colleagues were overcome by emotion: David Waddington was in tears, as were John Gummer and Michael Howard. Few others could have trusted themselves to speak. When she finished, James Mackay delivered a brief tribute. So did Cecil Parkinson, with a catch in his voice. She listened impassively, eyes front, and then said, 'Well, now that's out of the way, let's get on with the rest of the business.'

It was a brief discussion. None had much appetite for the usual routine of Cabinet: the latest Gulf developments, next week's parliamentary schedule *et al*. Margaret Thatcher had never used Cabinet as a sounding-board; under her, its discussions had always been firmly focused on the agenda. Her last Cabinet meeting was no exception; all the colleagues were united in their desire to bring it to a close as rapidly as possible. They succeeded; well within the hour, the agenda was concluded. 'Any other business?' the PM enquired (no one could remember any other business ever being raised at a Thatcher Cabinet) and then, virtually in the same breath: 'Let's have some coffee. I think we've all earned it.'

So ended Margaret Thatcher's last Cabinet. She went back to her study, and assembled her usual team – Dominic Morris, Peter Morrison, Charles Powell and John Whittingdale – to prepare for Prime Minister's Questions and go over the No Confidence speech. There was one thing she feared, she told them: she did not know whether she would be able to cope with sympathy. She was confident that she could deal with any amount of shouting and abuse from the Labour Party; it was people trying to comfort her that she would find hardest to bear.

There was indeed an awkward moment in Prime Minister's Questions. Dame Elaine Kellett-Bowman rose to ask a question, and broke down in tears. It was almost infectious. Those in the box were aware of Margaret Thatcher stifling a gulp and making a special effort to control her voice as she replied. Then the debate opened. Mr Kinnock performed adequately – but even if he had made a memorable speech, it would have been instantly forgotten. To judge by the version enbalmed in Hansard, Mrs Thatcher's speech does not seem remarkable – but fortunately, we are not dependent on cold print; the speech is recorded for ever on film, so that posterity will be able to appreciate its electrifying quality.

The speech was inseparable from the person and the occasion. It was characteristic of her that she should face trauma with triumph, and choose the moment of her downfall to deliver her greatest parliamentary performance. Rarely since the war has any speaker held all sides of the House spellbound for so long. Those who heard her will never forget the impact of every syllable. Perhaps the best moment, for it encapsulates both the scintillating exultant quality of the speech and its pathos, was when she said after Dennis Skinner had suggested that she became Governor of the European Central Bank: 'Now where were we; I am enjoying this.'[1]

When she sat down, the Tory benches behind her were torn between emotional exhaustion and foreboding. Even many of those who had been convinced that she must resign were now overcome with dismay. What they had just heard was no longer the Margaret Thatcher of by-election losses, adverse opinion polls, political crises and ministerial resignations. In her last speech as Prime Minister, she had brushed aside transient adversity, brushed aside even her own resignation to assert herself once again as a talismanic world-historical figure. If the Tory Party had voted at that moment, she would have been swept back to re-election.

If she *had* been standing for re-election, she could not have made that speech. The Labour Party had learned from that morning's newspapers that a majority of the Cabinet were against her. They would have reminded her of it, again and again. Mr Kinnock could have found enough material in that fact alone for a half-hour (not that there is any relationship between the length of his speeches and the quality of his material). Had Mrs Thatcher been a candidate, at least one Cabinet minister would have resigned, and everyone would have been waiting to see whether Ken Clarke would speak in the debate. Mr Kinnock would no doubt have heaped congratulations on Mr Clarke, and taunted the other eleven for their cowardice. In such circumstances, Michael Heseltine would have spoken, as might Nigel Lawson. Her supporters might have prayed for a hostile intervention from Ted Heath – not even that could have saved her performance. The atmosphere and the outcome would have been entirely different.

Speeches in the House of Commons are not timeless, senatorial

---

1 *Hansard*, 22 November 1990, col. 451.

texts. Timing and occasion are all. Had Margaret Thatcher still been a candidate, she might have used large sections of the speech she did deliver. But there would have been none of the brio or the bravura. Barracking in front of her, rows of grim faces behind her, colleagues looking round to see how Michael or Ken or Nigel were reacting. In those very different circumstances, even fighting for her life, not even she could have dominated the House of Commons, as she did that day.

Bad Luck and Bad Judgement

Margaret Thatcher's hatred of inflation is second in intensity only to her love of her country. It was a tragic irony, therefore, that her premiership should have been destroyed by the resurgence of inflation. Had it been under control, Mrs Thatcher could have survived the community charge – and retained it – while coping easily with the various European controversies. She would still be Prime Minister, on course for a fourth election win.

Inflation exacerbated all the Government's other problems. Many of those who protested about the community charge were facing increases in their mortgage costs which were greater than their entire community charge bill. Equally the European issue would not have been so damaging but for the markets' nervousness: the markets would not have been so nervous but for inflation. Despite all the Government's difficulties, however, there was nothing inevitable about her defeat; she fell inches short of victory. Bad economics brought her in peril: it took bad politics – and bad luck – to finish her off.

Mrs Thatcher's grotesquely inadequate campaign for re-election was only the culmination of months of misjudgement and ill-fortune. If she had appointed either Tristan Garel-Jones or Richard Ryder as Chief Whip in November 1989, she would still be Prime Minister. Even with the wrong Chief Whip, she could have won if she had appointed almost anyone but Peter Morrison as her PPS. Then again, if she had either cancelled her trip to Paris, or held the ballot slightly later, she could even have survived Mr Morrison.

The IRA can also claim a role in her downfall. Had Ian Gow still been alive, the first ballot campaign would have been properly run. Ian was also a close friend of Geoffrey Howe; even if he had not been able to prevent Sir Geoffrey from resigning, he might have persuaded him to make a less destructive speech.

In the early phase of her premiership, Margaret Thatcher owed much to good luck. Michael Foot's defeat of Denis Healey; Galtieri's rejection of the Peruvian peace terms: Scargill's rejection of the NACODs deal – all had made her task immeasurably easier. But in her final eighteen months, it seemed that everything which could go wrong did go wrong. Mrs Thatcher had believed her position to be invulnerable. In the event, she was almost proved right; it took an extraordinary sequence of misfortune to unseat her. Her party was fortunate in her misfortune.

By last November, the Tory Party was in desperate straits, and it is hard to see how an electoral recovery would have been possible under Margaret Thatcher. With a decent campaign, she could have won 220 votes – but she could neither have reunited the Party nor led it to victory. So when the Tories win the next General Election under John Major, a considerable degree of credit will be due to Peter Morrison.

Over the previous twelve months, it had often seemed that the Tory Parliamentary Party was bent on electoral suicide; at moments, the Whips had feared that discipline was on the point of collapse. It now appears that the MPs concerned were inspired, not by self-destruction, but by the wisdom of the Party's collective unconscious. Their rebelliousness was an expression, not of defeatism, but of that strongest of Tory emotions, a will to win. At the end of her premiership, Margaret Thatcher at last encountered a will stronger than her own.

7 The Major Campaign

Earlier that evening, while Mrs Thatcher was hearing her fate in the Commons, the MP's Downing Street staff were trying to organise her re-election bid. There was a logistical problem. John Major had to sign her nomination paper, but he was in Huntingdon. Andrew Turnbull, the Principal Private Secretary in No.10, ruled that it would not be possible to send the paper to Huntingdon by Government car: this was a Party matter. However, Jeffrey Archer, who was in No. 10, happened to overhear this conversation, and promptly volunteered the use of his Jaguar. Shortly afterwards, Bob Slade, Mr Archer's driver, set off for Mr Major's house. By the time he arrived, at around 9.00, Mr Morrison had spoken to Mr Major; John Major was no longer clear whether Mrs Thatcher still wanted him to sign the nomination paper, so he asked Mr Slade to wait.

During Mr Morrison's 10.30 'phone call, he and Mr Major discussed the question of the nomination paper. They decided that John Major might as well go ahead and sign it; there was still a faint chance that it would be used. So Bob set off back to London, with the signed paper in an envelope.

At around midnight, he delivered the paper to Mr Archer, who put it by his bed intending to hand it in to No. 10 in the morning. Jeffrey Archer is normally a sound sleeper, who likes to be in bed before midnight. That night, he found himself unable to sleep; although he knew it was absurd to do so, he could not stop worrying about the nomination paper. He finally decided that there would be no rest for him until he delivered it to Downing Street. So he dressed and drove across.

It was now about 1.30. Peter Morrison was still up, but when Jeffrey handed him the paper, he showed an absolute lack of interest. At that moment, Mr Archer knew that Margaret Thatcher was going to resign.

Norma Major occasionally looks at magazine horoscope columns. Earlier in the year, she had read that she ought to expect further career upheavals in the family. 'Not the Premiership, surely' she remembers thinking: after the Foreign Office and the Treasury, it was about the only upheaval left. She then dismissed astrology from her mind. Although she had no desire to hasten Margaret Thatcher's departure from No. 10, Mrs Major remembers one thought that occasionally crossed her mind. It was certain that Mrs Thatcher's successor would be a good friend of the Majors, so Mrs Major vaguely looked forward to the day when she would be on first-name terms with a Prime Minister. These days, she laughs when she tells that story.

By the time the Majors were roused by their alarm clock, at 7.30a.m. on Wednesday 21 November 1990, the horoscope writer had been vindicated. At 8.00, Peter Morrison 'phoned for the final time – to confirm that in an hour's time, Mr Thatcher would be informing the Cabinet of her decision to resign. At 8.15, Norman Lamont spoke to John Major. Mr Major told him that he would shortly be leaving for London, and that he had more or less decided to let his name go forward. One factor which helped him to make up his mind was Mr Thatcher's attitude. Although Peter Morrison had never actually told John Major that he regarded him as her chosen successor, that was the implication of the 'phone calls.

It is not clear when exactly Mrs Thatcher decided that John Major ought to be her Crown Prince – but by 1987, she had concluded that he was 'One of Us' – a talented young Thatcherite whose career she ought to advance. She seems to have come to this conclusion quickly and almost instinctively. It was certainly not based on any prolonged probing of John Major's opinions; Mr Major had never said or done anything to suggest that he was a radical Thatcherite.

Mrs Thatcher, however, had made up her mind, and once she took a view on one of her colleagues, she was always reluctant to change her mind. Mr Major's record as Chief Secretary also impressed her – but in order to control public spending, every Chief Secretary has to appear to be a hard-liner, and Mr Major was no exception. This helped to confirm Margaret Thatcher in her judgment.

Mr Major arrived in London to find everything in confusion. Once Cabinet had ended, and the Ministers were having coffee, Mr Hurd rose and excused himself, saying that he had some telephone calls to make. Michael Howard and Norman Lamont, at opposite ends of the table, gave each other a despairing look. They knew how much there was to do in such a short time – nominations closed at twelve noon – but neither felt that they could leave the table. It would have seemed indecent to have a succession of Ministers slipping away from Margaret Thatcher's Cabinet to organize the battle for the succession. To both Mr Lamont and Mr Howard, the next ten minutes seemed to last a century. Finally, Mrs Thatcher put down her coffee cup and rose; everyone else could now take their departure in proper form. The end of that Cabinet meeting also marked the official beginning of the Major campaign.

The first stage was one of primal chaos. Anyone who still believes that the Major campaign was a deep-laid conspiracy should have witnessed its first hour. By about 11.30 a.m. on that Thursday, those who were actually running the campaign were becoming anxious about their complete and elementary disorganization. In the first place, the Majorites assembled in three different rooms.

A number of MPs turned up at Mr Major's office, where Robert Atkins, Graham Bright, David Davis and Francis Maude had been meeting. A second group consisting of Michael Howard, Norman Lamont, Peter Lilley and John Gummer went straight from the Cabinet meeting in the Chancellor's office in the Treasury. But Mr Major himself had still not arrived, and John Gieve, his private secretary, would not allow his office to be used on his absence. After briefly protesting, Mr Lamont then moved on to his own office, where the group began to discuss the form a Major campaign should take; Messrs Atkins, Bright and Maude joined them, as did Terence Higgins and William Hague.

The discussion focused on two issues; who should nominate John Major, and how the campaign should be organised. At this point, John Major arrived. His initial instincts were to have as broadly-based a campaign as possible, with a minimum of hierarchy. Originally, he was intending that his nomination papers be signed by two backbenchers – Terry Higgins was standing by to be one of them – with the aim of countering Michael Heseltine's claim to be the backbencher's champion. Norman Lamont was doubtful about the wisdom of all this. He felt that it would look odd if John Major were not proposed and seconded by Cabinet colleagues. He was also convinced that the campaign had to be properly run; that meant someone in charge. The previous night, he had discussed the matter with Norman Fowler, and inquired whether Sir Norman might be prepared to run the Major campaign. But Norman Fowler told him that though he had a high regard for Mr Major, he felt committed to Michael Heseltine. Mr Lamont then decided that he himself ought to take charge of the campaign.

Mr Major accepted the argument that the nomination papers should be signed by Cabinet ministers. He telephoned David Waddington, and asked him to be one of the two. But Mr Waddington had already been asked to second Douglas Hurd, and though he had refused, gently informing Mr Hurd that he was a Major supporter, he felt that it would be a snub to Mr Hurd if he then nominated Mr Major. Mr Major told him that he perfectly understood. Mr Waddington assured him that he was at the Major camp's disposal, and would declare his support whenever John Major and his strategists thought it would have most impact.

By now Norman Lamont had emerged as not only Mr Major's Chief of Staff, but his proposer as well; there was a general view that the same man should do both jobs. At one point, it seemed that Michael Howard might be the seconder. But though they had nothing against Mr Howard *per se*, David Mellor, Robert Atkins and Graham Bright all thought that a Lamont/Howard nomination would not have been a balanced ticket; they might come across as a pair of Treasury dries. So John Gummer emerged as the seconder. Though Mr Gummer was personally loyal to the outgoing Prime Minister, in economic terms he was more of a pragmatic Thatcherite than an ideological one. Mr Gummer was also an unequivocal supporter of EEC membership, whereas Mr Howard shared Mr Lamont's Gaullist opinions. In terms of representing a spectrum of Party opinion, Lamont/Gummer was better than Lamont/Howard.

It was now 11.30; the noon deadline was approaching. Once the nomination form was signed, Graham Bright took it across to Cranley Onslow at the House. In so doing he came close to causing an almighty panic – if not indeed to changing the course of British political history.

As Mr Bright got into a Commons lift, the nomination form slipped from his grasp. He made desperate lunges to retrieve it, but the piece of paper swirled and fluttered before coming to rest on the floor of the lift. A blushing, embarrassed Graham Bright hurriedly scooped it up, while the lift's other occupants – secretaries – giggled at his confusion. They little realized the importance of the dropped document. Given the state of some Commons lifts, it might well have been possible for the paper to find its way via some crevice to the lift-shaft, where it would still be mouldering. If that had happened, there could still have been time – just – for Mr Bright to rush back to the Treasury, have a second form signed, and deliver it to Mr Onslow. He might even have had two or three minutes to spare. Mr Bright says that when he relives the moment of dropping the nomination form, he still shudders. Cranley Onslow almost shuddered when he arrived with it: 'What! Another one?' was the '22 Chairman's response. He had assumed that the election would be between Messrs Heseltine and Hurd.

John Major was now a candidate. With each passing moment, he was also a candidate with a campaign. From the first, Norman Lamont had been unmoved by his Chief's democratic aspirations; Mr Lamont knew how he wanted things run. It was still not certain that he would get his way until someone switched on a midday television news programme. It stated that Michael Stern was in charge of the

Major campaign. Mr Stern, a Bristol MP, is a respected and popular backbencher, who has since become a vice-chairman of the Tory Party, but he himself would not claim to be Chief of Staff material. After the television programme there was a sudden burst of decision-taking in the Treasury. Norman Lamont was appointed the campaign manager. He immediately displayed a Treasury minister's sense of priorities, and asked his friend Brian Wolfson, the Chairman of Wembley plc, whether he would meet the costs of the Major campaign. Mr Wolfson agreed: the eventual bill was just under £10,000. Mr Lamont was decided that at 8.00 a.m. every morning in No. 11 Downing Street – the Chancellor's official residence – campaign strategy would be discussed by a small group consisting of any Cabinet Minister in the Major team who was able to attend, plus Robert Atkins, Graham Bright, William Hague, Terence Higgins, Francis Maude, David Mellor, Richard Ryder and Andrew Tyrie.

As the campaign went on, that group became less small as others joined it on an ad hoc basis, either for some or all of its meetings. Those included Rob Hayward; Gordon Reece, the communications maestro; Angie Bray, the campaign press officer; and Bruce Anderson. The minutes were taken by Sue Dennis, Peter Lilley's secretary. As with minutes of the real Cabinet, they were taken in telegraphic form and concentrated on points for action. Because they were intended as an *aide-mémoire* for Mr Lamont rather than for general circulation, only one copy was made; at the time of writing, it has not come to light. During the end-of-campaign clear-up operation in No. 11, Mr Bright gathered together a number of relics which he took to No. 10: the minutes are not among them.

As well as the 'Cabinet', Mr Lamont appointed an inner cabinet, consisting of himself, Francis Maude and Richard Ryder. Francis Maude was designated Chief Whip, taking command of the canvassing operation. Richard Ryder was to be press supremo – the Major campaign's Bernard Ingham. But Mr Ryder had valuable assistance. Back in August, Norman Lamont had met Angie Bray, the Chief Broadcasting Officer in Tory Central Office; they had both been guests of David Hart's at a shooting lodge in Aberdeenshire. After dinner, while the rest of the house-party pursued low avocations such as bridge, Mr Lamont and Miss Bray discussed politics, and found themselves substantially in agreement. Around lunchtime on Thursday, Angie Bray telephoned Mr Lamont at the Treasury and offered her services. He replied: 'You are manna from heaven, Angie.'

Central Office, of course, remained firmly neutral during the campaign, and Miss Bray had to resign her job to join the Major campaign. Brendan Bruce, then the Party's Director of Communications, told her privately that he himself was not unsympathetic, and hinted that Kenneth Baker took the same view. But Mr Bruce made it clear to Angie that she was leaving at her own risk; there could be no guarantee that she would be given her job back, especially if Michael Heseltine were to win. Angie Bray brushed aside such doubts and reported for duty at the newly-acquired campaign headquarters. Michael Jack, now Parliamentary Secretary for Social Security, also did valuable work on the press side.

In the earlier Treasury meeting, Mr Lamont had raised the question of an HQ. A house within the division-bell zone would be ideal, he said; did anyone know of a suitable one? William Hague did. Mr Hague is an old friend of Alan Duncan, an oil trader and prospective Tory candidate. Mr Duncan owns a house in Gayfere Street, five minutes from the House; Roy Hattersley is another Gayfere Street inhabitant. During the week, Mr Hague had sometimes used Mr Duncan's spare bedroom, and he knew that the house was just what Mr Lamont had in mind.

He telephoned Alan Duncan at his office: Mr Duncan was at his tailors. At this, Mr Hague uttered a few incredulous expletives, and left instructions for Mr Duncan to 'phone the Chancellor's office as soon as he deigned to return to his own. Mr Duncan arrived back, and a secretary said that he was to telephone the Chancellor of the Exchequer's office. Alan Duncan, who had only met John Major once before, assumed that someone was taking the mickey. But the secretary handed him a scrap of paper with the number, and Mr Duncan, recognizing the Treasury code, thought he had better make sure that it was a joke. He was quickly talking to Mr Hague who, after dwelling briefly on the fatuity of those who chose such an absurd moment to disappear off to their tailor's, told him that his house was required for the duration of the Major campaign. Mr Duncan instantly agreed. David Davis and Francis Maude went immediately with Mr Hague to inspect the premises, while Mr Duncan, who had decided that Leadership campaigning sounded more exciting than oil trading, set off for home. By the time he arrived, Mr Maude and Mr Ryder had departed, well satisfied; 18 Gayfere Street was about to earn a niche in the annals of British political addresses.

Within minutes, the first wave of Major supporters came ashore.

They included a detachment of 'Majorettes', of whom there were to be five in all. These were House of Commons secretaries whose bosses had seconded them to the campaign, and who spent most hours of the next five days ensuring that 18 Gayfere Street and its inhabitants functioned smoothly. It would have been impossible to recruit a better or more delightful group; cheerful, charming, worldly-wise, efficient, immensely hard-working and equally good-humoured, they performed an indispensable role. Julia White – Francis Maude's secretary – was the first to arrive. Jules is a Brigadier's daughter; she had worked in pantomime, and then served in the Wrens: it was never clear which of the two had been the more valuable training for the Major campaign. She was closely followed by Katy Altman, Claire Gibson, Barbara Kyriakou, and Alison Ramage, who work for Richard Ryder, William Hague, Graham Bright and Jacques Arnold respectively.

No. 18 had another great advantage. Because of Mr Duncan's trading activities he had already installed a fax machine and two telephone lines, with capacity for several more. All that remained was for British Telecom to put the additional lines into service. Simon Blackman undertook the liaison with British Telecom. He is an undergraduate studying philosophy at London University, who also runs a security business employing thirty people; he had been installing new locks for Alan Duncan at 18 Gayfere Street. Mr Blackman also joined the Major campaign, and 'phoned the area manager of British Telecom, who sprang into action. In little over an hour, two crews of telephone engineers arrived – one for the house, the other for the roadway. Shortly afterwards, 18 Gayfere Street had six fully functioning telephones, on all floors of the house, as well as the fax machine. The Majorettes, meanwhile, were bringing over personal computers and typewriters from their offices in the House; a photocopier was also acquired. Mr Blackman also telephoned Special Branch to alert them to the likelihood that Gayfere Street would soon be full of Cabinet Ministers and other notables. They thanked him for letting them know, and shortly afterwards a police inspector arrived to look over the premises, while a number of metal crowd-barriers were piled up in a corner of Smith Square.

The first phase of the Major campaign was now over. Confusion had given way to organization, strategy and momentum. There were three main focal points. The first was John Major himself, who stayed in No. 11, when he made himself available to the large number of backbenchers who wanted to see him. This canvassing exercise was reinforced – and organized – by Gayfere Street.

By late afternoon, Richard Ryder, Angie Bray and Michael Jack were almost continually on the telephone; it seemed as if all the world's media wanted to interview John Major. It had already been decided, however, that Mr Major should concentrate on his electorate of 372 Tory MPs. He would have to appear on the main Sunday current affairs programmes, as well as seeing one or two editors and senior journalists, but beyond that, he intended to keep his media activities to a minimum. So Richard Ryder's and Angie Bray's main task was to say 'no' politely, but firmly, and to offer substitutes. Predictably, they found that the smaller the newspaper, or the more obscurely provincial the radio station, the more it insisted that nobody but John Major would do. But Mr Ryder and Miss Bray were immovable.

They had no shortage of alternative spokesmen. As Chief of Staff, Norman Lamont played the most prominent role, but he was reinforced by John Gummer, Michael Howard, Ian Lang, Peter Lilley, David Mellor, Tony Newton, Gill Shephard, and half a dozen others. Mr Mellor was particularly willing to help; he does not suffer from shyness. His willingness to appear anytime, anywhere earned him a nickname: there was no question of a sound bite where Mr Mellor was concerned; he was the sound meal. But the pressure of requests was such that Miss Bray occasionally ran out of Ministers. On one occasion, she answered the 'phone, listened briefly, then put her hand over the mouthpiece and looked desperately round the room. She hailed Alan Duncan – 'Alan!' then handed him the telephone. 'It's Radio Iceland – you're on air, live.'

However, the media operation, though essential, was not as important as the canvassing of MPs. This was the other main activity in Gayfere Street, and was organized from Alan Duncan's basement dining room, which immediately became known as the bunker. By the end of five days, it resembled one. Francis Maude was in charge of the bunker. As a former Whip – and a very good one – he organized his operations on Whips' Office lines. The Tory Whips' Office consists of fourteen men sitting round a table, discussing their colleagues and trying to solve problems. The bunker team was smaller, but it operated in a similar fashion. Apart from Mr Maude, its core members were David Davis, Rob Hayward and (later on) Andrew Mitchell, all three of whom managed to stand down all other activities. Between Thursday afternoon and Tuesday evening, they were in almost continuous session, leaving Gayfere Street only to go to No. 11, or to go home and sleep.

They were assisted by David Maclean, a Parliamentary Secretary at the ministry of Agriculture. Mr Maclean, a shrewd, witty, tough-minded Highlander who, had also been a Whip, was an admirable member of the bunker, but had to spend part of the weekend on constituency engagements. Among the others who joined the team at various stages were: Alan Duncan, Cecil Franks, John Gummer, William Hague, Archie Hamilton, Bob Hughes, Terence Higgins, Gill Shephard, David Wilshire and Bruce Anderson. But most MPs who called in at Gayfere Street participated in the bunker's deliberations, partly to enjoy the free theatre. The discussions never remained solemn for long. Every few minutes, the room would erupt with laughter, usually at some bleary-eyed sarcasm from David Davis. Francis Maude, laughing louder than anyone, would then restore order and readdress everyone's mind to business.

So the bunker's reputation spread as a cross between Dorothy Parker's table at the Algonquin and a visit to the lunatics at Bedlam. But the humour never obstructed the serious purpose; to organize a comprehensive, rigorous and reliable canvass of the Tory Parliamentary Party. As soon as the campaign started, constituency pressure was beginning to build up in favour of John Major and against Michael Heseltine. Though this was obviously going to help the Major campaign, there was also a risk that some MPs would declare for Major to keep their constituency happy, but then vote for Michael Heseltine; it was a secret ballot. After all, Peter Morrison had not invented his figures: he must have had reason to believe that 230 or so Tory MPs would vote for Margaret Thatcher. Mr Maude was determined not to repeat Mr Morrison's mistake.

By Thursday evening, his operation was already under way. He had been shown Peter Morrison's campaign files from the first ballot – a dubious benefit – and he had also debriefed Graham Bright, who had made a note of the names of many of those who had told him that they would support a Major candidacy. Moreover, MPs were continually telephoning Gayfere Street to pledge their votes, and offer their help.

Mr Major was also well supported at Cabinet level. In addition to Messrs Gummer and Lamont, he was endorsed by Michael Howard, Peter Lilley, John MacGregor, Tony Newton, Cecil Parkinson and

David Waddington. It was decided to hold back the announcement of Messrs Waddington and Parkinson's support until Sunday and Monday respectively, so as to maintain the impression of momentum. The Major camp also had the support of three other Cabinet ministers, none of whom felt able to make a public declaration: Ken Baker, John Wakeham – and Margaret Thatcher. So John Major had a clear majority of Mrs Thatcher's Cabinet.

In those first stages of the Major campaign, there were two objectives. The first was to win the battle for second place. If nobody won outright in the second ballot, all three candidates could, in theory, run again in the third ballot, in practice, however, the man who came third would be under great pressure to withdraw, and would find his support melting away. Mr Major needed to establish a clear lead over Douglas Hurd and become the main challenge to Michael Heseltine. The second objective was to arrest Mr Heseltine's momentum. As long as Michael Heseltine's vote was below his first ballot total of 152, then even if he still topped the poll, there would be an impression that his campaign had peaked.

Very early on, it was clear to the bunker that the first objective had been attained. The battle for second place was won before dinner on Thursday, with the Major camp already confident that their candidate was bound to win more than one-third of the vote. They were also confident that they were closing the gap on Michael Heseltine. So Francis Maude's task was to build on these initial advantages.

He began by organizing the technology of canvassing, and decided to adopt the same simple method of storing data that the Garel-Jones/Gow/Ryder team had used in 1989. Every MP had his own sheet of paper, on which all contacts with him were logged. These sheets were stored in six ring-files, arranged alphabetically. The bunker sessions consisted primarily of going through those files, name by name. Between them, the bunker's inhabitants had a vast store of information about the Tory Parliamentary Party. When any MP was discussed, someone in the room was bound to know who his good friends were, which Cabinet ministers he particularly respected, what policy issues were troubling him *et al*. In the course of these free-ranging sessions, the participants often remembered trivial information: MPs who regularly travelled down from their constituencies together, who had once shared a London flat, or who invited one another to shoot.

Enmities were at least as important. It was generally assumed that

Cabinet ministers would be the right men to talk to their junior ministers – indeed, in both the Major and the Hurd campaigns, a high proportion of the Cabinet ministers were able to deliver their whole departments, just as if they had been feudal magnates summoning their tenantry. But there were exceptions. It had just been decided that one right-wing Parliamentary Secretary, who was still shocked by Mrs Thatcher's departure should be reassured and canvassed by his Cabinet minister, a Major supporter, when a new arrival in the bunker disagreed strongly; the junior minister in question had no respect for his boss.

All this information helped to create a network of persuasion, plus the means of checking on the effectiveness of that persuasion. On the basis of the information that was rapidly being assembled, the bunker was able to decide not only who should canvass whom, but which old friends should follow up the canvass by a 'phone call in which it would be only natural to move on from family gossip to the question of the leadership. Mindful of what had befallen Peter Morrison, Francis Maude was reluctant to accept any information until it had been checked and double-checked. By Monday, much of the data available to the bunker had gone through as many sifting and refining processes as London drinking water: sometimes for similar reasons.

Every political party has its dubious characters. In that respect, the Conservative Party is no worse off than its rivals, but there is a small group of Tory MPs who are unsatisfactory members of the human race, and of whom one would not ask the time of day without subsequently checking the information with Big Ben. The idea of trusting their word as to their voting intentions in a secret ballot was risible. The names of this handful of miscreants were well-known to that fraternity of special constables who had served in the Whips' Office. Indeed, at the end of the campaign, David Maclean pointed out one disadvantage in the bunker procedure; the Whips' Office secret shits' list had now been widely disseminated. However, none of the names on it had come as a surprise to the bunker's other inmates.

As the lists were read out and discussed, two more schedules were compiled. The first consisted of points for action – mainly who should telephone whom. When that check-list overflowed, someone would go off and work through it. The second was a typed list of Conservative MPs. This was kept by Francis Maude, with the aid of three felt-tipped highlighter pens; blue for Major, yellow for Hurd, and pink for Heseltine. Firm supporters were given a heavy ink rectangle by their names; waverers received a lightly-coloured one. As the days went on, more and more of the light colours were re-inked definitively, and there were fewer and fewer names without any marking. On the basis of his colourings, Francis was able to provide regular running totals as to how the campaign was going. He arrived at these by counting the ink marks and then applying the Maude discount formula. He never discussed exactly how he arrived at this, but it was always used to reduce the raw figures for Major support.

There was always a certain amount of controversy about Francis Maude's figures, however, and not only because of of his formula. Several of his colleagues in the bunker were not convinced that Francis could add up, except on his fingers. It was widely believed that as soon as he had to count beyond ten, a margin of error would creep in. Mr Maude himself hotly disputes this, though it might explain why he is such a good Treasury Minister. It is certainly true that throughout the campaign, he consistently fed false information to the press and to John Major himself, but that was done deliberately. From first to last, all the figures Mr Maude issued were calculated underestimates.

The daily totals issued by the Major campaign were as follows:

Thursday evening 100
Friday evening   124
Saturday evening 140
Sunday evening   150+
Monday evening   160+
Tuesday midday   175

On each of these occasions, Francis Maude could quite legitimately have claimed a higher figure. By midday on Tuesday he had 197 firm pledges. He preferred his pessimistic discounting, knowing that it was less important to go for sensationalist headlines – which even if true, might not be believed – than to maintain both credibility and the impression of steady upward progress.

Considerable trouble was taken to brief selected journalists about the accuracy of the figures. Although they were not given a comprehensive account of the bunker's operations, they were assured that the Major campaign's claims were true. It was easy for those giving such assurances to sound sincere; they were. Naturally enough, the bunker briefers invited the press to contrast the probity of the Major figures with the evasive attitudes of Heseltine and Hurd camps. On Friday and Saturday, Mr Heseltine's supporters announced that he had made 'significant advances' from his first ballot total – but the Heseltine camp's figures were always vague. On Friday, Mr Hurd's camp declared that they were approaching the hundred mark; at intermittent intervals during the rest of the campaign, that claim was repeated with steadily diminishing conviction. If all these claims were added to the Major camp's figures, the resulting total – in excess of 400 – could not be reconciled with the fact that there were only 372 Tory MPs. On the whole, the bunker was able to convince the press that it was not we who were overestimating.

Late on the Thursday evening, for the first and last time during the campaign, Francis Maude was more optimistic than John Major. He told Mr Major that there was a possibility of him winning outright on the first ballot. Mr Major responded with surprise and scepticism, but also a certain cautious enthusiasm. By the next day, however, their roles were reversed. John Major's Chief Whip's nose told him that he was doing well; he could sense the surge towards him. He quickly realized that the figures he was receiving from the bunker were doctored – as he often protested. 'Get hold of Francis,' he would tell Graham Bright or William Hague, 'and tell him to give me the real figures. I know these are cooked.' Mr Maude's response was a sardonic smile, and an occasional concession: 'Yes, you can tell him that it could be one or two higher.'

Mr Major's expressions of mock irritation – it was never more than mock – were particularly vehement when after a hard day's telephoning during which he had been given half a dozen new pledges, and had been assured by several MPs that everything was moving in his direction, he would be told that his total of supporters had increased by three.

Mr Major's 'phone calls were a crucial element in the campaign. Messrs Lamont, Maude and Ryder were determined that he should spend as many hours as possible on the telephone: Mr Major himself concurred, though there were sometimes rueful protests about Mr Lamont's slave-driving tactics. The problem remained as to who should receive the 'phone calls. Even if John Major had telephoned for twelve or fourteen hours a day, there would still only be time to contact a limited number. So his time had to be allocated carefully.

There were a number of groups who had priority. First, the Party's grandees, who were entitled to expect a 'phone call. Second, there were those who thought they had grandee status, and would be offended if they were not telephoned. Third, there were insignificant, passed-over backbenchers prone to pomposity, and determined to enjoy this brief interlude in which they could make the bigwigs play court to them. Then there were the swing voters, whom earlier canvassing had revealed as anxious on particular topics, or as genuinely undecided. Finally, there were those who had declared themselves to be firm Major supporters, but whom the bunker felt might be made even firmer by a few words from John Major.

Fortunately, a large number of names could be eliminated. There was no need to 'phone those active in the Major campaign: they could receive their thanks after polling day. Equally, there was no point in contacting those known to be working for Michael Heseltine or Douglas Hurd. But that still left plenty to do. In all, Mr Major telephoned about sixty colleagues; no doubt there are others who are still grumbling that they were not contacted. Some MPs, of course, forced themselves on Mr Major's attention. During the entire campaign, nothing infuriated the bunker more than the behaviour of one or two individuals – one of them a minister – who while declaring that they were firm Major voters, also insisted that they needed a few minutes with John. They could not resist the opportunity to show off in front of the future PM. The bunker's view was that these characters should be offering their own time, not taking up John Major's – and that if the aim was to impress him, their behaviour might well be counterproductive. But they were voters; the bunker gritted its teeth and gave way.

Thirty MPs also came to see John Major. One of them was David Shaw, the MP for Dover, who easily won the prize for the most outrageous piece of lobbying during the entire campaign. The price of his vote turned out to be: a new by-pass around Dover; a new wing for a local hospital; a guarantee that no public money would ever be spent on the Channel tunnel link; and the designation of a local site as a 'green area'. Mr Shaw was received politely: no promises were made, to him or to anyone else. Above all, no one was promised a ministerial appointment. For years, Michael Heseltine had been commiserating with backbenchers about the way in which their claims to office had been overlooked. John Major did not adopt this tactic – nor did Douglas Hurd.

Other MPs who came to see Mr Major had their own concerns. Richard Holt is the MP for Langbaurgh, a constituency recently invented by the boundary commissioners. Mr Holt suspected, with much justice, that very few of his Parliamentary colleagues could either pronounce Langbaurgh (Lang-bar), spell it, or find it on a map. So he decided to test all three Leadership candidates on their knowledge of the geography of Langbaurgh. Over that weekend, he boasted extensively of his intention – Mr Holt is not a retiring figure – and news of it reached William Hague, a fellow Northerner. Mr Hague photocopied the relevant page from Robert Waller's *Handbook of British Politics*, and gave it to Mr Major. Mr Holt arrived, and bustled into the Chancellor's study. He emerged beaming. 'Good man, you've got there,' he announced. 'Very well informed.' Another vote was in the bag.

Busy men have little time to question the purpose of their activities. Mr Major and the bunker team both set about campaigning as if every vote was undecided. However, those involved knew that MPs are not infinitely malleable; most of them would make up their own mind how to vote, for their own reasons. In Francis Maude's view, no more than 40 MPs were truly open-minded. Then again, those 40 votes were the ones that would determine the result of the election.

There were also negative reasons for running a forceful campaign. This particular electorate expected to be taken seriously; it wanted to see the candidates working hard. The Major campaign was determined to ensure that it was only criticized for overkill, never for lassitude. Above all, Francis Maude was determined that he would never be responsible for misleading his candidate. The entire bunker exercise was at least as concerned with information as with persuasion.

Meanwhile, offers of help came pouring into Gayfere Street. Mostly these came from MPs, but half a dozen others also joined in the fun. I was one of them, having just parted company from the *Sunday Telegraph* due to a little local difficulty. Over the next few days, the *Evening Standard* invited me to write a couple of pieces on the campaign. These were supposed to be neutral. They did forecast the outcome correctly.

Then there was Lord Cardigan. David Cardigan is not a member of the House of Lords; his title is a courtesy one, as the eldest son of the Marquess of Ailesbury. He is fascinated by politics, and in the long fullness – although he now protests to the contrary – will undoubtedly be a minister in the Upper House. For years, Lord Cardigan has volunteered to drive Ministers during General Elections and at Party Conferences; one hates to think how many jokes about the Charge of the Light Brigade he has had to endure in the process. On the Friday, he turned up at Gayfere Street, with his car, ready to do anything. Over the next few days, he answered telephones, drove bunkerites backwards and forwards to No. 11, won the admiration of all the Majorettes and generally made himself useful.

The most bizarre inhabitant of Gayfere Street was undoubtedly Derek Laud. Mr Laud is an immaculate, somewhat precious figure with an exquisite, dandified drawl. He is also black: all he would need is a monocle and a buttonhole to be the first black Bertie Wooster. Matthew Parris tells a story of Derek Laud staying with him in Derbyshire. They encountered an old-fashioned Derbyshire farmer. After gaping open-mouthed at Mr Laud for several minutes, his comment was: ''E moost 'av eaten a fookin' posh missionary.'

Mr Laud is also a hard-line right-winger, and research assistant to Michael Brown, the NTBer. At Gayfere Street, he sometimes manned the 'phone, garnering the occasional pledge of support. Appropriately enough, one of these was from Peter Griffiths. Since 1979, Peter Griffiths has been MP for Portsmouth North. A diligent constituency member, he has never sought prominence at Westminster; perhaps he had had his fill of it in a previous Parliamentary incarnation. In the 1964 Election, against the tide, Mr Griffiths gained Smethwick from Labour, unseating Patrick Gordon-Walker, Harold Wilson's choice as Foreign Secretary. He was only to hold the seat until the 1966 Election, but his tenure was as notorious as it was brief. It was alleged that he had won by stirring up the race issue, and that some of his supporters had used the slogan 'If you want a nigger for your neighbour, vote Labour'. Mr Wilson promptly dubbed Mr Griffiths a 'Parliamentary leper'. Twenty-six years later in Gayfere Street, he was merely recorded as a Major supporter. But the coincidence that Derek Laud should have answered Peter Griffiths' telephone call occasioned a certain wry amusement.

Ian Greer, the lobbyist, also helped out, as did a couple of Parliamentary candidates. One of these, Iain Sproat, is a senior figure in the Party. MP for Aberdeen South from 1970 to 1983, he held junior ministerial office before becoming a victim of the anti-Tory mood in Scotland. Mr Sproat, who is now the candidate for Harwich, got to know and respect John Major when they overlapped in the Commons during Mr Major's first Parliament. They share an enthusiasm for cricket. The other candidate was Dr Liam Fox, another refugee from Scotland. Liam, a GP, has a fund of stories, a few of which would be suitable for broad-minded mixed-company occasions. He often found himself accompanying the Majorettes on shopping expeditions, while deploring the cholesterol content of most of their purchases.

Apart from a fairly constant flow of tea and coffee, the bunker mainly survived on bread, cheese, pizzas, hamburgers, beer and whisky – until Francis Maude discovered Alan Duncan's claret. This exiguous diet was supplemented by the Majorettes' cooking endeavours which mainly consisted of heating up Marks & Spencer's lasagne and shepherd's pie, though on the Saturday evening they did cook some chicken. There were also Judith Mellor's fruit cakes. On the Friday, Judy, David Mellor's wife, arrived with a delicious cake, which was much admired and quickly scoffed. Another cake appeared; by Monday, it too had largely disappeared. So Judy asked whether we would like a third cake, inviting comparisons with Sherlock Holmes and his three-pipe problems. We decided that this would be a two-cake election.

Even by Thursday evening, life and work in Gayfere Street had dropped into a rhythm which was not to alter significantly for the rest of the campaign. Gone was the confusion of the morning; in its place, purpose and drive. This was only possible in such a short time because of the number and calibre of the volunteers whom the Major campaign had attracted. Even by Thursday evening, over forty MPs had offered their assistance; in all, forty-two MPs worked on the Major campaign. At times, this was an embarrassment of riches; there was not enough work to go round. The bunker felt – quite rightly – that to turn away offers of help from MPs would give a damaging impression of complacency. So tasks were found, or invented, for all who sought them. This sometimes led to duplication. By Sunday, pleas were reaching the bunker from MPs who said they had surrendered to Major forces forty-eight hours earlier; why then were they still being bombarded with telephone calls? John Maples, a core member of the Major team, telephoned one MP who replied: 'John, I'm with you, as I told the three Major supporters who've already 'phoned me. I'm not sure what I shall be telling numbers five and six.'

There was only one occasion on which the even tenor of the Major campaign was disrupted. On Saturday, we were informed that Geoffrey Howe and Nigel Lawson were going to support Mr Hurd. Sir Geoffrey's decision occasioned no surprise; nor, in the bunker's view, would it work to our disadvantage. But John Major felt a little hurt by Nigel Lawson's decision – and Norman Lamont reacted with fury.

He telephoned Mr Lawson, and reminded him of the caustically adverse comments he had regularly made about Michael Heseltine's economic views. Norman Lamont also accused Mr Lawson of disloyalty to his former deputy. As the conversation proceeded, Mr Lamont became increasingly angrier. He ended the conversation by slamming down the telephone, and continued to seethe throughout Saturday evening. Indeed, he was so annoyed as to be unable to sleep: to relieve his feelings, he telephoned Sam Brittan in the small hours and harangued him for twenty minutes on the subject of Nigel Lawson's iniquities.

By Saturday, the bunker was trying to curb over-enthusiasm in the telephone campaign. It was generally felt that backbenchers should confine their telephoning to close friends, associates, or Parliamentary neighbours. The wider 'phone canvass should be left to the 'big beasts' – our Cabinet Ministers, plus Norman Tebbit – or to John Major himself. (The term 'big beasts' derived from a Douglas Hurd usage: big beasts of the jungle, to describe politicians of the front rank.) Drawing on its knowledge of the Party, the bunker regularly drew up lists of names for the big beasts, allocating each of them the most appropriate targets. This was done partly on personal and partly on ideological grounds.

Ideology played little part in the Major election strategy. Obviously, Mr Major could not win without the votes of the Party's right, but he and his strategists were also determined to run a broadly-based campaign which would have wider appeal. This was made easier by Mr Major's success in attracting prominent supporters from across the Party. Michael Howard, Norman Lamont, Peter Lilley and John Major himself could reassure the dries, while John Gummer, Terence Higgins, Ian Lang and John MacGregor are middle-of-the-road figures. Robert Atkins, David Mellor and Tony Newton are on the left of the Party, as is Bob Hughes, a surprising recruit to the

Major camp. Mr Hughes, who was Ted Heath's PPS and had his proxy vote (Mr Heath being in China), is generally assumed to be one of the more left-wing members of the Parliamentary Party. But he was attracted by John Major's classless appeal, and believed that an examination of the record showed Mr Major to be a more pragmatic figure than some of his ultra-Thatcherite supporters believed. So when the Major campaign had a team photograph, there was something for everyone. Steps were taken to ensure that the same balance was achieved in media spokesmen. There is at least as much intolerance on the left of the Tory Party as on the right. David Mellor and Robert Atkins in particular seemed to protest every time they saw a right-winger on television endorsing Mr Major; they thought this would drive away their own friends. In practice, though, the diverse nature of Mr Major's support was well reflected in the press and TV coverage.

There remained the question of Mrs Thatcher. For some time, she had regarded John Major as the man she would like to succeed her, in due course. Now, even though she felt cheated of her due by the course the Party had chosen, she was ready to give Mr Major her support and help. After her speech on Thursday, she returned to Downing Street to begin packing. For the next four days, that melancholy process continued. Mark and Carol Thatcher came to help, though Mark was less effective at filling packing cases than at fulminating against the Tory Party. Charles and Carla Powell also lent support, as did 'Crawfie' – Cynthia Crawford, David Wolfson's secretary – who for many years had helped Margaret Thatcher with her wardrobe. On the Saturday, after calling on John Major in No. 11, Jeffrey Archer popped through the connecting door to No. 10, where he found golf bags stacked in the passageway, plus Denis Thatcher, contemplating a pack of five golf balls. 'I keep on finding these things in the strangest places,' he said wistfully.

Over the years, many memorabilia of Prime Ministerial visits and other personal gifts to Mrs Thatcher had found their way to the public rooms of No. 10. During the weekend, Mrs Thatcher carried out an audit, deciding which to take with her and which she would leave. 'If that man gets in,' she would announce fiercely, referring to Michael Heseltine, 'I'm taking the lot.' She was determined to do what she could to stop 'that man' getting in, and to help John Major beat him.

Most of the Major campaign's strategists found this willingness to rise above her own grief moving and inspiring; the question of how to deploy her still had to be considered in a clear-eyed fashion. The fact that Mr Major was her choice could win him many votes; it could also alienate some MPs. At that juncture, most Tory MPs attitudes to the Thatcher question could have been classified in one of five broad groups. First, there were the bitter-enders – ultra-loyal Thatcherites who could not forgive their colleagues or their Party for the way the PM had been treated. None of them was interested in addressing the question of a post-Thatcher future; some of them frankly did not give a damn whether there was a post-Thatcher future. They felt their world had ended with her. There were only about twenty or thirty bitter-enders, but the Major campaign felt entitled to all their votes. It was clear that in many cases we would have to rely on Margaret Thatcher to deliver those votes, though Norman Tebbit could also be of enormous value.

Then there was the calmer element among Mrs Thatcher's erstwhile supporters. Most of the Major campaign's key workers fell into this category. However much they regretted both the fact and the manner of Mrs Thatcher's departure, they were prepared to adjust to the new circumstances, and to transfer their allegiance to John Major. It was not necessary for Mrs Thatcher to make any special effort with them; all that would be necessary was press reports that she had endorsed him. That second group numbered around 120, almost all of whom voted for John Major.

The third group was mainly concerned with Party unity – and electability. They had no strong preferences for any of the three candidates, but might have been tempted to choose Douglas Hurd's experience or Michael Heseltine's bravura over the relatively untried John Major. With these characters, the Major camp's strong-est argument was that their man would be best at holding the Party together. In this, John Major's claim to apostolic succession was important. It was easy to make the case that, in order to achieve Party unity post-Thatcher, continuity was at least as important as change. About 100 MPs fell into this third category, half of whom voted for John Major. This was also the group from whom Douglas Hurd picked up most of his vote.

When it came to the fourth group, Mrs Thatcher's support was a disadvantage. These 100 or so MPs had voted for Michael Heseltine in the first ballot because they were disillusioned with Margaret

Thatcher. They wanted a change: a change in the community charge, a change on Europe, a change on public spending – a change in the entire style of government. Many of them were not persuaded that Mr Major could offer such a transformation; any sign of his being tied to Mrs Thatcher would reinforce their doubts. Most of this group ended up by voting for Michael Heseltine.

That was also the case with the fifth group – twenty-five or so MPs who *hated* Margaret Thatcher. Many of these – Ian Gilmour, David Knox, Charles Morrison *et al* – had been in internal exile since 1975. They had always regarded Margaret Thatcher as a usurper – so they were not interested in continuity: they wanted the maximum discontinuity. Their attitude to Party unity resembled that of the bitter-enders; they wanted it on their own terms, with no quarter to their enemies. So the fifth group was not fruitful territory for John Major. Most of them had long since been signed up by Michael Heseltine; the only question was whether Douglas Hurd could dislodge some of them. This he failed to do; they voted for Mr Heseltine virtually to a man.

There was one exception. It might have been assumed that since Saddam Hussein was not entitled to run, Ted Heath would support Mr Heseltine as the candidate most repugnant to Margaret Thatcher. But Mr Heath had never really taken to Mr Heseltine. Indeed, the word from Bob Hughes was that the Grocer had a certain regard for John Major, and that though he was leaning towards Douglas Hurd – his former chief of staff in No. 10 – he might even be won over, and was almost certain to come our way in the third ballot. It was resolved, therefore, that John Major should try to telephone Mr Heath in Peking; but Mr Major was unable to make contact with Mr Heath. (It was also resolved that the Tory Party at large should not be informed of Mr Heath's benevolent attitude to the Major campaign; an endorsement from him would not be helpful.)

Meanwhile Mrs Thatcher was making her contribution to the Major campaign. The irony is that she did more to assist Mr Major than she had done to help herself win re-election. Over the weekend, she interrupted her packing to make telephone calls and, on Monday, she used her last lunch party in No. 10 to lobby some of the Thatcherite irredentists. Ostensibly, this was a farewell lunch for some of her most ardent supporters; the No Turning Back Group was well represented. But the guest list was drawn up specifically to target right-wingers who were still reluctant to transfer their allegiance to Mr Major. Michael Brown, Chris Chope, Edward Leigh and David Evans were all present. Mrs Thatcher spoke to them all, collectively and individually. Gently but firmly, she reminded them of their obligations to her, and asked them to perform one final service on her behalf. All of them found it an emotional occasion anyway, and few could resist the added emotion of Mrs Thatcher's appeal.

Chris Chope, Eric Forth, Michael Forsyth, Neil Hamilton and Michael Portillo were among those whose enthusiasm for a Conservative Government had briefly waned after Margaret Thatcher's resignation. Most of them could not forgive Mr Major's Cabinet supporters for recommending that she resign; some of them were even ready to believe that leading Majorites had conspired to oust her. It is quite likely that without Margaret Thatcher's intervention, none of them would have voted for John Major; the same is true of Cecil Parkinson. Some might not have voted at all: others were tempted to support Michael Heseltine, on the grounds that at least he had conspired openly. But Margaret Thatcher made her distaste for Michael Heseltine plain. Without quite expressing herself in such terms, she pointed out that if those who protested their undying devotion to her went on to vote for the candidate she most abhorred, this would be a bizarre way of expressing their loyalty. Extraordinarily enough, one or two of them were actually able to resist that appeal.

Michael Brown and Edward Leigh voted for Michael Heseltine; Mr Leigh insisted that at least Mr Heseltine had stabbed her in the front. Mr Brown, who thought likewise, snubbed all attempts by his friends in the Major camp to persuade him of the error of his ways. Consumed by misery and bitterness, he would have nothing to do with any campaign to choose Margaret Thatcher's successor. Over the weekend he left a scornful message on his answerphone: 'If that is a candidate, I want to be Governor of the Cayman Islands.' Jill Knight and David Evans also held out against Mrs Thatcher's appeal. Mr Evans, indeed, displayed an adamantine resistance to pressure which the bunker team found infuriating, though we could not help feeling a rueful respect for his bloody-minded obstinacy.

David Evans is a new Tory. He looks and sounds like Labour MPs used to in the days when Labour recruited MPs from the proletariat rather than the polytariat. Mr Evans is also a successful businessman; he has made several million pounds out of an industrial cleaning company, and for a time was chairman of Luton Town football club. Unlike some of the Tory Party's self-proclaimed populists, Mr Evans understands political popularity; he is also excellent company. But on this occasion, his shrewdness had deserted him. Convinced that Mrs Thatcher had been the victim of an upper-class plot – orchestrated by Tristan Garel-Jones – to make Douglas Hurd Prime Minister and thus ensure that Eton once more held sway over the Tory Party, David Evans thought that the only faint hope of thwarting Mr Garel-Jones's machinations was to vote for Michael Heseltine. Pledging their judgement and their honour – offering to reinforce both by substantial bets – the bunkerites would assure him that whatever happened, Douglas Hurd could not win. In response, Mr Evans would merely utter a melancholy chuckle. He told us that we were poor, deluded fools: our figures fantasy, our supporters phantasms. The Tory Party was bought and sold; there was nothing we or that nice young fellow Major could do about it.

The bunker failed; Margaret Thatcher failed; even a session with John Major made no impression. David Evans assured Mr Major that 'if the Commies ever march down Pall Mall, I'll be alongside you, John.' But he could not support any member of the Cabinet: 'They've done my leader.' The only remaining hope of persuading Mr Evans was to deploy Lord Hesketh. Alexander Hesketh, who was then Minister of State at Industry and is now Government Chief Whip in the House of Lords, is no mean populist himself – had chosen David Evans as his PPS, and used to relish the robust manner in which Mr Evans would express his views at DTI prayers meetings,[1] making no concession to the conventional blandnesses of Whitehall parlance. Mr Evans was also known to hold his boss in high esteem. So Lord Hesketh was telephoned, and instructed to sort out his PPS. He promised to do so, and was confident of the outcome; wrongly. David Evans remained obdurate. Partly because he had been regarded as a bankable Major supporter, he had taken up more of the bunker's time than any other member of the Parliamentary Party, to no purpose. We cursed him, admired his unique qualities, and thanked God that they were unique.

The second most discussed figure in the bunker was Michael Fallon. Mr Fallon, another NTBer from St Andrews, is a clever fellow, but in his early years as an MP tended to economize on charm. He was always ready with a sharp, sarcastic quip, and the only provocation he needed to utter one was to be wished 'Good morning' or 'Hello'. He once wrote that the process of questioning ministers resembled

---

1 In most Government departments, it is now the practice for the ministerial team plus advisors and PPSs to meet first thing on several mornings a week for 'morning prayers', a free-ranging discussion of the issues facing the department, concentrating on the political implications. Civil servants are often excluded from such meetings.

setting pet mice to work on a toy treadmill. A minister retorted that being questioned by Mr Fallon was like having a noxious insect crawl up one's nostril.

The Whips decided, however, that Mr Fallon was too able to be allowed to fester on the backbenches, so they employed the usual treatment in such cases; they made him a Whip. There is a little-known special unit in the Whips' Office, analogous to the special unit in Barlinnie Prison; both are used to realign difficult characters with the human race. In Mr Fallon's case, the treatment was adjudged successful. After two years, he was released on licence as a junior minister. During his stay in the Whips' Office, however – as often happens to prisoners – he seems to have become psychologically dependent on his captors, and especially on Tristan Garel-Jones. In the Leadership campaign, Mr Fallon followed his master, and so became a psephological impossibility: an NTBer who supported Douglas Hurd.

The bunker intended to twist his tail for that. Many bunkerites had scores to settle with Mr Fallon – the Whips' Office had not cured his sarcasm – and now saw their chance. Insults were prepared, some of them printable. Michael Fallon was to be told that he would be excluded from the general amnesty, that his provisional membership of the human race had been withdrawn, that David Davis was in charge of the prisoners, but that he need not worry about his political future: he would *remain* a Parliamentary Under-Secretary of State.

Mr Fallon provided the bunker with much idle amusement. But the serious work was never neglected. On Thursday and Friday, two key strategic decisions were taken – one of them more or less by accident. The first concerned the community charge. With the fall of Margaret Thatcher, the community charge was dead, as John Major instantly appreciated. It was also clear that Michael Heseltine, who had always opposed the charge, was going to commit himself to fundamental reform. Mr Major and his strategists decided that they must match that pledge, and so deny Mr Heseltine any advantage. That decision was taken on Thursday, and confirmed at the 8.00 a.m. strategy meeting on Friday morning. It was successfully implemented; the Parliamentary Party was informed that John Major would recognize political necessity when he saw it; the community charge was finished. Thereafter, crucial to the entire progress of the Leadership contest, it was also finished as an issue in the campaign. Everyone was uneasily aware that the real bomb disposal exercise had not begun, and that the commitment to replace the tax was easier to give than to execute, but that problem could wait: sufficient unto the day was the evil thereof.

The second decision was the accidental one. Andrew Tyrie was formerly a Treasury special advisor to both Mr Lawson and Mr Major, but there is an absurd rule that special advisors cannot be Parliamentary candidates, so Mr Tyrie had to quit his post on being adopted as a candidate to fight the safe Labour seat of Houghton and Washington. But Mr Tyrie, by now a consultant and a Fellow of Nuffield, Oxford, returned to No. 11 as soon as the Leadership campaign began. He remembered an unreported passage in Mrs Thatcher's last Party Conference speech. In it, she had talked of the need to ' . . . break down barriers – barriers between workers and bosses, skilled and unskilled, tenants and owners, barriers between private and public. That's the kind of open, classless Britain I want to see.' Mr Tyrie thought that an excellent theme for Mr Major. John Major concurred, and the press agreed. At his Friday morning press conference, Mr Major issued a statement affirming his belief in a 'genuinely classless society'. It received approving comment and headlines throughout the press.

John Major himself was a little uneasy, partly because he genuinely does believe in a classless society. He did not think Douglas Hurd was entitled to be Prime Minister merely because he went to Eton – neither, of course, did Mr Hurd – nor did he regard himself as entitled to the premiership merely because he came from Brixton. He thought that it was foreground which ought to count, not background. As he told Jonathan Dimbleby: 'It is the ability to do the job that matters, not where you come from.'[2]

Nor did John Major wish to seem to be sniping at Douglas Hurd. He has the highest regard for Mr Hurd; they are good friends, and both of them were determined that the contest should be fought in a sporting manner. On Friday and Saturday, one or two of those drafting newspaper articles for Mr Major sought to exploit the classlessness theme and press home the attack. In every case, John Major watered down the draft and removed all the edge. He thought the attack had gone too far already.

It may have, but it worked, throwing Douglas Hurd on the defensive about his social origins. Mr Hurd did come up with a good line, also to Jonathan Dimbleby: 'This is inverted snobbery. I thought I was

---

running [to be] . . . Leader of the Conservative Party, not some demented Marxist outfit.'[3] But apart from that, he was reduced to claiming that he was the son of a tenant farmer – a somewhat incomplete account of the career of his father, Anthony Hurd, son of Sir Percy, sometime Conservative MP for Newbury, and subsequently a Life Peer.

The class issue did damage Douglas Hurd. A large number of Tory MPs who had a high regard for Mr Hurd doubted whether he was the best man to appeal to their constituents. Eton was used as a shorthand method of expressing these doubts, but they may have related as much to Mr Hurd's personality as to his origins. On television, Mr Hurd comes across as mandarin rather than patrician, remote rather than grand. Anyway, many Etonians would insist that all tugs – King's Scholars – such as Mr Hurd are really Wykehamists in a top hat.

That Eton should have counted against Mr Hurd caused pain in some traditionally-minded quarters. Only a quarter of a century ago, Alec Douglas-Home had still been Leader of the Party: the third Etonian in succession to hold the post. Mournful analogies were drawn with the House of Lords. In 1902, Salisbury was PM in the Lords; by 1923, Curzon was blocked from succeeding Bonar Law because he was a peer. However, Curzon was also denied the succession because he was Curzon, just as Halifax's record and personality counted against him in 1940. As regards Eton, it remains to be seen whether a less inhibited character, with a gift for vulgar self-projection, would find his background such a handicap.

Mr Hurd was handicapped – while Mr Major's classless rhetoric did not deter a small but significant group of his own supporters: the 'toffs for Major' movement. These included Lords Cardigan, Hesketh and Cranborne, plus Alan Clark, Archie Hamilton, Mark Lennox-Boyd, Nick Ridley, and Tom Sackville – all Etonians and sons of peers – plus James Arbuthnot, another OE. Lord Caithness, who had become an admirer of Mr Major's when he served under him in the Treasury, was also an enthusiastic supporter, but decided reluctantly not to give Mr Major a public endorsement, for two reasons. First, he was one of Mr Hurd's Ministers of State at the FO, and he liked and admired the Foreign Secretary, though his allegiance remained unshaken. Second, Malcolm Caithness is President of Douglas Hurd's constituency association. Lord Caithness's reluctance to make views public was typical of the chivalrous spirit in

---

3 Ibid.

which the campaign was – mostly – conducted. All three candidates were aware that in a week's time, they would be serving together in a Cabinet, one of them charged with the task of healing wounds and reuniting the Party. They were determined that the campaign would leave no fresh scars.

In the various interviews they gave, the candidates had the delicate task of asserting their own claims without disparaging their rivals. Naturally, the interviewers tried to lure them into indiscretion: surely Douglas was a little old-fashioned; surely John was somewhat inexperienced; surely Michael was a bit excitable? All such tempting lobs were greeted with an immaculate dead bat. This was not a pretence; the three men did respect one another, though in the case of Messrs Hurd and Major *vis-à-vis* Mr Heseltine, it was a wary respect. They admired his bravura, but neither of them thought he could unite the Party. Mr Major also shared the Treasury's long-standing suspicion of Michael Heseltine. In Mr Heseltine's days as a minister, many Treasury officials believed that if they took their eye off him for half an hour he would have spent the national income three times over.

Michael Heseltine had always liked Douglas Hurd. He hardly knew John Major, who had been a mere Parliamentary Secretary when Mr Heseltine resigned over Westland. He had always regarded both his rivals, and most of his colleagues, as creatures of a lesser destiny, but he would not have resented their standing against him, as long as he had won.

John Major had a considerable respect and affection for Douglas Hurd, which was fully reciprocated. In the year that had just passed, they had worked closely together and had become good friends; John Major would have been happy to serve under Douglas Hurd. He felt, however, that he himself would have a broader electoral appeal, and doubted whether Mr Hurd could have beaten Mr Heseltine.

Without in any way disparaging Mr Major, some Hurd campaigners made the obvious contrast between their man's experience and John Major's. After being Ted Heath's Chief of Staff, Douglas Hurd had served as a Minister of State and then as a Cabinet minister for eleven years, to John Major's four. They went on to point out that there was no need to choose between Douglas Hurd and John Major: the Party could have both. Mr Hurd was thirteen years older; Mr Major's day would come, after several rewarding years as Chancellor of the Exchequer. Not every Hurd supporter was so restrained, however. On Thursday morning, Norman Lamont and other sincere Major supporters had been angered by some comments William Waldegrave had made apparently disparaging Mr Major's abilities. Throughout Thursday and Friday, reports reached the Major camp that Mr Waldegrave was continuing to belittle Mr Major's claims. These may have been exaggerated, for many of them came via journalistic sources, but Norman Lamont complained to Douglas Hurd, who apologized and promised to rein in William. Some weeks afterwards, Mr Hurd commented that in any such campaign, there would inevitably be a certain amount of scragging behind the bikesheds. But the Major campaign could claim to have cleaner hands. The bunkerites never wanted to scrag anyone, except Fallon.

Once classlessness was in circulation, Mr Major was able to concentrate on telephoning. However, there was constant pressure from the media for photo-opportunities, and it was decided to hold one on Saturday morning. Angie Bray proposed a visit to Brixton market, which would have made excellent footage. But the decision went against Brixton, partly because of John Major's reluctance to dwell on his background. There was also the time factor; Norman Lamont and Richard Ryder both felt that John Major should be on the 'phone, not wasting valuable minutes driving from Westminster to Brixton. The alternative was a walkabout in St James's Park – hardly the most novel event, or original location. There were suggestions that it might be possible to enliven the occasion and perhaps even find a role for Angie Bray's dog, Tuppence, an appealing and moderately well-behaved graduate of Battersea Dogs' Home.

Wiser counsels prevailed. We wanted front-page pictures of John Major, not of Tuppence biting a Cabinet Minister or peeing on a cameraman – or vice versa. Norma Major arrived from Huntingdon to take part in the walkabout; she also brought supplies of food for No. 11. Richard Ryder asked Alan Duncan if he would drive the Majors to St James's Park. Alan thought that unwise, as he has a BMW, so Ian Greer's Jaguar was used instead. The walkabout was uneventful. One or two cameramen grumbled, and asked whether we could not persuade Mr Major to do something more interesting, but the newspapers and TV stations gave the event full coverage. On Sunday, Mr Major particpated in another photo opportunity – this time by strolling from Downing Street to Gayfere Street, a seven-minute walk. But Sunday's news coverage was dominated by the interviews with Brian Walden and Jonathan Dimbleby.

The two interviewers had markedly different styles. Mr Walden, as usual, was conversational and beguiling, as if he was trying to lull his guest into a false sense of security before pinning him with a deadly thrust. He enquired of Mr Major whether he was the 'Thatcherite candidate' in this election, an apparently straightforward question, which had several pitfalls. If Mr Major had responded with an enthusiastic 'yes', Mr Walden would have followed up rapidly by suggesting that if Tory MPs had wanted a Thatcherite Leader, they should have stuck with the Thatcherite who had led them for fifteen years. He would have gone on to point out that Mr Major was offering no comfort to the large number of MPs who wanted a change. If Mr Major had tried to avoid those dangers by sounding unenthusiastic about Mrs Thatcher, Mr Walden would have claimed that he was repudiating her, and asked him how that would go down with the very many MPs who still revered her.

John Major spotted Brian Walden's game. Though he remained on the defensive for much of the interview, Mr Major managed to portray himself as someone who would build on the Thatcherite legacy, but in his own way. Mr Walden also had Messrs Heseltine and Hurd on the defensive in their interviews with him.

Jonathan Dimbleby's approach was more combative than Brian Walden's. In his second question, Mr Dimbleby made his intentions clear: 'Is it wise . . . to run against two such senior and very experienced politicians for the highest office?'[4] From then on, Mr Dimbleby sought to brow-beat Mr Major and to prove that he was a boy in a man's race. He failed. Despite all the hectoring and interruptions, Mr Major remained unruffled, and smiled throughout. Towards the end, indeed, it was the interviewer who wilted. Jonathan Dimbleby has not inherited a full share of his family's on-screen presence; when his attempts at impertinence miscarried, he looked increasingly like a cornered rodent.

Some of the watching bunkerites were angered by Mr Dimbleby's tone. Others pointed out that however offensive he had tried to be, his failure to discomfort Mr Major must have worked to our advantage, especially as a lot of Tory MPs were suspicious of Jonathan Dimbleby's left-wing past. In more sophisticated Tory circles, it is well-known that Mr Dimbleby is a good friend of Chris Patten, who was in the Hurd camp. It would be absurd to suppose that this

---

4 *On The Record*, BBC TV, 25 November 1990.

influenced the Dimbleby technique – but he did treat Mr Hurd more respectfully than Mr Major. That did not do Mr Major any harm with Tory backbenchers.

John Major did give one combative interview to Charles Moore of the *Daily Telegraph*. This time, far from smiling throughout, he hardly smiled at all; he found Mr Moore supercilious. Not surprisingly, the published interview is flat and uninteresting, though the refrigerated atmosphere in which it was conducted is apparent from the text. In reply to a question asking him whether he would invite Mrs Thatcher to join his Government, Mr Major snapped 'this is ludicrous'. He was referring, not to the question itself, but to the way the interview was being conducted.

Afterwards, John Major was furious. Richard Ryder and others who were with him all agreed that they had never seen him so angry. Mr Major said that Charles Moore's disdainful manner reminded him of the patronizing attitudes of some of those he had encountered in his early days in the City: he could not stand it then; he would not put up with it now. This marked the beginning of a quarrel between John Major and some sections of the Conservative press – and of an unworthy phase in Tory journalism.

Richard Ryder attempted to restore relations with the *Daily Telegraph* by talking to its editor, Max Hastings. In the short-run this was not successful. Mr Ryder's telephone manner was eirenic; he did not receive a similar response – or an apology.

In general, however, the Major camp had good relations with the press. Mr Major was endorsed by *The Times*, the *Daily Mail* – particularly supportive – the *Daily* and *Sunday Expresses*, the *Sun*, the *News of the World*, the *Sunday Telegraph* and the *Evening Standard*. The *Sunday Times* and *Mail on Sunday*, though supporting Mr Heseltine, were complimentary about Mr Major, as was the *Daily Telegraph*, which supported Douglas Hurd.

Conrad Black, proprietor of the *Telegraphs*, was a devoted admirer of Margaret Thatcher's. On the day after the first ballot, he, Tim Bell, Alistair McAlpine and Gordon Reece lunched in a private room in Harry's Bar; all four were trying desperately to devise a strategy which could enable her to survive. Mr Black suggested that she invite Mr Heseltine to rejoin her Cabinet, as well as promising a fundamental review of the community charge. He also argued that Mrs Thatcher should threaten that if she were defeated in a Leadership ballot, she should ask the Queen to dissolve Parliament. The others thought this excessively robust, but promised to convey his views to the Prime Minister.

After Mrs Thatcher resigned, Mr Black discussed the new situation with his editors, Max Hastings and (now Sir) Perry Worsthorne. Between them, they agreed that the *Daily Telegraph* should back Mr Hurd, while writing favourably about Mr Major – and the *Sunday* should support Mr Major, but also give Mr Hurd a respectful mention. Michael Heseltine was not to receive any support. He himself 'phoned Conrad Black and put his case – but Mr Black, though assuring him that there was no question of personal animosity, remained unconverted.

Yet the biggest boost the Major camp received from the press was not in the editorial pages, but in the opinion polls. Michael Heseltine was one of the three or four best-known faces in British politics, and Douglas Hurd had not only been a senior Minister for much longer than John Major, he had been on television a great deal during the Gulf crisis, performing well, and effortlessly projecting an aura of experience, authority and calm. Eighteen months earlier, however, John Major had been largely unknown, and he was still only beginning to build his public reputation. It seemed inevitable therefore that Mr Heseltine would be the public's choice as Party Leader, followed by Mr Hurd, with Mr Major in third place. In Gayfere Street, our only hope was to avoid coming a bad third in the public opinion polls. We were preparing defensive briefing, concentrating on the point that whatever Mr Heseltine's current popularity, he would not be able to retain it as Leader of a riven party.

The defensive briefing was not needed. Six Sunday newspapers commissioned polls to test the electoral popularity of the three candidates. The six polls all showed divergent totals, but on average, it appeared that if Michael Heseltine were to become Leader, the Tories would enjoy an eight per cent lead over Labour – as opposed to five and a half per cent under John Major: an insignificant margin. (With Douglas Hurd, the two parties would have been neck and neck.) All this was a boost for the Major camp, and bad news for Michael Heseltine. A commanding lead in the polls would have given him ammunition for a final push; the actual result helped John Major in his final push.

Though no one in Gayfere Street made such a claim at the time, the campaign was over by lunchtime on Sunday. The polls were helpful, the interviews had gone well, and Mr Major had pulled into a clear lead. The only remaining question was whether he could win outright on the first ballot. In the bunker there was no complacency – we left that to John Major. The bunker was increasingly aware of the strength of its position, which led to a switch in tactics; there was a new argument to deploy.

It was thought that a number of Tory MPs who had been intending to vote for Mr Hurd rather than Mr Major might change their mind if they thought he could win on the first ballot. There were obvious grounds for doing so: the quicker the Party got its own election out of the way, the sooner it could concentrate on the next General Election. Mr Hurd was clearly going to come third, so he was vulnerable to a classic by-election third party squeeze. A small list was drawn up, including names such as Michael Jopling: in each case, a trusted friend in the Major camp made the 'phone call. David Maclean was particularly good at that task, for he brought to it the authority of an ex-Whip; Whips are known to be good head-counters.

At the Monday morning strategy meeting, John Major was informed of all this. To everyone's surprise, he did not approve. He declared that he wanted Douglas Hurd to be a Foreign Secretary with authority in the Party, and so did wish to see his position undermined. The more partisan members of the team were momentarily taken aback; they were also impressed by the way that their candidate was already thinking like a Prime Minister.

Late on Monday night, William Hague started to give John Major a list of applicants for the next day. John Major interrupted him: 'William, you must leave me some free time. In twenty-four hours time, I'll have to clean up my Cabinet.' At that stage the mood in Gayfere Street was also optimistic.

That was to change on the Tuesday morning. Once the campaigning ended, the worrying started. By mid-morning, at the last strategy meeting in No. 11, the tone was gloomy and nervy. On Monday, Mrs Thatcher had visited Central Office to say goodbye to the staff. In the course of an impromptu speech, she announced her intention of being a 'good back-seat driver'. She had the forthcoming Gulf War in mind. Her remarks were leaked to the Press, and the Heseltine camp naturally tried to claim that she regarded John Major as merely her front-man. Some Major supporters worried that all this would unsettle the Parliamentary Party; Lynda Chalker feared that it would cost us ten votes.

At the final meeting no one believed in the possibility of a second ballot win, we reinforced one another's anxieties. Then John Gummer called us to order. He said that everyone was suffering from election-day nerves, which everyone in the room had experienced. We had fought a splendid campaign, and were going to win. As we left No. 11, the television cameras would be filming us, and it would be unhelpful if we all had gloomy expressions on our faces.

John Gummer's advice was taken: six hours later his judgement was vindicated.

The Heseltine and Hurd Campaigns

Douglas Hurd and Michael Heseltine also organized leadership campaigns – though neither of them approached the Major team's level of activity. The Heseltine camp took the view that they were not so dependent on a five day campaign; their man had been campaigning for the past five years. Equally, the Heseltine team were less dependent on written material: their impetus would come from Big H himself, and their data was stored in his head.

Michael Mates missed the first part of the campaign; Col Mates is Chairman of the Commons Defence Select Committee, and was leading a delegation to the Gulf: he thought that campaign ought to take priority. In his absence, Keith Hampson, Anthony Nelson, William Powell and Peter Tapsell canvassed vigorously – but the key player was Mr Heseltine. Early on the Thursday evening, he addressed the No Turning Back group, assuring them of his commitment to Thatcherite radicalism – and insisting that he would be dependent on their support. He also made the point that *he* had been open in his opposition to Mrs Thatcher, and could not be accused of conspiracy. He had a polite reception – but the majority of the NTBers remained loyal to John Major.

From the beginning, however, Michael Heseltine and his intimates were aware that they were losing momentum. In particular, Mr Heseltine was disappointed by the lack of Cabinet support. He did receive one Cabinet endorsement. David Hunt, a Euro-enthusiast who believed that Mr Heseltine would have great electoral appeal, is also a Merseyside MP; he had been impressed by Mr Heseltine's efforts in his days as Minister for Merseyside.

Mr Hunt was Mr Heseltine's sole Cabinet supporter – much to Michael's chagrin. Mr Heseltine has great faith in his own powers of persuasion, and had always believed that when he finally raised his standard, many former associates would rally to him. He had hoped to win over some or all of Tom King, Norman Lamont, David Mellor, Chris Patten and Malcolm Rifkind; in the event, he won none of them. He did pull in some former Cabinet Ministers including Norman Fowler, Geoffrey Howe and Nigel Lawson: by November 1990, however, a Howe/Lawson endorsement was not worth a single vote – and may even have been counter-productive. By the weekend, Michael Heseltine knew that John Major had pulled into a clear lead. So did Douglas Hurd.

Mr Hurd had not started out with much enthusiasm for campaigning; he had never been certain that he did want to be Prime Minister. He decided, however, that if he did not take his chance, he would subsequently feel that he had been somewhat cowardly. In the event, he enjoyed campaigning much more than he had expected to. In particular, he was touched by the tributes paid to him by colleagues, some of whom he hardly knew.

But is was clear to Mr Hurd from very early on that he was not going to win. From the start, Tristan Garel-Jones took a pessimistic view of his candidate's chances. He did not wish to lower Mr Hurd's morale by giving him excessively disillusioning information; nor did he wish to encourage false hopes.

The Hurd campaign was run from Mr Hurd's office in the Commons. Mr Garel-Jones briefly considered the possibility of using his own house in Catherine Place as a headquaters, but decided against it for two reasons: it is slightly too far from the Commons, and the earlier Catherine Place meeting had been too well publicized. Mr Garel-Jones did not want Hurd HQ to have conspiratorial overtones.

Giles Shaw was Douglas Hurd's Chief of Staff, though John Patten was effectively the campaign manager. Ann Widdecombe and Tim Yeo were also key members of the team – though there is no truth in the rumour that Miss Widdecombe was responsible for the catering.

Mr Garel-Jones's first objective was to gain the support of the senior Wets – Ian Gilmour, Charlie Morrison, Dennis Walters and others – who had supported Mr Heseltine in the first ballot. All of them are good friends of Chris Patten's, and Mr Patten was deployed to win them over. He failed. None of them could be shaken from their

Heseltine allegiance. That was a fatal blow to Mr Hurd's remaining hopes, for it meant that he was unable to advance beyond the fifty or sixty supporters with whom he had started the campaign.

Mr Hurd was well supported at Cabinet level. He had been proposed by Tom King, and seconded by Chris Patten, and was also endorsed by Messrs Brooke, Clarke, Rifkind and Waldegrave. Ken Clarke's decision to support Douglas Hurd came as a surprise to the Major camp, and he came in for some gentle teasing: what was a grammar-school boy doing with all the toffs? Mr Clarke replied that the Hurd camp had needed one peasant to pour the drinks.

Mr Hurd and almost all of his supporters accepted defeat graciously. Miss Widdecombe and Tim Yeo were both made junior ministers, as was Jeremy Hanley, another Hurd supporter. A few days after the result, Tristan Garel-Jones wrote everyone a letter of thanks in which he summarized most of the Hurd camp's attitude to their defeat: 'Sometimes, when you lose, you win.'

8 The Young John Major

An Aftershock

In January 1943, Gwen Major went to her doctor, complaining of indigestion and stomach trouble. She was astonished to learn that there was nothing wrong with her digestive system; she was merely seven months pregnant. John Major was correct when he described his arrival as not only an afterthought but an 'aftershock'. It was an unusual pregnancy.

Tom Major, John's father, was almost sixty-four, Gwen, his second wife, was almost thirty-eight. They already had two children, Patricia (Pat), aged almost thirteen, and Terry, aged ten. In view of Mr Major's age – and the war – it hardly seemed a propitious moment to add to family responsibilities. There nearly was no addition. At the Surrey County Hospital in Carshalton, the new infant caught an infection from the midwife. As a result, his body was covered in scabs, and his blood had to be changed several times: there are still scars on his ankles from the blood transfusion needles. For a time, his life was despaired of. Meanwhile, Gwen Major, who had never been strong, contracted double pneumonia and pleurisy. It seemed that this unexpected pregnancy would end in tragedy.

Mother and child slowly recovered, however. The question then arose as to what the new infant was to be called – both Christian name and surname. Tom Major had been born Abraham Thomas Ball. He later took the surname Major, but for official purposes, he changed his name to Major-Ball. Gwen thought this pretentious, and they were known as Mr and Mrs Major – though she always regarded Major-Ball as the name to be used in all solemn or legal contexts. Terry had been registered as Terry Major Ball, without the hyphen, thus leaving his options open. When it came to John, Gwen's enthusiasm for the 'Ball' element was overriden; perhaps she was too weak to argue her corner. The new infant was to be named simply 'John Major'. It would have been an irony if the subsequent exponent of classlessness had started life as John Ball, the same name as one of the leaders of the Peasants' Revolt of 1381, and supposed author of the lines:

> When Adam delved, and Eve span,
> Who was then the gentleman?

The name issue was still not resolved. John had a godmother, one Miss Pink, a formidable and opinionated lady, who thought that to call the infant 'John Major' was an excessively short ration of nomenclature. At the font, when she was asked for the name, she therefore replied 'John Roy Major'; he was duly christened and baptized accordingly. Tom Major was very angry, but felt he could hardly interrupt the baptism with a scene. The child continued to be known as 'John Major' according to Tom's wishes, but Gwen seems to have registered him as John Roy Major when he went to school. He himself never liked the name Roy, and has generally preferred the version registered on his birth certificate: plain John Major.

No sooner had the new infant acquired a name, recovered his health and arrived at his parents' home than he nearly became a war victim. Early in 1944, a V-1 rocket landed within a few hundred feet of the Majors' house and young John's cot was spattered with broken glass. That was enough for Gwen Major, still weak after her pregnancy and illness. Like many Londoners who had endured the bombing blitz of 1940, she was filled with dismay at the prospect of a rocket blitz in 1944. The family moved to Norfolk for the final year of the war.

Tom Major worked on a US aerodrome near Thetford; he was in charge of the pump house. Needless to say, John Major can recall nothing of this, his first visit to East Anglia. He was not to return to the area until more than thirty years later, when the time came for him to find a seat in Parliament.

The second blitz ended: the war in Europe was won; the Majors went home. After the alarms and excitements of his first two years, little John settled down to a normal, contented childhood. In a sense, this was surprising, since Tom Major was anything but a normal father.

Abraham and Sarah

Abraham Thomas Ball was born in Walsall on 18 May 1879. His parents were Abraham Ball, a master bricklayer, and Sarah Anne

Omarah or O'Mara – both spellings exist – who, at least at the time of her son's birth, could not write. She witnessed the registration of his birth, but only with an 'x'. Sarah's father was Andrew O'Mara or Mara, a miner, later, a bookmaker. As a child, Tom Major was told that the O'Maras had been a moneyed Irish family, ruined about the time of the famine – but Irishmen seldom admit to an uninteresting lineage.

Abraham Ball senior was the son of John Ball, a locksmith and inn-keeper; at one stage, he kept the Bridge tavern at Willenhall, which still exists. John Ball's father was also an Abraham Ball, another bricklayer. With him, we are back in the vanished world of the early-nineteenth-century artisan, the sort of figure who might have had a walk-on part in a George Eliot novel: one of Adam Bede's work-mates, perhaps. Before Abraham the first, the Balls disappear into the unrecorded history of England.

The little that is known of Abraham Ball the second is greatly to his credit; he had characteristics which his grandson was to inherit. Thomas Ball remembered his father as a perfectionist: if he was in charge of building a wall, the wall was not completed until it met his standards. When Abraham Thomas was born, Abraham was in America, building blast furnaces for Andrew Carnegie in the foot-hills of the Alleghenies in Pennsylvania. Tom Major told his children that in 1878 Sarah had returned to England while pregnant so that he could be born in his native land. It seems extraordinary that Tom's parents should have gone to such inconvenience, expense, and even risk; in the 1870s, travel and pregnancy were much more troublesome processes than they are today. Moreover, if Sarah's family had been driven from Ireland by the famine, it is hard to imagine her nursing kindly feelings for England; she may easily have met many fellow Irish exiles in the United States. The journey sounds like Abraham's idea; it certainly ties in with Tom Major's account of his father's character.

Not long after Tom was born, mother and child left Walsall and returned to America, where Tom spent a large part of his boyhood – though he had lost all trace of an American accent by the time his own children were growing up in England. The family may have crossed and recrossed the Atlantic during the 1880s and early 1890s, but Tom had much of his education in the States. He played baseball for a Philadelphia junior league, and was drum major in a Philadelphia brass band. He seems to have thought of a military career, and indeed won a Girard Scholarship to West Point, the American equivalent of Sandhurst, though he did not take it up.

By 1897, Tom was back in Walsall, where he spent the next few years working in the building trade, as well as swimming and playing water polo in local leagues. At some stage in his late teens, a doctor told him that he had a weak heart. On the evidence of the rest of his life, that was not an accurate diagnosis. Tom Major himself does not seem to have taken any notice of it, though it did keep him out of the First World War. Abraham had concluded that his son's best career prospects lay in building; Tom had other ideas. In 1901, against parental opposition, he took up a new career – in the theatre, taking Tom Major as a stage name.

Between then and 1929, when he left the stage, there seems to have been little that Tom Major did not attempt, and nothing that he would not turn his hand to. He was a singer and dancer and conjurer. He performed comic sketches, either solo or in a double act, and he appeared in plays. In the early days, he was also a trapeze artist – Terry Major has records of his career – appearing both outdoors and in big tops. Once, indeed, he had a fall, though his harness saved him from death or serious injury. The manager of that particular show was so struck by the audience's horrified reaction that he wanted to keep the fall in the act.

In 1910, Tom married his first wife Kitty Drum, an actress. There were no children of that marriage. Husband and wife regularly worked together, frequently as Drum and Major, a music-hall double act with an extensive repertoire, though they also performed separately. Kitty, who sometimes used 'Ginger' as a stage name, had a good line in monologues – sometimes comic, sometimes patriotic. Towards the end of his life, Tom Major claimed to have performed in every theatre and music hall throughout the length and breadth of Great Britain and Ireland. He also travelled abroad as a performer, especially to the United States. Some of his trapeze artist's tights, discovered after his death by Terry Major, had the Stars and Stripes emblazoned on them, possibly for use in the US. On another occasion, he visited the Argentine, where he claims to have been employed by something he described as the 'Millionaire's Club' in Buenos Aires. According to his own account, his duties were to assist good order and discipline by using his skill at card tricks to outsharp the card-sharpers, regaining from them the money they had won by cheating honest patrons; the cash would then be restored to its rightful owners.

It must be remembered that some of the details of Tom Major's life derive from stories he told his wide-eyed children; there must occasionally have been an element of Baron Munchhausen. But Tom Major's life needed little embroidering to make it interesting. John Major is pretty sure that at various stages in his life, his father had a fair amount of money, but that he enjoyed spending it, on others as well as himself. This prodigality was coupled with a serene confidence in his ability to earn money whenever it was needed. In his essay 'On Actors and Acting', Hazlitt observed: 'With respect to the extravagance of actors, as a traditional character, it is not to be wondered at. They live from hand to mouth, they plunge from want into luxury. Uncertain of the future, they make sure of the present moment.' Judging by his son's account, that was a fair description of Tom Major's philosophy.

Not that there was much want. For a man as fit and versatile as Tom, there was always plenty of work, with the guarantee of a good standard of living. Neither he nor Kitty ever achieved stardom, though they did once appear on the same bill as Marie Lloyd. But they seem to have had a secure niche in the middle parts of fortune.

In 1910, when Tom was thirty-one, the Majors moved to Meadow Farm, at Catshill, near Bromsgrove. As a child, Terry Major remembers seeing photographs of Grandma Sarah feeding chickens. Tom Major enjoyed rural life, as he enjoyed everything he did; he was a good shot. By the First World War, the Majors had moved to a bungalow in Shropshire, for which Tom found a name at once humorous and sentimental: Drumcote. Abraham settled there with them after Sarah's death in 1919; he lived until 1931. In his last years, Abraham was almost blind, though still active. He was once discovered up a tree, vigorously sawing away at a branch – sitting on the wrong side of the cut.

At Drumcote, as a hobby, Tom started modelling in cement. He also showed a flair for design, embroidering mantle cloths from designs obtained by copying floral postcards. The stage remained his first love, however, until he lost his partner, in sad circumstances. Sometime during the mid-1920s, in an accident during rehearsal, Kitty was struck on the head by a falling steel girder. She never properly recovered, and died in 1928.

Before her death, Kitty had already made plans for Tom's future well-being. She had decided that he must remarry, and selected a candidate: Gwendoline Coates, a singer and dancer with the troupe to which the Majors were also attached. Tom took his wife's advice. The next year, he married Gwen, and shortly afterwards their first child, Thomas Aston, was born. He lived for only twelve hours.

In Terry Major's view, the speed with which Tom Major remarried, far from revealing any lack of warmth in his attachment to Kitty, proves the opposite. Tom Major had been so devoted to Kitty that he was bereft without her. She herself realized that he must remarry – he would have been lost without a wife. Tom Major's second marriage was equally happy, but it was accompanied by a change of career. When Kitty died, he lost not only a wife, but a stage partner; without the well-practised other half of his double act, he would have had to rebuild his repertoire, no easy task at fifty. Equally, he and Gwen wanted children, and Gwen was adamant that she was not going to tour the country with a young family.

Garden Ornaments in the Suburbs

Tom Major settled down, and the family moved to the Surrey suburbs of London. In the early 1930s, Tom bought a bungalow at 260 Longfellow Road in Worcester Park. Today, Worcester Park is part of London, but as late as the 1920s, there were still farms in the vicinity: some of the older residents can remember hay-making and fields of cattle. By the 1930s, the pace of suburbanization was accelerating; that gave Tom Major his opportunity.

In Britain, there were two 1930s. There were the 1930s which have passed into mythology: of Jarrow, the means test, and *The Road to Wigan Pier*. But, especially in the south of England, there was also a 1930s of rapid economic recovery, the spread of light industry – and of increasing prosperity. Hence the growth of the suburbs. In Worcester Park, as over much of outer London, a great deal of housing development took place. In the 1930s, the cost of housing relative to income was much smaller than it is today, so the proud new residents of suburbia had cash to spend; in Worcester Park, most of them also had little gardens. Tom Major saw a money-making opportunity in all this; he set up a garden ornament business. Mr Major made his own moulds, filled them with cement – and, once the cement had set, painted the ornaments. He made bird tables, ducks, frogs, animals – as well as some garden gnomes. To begin with, he sold these by getting on his bike and cycling around Worcester Park with samples in the panier of a bicycle. The demand for his ornaments grew rapidly.

There were problems with the local council, for Mr Major was running the business from home; the back garden had become a workshop. Some busybody, doubtless, complained, and so Tom Major had to find other premises, but quite a lot of activity continued to take place in Longfellow Road. Phyllis Swain, who was brought up next to the Majors and still lives there, remembers how she and other children would watch as Tom and Gwen Major painted and pre-pared models. Under council pressure, Tom Major found other workshops. This helped his business to expand; by 1939, he had two vans, and employed a driver as well as occasional labourers. He was also able to send his two older children, Pat and Terry to the junior department of the fee-paying Worcester Park High School.

War and Old Age

Then came the war, with instant and drastic consequences for a manufacturer of garden ornaments. Mr Major could no longer obtain cement, and even if he had been able to do so, would not have found any customers. In wartime, gardens were for vegetables and Anderson shelters – not for bird tables and ornaments. So the business closed down for the duration of hostilities, and Mr Major became a senior air-raid warden. Because of the decline in the family's income, Pat and Terry were moved to state schools. Pat later won a coveted place at the Nonsuch Girls' Grammar School. Terry, who did not pass his eleven-plus, went to a secondary modern. In 1943, not long after John was born, Tom Major had a bad fall on Cheam Common one night during the blackout. He landed heavily on his steel helmet, which was strapped to his side. This may have damaged his heart. After the fall, old age suddenly caught up with a man who had hitherto seemed much younger than his years.

Once the war was over, the Majors resumed life in Longfellow Road, and Tom Major tried to rebuild his business. From the first, there were problems. Demand was not as buoyant as in the pre-war years, and Tom Major, now approaching seventy, refused to adjust to post-war conditions. He would neither increase his prices nor lower his standards. If he thought a model was in any way defective, he discarded it. The back garden of Longfellow Road became a gra-veyard for cement models which had failed Tom Major's quality-control test. After he left school and joined the business in 1947, Terry Major suggested various changes, such as the use of rubber moulds – easier to use than plastic ones – in order to increase output; Tom would not alter his habits. He did take steps to stabilize the family's finances, however. Tom Major disliked the Attlee Government, and came to the view that it was impossible for a small businessman to flourish in a climate of austerity and excessive regulation. Concluding that Attlee's Britain was no country for old men, he decided to set sail for Canada and build a new life there.

In preparation for departure, and to raise capital for Canada, he sold the business for three thousand pounds. The purchasers were two women, one of whom had a boyfriend who would run the business. The three thousand pounds was to be paid in instalments, and Tom and Terry Major were to teach the boyfriend how to produce and sell garden ornaments. Then everything went wrong. Tom had a medical examination – a sensible precaution for a seventy-year-old preparing to emigrate. It was discovered that his eyesight was deteriorating rapidly: he would be likely to die blind, like his father. He might still have pressed ahead – except that the sale of his business also collapsed. The boyfriend had discovered that he did not enjoy making garden ornaments. He also fell out with his girlfriend: she and her partner not only repudiated their agreement; they demanded the return of the money already paid.

John Major vividly remembers an incident that occurred around this time – in 1950 or early 1951. His father was standing on a kitchen chair, changing a lightbulb, when he slipped and fell to the ground. Gwen was distraught, and John Major recalls that though they tried – unsuccessfully – to conceal the fact from him, everyone in the family was upset that day. As a result of this second fall, Mr Major's eyesight became markedly worse, as did his general health. This made it hard for him to assert his rights against the two ladies. His lawyer thought that he would win a court action, but his doctor told Gwen and him that his heart would not stand up to the strain of going to court. So the Major family surrendered. Much of the money received from the two women had been used to pay off other liabilities and bills, Pat Major announced that she would be responsible for repaying the debt. It was to take her eight years.

The family's difficulties helped to shape John Major's personality as well as disrupting his education, but the effects on Pat and Terry were more severe. They were older, and took more of the burdens.

Terry spent a dozen years when he could have been building his own career in an ultimately futile attempt to keep his father's business afloat. He later worked for the electricity board and for Phillips' Services, but his own working life never recovered from that early loss of momentum.

In 1951, Pat met her future husband, but because she was saddled with the family's debts, she did not feel free to marry him until 1959, after she had made the final repayment. Unlike their younger brother, neither Pat nor Terry was ever to recoup the sacrifices that they made in the 1950s; but they do not feel bitter. Both comfort themselves that in all its troubles, they stood by their family.

In the early 1950s, the youngest Major was unaware of those troubles. Looking back, John Major is grateful for the way the grown-ups avoided burdening his boyhood with adult problems. For him, Longfellow Road remained a tranquil environment; there was nothing to disturb the stability of life. Children take their surroundings for granted. John Major is sure that it never worried him if his friends, meeting his father for the first time, thought that this must be John's grandfather, and there were compensations in having a father as old as a grandfather. Because of Tom Major's poor eyesight, he needed a navigator if he was walking anywhere; young John often accompanied him. As they walked along hand in hand, old Mr Major would tell the little boy stories from his earlier life. John Major remembers his father as the best raconteur he has ever met.

The children in Longfellow Road formed a happy community, playing in one another's gardens, or in the road itself; in those days, there were very few cars. At one end of Longfellow Road, not far from the Majors' house, there is a brook: an endless source of diversion for children. Phyllis Swain remembers John Major as 'just a normal little boy', 'a cheerful little nipper'. A gate connected the Swains' and the Majors' back gardens, and John, a favourite with the Swain parents, would often pop next door. Later on, Mr Swain – who worked for the post office – helped him with his homework, especially arithmetic. John Major remembers Mr Swain with great affection. A bald, ruddy-faced but slim man who smoked a pipe, he always had time for young John. Indeed, John Major seems to have been a popular little boy. When a playmate's ball ended up in the garden of one of the less benevolent neighbours, John was often chosen as the emissary to apologize and avert confiscation.

Until he was eleven or twelve, John Major had an ordered and happy childhood – resting on the secure foundations of two loving parents. Tom and Gwen were a warm, affectionate couple; their home was an attractive place. They stood out among the residents of Longfellow Road, bringing a breath of Bohemia to an otherwise conventional surburban setting. They seem to have been a source of fascination to their neighbours, especially the younger ones. Tom liked an audience when he painted his models, while Gwen often did acrobatics in the garden. When work was over, Tom would sometimes sing, do card tricks, or – until his health declined – perform with Indian clubs. Then there were his stories – of the big top, the music hall, and his early days in America. The old trouper turned businessman found an outlet for his theatricality in entertaining his friends and his family.

The Majors were a generous couple. When they had money, they enjoyed spending it. No. 260 was a hub of the neighbourhood's social life. In 1953, the Majors were one of the first families in Longfellow Road to acquire a television set; they wanted to watch the Coronation. Naturally, they invited in as many neighbours as their living room would hold to watch with them and the room was so crowded that John Major himself saw little. He was stuck at the back, ferrying cups of tea.

There was always something going on at the Majors', including good works. Gwen Major generally had a clientele of lame ducks: an elderly neighbour who was becoming a bit confused, someone down on his luck, a family afflicted with illness. If anyone in the immediate vicinity needed help, the likelihood was that Gwen Major would provide it.

John started his schooldays at Cheam Common primary school, an easy walk from home. In those days, one building still had a corrugated-iron roof, but it seems to have been a well-run school, where John Major thrived. He was elected form captain of football, and did well enough in the eleven-plus examination to win a coveted place at Rutlish Grammar School. That marked the end of the first phase of young John's boyhood; the second was to be very different.

Since the age of twelve, John Major's life has consisted of stress, strain, challenge – and ultimately, achievement. Those early Worcester Park years were crucial in laying the foundations of a character which enabled him to stand up to the strain, surmount the challenges, and reach the summit. By the age of twelve, he had imbibed a strong sense of identity and of values, and this enabled him to survive the next difficult years. He had absorbed those values, not through formal moral instruction, but from the example of his parents. They also taught him another lesson, which he has had a diminishing amount of time to put into practice: that life should consist, not only of hard work, but of having fun.

The Business Finally Collapses

Even by the time John Major won his place at Rutlish, he was aware that the family's finances were in trouble; he overheard his parents talking about whether they could afford to send him there. The business was failing, and some of the workshop equipment was wearing out; the Majors' debts were increasing. In 1955, Tom Major's affairs reached crisis point; there was no alternative to drawing on the family's only other capital asset; 260 Longfellow Road itself. The house was sold for £2,150, and in the summer of 1955, the Major family moved to a rooming house in Brixton, from which Tom Major intended to keep his business going.

The house at 144 Coldharbour Lane is only eight miles from 260 Longfellow Road; to the twelve-year-old John Major, Brixton seemed like another planet. It was indeed a cold harbour in which poor Tom Major's last voyage had ended. The Majors were living in two rooms, with a gas ring on a landing and the lavatory three floors below. John and his father slept in bunk beds in one room, Gwen and Pat in the other. Terry moved out to make room for the others. He assured them cheerfully that he had found comfortable lodgings, though he was evasive as to exactly where these were; later on, the Major parents discovered that he had been sleeping in workshops and garages, to save every penny he could for the family budget.

Tom Major was slipping downhill into old age. By then, he had little sight left and was registered as blind. He had heart trouble; he was seventy-six, in the last chapter of his life, which was not as he would have wished it. But he remained serene and humorous; if he could do little else for his family, he at least kept them cheerful. John Major remembers no rows or recriminations, only his parents' determination that however little money and space they had, the warmth of family life would continue. As he said recently: 'My mother had the capacity to throw a girdle around the family and the world could go drifting by.'[1]

---

1 *Harpers & Queen*, December 1990.

His parents tried as far as possible to shield their youngest child, but the family's changed circumstances could not be concealed from him. The adult John Major has claimed on several occasions that he took the move in his stride, but that is not so, however stoical he may have been at the time, and subsequently. One indication of the effect it had on him is that John Major cannot remember much about his early teens, and clearly does not wish to do so. Just at the age when he was beginning to think about his place in the world, that world fell apart. He lost the friends and the neighbourhood he had grown up in; he also lost his sense of security. He was plunged into circumstances that must have been not only unfamiliar and disagreeable, but at times frightening.

Brixton then was much more Cockney, even Dickensian, than it is now. At one stage, an illicit bookmaker was running his operation from under the arches at Loughborough Junction railway station, about 200 yards from 144 Coldharbour Lane. One of the Majors' fellow tenants in 144 asked John if he would like to earn some extra pocket money by helping the bookie; he would be paid sixpence a time for keeping an eye out for the arrival of the constabulary. One day the neighbour called upstairs, and asked John if he would slip outside and see if there were any policemen about. John's father overheard, and intervened. He had always been suspicious of that particular neighbour, and was shocked when John told him about the bookie. He instructed his son to have nothing more to do with either of them. So a future Prime Minister's burgeoning career in crime was terminated. Shortly afterwards, the neighbour was arrested, and turned out to have had a flourishing practice as a cat-burglar. John Major was to become the youngest Prime Minister since Rosebery. Lord Rosebery was the last Prime Minister to own a Derby winner; Mr Major must be the first PM to have acted as an illegal bookie's look-out man.

When the cat-burglar was sent to prison, his supposed wife was left destitute, with their child. Her circumstances were not made easier by the arrival of a woman who seemed to have the legal title to call herself his wife, and adopted a forcefully unsympathetic attitude to her rival. Characteristically, Gwen Major calmed down the two women, and then did what she could to help the common-law wife and child.

Even in the reduced circumstances of Brixton, Mrs Major still had her clientele of lame dogs – although her own health was beginning to fail, and Tom was also requiring an increasing amount of help. John Major thinks that during the late 1950s at least two men who lived at No. 144 were sent to prison. Another resident, an elderly Irishman, was in the habit of giving the Majors a late-night salutation, possibly as a jibe at Tom Major's theatrical past. After closing-time, this character would break his journey from the pub to his bed, push open the Majors' door – the lock was flimsy – and present them with a disembodied hand waggling a pair of false teeth.

Gilt Buttons

For the young John Major, these experiences were an education of sorts. From then onwards, he was enrolled in the University of Life. But his actual schoolwork suffered. Rutlish had been founded in 1895. In the 1950s, it was run on similar lines to most grammar schools: priding itself, not only on high academic standards, but on traditions derived from the example of the nineteenth-century public school, with its ethos of patriotism plus muscular Christianity. As far as possible in a London day-school setting, Rutlish tried to reproduce the trappings of public-school life: prefects in mortar-boards, corporal punishment, a prominent role for the playing field and the cadet corps. A Rutlish education was supposed to be about character-building as well as classroom success. A few sensitive souls who went through that process in the 1950s still shudder at the memory. To them, Rutlish typified the stuffiness, complacency and oppressiveness of pre-1960s English life. But a large number of Rutlish old boys think that the place served them well, and have fond recollections of their schooldays.

John Major did not enjoy his schooldays – despite being good at games, normally a route to popularity with schoolmates and to official approval. Although he was not a disruptive pupil, he stopped working. At least in class, he became a quiescent drop-out. One reason for this was social insecurity. He arrived at Rutlish in September 1954. Though the family were still living in Worcester Park, their finances were already on the verge of crisis. John Major acquits the school of any intention to make him feel inferior, but the knowledge that he was one of the poorest boys in the place oppressed his spirits. He also felt guilty about the strains imposed on the family budget by the extra bills involved in going to Rutlish – the cost of school outings, a straw boater for the summer, the price of the uniform itself.

That guilt overshadowed his schooldays from the start. When Gwen Major was kitting John out for Rutlish, she bought him a second-hand blazer in good condition. Mrs Major was pleased with the purchase – and the resultant saving. But there was a problem: Rutlish blazers had a distinctive gilt button, and the buttons on the blazer Gwen Major had bought were subtly different. John Major did not want to put his mother to the expense of an extra few shillings, even though his buttons aroused comment at school.

At one stage, the school secretary, a Mr Windsor, stopped young John Major in a corridor and told him that money to buy the right buttons would be available from a school fund. This was intended as a kindly gesture, but it only added to John Major's embarrassments. He knew that his parents would be mortified if he took such a message home, so he assured Mr Windsor that no such assistance was necessary. Mr Windsor may have perceived the true state of affairs and sympathized with the boy's pride; John Major was not to know that. The matter was only resolved when one of John's friends asked him in his mother's hearing when he was going to get a proper set of buttons. Gwen went to a school jumble sale, bought an ancient, worn-out blazer, and transferred its buttons to John's blazer. The affair of the buttons might seem absurd, but John Major was only eleven at the time: such matters can fill an eleven-year-old's horizon and poison his entire outlook. It was nobody's fault – yet it was also the worst possible beginning to John Major's schooldays.

There were other poor boys at the school – as the existence of jumble sales and a school fund demonstrate. However, John Major's family circumstances made him over-sensitive and rather shy: he was an unhappy schoolboy. Most small boys in a large school quickly develop an unthinking acceptance of their school environment. Not John Major. He had been rudely jolted out of the security of childhood, and thereafter he took nothing for granted. He did not adapt to Rutlish; he disliked the regimentation and the authorities' overbearing attitude. In his sister Pat's words, 'Majors aren't very good at doing what they are told.' John Major decided not to join the cadet corps because of the cost of the uniform, but thinks he would have refused to join anyway. In its regimentation, however, Rutlish was no different from most schools of its type: if John Major had been less unhappy, he would have been better able to cope.

John Major's unhappiness also manifested itself in poor work. Rutlish encouraged competition in class as well as in sport – but over-sensitive children may not always flourish in a competitive environment; they are not psychically robust enough to cope with the possibility of failure. One way to avoid the risk of failure is not to try to succeed; that was John Major's approach to classroom life at Rutlish. He did just enough work to avoid large-scale disciplinary consequences, but drifted down to the bottom of the form. By his third year, he had been demoted to the 'C' stream. Academically, he had written himself off; the school was too ready to concur. He was a likeable boy who did not draw attention to himself by gross misbehaviour, so most of his masters, concluding that young Major was a nice enough chap but no great shakes, saw little point in pushing him. None of his teachers spotted the potential that ought to have been developed.

The treatment of 'C'-stream children was one weakness in the grammar-school system. Schoolmasters were too ready to forget that only a quarter of the population won a grammar-school place. So although 'C'-stream pupils may have been the bottom of the grammar-school pile, they should still have been expected to perform adequately: any failure rate was an unacceptably high failure rate. Anyway, a boy of John Major's potential ought never have been allowed to sink down to the 'C' stream. He did enjoy some subjects, including English, history and maths; the rest made no impression. But the only really pleasurable moments of his schooldays took place on the games field. John Major was a good performer at rugby, cricket and athletics. A bowling analysis of 7 wickets for 9 runs, including a hat-trick, once won him a cricket bat in an *Evening Standard* competition. On the rugger field, he was an effective, hard-tackling full-back. Had he stayed longer at school, he would have been in the cricket XI and the rugger XV.

He enjoyed watching sport as well as playing it. During the football season, he went to almost all Chelsea's home matches. He would take a 45 bus from Brixton to Battersea, walk across Battersea Bridge to the Chelsea ground at Stamford Bridge, and then stand on the terraces. In those days, no one had to worry about the safety of youngsters in football grounds. In the summer, John Major was able to find one compensation in the move to Brixton. Coldharbour Lane is only twenty minutes' walk from the Oval, the headquarters of Surrey County Cricket Club; the Oval is also a Test ground. Those were the greatest years in the history of Surrey cricket. Between 1952 and 1958, Surrey were county champions for a record seven times in succession. John Major, who can still recite the names of that

Surrey XI, thinks it was the greatest championship side ever – a view widely shared, though not in Yorkshire.

Young John Major was able to watch some of the greatest English cricketers of modern times. There was Peter May, England's finest post-war batsman, and Jim Laker, the best slow bowler. Ken Barrington would also qualify for a post-war England XI, as might Alec Bedser. Several other members of that side played Test cricket, and even its less-well-known names would be regular fixtures in the current England XI. John Major spent some of the happiest days of his boyhood at the Oval. Like many boys, he dreamt of playing for England, and attended some of Alf Gover's coaching sessions on East Hill, Wandsworth. In his heyday, Mr Gover, himself Surrey and England, was one of the most respected cricket coaches in the world. As John Major himself came to recognise, however: 'I had Surrey ambitions, but not Surrey abilities.' He became a useful opening bowler who could bat a bit, but was never more than club standard.

Cricket would not provide him with a career; he had to turn his mind elsewhere. There was no lack of eagerness to set about earning a living; he had decided quite early on in his schooldays to leave Rutlish as soon as possible, and did so when he was sixteen. His parents were strongly opposed to his leaving school. They both believed in the value of education, and had been proud when he won a place at Rutlish; they wanted him to gain as many qualifications as possible. There were many family arguments on the subject. John insisted that school was doing him no good, and that he had had enough of it – but he could not persuade Tom and Gwen. Finally, John acted and simply informed the school he was leaving at the end of the Easter term. Only then did he tell his parents what he had told the school. Reluctantly, they gave way. Looking back, John Major thinks that 'they were too sick to prevail'.

Conservative Politics and Manual Labour

John Major left school in March 1959; he would have been due to sit 'O' levels that summer. He returned to school in June and July to sit 'O' levels: he passed three. After leaving school, he used the 'Rapid Results' correspondence course to acquire three more 'O' levels, thus bringing his total up to six. His parents' anxieties about his decision to leave school were assuaged when he got his first job – as a clerk at Price Forbes, the City insurance brokers. It was not a success. In his one, ill-fitting suit, John Major felt gauche and lacking in social assurance. Worse still, he found some of his colleagues patronizing. In retrospect, he thinks he was exaggerating; adolescents are prone to blame the attitudes of others for their own insecurities. But he was ill-at-ease at Price Forbes. Painfully self-conscious, he also felt that he was merely an anonymous junior in a clerical ant-hill. He had wanted a change from school, yet found himself stuck once more behind a desk, still bottom of the heap. He quit. John Major now thinks that at sixteen he had not been mature enough to cope with such a job. By the time he returned to the City in 1965, he knew a lot more about himself, and had grown in self-confidence.

Since the move to Brixton, Terry Major had worked hard to keep the garden ornaments business going – and keep the rest of the family on its earnings. Eventually he was bought out. A retired naval officer, Commander David, who ran David's Rural Industries – in effect a garden centre – made an offer for Tom and Terry Major's firm. They accepted. The proceeds from the sale helped to pay off Tom Major's remaining debts, and also financed a move to a three-bedroom flat, at No. 80 Burton Road. This meant that Tom Major was able to live out his last few years in relative comfort.

Pat Major married in 1959, after which she and her husband Peter Dessoy set up home in Croydon. But Pat continued to spend a great deal of time in Burton Road; Peter suggested that they move back there. The appearance of their names on the electoral roll gave rise to newspaper reports about the Majors taking in lodgers. After Tom's death in March 1962, Pat and Peter wanted to start a family. They decided to move out of Brixton, and bought a house in Thornton Heath. Gwen went too, and lived with the Dessoys until her death in 1970.

After the sale of the business, Terry Major then went to work for Commander David; John Major followed him, as a labourer. This earned him eight pounds a week, compared to clerking at Price Forbes which had paid only five pounds a week; he was much happier than he had been in the City. He liked Commander David, and enjoyed working with Terry. He also took pleasure in using his muscles, and he did not mind hard work. When orders were brisk, the Major brothers put in long hours, and sometimes six- or even seven-day weeks. John Major was content: the overtime pay was good. Mr Major still looks back to those days with nostalgia, and seems to have enjoyed every minute of his time at David's Rural Industries. For the first time since the family fortunes had crashed, he was happy. No one was patronizing him or looking down on him. He could see the relationship between effort and reward, and enjoyed putting in the effort; John Major was beginning to feel that he was master of his own destiny.

A Young Conservative

John Major was also laying the foundations of his political career. Like most politicians, his interest in politics was aroused early. Tom and Gwen Major had not been particularly interested in politics, though they were instinctive Tories who believed in patriotism and the British Empire. But as soon as young John Major began to think, he began to think about politics – a process quickened by the move to Brixton – and realized instantly that he was a Conservative. At no stage, however briefly, did he have a left-wing phase.

It might have seemed more natural for a poor boy from a poor part of London to resent the status quo and identify with the Labour Party, which claimed to represent the poor – but John Major rejected these claims. Like most teenagers, he did have radical enthusiasms, and was instinctively anti-establishment, but in his south London, the establishment was a Labour one; in his eyes, Labour was the party of the status quo. In those days, much of south London was a Labour Party fiefdom. Labour controlled the borough councils and held almost all the parliamentary seats, generally with large majorities. John Major could not see what benefits the poor derived from Labour rule. He liked and admired individual Labour politicians, especially Colonel Marcus Lipton, whose constituency included Brixton. He also believed that, however unintentionally, Colonel Lipton and other Labour politicians were adopting a patronizing attitude towards the poor. He hated the way Labour politicians would speak about 'their people' as if they owned them, and believed that Labour's attitude towards his fellow Brixtonians was essentially one of benevolent feudalism. He also suspected that the Labour Party did not want to see Brixtonians' economic circumstances improve – for economic and social mobility might also lead to political mobility (as has happened across south London over the past dozen years). The Labour Party wanted to keep its political tenantry poor and Labour; the poor always ye have voting for you.

When he was thirteen, he met Marcus Lipton at a church fete in Brixton. Colonel Lipton offered to give him a tour of the Palace of Westminster. John Major was enthralled by the place; he listened to part of a Budget debate, and thinks that he formed the ambition to become an MP there and then. Not much later, he ran into some Young Conservatives canvassing in Brixton market – and began to help them. At the age of fourteen, he had another meeting with Marcus Lipton, who happened to visit Brixton market while young John Major was speaking from a soap-box, in the Conservative interest. The Colonel was amused.[2]

On his sixteenth birthday – the minimum age for membership – John Major joined the Young Conservatives. In the leafier Tory constituencies, many YC branches were primarily social clubs, an urban equivalent of the Young Farmers. They organized dances, tennis parties and other such pre-1960s boy-meets-girl events. Not in Brixton. John Major and his fellow YCs took their politics seriously – despite the difficult task they faced.

During the late 1950s and early 1960s, Brixton offered an interesting political challenge to younger Conservatives. It was a divided constituency. Towards the Clapham end, there were areas of solid Conservative support, and in 1959 – a good election for the Tories who won a majority of 100 – Colonel Lipton's majority fell to 2,000. But in the poorer areas of the constituency – Brixton proper – there was no Conservative organization. John Major and his fellow Brixton YCs were like special forces operating behind enemy lines; they enjoyed themselves.

John Major displayed a taste for the slog-work of constituency politics. In particular, he showed a tireless enthusiasm for canvassing, and was happy to knock on doors in the roughest bits of Brixton on the filthiest November evening. In the small world of Brixton Young Conservatives, he began to develop the reputation that has stayed with him throughout his political career, at each successive level; of a man who could be relied on to get things done.

After the 1959 election, largely because of the good result, the Conservative Party hierarchy suddenly took more of an interest in Brixton. The London County Council elections were due in April 1961, and someone in Tory Central Office had calculated that if the Conservatives could capture the three Brixton seats, they might win a majority on the LCC for the first time since the war. A number of able candidates were selected, including Ken Payne, a promising young south London Tory who was unlucky not to become an MP.

Mr Payne quickly recognized John Major's value, and he came to

---

2 Marcus Lipton usually adopted a bene-volent attitude towards promising young political opponents. In February 1974, his Conservative challenger was Chris Patten, who found him genial and encouraging. Mr Patten thought that these qualities reflected his good nature rather than his safe seat.

depend on the boy's inexhaustible energy. Ken Payne used to enjoy speaking from a soap-box opposite Brixton Town Hall on Saturday mornings; it was a good way to attract attention, as there were always crowds of shoppers. John Major would often help; when Ken Payne felt his inspiration waning, John would take over. This was John Major's first experience of public speaking; it was a good training ground. It was not easy to persuade passers-by to stop and listen – unless they were in search of cheap amusement, and hoping to make a fool of the speaker. Ken Payne remembers the seventeen-year-old John Major improving his technique week by week.

All in all, John Major was an important volunteer in Ken Payne's campaign, which was unsuccessful: Brixton – and the LCC – remained Labour. Ken Payne's efforts were not unrewarded; he was invited to become the Brixton Tories' parliamentary candidate at the next General Election, and John Major continued to work hard on his behalf. Mr Payne does not claim to have spotted a future Prime Minister in his young assistant, but he was convinced that the lad would have a bright future. He knew that John Major was a labourer, and occasionally suggested to him that he would be well advised to find a job with prospects. Mr Payne was certain that once John Major decided what he wanted to do, he would carve out a successful career for himself.

By the time he was twenty-one, John Major was already one of the most prominent figures in the Brixton Conservative Association – and the most energetic. In 1964 he fought his own first election – for the new Lambeth borough council, contesting Larkhall Ward, Brixton. He was only just old enough to do so: had his birthday taken place even a fortnight later, he could not have met the minimum age qualification (twenty-one). There had never been any serious chance of his winning the seat; that he was chosen to contest it at such an early age was a mark of recognition.

During the 1964 General Election, John Major took a Saturday morning off from serious campaigning in Brixton to help the Conservative candidate in Bermondsey – an overwhelmingly safe Labour seat. In those days, the Labour MP was Bob Mellish (now Lord Mellish). John had an enjoyable time in the back of a primitive loudspeaker van, pursuing Mr Mellish across Bermondsey and trying to drown out his efforts on the doorstep by broadcasting taunts and Tory propaganda, until a loudspeaker van arrived for Mr Mellish, with much better equipment. Suddenly Bob Mellish was in the ascendant, his stevedore's lungs reinforced by a more powerful loudspeaker. Cheerfully and with interest, he flung back the Young Conservatives' taunts – pointing out to them that he was going to win: he had the bigger loudspeaker.

With most youngsters, the late teens are a period of rapid development. That was certainly so in John Major's case. The lad whom Ken Payne and others encountered around 1961 or 1962 was a much more impressive character than the sensitive schoolboy or the unhappy bank clerk of two or three years previously. Like much of John Major's early life, it had been an unusual process of development, abetted by two activities that rarely coexist: Conservative politics and manual labour. John Major's years at David's Rural Industries had been a vital part of his education and his development.

Life on the Dole

John Major's first journey from David's Royal Industry was rather a step backwards. Commander David ran his business more as a hobby than as a ruthlessly commercial operation; in about 1962, he decided to retire, and David's Rural Industries went out of business. Terry Major quickly found other work making bottle caps – but the closure of David's Rural Industries was the beginning of another difficult period in John Major's career. He took one or two other short-term labouring jobs, but then had a period of unemployment.

This began as a deliberate decision not to seek work. Tom Major was growing frailer and frailer, and Gwen Major was not well enough to look after him. Indeed, there were fears that Gwen might also be becoming an invalid; she had never been strong and was increasingly afflicted with lung trouble. The Majors needed help and for some weeks John provided it. In 1962, he spent some weeks looking after Tom and Gwen. Terry's wife Shirley, who worked at Woolworth's in Brixton, often slipped round to Burton Road during her lunch hour, to help keep an eye on things. She was regularly subjected to John's cooking, which was heavily dependent on the frying pan.

Gwen Major rallied, however, although her cheerful nature almost certainly made the recovery seem more complete than it was. John Major was no longer required as a home help: he could once again seek work. By then, he had decided to look for a white-collar job, but it was not an easy search. This was hardly surprising. He had been unsuccessful at school, and possessed minimal academic qualifications. He had thrown up a City job to go labouring, and was currently unemployed. Potential employers could hardly be blamed for failing to see beyond a threadbare CV and a diffident manner.

John Major's period of unemployment spanned the exceptionally hard winter of 1962/63; once he became disillusioned after a series of rebuffs from clerical employers, he could not even find a labouring job. For all his job-hunting endeavours, he stayed on the dole for about nine months, receiving £2 17s 6d (£2.87) a week in unemployment benefit. At one stage, he was even unsuccessful in an attempt to become a bus conductor. Three candidates were summoned to Camberwell bus depot for an aptitude test; there was one vacancy. The first test involved arithmetic – adding up fares and issuing tickets with the aid of a bus conductor's ticket-machine. John Major thinks he performed passably – though he is not sure that he was the best of the three candidates. What really counted against him was his height – a six-foot bus conductor is at a disadvantage when it comes to rushing up and down stairs. His movements were ungainly, especially in comparison to Barbara Laguerre, a chubby little West Indian woman who seemed to have 'London clippie' written all over her. She got the job, and John Major recalls that her obvious delight as she danced around proclaiming 'I got de job, I got de job' was some compensation for his disappointment.

He devoted his mornings to job-hunting, and many evenings to politics. The afternoons often found him in the Grand Cinema, Brixton, where the price of admission was only a shilling. *The Flame and the Arrow*, starring Burt Lancaster, had a long run; John Major saw it several times. This was a dispiriting period in his life. He had no job, no money and, seemingly, no prospects. He did not enjoy queueing up at the Labour Exchange and being treated in an offhand manner by petty officials. But he never lost hope, or determination. He remembers comparing his position to that of a man on a bicycle; he felt that as long as he kept on pedalling, he was bound to arrive somewhere.

Finally he found a job, as a clerk at the Electricity Board. The work was routine, undemanding and dull, but at least he was no longer on the dole. Nor did he stay long there. In 1965, he applied for and got a job as a bank clerk at the District Bank (now part of the National Westminister Bank). The twenty-two-year-old who returned to the City was much better equipped to cope than he had been in his Price

Forbes days, and though John Major began banking on a low rung, he was now part of a professional structure which would enable him to have a successful career for the next couple of decades. It was also a career which harmonized with his political ambitions. If it had not been for them, he would probably have taken longer to reconcile himself to working behind a desk.

A Core of Steel

John Major never kept a diary. His memories of his early years are vague – and on dates, unreliable; there is much that he does not want to remember. It is possible, however, to reconstruct an impression of John Major at this stage of his career from the memories of those who observed him closely.

Apart from Ken Payne, they included Clive Jones, another Brixton YC who was to become one of John's closest friends. In the mid-1960s, Clive Jones was in the Foreign Office; soon afterwards, he left it for the private sector, so that he could pursue his political ambitions.

Peter Golds was also to become a good friend of John Major's. He introduced him to a girl called Norma Johnson. Peter Golds, then still at school and eight years younger than John Major, met him through the Young Conservatives; the schoolboy developed an instant admiration for the young man, and thereafter to some extent modelled himself on John. One of the many things that he found impressive about John Major was the calm assurance which he displayed in his dealings with older people, including the MPs who would occasionally turn up in Brixton to address public meetings. Peter Golds can claim to have been the first person to predict that John Major would become Prime Minister.

Although they were dedicated politicians, the youngsters also knew how to enjoy themselves. In July 1965, the Brixton Young Conservatives hosted a dinner for some luminaries of the Greater London Young Conservatives – and John Major brought along a special guest. This was none other than the Hotep of the Aquarian Dawn, an important spiritual leader from the Middle East. It must be said that the visitors were not entirely convinced by the Hotep's credentials, despite his turban and Arab robes; someone noticed that he was also wearing 'hush puppy' shoes, which did not seem in character. But no one was sufficiently convinced of his inauthenticity to challenge him. The 'Hotep' was a former merchant seaman called Reg, who had been a colleague of John Major's at the Electricity Board. Reg had visited many Arab ports, and had a weather-beaten nut-brown complexion, which helped him carry off the impersonation.

Around this time, John Major, Derek Stone and others started a magazine. They named it BAYC – the initials of the Brixton Association of Young Conservatives. It was produced with old-fashioned equipment, a tiny budget, and in very limited editions. The process was enjoyable, however. On one occasion, it necessitated a female volunteer removing one of her stockings and using it to strain the printer's ink. Such devotion to duty ought to have been better rewarded – but BAYC lasted only for a few months, and no copies seem to have survived. It must be unlikely that these first printed expressions of John Major's political thinking will ever come to light.

In 1965 and 1966, John Major spent a lot of time with someone from an entirely different background. After the 1964 election, Ken Payne felt that he should leave Brixton politics to look for a more promising constituency. His replacement as candidate was Piers Dixon, son of Sir Pierson ('Bob') Dixon, one of the most distinguished post-war diplomats. Piers Dixon, then Duncan Sandys's son-in-law, was the first Old Etonian John Major had ever met. He introduced John Major to Lady Churchill, Sir Winston's widow; through family connections, Mr Dixon had persuaded her to open a fete in Brixton. She confided in him that she rarely undertook such tasks – partly because she still regarded herself as a Liberal.

Mr Dixon formed a high opinion of young John Major. He was impressed by his energy, his enthusiasm, his dedication to politics – and by his charming manners. He noticed that however busy John Major was in the committee rooms, he always had time for even the most insignificant visitor – and could simulate not only patience but enthusiasm when listening to some bumbling exposition of the obvious or the irrelevant. Above all, Piers Dixon came to respect John Major's judgement. Mr Dixon is not sure whether the respect was returned; he felt that John Major would have preferred a more aggressive approach to canvassing. Mr Major now insists that he has fond memories of canvassing with Piers Dixon, but Mr Dixon is sure that he remembers a certain amount of concealed impatience. This would not have been surprising; there were crucial differences between the two men. John Major was twenty-two: he had spent his whole political life in Brixton. With that background plus the natural optimism of youth, he was still thinking in terms of winning Brixton for the Conservatives. Piers Dixon was in his late thirties. He had appraised the political situation realistically, and knew that the Conservatives had little hope of winning the next election, and none of capturing Brixton. He was also aware that he himself would only be a bird of passage in Brixton. His aim – like that of most young Tories who fight safe Labour seats – was to put in a good performance which would count in his favour when he went hunting for a safe seat.

Piers remembers that one evening when they were having a drink after canvassing, John Major told him that he too wanted to be an MP. Mr Dixon recalls an initial reaction of surprise, because of John's background. At that time, it was much less common for those of lowly origins to aspire to become Tory MPs. The few Tory MPs from poor backgrounds tended to have become either rich or eccentric – or sometimes both, like Ernest Marples and Gerald Nabarro (nicknamed 'Nabarro-boy') – or to be obviously token figures such as Ted Brown and Ray Mawby. Piers Dixon reflected, however, that there was also a fellow called Ted Heath. Admittedly, he had been to Oxford – but his social origins were much humbler than those of any previous Tory leader. 'The Conservative Party is changing,' he told John Major. 'But you won't find it easy to become a Tory MP, and it would help if you could make a bit of money.' This was becoming familiar advice; John Major intended to try and take it. He does not seem to have been deterred by the social gulf that separated him and most of his Brixtonian friends from the Tory Party at Westminster, most of whom would have been much more at ease in Belgravia – or Blenheim – than in Brixton market. Yet John Major felt no sense of exclusion.

Messrs Dixon, Golds, Jones and Payne are four very different personalities, but their accounts of the young John Major converge, as do those of other friends such as Alan Milne and Derek Stone. Even by this early stage in his development, the young Major had developed, at least in embryo, most of the habits, attributes, beliefs and values which were to become the foundations of his personality. There was his capacity for hard work. He may have been an idle schoolboy, but thereafter, apart from his involuntary period of unemployment, he was happy to put in long hours. While taking his 'O' levels, and later his banking exams, he would very often get up early to study before beginning the day's work. Afterwards, there would be a long evening's politics. In this, John Major displayed mental toughness as well as physical toughness. Even by the time he was twenty, he was a self-disciplined, self-controlled character. John Major developed those qualities because he knew he had to do so. He was determined to live his life on his own terms; he had a fastidious dislike of being a creature of circumstances or a pawn serving others' purposes. John Major had absorbed the lesson that life was a hard school. After 1955, his family had been trapped in poverty; that experience had left him with an abiding social claustrophobia. He was determined that he would never be trapped.

The Brixton years had built a steel core into John Major's character. This steeliness was something of which his friends gradually became aware. Though it did and still does shape his economic views, it never manifested itself in either his social relations or his social attitudes. As one would expect from a child of Tom and Gwen Major, John Major is an immensely warm and affable character. All those who knew him in the middle 1960s remember his friendliness; he could always be relied on to create a cheerful and good-humoured atmosphere. This is not an attribute often associated with ambitious young men, a breed more often inclined to self-centred-ness than to consideration for others. The young John Major was ambitious. His political career in Brixton did not develop by acci-dent: like most striving politicians, he was good at organizing his way to committee posts and chairmanships. But he never came across as self-centred. Somewhere in the wake of most successful men one can find youthful companions, now abandoned, who feel used and bruised. This is not the case with John Major. Throughout his entire career, he appears never to have made any enemies; many of his early colleagues became friends for life.

John Major's benevolence was not confined to private life: it per-meated his political attitudes. Again, this might seem surprising. Such social generosity is more often the product of guilt feelings arising from an affluent background. Especially in the Conservative Party, many men – and women – who have fought their way up from adversity tend not to sympathize with those who failed to do so. Unable to forget the immense effort they put into their own early struggles, they are inclined to think that many of those left behind could have tried harder. John Major has no such feelings. His attitude to those who remained poor in the inner city has always been 'there but for the grace of God'. It is a subject on which he is easily stirred to eloquence, especially when talking of those whose circum-stances have locked them into a position from which they cannot escape. People trapped by young children or elderly relatives; those who are forced to hang on to a job they dislike, because moving to an enjoyable job would involve a cut in pay; families penned up in squalid council houses – John Major met all of them in his Brixton days, and became convinced that, in most cases, their poor living conditions were not their own fault.

Nor did he believe that the solution lay in additional public spending. He had too much personal experience of the Welfare State's treatment of the poor to believe that its faults could be cured by extra cash alone. In his view, the Welfare State's problems stemmed, not from lack of resources, but from misuse of resources. John Major knew all about the incomprehensible forms; the take-it-or-leave-it attitudes of contemptuous petty officials; the third-rate quality of so much that the Welfare State provided. He came to the conclusion that, above all, the poor needed empowerment. The Welfare State's problem was that its priorities were determined by bureaucrats and middle-class pressure groups, whose attitude to its voiceless customers was essentially patronizing.

One obvious method of empowerment was to allow the less well-off to keep more of their own money. John Major knew that while Brixton families were finding it hard to scrape together the pennies to buy the necessities of life, central and local government were wasting millions. Out of all this, he evolved his own philosophy. He believed in a Welfare State and enhanced state provision for the poor. But he also believed that the existing Welfare State needed to be reformed, so that it was run in the interests of clients – with the clients themselves determining the priorities.

Throughout the 1960s, John Major's political ideas evolved out of his experience. Although when time permitted he read novels and biographies, he took little interest in political philosophy. As he has described it: 'I absorbed my ideas not from someone else's intellect, but from the ether, by instinct, and through experience.' During the late 1960s, however, he did pay a couple of visits to Swinton. At that stage, Lord Swinton's Yorkshire house also accommodated the Swinton Conservative College. Those who attended courses or conferences there remember both the intellectual stimulus and the *après-ski* with great affection.

One politician had a considerable influence on John Major, as he did on many of his contemporaries. Iain Macleod, a practitioner of politics rather than a theorist, was one of the most effective Tory politicians of the 1950s and 1960s. A superb platform performer, he is etched on the memory of almost everyone who heard him, yet he remains an elusive figure to those of a later generation. There are reasons for this: his early death – after only one month as Chancellor of the Exchequer; the difficulty of associating any specific body of ideas with his name; and the absence, thus far, of a major biographical study.[3]

Macleod was an inspiration to younger Tories in the 1960s. Particularly effective in Opposition, his attacks on the Wilson Government always restored his party's morale. Many Tories who came to admire him believe that his death was a grievous loss, and that if he had lived, the Heath Government would not have gone awry.[4]

Iain Macleod's thinking remained protean, and his views were often the product of the day's debate. This means that any contemporary politician wishing to give his text a touch of *gravitas* can dignify almost any Tory commonplace he chooses by attributing it to Macleod.[5] Even so, it is possible to identify, if not a Macleodism, a Macleodian disposition: one which the young John Major came to share, and which Prime Minister Major still endorses. Like Macmillan, Macleod understood that the Tory Party could survive only if it identified itself with the economic aspirations of the mass of the population. This meant a double platform – opportunity and social provision. On the one hand, the party must advocate free enterprise to promote higher living standards and the growth of property ownership; on the other hand, Tories must also sustain the Welfare State, which most ordinary people now regarded as part of the natural order. As for the exact balance to be struck between the claims of public spending and the desirability of reducing taxes, that was a matter for pragmatic decision. With Tory economic management, and the elimination of public sector waste, both might be possible. Though many of his economic assumptions remained Keynesian, Macleod was instinctively an individualist; in his dislike of bureaucracy and regulation, he could almost sound like a proto-Friedmanite.

His views on social policy were little different to those of Roy Jenkins. He was opposed to capital punishment and in favour of the other 1960s liberal reforms. He broke off relations with his once close friend Enoch Powell because of his views on race, and he fell out with the party's Imperialist wing over the decolonization of Africa. (He does seem to have believed that some of the nations he was assisting

---

3 Robert Shepherd's forthcoming work may rectify this.

4 If Macleod's health had been better and he had not lost his head in October 1963, Mr

Heath might never have become leader of the Party.

5 Disraeli has been used in this way for more than a century. No one knows what, if anything, he believed.

to independence would remain democratic.)[6] In other words, Iain Macleod was a social liberal. Partly because of his silly comments about Etonians. Mr Macleod seemed to be a principal exponent of the Tory Party's new, classless identity. He also gave that identity a human face, which poor Mr Heath could never do. He excited the young – and then himself died at only fifty-six, adding to his reputation the allure of unfulfilled promise. It is easy to see why a Prime Minister who remembers Macleod in his prime, and who shares his general outlook on politics, should revere his memory.

Jos

The young John Major was not a monoglot politician, however. Although he found that there was too little time to play and watch as much cricket as he would have liked to, he did have a social life. There were a number of girlfriends, and at one stage Piers Dixon even formed the impression that his young assistant was married. Mr Dixon was in error; until Norma came along, John's girlfriends were merely transient enthusiasms.

Moreover, John Major had still not reconciled himself to life behind a desk. Above all, he wanted to travel. At the age of twenty-three, he had hardly been out of London; he thinks that the longest journey he had ever undertaken was to East Anglia and back, when he was an infant. His second stint as a banker was going well, and he was now preparing to take the Institute of Bankers' examinations, which would give him a professional qualification. It would have been folly to leave banking; he would not do so until he joined the Government. It was possible, however, to combine banking and travel. In 1966, he moved to the Standard Bank.

The Standard Bank was a creation of the British Empire. It had strong links with West Africa, and as late as the 1960s still retained a flavour of earlier days, when young men were trained in a London counting house before being sent to run branches in the colonies. The Standard Bank was also an avenue of advancement for men from modest backgrounds: traditionally, it had not recruited either from the universities or from the leading public schools – though by the 1960s, that was changing. But many of those in senior positions at Standard had themselves been denied a university education because their families could not afford one. In the 1960s, they had not yet reckoned with the consequences of student grants and the

---

6 It was the dispute over decolonization which led Lord Salisbury to describe Macleod as 'too clever by half' – a charge that has been levied at the Cecils since the reign of Elizabeth I.

expansion of university places, and still expected to employ younger versions of themselves. This worked to John Major's advantage.

John Major enjoyed his time at the Standard Bank. From the start, he showed promise, and within a few months, he felt that this was a job he could do well. He was still at the bottom of the ladder, but at least he could see the rungs above him, and that they were within his grasp. A foreign posting came up, in northern Nigeria. There was no rush of applicants, for this was the time of the Nigerian civil war caused by the attempted secession of Biafra. John Major makes a joke about this: 'There was a war on, and I was the most expendable member of the staff, so they sent me.' In fact, Jos, where the vacancy had occurred, was hundreds of miles from the front line, but as often in the case of foreign wars, people in Britain were using small-scale maps – and assuming that because Nigeria looked to be the size of a postage stamp and because they had seen something horrible on the TV screen, the whole country must be in flames. His colleagues' ignorance was John Major's opportunity: it also helped that he was unmarried.

He arrived in Nigeria in December 1966. The hill country around Jos is one of the more attractive parts of Nigeria. The people and the way of life in northern Nigeria in no way resembled the chaos, squalor and corruption of Lagos, while the bush, the skies, and the African landscape worked their magic on John Major. From the moment of his arrival, John Major enjoyed himself. Like most of those who took up a post in the colonies, he found that his standard of living immediately increased. He was sharing a large flat, which came complete with servants. To begin with, he found dealing with servants embarrassing; for the first time in his life, John Major felt that he was in danger of being patronizing. Like many liberal-minded Westerners visiting Africa for the first time, John Major may have assumed that as he felt guilty, the natives must feel resentful. In fact, those who worked for him would have taken their status for granted, and would have been grateful to work for such a pleasant and easy-going boss, who could be relied on to pay them their wages. His staff remember him with great affection.[7]

John Major continued the habit of getting up early to study. He would then walk the mile or so to his office, savouring the sights, the sounds and the sunlight. It was a very different journey to work from the one he was used to in London, especially in the months from December to March.

---

7 Some of their recollections were published in the (Nigerian) *Guardian* of 24 December 1990.

Although he did his job well and diligently, the pace of work in Jos was not as demanding as it had been in London – and there was no canvassing to occupy his evenings. He had time for social life, mainly centring round the Jos Club, which had film shows, with a white-washed wall as the screen. Of an evening, John and his friends would sit chatting over a few drinks, which in John Major's case would be Coca-Cola at least as often as beer. He also found time for cricket. Some of the local expatriates had formed a side which they called 'Northern Nigeria'. John Major says that this was a rather excessive claim for an XI of about village cricket standard. Anyway, he opened the bowling for Northern Nigeria, while batting down the order. In one match, however, he put together his best ever innings. He had made 77 and was going well, thinking of a century – when the mail plane arrived; the cricket pitch was also a landing strip. Unfortunately, Northern Nigeria was not nearly grand enough to have its exploits recorded in Wisden, otherwise Major – 77 not out, plane stopped play – would be an original entry, especially as it was to be John Major's last serious appearance at the wicket.

His flatmate and regular companion at the Jos Club, Richard Cock-ram, had a new Cortina. In it, they had visited a neighbouring club to watch a spy film. On the way home, the car ran off the road – due neither to excessive speed, let alone to drink, but to some defect in the road surface. John Major thinks he was thrown through the windscreen. He was briefly unconscious, but quickly came to, and found himself sitting by the roadside. His trousers were cut to ribbons, he had lost a lot of blood, and his left leg was in a mess: he thinks that one or two bones were protruding. He does not recall being in great pain, probably because he was in a state of shock, as was Richard Cockram, sitting beside him. He remembers thinking or saying, 'Oh God, I've done it this time.' Then he passed out. He was taken first to the local mission hospital, which did everything it could. The Standard Bank acted with admirable dispatch. He was flown first to Lagos – and then back to England, and the Mayday Hospital, Croydon, near Gwen's new home. The battle was on to save his leg.

As well as losing the kneecap, he had compound fractures of the thigh and ankle; other bones were also damaged. The injury was so extensive that, at first, the surgeons were not sure that it would ever heal. In such cases, there is always a danger of infection, and even of gangrene. In those early days in the Mayday Hospital, it was possible that John Major would lose his leg. He remembers one ward sister with gratitude and affection. When he arrived in his ward, there was a lot of clearing up going on, and things seemed a bit confused. Sister arrived; suddenly there was order and calm. During the period in which his leg was in jeopardy, she paid him a lot of attention, watching over his treatment, encouraging him, chivying him if he ever sounded gloomy. John Major thinks that as he began to recover, she gradually lost interest in him – but no doubt other serious cases were demanding her attention.

Slowly, the bones mended, but the leg has never regained its full strength. Once or twice over the next few years, it gave way beneath him. On one occasion, he collapsed in the street, and had to be helped into a local cinema while somebody organized transport. After his wedding, the leg again gave way; John Major had to sit on a chair for most of his wedding reception. Today, he still cannot walk for much more than a couple of miles without feeling discomfort – a nuisance during election campaigns. The accident also ended his cricket-playing days.

Mr Major was quite a good patient: he recalls that he was determined to keep his spirits up and that he banished all thought of amputation from his mind. He listened to music, both classical and pop. In particular, he remembers one Supremes record – 'The Happening'. He also used the time for reading – Jane Austen, a lot of Trollope, and large quantities of Agatha Christie, as well as some cricket books. He had taken about fifty books – a large proportion of his library – to Jos. They included novels as well as banking textbooks. But the books were left behind (hardly surprising, in the circumstances). It would be interesting to know whether any of them survive on the bookshelves of Jos.

To this day, he remains grateful for the way the bank treated him. It not only paid his salary, including any increases, but stayed in contact. Of course, any halfway decent employer ought to behave that way, but John Major recalls deriving reassurance from the regular visits – colleagues asking whether he needed anything, and insisting that though everyone was looking forward to having him back, he must take all the time he needed for a complete recovery. He also resumed his interest in politics. Clive Jones and Peter Golds often came to see him in hospital, and kept him in touch with events in Brixton. As it became clear that he was going to walk properly again, his thoughts turned to the Borough Council elections, due to take place in May 1968.

At this stage, he had his first sustained contact with an impressive political operator. For the past generation, Jean Lucas – who retired last year – was one of the most successful Tory agents in the country. She spent her career in Lambeth and Wandsworth, and her organizing skills entitle her to much of the credit for the Tory Party's successes in those boroughs. Over the years, she helped to train a large number of young politicians, including Chris Chope, the late Ian Gow, David Mellor, Dick Tracey – and John Major. She has a claim to being the Alf Gover of Tory politics.

John Major remembers Miss Lucas from the early 1960s, but at that time she was agent for Clapham, and did not have much to do with Brixton. In the run-up to the 1968 borough elections, however, she was involved on a Lambeth-wide basis. Peter Golds, by then a trainee agent, was one of her assistants. For the next few years, she and John Major worked closely together. Mr Major had already given much thought to the techniques of canvassing and campaigning, but he is happy to acknowledge that he learned a lot by watching Jean Lucas in action. The admiration was mutual. She quickly recognized that he had 'a maturity and a political instinct far in advance of his years. He had a sharp, quick appreciation of any situation, and he was a thoroughly nice person.'[8]

In those early days, John Major had neither a car nor a driving licence. Because of his gammy leg, he could not walk long distances to and from meetings, so Jean Lucas often ferried him. These journeys generally came at the end of a long evening, with Jean Lucas – and John Major – due for an early start the next morning. Unlike Mr Major, Miss Lucas wanted a decent ration of sleep. But when they arrived at John Major's flat, instead of saying 'good night' and getting out, he would carry on talking, oblivious to any hints. At the beginning, she tried keeping the engine running – but in his eagerness to continue discussing politics, he took no notice. Jean Lucas generally ended up by switching off the ignition – partly because his comments were so interesting.

John Major did not commit himself to running for the council until early in 1968, by which time all the wards in Lambeth that seemed decent prospects for the Conservatives had already chosen their candidates. This did not worry him: he was playing himself in again at the bank and completing his recovery. He did put his name forward to stand in Ferndale Ward, but even by stronghold standards, this was rock-solid safe Labour territory. There seemed no hope of John Major being elected.

---

8 Jean Lucas, *The Wandsworth Story*, 1990 (WCTA), p. 8. Miss Lucas's book is full of insights into constituency politics.

Having decided to stand, he threw himself into electioneering, with a dedicated band of helpers including Peter Golds, and an elderly lady called Miss Evans, a former Chairman of the Brixton Conservative Association. By the end of the campaign, John Major wanted to win, and at various stages during it, he thought he had a chance of doing so – a delusion commonly found in candidates for hopeless seats. It transpired, however, that there were no hopeless seats for the Conservatives in the London of May 1968. Harold Wilson's Government, at its most unpopular, was about to lose a succession of by-elections with adverse swings of 20 per cent or more, and in the London borough elections Labour suffered an overwhelming defeat. In the stauncher Labour boroughs, in order to give the impression that the party had a strong presence, the Tories had fielded a number of 'paper candidates' – people who were happy for their names to appear on the ballot paper but who had no intention of campaigning, and no wish to be elected. But in May 1968, a lot of them were elected. Embarrassments, resignations and by-elections followed.

Even by the standards of that exceptional year, the Lambeth result was remarkable. But there had been a special factor: race. Throughout the 1960s, large numbers of Commonwealth immigrants, especially West Indians, arrived in Lambeth. They were generally cheerful, God-fearing, small 'c' conservatives who brought to England the Victorian values which were still commonplace in the Caribbean. They came to England with the intention of working hard to build a better life for themselves and their children.

By 1968, an increasing number of the immigrants' neighbours disapproved of their presence. To an extent this was due to the overcrowding created by the new arrivals. Though they were not to blame, they intensified the pressure on scarce inner-city housing. But the whites' objections also arose from a dislike of black faces. Willy-nilly, the Conservative Party in Lambeth gained increased support as a result of racial tension. Then came Enoch Powell's famous 'rivers of blood' speech, a verbal hand grenade which exploded on 23 April, only ten days before polling day. The establishment, including the Tory front bench, rose up in horror; much of white working-class south London rose up in support. Dockers marched to Parliament to proclaim their devotion to Enoch. Though Mr Heath had instantly sacked him from the Shadow Cabinet, a lot of former Labour voters flocked to the polling booths in Lambeth to vote for Mr Powell's party. On the outgoing council, there had been forty-two Labour and eighteen Conservative councillors. The new council had only three Labour councillors, and fifty-seven Conservatives. Among them was John Major: he had won his seat by seventy-one votes.

It has been suggested[9] that his election to the council might have been invalid, because he had not fulfilled the residence qualifications. This is unfair: the confusion arose solely from his leg injury. Before he left for Nigeria, John Major had been living in a third floor flat in Binning Street, Westminster; the landlords had left his name on the electoral roll. But a man with a leg injury could not climb three flights of stairs; so after leaving hospital, John Major stayed with friends in Brixton while using Miss Rose Oliphant's house at 14 Templar Street, Brixton, as a mailing address (she was an old friend of Gwen's). Shortly afterwards, he moved in to a flat of his own at No. 9 Templar Street. The purpose of the residence qualification is to ensure that councillors are committed to the area they serve. In John Major's case, that commitment was not in doubt.

However, John Major's election did involve him in a brush with the law. Miss Evans had not been at the count; nor did she have a telephone, but John Major was determined to give her the news that night. At about 2.00 in the morning, after the victory party, he and Peter Golds decided to call on her. They arrived outside her flat, but did not ring the doorbell for fear of waking the neighbours. Instead, John Major shinned up a lamp-post, and started throwing gravel at her window. Mr Major has always been moderate in his consumption of strong waters, but that night he had had grounds to celebrate. It is hard to believe that someone who had nearly lost a leg only a year earlier would have climbed a lamp-post at 2 a.m. unless he had benefited from both the anaesthetic and the stimulating properties of alcohol.

In the excitement, however, John Major had forgotten the lessons he ought to have learned from the bookmaker and he had failed to post a look-out. Suddenly, a policeman arrived on the scene. It was quickly explained to the officer of the law that though the situation might seem unorthodox, he had nothing to worry about. It was merely a case of a newly-elected – Conservative – councillor communicating the result to an important party worker. 'What, Conservative? Round 'ere? Never. No Conservative'd ever win a council seat round 'ere. You're having me on, mate. Come down off of that lamp-post.'

---

9 'Panorama', 15 April 1991.

Miss Evans came to the rescue. She appeared at the window, peering doubtfully at the scene below – but brightened up when she saw John. She opened her window, and was informed of the result (probably half the street was awake by then). She congratulated him warmly, as did the police officer, whose first reaction was: 'Well, I'll be blowed.' The new candidate and the constable shook hands, but the policeman did issue one parting piece of guidance: 'As I say, sir, congratulations – but please, sir, don't go climbing no more lamp-posts.'

As soon as the new Tory councillors assembled, they started to quarrel. The group's leaders – Bernard Perkins, Peter Cary, Miss Hilary Jellie and one or two others – were all liberals on race. None of them agreed with Mr Powell's 'rivers of blood' speech, which they thought would only inflame the situation. This view was shared by many of the new intake, including Sir George Young and his wife Aurelia, who had both won seats in Clapham. But the Tory Group also contained a substantial Powellite[10] wing, mainly from wards in Vauxhall. Its unofficial leader was David Renwick, who had been Chairman of Brixton Conservative Association and, as such, had fired Piers Dixon as candidate. Mr Renwick is now dead, but those who remember him take little notice of '*de mortuis*': he seems to have been an unpleasant character.

Mr Renwick and his friends immediately tried to move Tory group policy in a Powellite direction. This was firmly resisted by Bernard Perkins and his allies – with the support of John Major. At that time, Bernard Perkins, George Young and others hardly knew John Major, so they had not been certain which view he would take – especially as he probably owed his own victory to Mr Powell's speech. But Mr Major's support for the liberal line was absolute, and well expressed. He spoke of his commitment to equality of opportunity for all. Men should be judged, not by colour, creed or class but by their efforts and their innate worth. Mr Renwick and his faction not only lost the vote; they lost the argument. Shortly afterwards, Mr Perkins issued a press statement critical of the Powellite rump's activities. This received widespread publicity, and helped confirm their political impotence. Contrary to some reports, none of the Powellites was expelled from the Tory group – and John Major was not directly involved in any public censure.

The debate with the Powellites brought John Major to Bernard Perkins's notice. That was the beginning of another important

---

10 'Powellite' entered the vocabulary of politics at this period. Mr Powell himself had only a limited responsibility for his supporters' views – and none for their actions.

friendship which was to have great influence on the young John Major's development. In 1968, Bernard Perkins was forty, and himself a local government official: he was Assistant Director of Housing in neighbouring Wandsworth. He had been the leader of the Conservative group on Lambeth Council since the previous year, when Charles Braxton, his predecessor, was eased out by the younger Tory councillors who wanted a more dynamic approach.

By all accounts, Mr Perkins proved a first-class council leader – shrewd, humorous and decisive, easily able to command the respect of all his colleagues, the Powellite dissidents excepted. Alas, his career was to be curtailed: in the late 1970s, he was stricken by multiple sclerosis. In *Who's Who*, Mr Perkins lists as his recreation: 'social service'. Over the years, he has indeed given much service to society.

Bernard Perkins decided that the twenty-five-year-old John Major should have immediate preferment, as Vice-Chairman of the Housing Committee. It was exactly the appointment John Major had dreamed of. Housing was not only a London borough's most important responsibility – Lambeth's budget for housing was £100 million over three years – it had the greatest impact on the lives of the borough's poorer residents, whose hopes for better accommodation could be realized only with council help. John Major had seen the arrogance with which the worst type of so-called public official treated the public; Councillor Major was now in a position to do something about it.

He would have the assistance of another remarkable public servant. At that time, Lambeth's Director of Housing – the most senior council official in the housing field – was Harry Simpson, then fifty-one, who had held the post since 1962. Mr Simpon, alas, died in 1988 but everyone who knew him testifies to his charm, common sense, efficiency – and humanity. He was a bureaucrat who was always aware of the limitations of bureaucracy, and of the importance of continuously reassessing the services a council provides to ensure that they meet the public's needs.

He and John Major took to one another instantly. Though Harry Simpson's own politics were probably old-fashioned Labour, he liked, admired and guided the new-fangled Tory. John Major reciprocated; later, Mr Simpson was to be Elizabeth Major's godfather. In the 1970s, both Harry Simpson and Bernard Perkins were to serve on a variety of public bodies: Mr Simpson ran the Northern Ireland Housing Executive for two years. These appointments were accolades, by no means over-generous, for their successes in Lambeth.

Before the new council could settle down to serious business, it had to cope with a farcical incident, which would have made an excellent basis for a television comedy series. By 1968, Lambeth was the only London borough which still permitted its dustmen to practise 'totting', an activity reminiscent of Henry Mayhew's London. When the dustmen set out on their rounds, they would attach a trailer to the back of the dustcart. The contents of promising-looking dustbins were then strewn on the trailer and raked over to discover if there was anything of value. Totting was unhygienic and malodorous; it also slowed down the process of emptying dustbins. Moreover, the dustmen were allowed to finish their totting – and to sell anything they had discovered – in the council's time. The new council felt that all this contributed to a general atmosphere of corruption which pervaded the dustbin department, and so totting was summarily banned.

The result was a dustmen's strike. The council was not deterred. Private contractors' vehicles were quickly hired, and the councillors themselves ran their own dustbin collection service on Saturdays. All the younger men took part, and some of the lady councillors, helped with the driving. John Major decided that his leg was not going to make him miss out on the fun; his job was to stand on the dustcart and empty bins as they were passed to him. During their journeys, the dustmen-councillors picked up a lot of interesting information. In particular, they found themselves declining many offers of payment, especially from shopkeepers, who seemed equally bewildered to learn that for years past, they had been paying for a free service. Within a couple of weeks, the councillors felt that they were emptying Lambeth's dustbins almost as reliably and far more honestly than the dustmen had done. The dustmen may have come to the same conclusion; they quickly surrendered. There was no more totting.

After that light-hearted distraction, the councillors were able to devote their full attention to serious business, which in John Major's case principally concerned housing. He proved such an effective Vice-Chairman that when Bernard Perkins had a reshuffle of committee posts after the Tories' second year in office, John Major became Chairman of Housing. He was one of the youngest men to hold that post in the history of London local government.

When contrasted with the Thatcher Government's approach to municipal housing, the policies Councillor Major and his colleagues pursued in Lambeth between 1968 and 1971 seem lacking in radical drive. But that would be an unfair comparison. By the standards of the times, the Lambeth Tories were radicals. They began by calling a halt to the destructive aspects of housing policy. Under the Labour council, municipal housing had been used as an instrument of social engineering. Much of old Lambeth survived the Luftwaffe only to fall victim to bulldozer socialism. Street after street of Victorian and Georgian terraces disappeared. No doubt many of the houses had been dilapidated, but that could have been put right in a couple of months by a yuppie owner, four builders and a skip. Very often, the demolished properties were replaced by the sort of buildings which have discredited modern architecture. John Major and his colleagues did not halt the bulldozers altogether, but they subjected proposals for redevelopment to a much greater degree of scrutiny. Plans to eradicate the pleasant Victorian houses of Clapham Manor Street were cancelled, and in general Mr Major and his committee encouraged renovation rather than demolition.

At that stage, the legislation permitting the sale of council houses on a large scale was not yet on the statute book: that happened under the Heath Government during Peter Walker's reign at the Department of the Environment. But under the cumbersome machinery then available, Mr Major was able to sell a few council houses; he also built one terrace of houses for sale. His principal innovation as Housing Chairman – enthusiastically endorsed by Harry Simpson – was designed to help those who were likely to remain council tenants. John Major decided that the housing department should listen to its clients. In 1969, Lambeth opened the country's first housing aid centre, giving free advice to council tenants and others with housing problems. The opening ceremony was performed by the then Opposition housing spokesman, Peter Walker. John Major also decided that there should be a touring housing aid centre, in the form of regular open meetings attended by himself, Harry Simpson, the Chief Executive of the Council, and the Director of Lettings. These proved popular, though there was an obvious temptation for the Labour Party to try to disrupt the meetings.

There was one dramatic attempt at sabotage. A striking-looking woman appeared in the audience, wearing a black leather hat and thigh-length boots. She was bouncing around excitedly in her seat; John Major could not decide whether she had partaken of excessive refreshment, or was a man in drag, or both. Suddenly, she shot to her feet, began haranguing the platform about the disgusting conditions in which she was forced to live, reached a climax – and flourished her proof. She opened her bag, pulled out a dead rat, and flung it at John Major. She missed. An investigation proved that the woman and the rat both came from Southwark. It was suggested to her that she should take her housing problems – and the evidence – to the proper quarter.

John Major's colleagues on Lambeth Council remember him as one of the Tory group's most effective performers in the council chamber. Of course, with a massive Tory majority, the political atmosphere was unreal, but even though he could take the vote for granted, Councillor Major still treated every debate as if he intended to win the argument. He never set out to be rude to his Labour opponents and if they made constructive speeches, he was quick to compliment them on doing so. If they tried to score points, however, especially personal points, he was quick to retaliate, though always with good humour. In this, he not only won the admiration of most of the other Tory councillors and of Peter Golds, who often listened to the proceedings, but of Ken Livingstone, who also spent a lot of time in the public gallery. His comments on the young John Major must be treated with a certain scepticism, however. Mr Livingstone has succumbed to a false syllogism: 'All Tories are monsters. John Major is charming. Therefore John Major cannot be a Tory.' Under the influence of Mr Major's charm, Mr Livingstone appears to have convinced himself that his Tory counterpart was really a crypto-socialist. Mr Livingstone ignored Mr Major's economic views – but Ken Livingstone is hardly a rigorous economic thinker.

If Ken Livingstone could develop such respect for John Major, it is hardly surprising that Mr Major's Tory contemporaries also did so. John Major became the acknowledged leader of a group of younger Tory councillors. They would often have a beer together after council meetings – or alternatively pile into Clive Jones's car, and go via an Indian takeaway to John Major's flat. On arrival, there would be a rush for the one chair; the rest would sit round the walls. In those days, John Major seems to have lived on a diet of curry and political discussion. As on most such occasions, the talk ranged from issues to personalities to 'who's up, who's down': which committee chairmanships might be coming up and who might get them. Peter Golds says that on those questions, John Major always seemed to have thought three moves ahead of everybody else. Even then, Mr Major knew that it was impossible to treat issues in isolation from their political implications and the from personalities involved. To run any sort of administration successfully, all three elements had to be in harmony.

In 1969, John Major became Vice-Chairman of the Brixton Conservative Association; he succeeded to the Chairmanship the following year, in the period before the association was wound up as a result of constituency boundary changes. All aspiring Conservative politicians must collect – or invent – the material for an impressive curriculum vitae. By the age of twenty-six or twenty-seven, John Major's CV must have been as good as that of almost any of his Tory contemporaries; he could also list a range of school governorships and other voluntary activities. In terms of his ambition to become an MP, the political side of his life was on track.

Jean Lucas reinforced the advice he had often received not to neglect other aspects of life. She stressed the expense involved in being a Member of Parliament: the more money he could earn before becoming an MP, the better. She also advised him to buy property, which he did. His first flat was in Primrose Court, Brixton, and it became the headquarters of the curry club. Apart from the chair, the living room contained a record player and a carpet; the bedroom was less lavishly furnished. All his friends recall the Primrose Court days with great affection.

At the bank, John Major was making progress; he had passed most of the Institute of Bankers examinations. From his earliest days at Standard, he fitted in well and was regarded as a chap who would go far. But there may have been a few difficulties around 1969/70, caused by his Chairmanship of the Housing Committee, which took up a lot of his time and necessitated occasional days off. Senior figures at Standard Chartered felt that the bank ought to encourage its employees to involve themselves in public service, so they approved of John Major's council activities, but there do seem to have been some snide comments from one or two of John Major's contemporaries, possibly motivated by jealousy. He took this sufficiently seriously to confide in Jean Lucas. Will Manser, now Head of Public Affairs at Standard Chartered,[11] can

11 In 1970, the Standard Bank merged with the Chartered Bank to form Standard Chartered.

find nothing in the bank's records to suggest that there was a problem, and it is possible that John Major was paying more attention than he need have done to a few casual comments.

Sir Peter Graham, now Chairman of Standard Chartered, met John Major as soon as the two banks merged; he was a senior figure from the Chartered side. In Sir Peter's opinion, by 1970, John Major had reached more or less the level he would have done had he joined the bank with a good degree. Meanwhile, his progress in politics had been exceptional – and he had gained valuable experience along the way. However, he did lack one attribute a university education would have given him: intellectual self-confidence. Apart from the social life a strong argument for going to university is that those who do so will never regret not having gone to university. A surprising number of non-university men who have had very successful careers still have an inner uncertainty about their intellectual abilities, and tend to think of university as a challenge which might have found them wanting. This was true of the younger John Major, and though his defensiveness about not having a degree was largely cured by his time in the Treasury, it is something he has never entirely lost.

The Tories had won Lambeth when the Labour Government was desperately unpopular, but by the time they came to defend their seats in 1971, Mr Heath was in No. 10, and already encountering the usual mid-term problems. So the Lambeth Tories' task was hopeless – and nowhere more so than in Ferndale Ward. As Councillor Major was enjoying local government and would have been happy to stay on in Opposition, he abandoned Ferndale Ward for Clapham Park Ward. This was a better prospect: but still not good enough. John Major lost, the Tories lost, and the Labour Party regained control of Lambeth, which it has held to this day, despite the annual contest with Liverpool for the title of the worst-run local authority in Britain.

After his defeat, John Major wasted no time. So as long as he was Chairman of Housing, he felt that it would have been impossible to think in terms of Parliament; even for a man of his energy, there would not have been enough hours in the week to work, run the Housing Committee and nurse a constituency. Now that he was no longer a councillor, however, the path to Westminster was open. He immediately applied to join Conservative Central Office's candidates list, and on 20 July 1971, Jean Lucas wrote a letter in support of his application.

The central organization of the Tory Party has virtually no powers over the constituency associations, which are all independent, most of them jealously so. Short of the *News of the World* featuring his private life, almost the worst misfortune that can befall someone applying for a Tory seat is to be described in the 'Crossbencher' column of the *Sunday Express* as the man favoured by Central Office. Technically, the candidates list itself is issued only as guidance to Tory associations; there is nothing to prevent them from choosing someone not on the list. In practice, this happens very rarely, and usually only if the person in question has powerful local connections. Getting on the candidates list is one of the first tasks aspirant Tory politicians set themselves.

Jean Lucas wrote in a matter-of-fact manner; there were no rhetorical extravagances. But there was one key phrase, to which she drew my attention: 'first-class'. After all her years in the field, Miss Lucas believed in weighing out her praise of young politicians on troy scales. She rarely used the term 'first-class'; when she did, she meant it.

John Major also needed an MP to recommend him: Jill Knight performed that role. With his track record, he expected little difficulty in finding his way on to the list, and there was none. A key factor in his success was the approval of Tory agents, who have the power to make or break young politicians. The agents who had seen John Major in action were impressed, and Jean Lucas's good opinion counted for a great deal. By 1971, John Major was a rising man.

Mr Major had a respectable career. He had a good track record in politics. By 1971, he had also acquired the third asset which any hopeful young Tory ought to have: a wife.

Norma Johnson was born as Norma Wagstaff, on 12 February 1942 the daughter of Norman Wagstaff, then a sergeant in the Royal Artillery, and his wife Edith née Johnson. But just before the end of the war Norman Wagstaff, by then commissioned, was killed in a road accident. He had been a talented pianist, who intended to try to make a living as a professional musician once the war was over. He passed on some of his talent and all of his interest to the daughter who never knew him.

After the war, Edith reverted to her maiden name. With no paternal income, the Johnsons' little household was short of money. Edith went out to work. At one stage, she was doing three jobs at the same time. The four-year-old Norma was sent to boarding school, paid for by Royal Artillery charities. That might sound cruel – but little Norma enjoyed herself. The school seems to have been a kindly institution; she liked her playmates, and perhaps because she had been sent away from home so early, does not remember ever resenting it. Unlike her future husband, Norma was a diligent pupil. Her first love was music; and like her father, she played the piano. By her mid-teens, however, she realized that she was not sufficiently gifted to think of a professional career. She went to Battersea Teacher's Training College, and thereafter taught domestic science.

At this stage, Norma was not strongly interested in politics, though she was always an instinctive Conservative. But she was drawn into the periphery of Conservative politics by two non-political friendships. Norma, who had always been good with her hands, had an excellent sense of design. Like many girls whose taste for dresses outruns their budget, she began to make some of her own clothes. Friends admired the result; she made dresses for them as well. Then their friends started contacting her, and soon after she decided to give up teaching for dressmaking. One of her main clients was Diana Geddes, the Tory candidate for Putney in the 1970 GLC elections.

Norma had also met Peter Golds; they shared an addiction to opera. In 1970, Peter Golds was working on the Tory campaign in Putney; he persuaded Norma to help man a committee room. John Major was also helping in Putney, for it was a better prospect for the Tories than Brixton. He arrived at Norma Johnson's committee room, spotted her, and liked what he saw. 'Who is that pretty girl?' he said to Peter Golds, who was able to tell him, and then introduced them. They had a couple of minutes' chat in a busy committee room; both of them wanted to prolong the conversation. 'See if you can get her into the count tonight,' were John Major's parting words to Peter Golds. The Tory Party's allocation of places at the count had already been filled up, but agents have their ways of arranging such matters. Norma went to the count under false pretences, as Clive Jones' girlfriend. By the time the count was over, she was John Major's girlfriend.

The attraction was instant, powerful and mutual. Strange to relate, there was a complete absence of dithering on John Major's part. Six weeks later the couple were engaged, and on 3 October they were married in St Matthew's, Brixton. June Bronhill, the opera singer, for whom Norma had made dresses, sang an aria during the service. Clive Jones was the best man, and Peter Golds signed the register.

Amid all the joy, there was also sadness. Gwen Major's health had been failing rapidly. She had spent much of 1970 in hospital, suffering from emphysema, but had hoped desperately to be well enough to attend her youngest child's wedding. It was not to be. Gwen died in September. But John Major's engagement had brightened her final weeks. John's first instinct was to postpone the wedding – but his sister Pat dissuaded him, pointing out that their mother would have hated to be responsible for delaying an event to which she had so looked forward.

Needless to say, politics also played a role in the proceedings. On the wedding morning, Councillors Major and Jones had been due to take part in a visit to a housing estate, which had been organized months earlier; those in charge had failed to allow for their impetuous young Chairman rushing off and becoming engaged. John Major, conscientious as ever, decided that they could not cancel the trip. Clive Jones, political as ever, decided that virtue should organize its own reward. He alerted the *South London Press*, a local newspaper. It sent a photographer – and the pair of them, in morning dress, were given excellent coverage.

Once, while interviewing John Major for the *Sunday Telegraph*, I asked him where he and Norma had gone on honeymoon. 'Ibiza,' he replied, but then a look of unease spread across his features. 'I *think* it was Ibiza.'

'Are you sure?' I replied, 'You might get into trouble if I print the wrong destination.'

'Oh no, I remember who I went with, that's the main thing.'

It was Ibiza, and it rained for much of the time. Since then, however, very little rain has fallen on the Major marriage. In many respects, their personalities are similar. To neither of them does a public face come easily and they both tend to be reserved on first acquaintance, though John Major conceals his reserve under a politician's bonhomie. As they come to know people, the reserve vanishes. Open and generous by nature, the Majors find it easy to form lasting friendships.

John Major is a private man who wanted to become a public figure; it was not until he became Prime Minister that he grew fully aware of the sacrifices public life involves. Norma Major was a private person who married an aspirant public man without realizing how far his aspirations would carry him. She was aware of the costs of public life earlier than her husband was. John Major believes as strongly as Norma does in the importance of roots and family; and anyone visiting the Majors is struck by an easy, affable domesticity, which reflects their deepest instincts and values. But the primary responsibility for maintaining that has fallen increasingly on Norma. The Majors smile and laugh a lot: both of them have a delightful sense of humour. Their conversation is full of light irony, banter and raillery. John Major is good at laughing at himself – and so he ought to be. He has had plenty of practice through being teased by his family.

Even in the early days, Norma Major showed her homemaking skills. Although the Majors had little money to spend, she set about the de-bachelorizing of Primrose Court. John's friends were amused and astonished at the way his hitherto sparsely furnished quarters were transformed into something out of a colour supplement.

Seat Hunting

John Major was now starting the search for a constituency. He was not expecting a Tory-held seat or even a marginal. Most Tory associations in safe seats would expect anyone seeking the nomination to have fought a seat already – a requirement which is occasionally waived for those with distinguished careers outside politics – but rarely for someone in his late twenties. Anyway, John Major wanted to advance his career in banking, settle down in married life and start a family before he went into Parliament. In 1971, he was thinking in terms of fighting a safe Labour seat at the next election – and entering Parliament at the election after that.

He did not have long to wait for the safe Labour seat, and he was selected at his second attempt for Holborn and St Pancras North. This was a good result for John Major; safe Labour seats in London are particularly sought after by young Tory hopefuls, many of whom are based in London.

John Major now set to work. Though it would have required a result almost on the Lambeth 1968 scale to dislodge the Labour incumbent, Jock Stallard, John Major was determined to suspend disbelief and fight the seat as if it were a marginal. By this stage, his reputation had spread beyond Lambeth. He was becoming widely known on the candidates' circuit – and widely recognized as a coming man. Once again, as in his Lambeth council days, he became the unofficial leader of a group of young politicians, including Graham Bright, now his PPS, Dick Tracy, the former Sports Minister, Nick Bennett, appointed a Parliamentary Secretary at the Welsh Office in Premier Major's first reshuffle – plus Margaret Marshall and Gerry Wade, who didn't succeed in getting into the Commons. As Margaret Marshall describes it: 'We all found ourselves turning to him for advice. If in the course of a general chit-chat, the rest of us realized that John was making serious points, other conversations would stop – because we wanted to hear what he had to say. He often found himself holding the floor without trying to.'

Long before the word 'networking' crossed the Atlantic, John Major was a natural networker. In his case, this is more an indication of good nature and a gift for friendship than of calculation. As Margaret Marshall puts it: 'At party conference receptions you'd see some ambitious characters looking round the room and making a quick check-list of the six people – area agents, constituency chairmen and what have you – that they wanted to speak to in the next twenty minutes, before moving on to do the same at another party. John wasn't like that at all: he'd happily stand chatting to some old dear for twenty minutes.' Even so, he built up a long list of political contacts and admirers.

John Major took no part in the debates and splits of the Heath era. Had he expressed his views on topics such as the U-turn and the introduction of an incomes policy, no one would have taken any notice – but that did not prevent other parliamentary candidates expressing *themselves*. Mr Major may simply have supported Government policy; most Tory MPs did. There were a few dissidents, notably Enoch Powell, John Biffen, Jock Bruce-Gardyne, Teddy Taylor and – after Mr Heath fired him – Nicholas Ridley. There was also a revolt over the EEC, in which Messrs Biffen, Powell and Taylor took leading roles. But especially over economic policy, the extent of dissent in the Heath era has been greatly exaggerated. Keith Joseph and Mrs Thatcher remained loyal members of Mr Heath's Cabinet throughout; many others who later became Thatcherites were also loyal Heath supporters.

Around 1980, Margaret Thatcher was addressing a meeting of the 1922 Committee Executive, one of whose members was Ken Baker, not yet a Minister. Mr Baker found himself unable to resist making a remark which could well have postponed his joining the Thatcher Government. Mrs Thatcher had been assuring her audience that she would never commit a U-turn. 'You'll remember, Ken, what a terrible effect Ted's U-turn had on his Government?'

'Not really, Prime Minister,' replied Mr Baker. 'I didn't join Ted's Government until 1972, by which time the U-turn had already happened. You and Keith would be better able to remember its effects.'

It was not Ted Heath's U-turn which so upset the Tory Party, but the loss of the February 1974 election. Curiously, in 1974/75, when Mr Heath's position was deteriorating, the number of those who had always been opposed to him increased dramatically, just as membership of the French Resistance had done in 1944/45.

John Major neither was nor claimed to be a dissident. His February 1974 election address loyally followed the party line, stressing the need to combat industrial anarchy.

For that campaign, he neither had, nor expected much help. In General Elections, the Tory Party's resources are concentrated on the marginals. Mr Major was given the services of Sue Winter, a twenty-year-old trainee agent. Sue remembers that when she met John Major she thought he was a rather forbidding figure. With his serious manner and deliberate mode of speech, he seemed older than his age. That feeling lasted about a quarter of an hour – then all was laughter.

Miss Winter, who had never seen a parliamentary candidate in action before, was impressed and at times awestruck by John Major's capacity for work. He had been putting a great deal of energy into the constituency ever since his initial selection; during the February 1974 campaign, his efforts were redoubled – to no avail. Because of boundary changes, it is not possible to make an exact comparison between the February 1974 result and the June 1970 one, but John Major's result seems to have been an adequate one. Labour's majority went up by only 1,000.

As a result of that election, Harold Wilson formed a minority government. It was clear that another election would follow within months, and would be unlikely to go well for the Tories. As well as exploiting the war weariness resulting from the miners' strike, Mr Wilson would obviously highlight the attractive aspects of Labour's programme while concealing its cost. In the event, Ted Heath fought as effective a campaign as was possible in the circumstances, and Labour were able to win only a narrow overall majority. In

Holborn and St Pancras North, Jock Stallard secured a further increase in his vote. From the point of view of the Major campaign, however, the figures were not the most important element. In both February and October, John Major kept up the morale of his party workers. They may have been fighting a hopeless seat in two losing elections, but John Major at least made sure that they enjoyed themselves.

Sue Winter claims that during one campaign, a report reached her that John Major had canvassed a parrot. He knocked on the door, heard a cry of 'Who's that?' answered, 'John Major, your Conservative candidate.' The question 'Who's that?' was repeated; he gave the same answer. Only at the third repetition did he realize that he was talking, not to some quavering old crone, but to a parrot. However, Mr Major has no recollection of that story; it has been told before of other politicians in earlier elections.

In preparation for the October 1974 election, the Tories of Holborn and St Pancras North had whitewashed the wall of their constituency association headquarters, at the junction of Leighton Road and Falkland Road. After the election, the slogan 'not a Major success' was painted on top of the whitewashing in large letters; the whitewashing had to be repeated.

John Major had acquitted himself honourably at the 1974 elections. He was now ready to move on to the next stage. In early 1975, sitting Tory MPs began to announce that they would not be contesting the next election; John Major began to apply for their seats. Any vacancy at a Tory-held seat will attract at least 200 applicants. The association concerned will begin by whittling that list down to around twenty names, whom it will interview. So the priority for an aspirant candidate is to get himself interviewed.

In 1975, the first half-dozen seats John Major applied for rejected him out of hand, which not surprisingly depressed his spirits. He consulted Jean Lucas, and asked her what he was doing wrong. She suggested they examine his CV to see if it could be redrafted in a livelier style. She asked Central Office for a copy of the document – and was sent the CV of another John Major, who had never fought a Parliamentary seat, and who was merely trying to become a GLC councillor (he later succeeded). That explained the absence of interviews. Once the correct CV started arriving on associations' desks, John Major was invited to present himself for interview. He went to South Dorset, Ruislip Northwood and Portsmouth North –

and though none of them selected him, the regular interviews gave him grounds for optimism.

In early 1976, he had a nomination in his grasp. Jean Lucas, now in charge of the Tory organization in Wandsworth, was involved in selecting a candidate to fight Putney, then a Labour marginal, but a seat likely to fall to the Conservatives in the event of an election victory. Miss Lucas suggested that John Major apply; he did, and became the clear favourite to win. David Mellor was in second place, but some way behind; he was six years younger than John Major and had not previously fought a seat. Mr Mellor, never noted for an excess of modesty, thinks he stood no chance of defeating Mr Major.

While Putney was selecting, however, the Tories of Charshalton were interviewing candidates to fight a by-election caused by the retirement of Robert Carr. John Major was also doing well in the preliminary stages there, and therefore he withdrew from Putney, leaving the race to David Mellor, who won the nomination and went on to capture the seat. Carshalton, meanwhile, selected Nigel Forman of the Conservative Research Department. John Major was still without a constituency. He did not have much longer to wait. In June 1976, Sir David Renton, who had been the Member for Huntingdon since 1945, announced that he would not be contesting the next election. Though Sir David's majority had fallen to 9,250 in October 1974, the candidate selected for Huntingdon would be winning a safe seat for the rest of his Commons career. John Major immediately applied, along with 280 other hopefuls.

Initially, he himself was not that hopeful. He assumed Huntingdon would be an agricultural, even squirearchical constituency, with a traditional Tory Association looking for a traditional Tory candidate, not a meritocrat from south London. Peter Golds knew better. Peter, by then Rhodes Boyson's agent in Brent North, spotted that Huntingdon's population had been growing rapidly. This was due, not to philoprogenitive farmers and squires, but to London overspill. Indeed, there was a substantial commuter population: Huntingdon was only an hour by train from King's Cross. Some Londoners had migrated north, in search of green fields and affordable family accommodation; some council tenants had been transplanted to new housing estates, especially around St Neots and on the outskirts of Peterborough. So a candidate from south London would find a lot of former south Londoners among his potential constituents. He would also find some disgruntled aboriginal inhabitants.

Around that time, there were a lot of complaints in the eighty villages of the Huntingdon constituency about the social imperialism of the newly-arrived Londoners, who were accused of appalling crimes such as monopolizing the badminton evenings at the church hall. However trifling the grievances might sound, they attested to a divided community. This would be dangerous for a candidate from London.

Rarely if ever has a Tory Association had such a strong field of applicants to choose from as Huntingdon did in 1976. Apart from some good local candidates, there were at least six former MPs including, ironically, Piers Dixon, John Major's sometime mentor in Brixton. The others were Jock Bruce-Gardyne and Alan Haselhurst – who were both to return to the Commons after by-elections in 1977 – Sydney Chapman and John Wilkinson, who won seats in 1979, and Tony Trafford. Mr Trafford, a surgeon, who in 1984 treated the Brighton bomb victims, was briefly a Minister of State in the House of Lords before his unfortunate early death in 1989. There were also four future members of John Major's Cabinet – Peter Brooke, Michael Howard, Peter Lilley and Chris Patten – plus the Marquess of Douro, heir to the Duke of Wellington.

After sifting the names, the association decided to interview twenty-one applicants, who were also invited to a cocktail party with their wives. Andrew Thompson, then agent for Huntingdon, recalls that Norma Major did not shine at the cocktail party. She seemed nervous, as if afraid that she might say something to jeopardize John's chances; she lacked the surface glitter and the self-assurance among strangers of some of the other wives. Mrs Major did not give the impression that she either wanted to be a political wife, or would be particularly good at it. Nor did John Major give an outstanding performance. On the basis of the first set of interviews, three men had a strong following: Jock Bruce-Gardyne, Charles Douro and Alan Haselhurst. But the selection committee decided that they ought also to see a fourth candidate. The three front-runners for that slot were Michael Howard, John Major and Tony Trafford. Dr Elizabeth Cottrell, now Head of the Economic Section at Conservative Research Department, formed the impression that Tony Trafford was ahead. But the partisans of Mr Howard and of Mr Major – she was a Major supporter – would not give up. The argument was meandering inconclusively. It had been a long evening; some people wanted to go home, others wanted a drink. Suddenly Roger Juggins, who was chairing the meeting, suggested that they hold a ballot according to a system of transferable voting which he devised on the spot. This was done: John Major emerged the winner. Some non-Majorites looked as if they were about to question the reliability of the Juggins method of balloting, but the majority instantly adjourned to the door, or to the bar.

One evening, between the first and second ballots, John Major was sitting at home when the telephone rang. It was Mary-Jo Elphick, a prominent member of the Huntingdon District Council. She told him that he was her choice to be their next MP, and asked him if he had thought of attending a District Council meeting to brief himself on local issues; the next session would have an interesting agenda. John Major took her advice.

One hundred and eighty or so Huntingdonshire Tories assembled for the final round, which was open to all full members of the Association. The candidates were to speak in alphabetical order, which gave John Major the final slot, generally an advantage. At the beginning of the evening, Mr Bruce-Gardyne was the favourite; his first-ballot performance had been adjudged the best. The late Jock Bruce-Gardyne was a lovable character, and is much missed by all his friends. A courageous and witty fellow with an original mind, he wrote some good books on politics and ministerial life. At the height of his powers, his relish for life undiminished, Jock was stricken by a brain tumour. He faced his end with Roman fortitude. For all his virtues, however, Jock lacked some of the baser qualities necessary for success in politics. He had no political common sense and no instinct for self-preservation. As a result, his career suffered several reverses, mostly self-inflicted. Thus it was at Huntingdon. At the second ballot, Jock performed abominably. A bad speech was followed by flippant answers to questions. In about half an hour, he had moved from first place to the bottom of the poll: his eventual vote was barely in double figures.

Lord Douro made a nervous speech, but Mr Haselhurst performed well, and became the new favourite. Now it was John Major's chance; he was determined to take it. His themes were unity and opportunity. He said that the newly-adopted Conservative candidate's first task would be to reunite Huntingdon, just as the incoming Conservative Government's first task would be to reunite the nation. By its denial of opportunity, the Labour Government was responsible for exacerbating social divisions: that was something the Tory Party would tackle and put right.

It was the right subject for his audience, and John Major put his points across with conviction. Long before he had finished, the audience was humming with approval. There was only one awkward moment, during questioning. A farmer put a point about the Green Pound,[12] and John Major's reply was unconvincing. 'It strikes me, Mr Major,' said the farmer, 'that you don't know much about agriculture.'

'You're right, sir,' came the reply. 'I don't know one end of a cow from the other. But I promise you this. If you adopt me as your candidate, I'll be an expert on cattle-breeding within twenty-four hours.'

That answer was well received, even though there is very little cattle-breeding in predominantly arable Huntingdonshire. Moreover, John Major has fulfilled his pledge, albeit vicariously. His daughter Elizabeth, who is now training to be a veterinary nurse, will be an expert on cattle-breeding. Then it was time to vote, under a procedure similar to the second and third ballots for the Tory leadership. In order to win, it was necessary to gain an overall majority. There could be up to three ballots; at each stage, the candidate who finished last would be eliminated. Andrew Thompson had indeed prepared three sets of ballot papers, while John and Norma Major, assuming that the balloting would take some time, slipped out of the hall for a brief stroll in order to unwind.

As they were making their way back, they spotted someone who had obviously been sent to find them; he was waving excitedly. They arrived to find the hall in uproar; they entered to applause and cheering. Mr Thompson had two unused sets of ballot papers: John Major had won outright, with 60 per cent of the vote. He was almost overcome, but there was another brief speech to make. 'It's a long way from the back streets of Brixton to the green fields of Huntingdon,' he began – and was promptly interrupted: 'yes, John, and some of us made it before you.' Rarely does the selection of a Tory candidate generate so much emotion. All this south London triumphalism was too much for one or two of the more old-fashioned Huntingdonians – Peter Crossman, later Sir Peter, left the platform, complaining that he felt ill. Some suspected the ailment was not physical.

---

12 The EEC's unit of exchange for agricultural prices.

John Major had pledged himself to be the unity candidate; in his initial attempts to honour that pledge, he encountered a certain amount of snobbery. This was not a simple matter of the squires versus the plebs. Some squires took the view that in the modern Tory Party, Huntingdon ought to find a candidate from an ordinary background – whereas a number of middle- and lower-middle-class Tories would have preferred to be represented by the son of the Duke than by someone like themselves (there is an analogy with the problems local men have in being adopted for Tory seats; their candidature almost always arouses jealousy). In John Major's early days, there were some mutterings about 'the bank clerk' – but not for long. Andrew Thompson believes that by the late spring of 1977, John and Norma Major had assuaged any remaining doubts.

As regards the squirearchy, Mr Major was fortunate to have the help of his predecessor. Sir David (now Lord) Renton was a distinguished lawyer who had served as a Minister of State. Unlucky never to have become a Law Officer, he was one of the non-Cabinet victims of Macmillan's 'Night of the Long Knives' in July 1962. As a doctor's son who went to Oundle, Sir David could have passed as a self-made man in the Tory Party of the 1950s. By the 1970s, however, it would have been fair to describe him as a grandee; he could certainly deliver the grandee wing of Huntingdon Toryism. He did so, for John Major. During Mr Major's first few months as candidate, Sir David organized a number of dinner parties at which the new man met the old order; good relations were quickly established.

John Major now had a seat for life; no one would have guessed that from his demeanour. He quickly moved into the constituency, buying a house at Hemingford Grey, and set to work. As Andrew Thompson described it: 'He worked his guts out. You'd have thought he was fighting a marginal, not a safe seat.' It is always wise for a new candidate to treat the safest of seats as if it were a marginal, and to assume that he cannot rely on inheriting his predecessor's majority. But John Major's attitude reflected anxiety as well as prudence; Norma Major recalls that they both worried about losing the seat. Peter Golds tried to laugh them out of that nonsense, saying that he had better book two one-way tickets to America for the day after the election, for if they lost Huntingdon, they would have to flee the country. But the fears persisted. Well-meaning constituents would say to John and Norma: 'Of course, as it's your first time, no one expects you to do as well as dear David would have done.'

Though the Majors took no comfort in such low expectations, they entirely shared them.

If Huntingdon had been anyone else's constituency. John Major's political nose would instantly have told him that this was a safe Tory seat growing safer by the day. As it was his own, his political instincts were overriden by insecurity and self-doubt. Perhaps because John and Norma had worked so hard for their success, they had difficulty believing in it. After the long journey from the back streets to the broad acres, there was inevitably a certain amount of social and psychological jet-lag.

In fact, John Major was an outstanding candidate. He made friends everywhere, and was particularly effective with ex-Londoners living in council houses. They would usually preface the conversation by saying that they had not expected to find a Tory on their doorstep. John Major would counter by asking them where they came from, and was often able to discuss their old London haunts in detail. Very often, these were skilled workers and aspirant home-owners: the very C2s[13] on whom the Tories' prospects depended. In Huntingdon, John Major did not need their votes – but he won many of them.

Like a number of his future constituents, John Major commuted to King's Cross. His train journeys often turned into political meetings, and he also made other contacts. One day, a woman sat down opposite him at King's Cross, and promptly dissolved into tears. John Major asked her what was wrong; she told him she had been in London to see a specialist, and had been informed that she had to have an operation for cancer. Mr Major spent the rest of the journey trying to comfort and reassure her. He then drove her to Hemingford Grey, where Norma joined in the comforting. The woman lived on her own; by the time the Majors had given her a lift home that evening, she felt much more able to face the future than she had at King's Cross. John and Norma Major continued to visit her, both at home and in hospital, and have remained in close touch ever since.

The General Election was approaching. For all his good works and his hard work, John Major's doubts persisted right until the ballot boxes were opened on the evening of 3 May 1979. Then there were no more doubts. John Major had won a seven per cent swing in his favour and the Tory majority had increased from 9,244 to 21,563.

---

13 According to the Registrar-General's social classification.

Over the next couple of days, he and Norma, still hardly able to believe that he was now an MP, looked back over the years and marvelled at how far they had come. Their journey had hardly begun.

9 From Backbencher to Cabinet Minister

Blue Chips and Attendant Lords

The 1979 vintage of Tory MPs was among the finest of the century. Among the newly-elected MPs were at least a score of talented, amusing and interesting characters who quickly made an impact. They included five members of John Major's first Cabinet – the PM himself and Messrs Lang, Mellor, Chris Patten and Waldegrave – plus at least two strong candidates for early promotion to the Cabinet, Nick Lyell and John Patten. Three more '79ers of Cabinet ability – Robert Cranborne, Matthew Parris and John Watson – were to quit the House because, in their different ways, they could not adapt to the frustrations of life in the Commons.

Two of the '79 intake – Chris Patten and William Waldegrave – had been tipped as future Prime Ministers even before they arrived in the Commons. Many of the bright new members already knew one another well by 1979, and most of them had attended at least one of the Tory Party's nurseries for the talented young: Eton – declining, but still a power – Oxbridge, or the Conservative Research Department. So there was already a strong basis for group loyalty and a group ethos even before Tristan Garel-Jones started work. In the early years of the Thatcher era, Mr Garel-Jones played a crucial role in organizing and orchestrating his fellow '79ers' activities. This might seem paradoxical, for Tristan suffers from a failing which none of the others showed; he persistently underrates his intellectual ability. By the time he arrived at Westminster, Tristan had already decided that as he possessed only a second-class mind, nature had fashioned him for the role of attendant Lord. He would attend, therefore, on his brightest contemporaries, and help to organize their ascent.

He began this process in traditional Tory fashion by organizing a dining club, which was to meet about once a month (when the Commons was sitting), at Mr Garel-Jones's house in Catherine Place. Originally, there were thirteen members; Tristan had set out to recruit a dozen, but asked one person too many. The members were: Michael Ancram,[1] Robert Atkins, Jocelyn Cadbury,[2] Robert Cranborne, Peter Fraser, Tristan Garel-Jones, Nicholas Lyell, Richard Needham, Chris Patten, John Patten, Alex Pollock, William Waldegrave and John Watson.

It was a conspicuous group. Apart from its intellectual distinction, there was a social cachet which not even Robert Atkins's membership could expunge. Lords Ancram and Cranborne were heirs to Marquessates. Mr Needham is also the Earl of Kilmorey, an Irish title which he does not use – and the Hon. Mr Waldegrave is the younger son of an Earl. The group was quickly named the 'Blue Chip', a nickname which embarrassed its members, who tried to circulate the 'Dirty Dozen' as an alternative. The name Blue Chip stuck. It also aroused resentment. Any such group inevitably creates a feeling of exclusion among those not invited to join, and whatever disclaimers its individual members might make, the Blue Chip was seen at Westminster as a mutual admiration society of privileged, self-confident and ambitious young men who took it for granted that they would reach the heights.

The Blue Chips had no high opinion of Thatcherism – or of Margaret Thatcher. Though they accepted the need to curb inflation, control public spending, reduce taxes and reform the trade unions, they saw this as a necessary corrective to the economic failures of the 1970s – not as a decisive break with the whole of post-war policy. They took it for granted that whatever the Prime Minister's views, normal Tory service would be resumed as soon as possible – with them delivering it.

After 1979, the Blue Chip devoted much of its energy to preparing 'Changing Gear', a manifesto it published in the autumn of 1981, which expressed its opposition to the Government's economic policies. Though the Blue Chip's criticisms were not as forthright as those of Ian Gilmour, 'Changing Gear' was part of the Wet insurrectionary movement of 1981. This added to the Blue Chips' unpopularity among their Thatcherite colleagues. Then again, there were hardly any clever Thatcherites among the '79ers. No attempt was made to set up a Thatcherite alternative to the Blue Chip;[3] among the Tory MPs newly elected in 1979, Thatcherism was generally in inverse proportion to ability.

---

1 A Member of Parliament between March and October 1974.

2 A delightful, talented man whose charm concealed a losing battle against depression. He committed suicide in 1982.

3 The ablest members of the 1983 intake were almost all Thatcherites. They established the 'No Turning Back' Group; the name defines their views.

Guy Fawkes

John Major was not invited to become a member of the Blue Chip in 1979; its leading members did not yet know him. By the time he did join the group, in 1985, its character had changed.

A majority of the group were now in the Government, and paradoxically, the more important its members became, the less seriously the Blue Chip took itself. By 1985, it had ceased to be a focal point for anti-Thatcherite activities, and was purely a dining club. Through not being a member from the beginning, John Major missed many enjoyable evenings and much good talk: he was also kept out of danger. If Mr Major had belonged to the Blue Chip, he would have been on the group's right wing, but it is unlikely that he would either have changed its outlook, or resigned from it. As a Blue Chip, he could not have escaped the taint of Wettery, and would almost certainly have been regarded with suspicion by Margaret Thatcher and her acolytes. He might still have been in a position to succeed her, but his task would have been harder. The fact that John Major was not yet a friend of Tristan Garel-Jones's in 1979 was one of those happy accidents which helped his career.

He did join another dining club, however. John Watson, a member of the Blue Chip, was sensitive to the charge of cliquiness and aloofness which other MPs were levelling at the group, and wanted to expand its membership. The other members were against him, but not out of disdain for their colleagues; they felt that it was necessary to limit their numbers to a figure which could be comfortably accommodated around Mr Garel-Jones's dining table. Mr Watson decided to set up another club, which he called the 'Guy Fawkes'; John Major was one of the founder members. It held its meetings over dinner in L'Amico restaurant in Horseferry Road which is on the division bell, and where Mr Gorbachev dined on one occasion. Apart from Messrs Major and Watson, the Fawkes's members included: Graham Bright, John Butcher, Stephen Dorrell, John Lee, Peter Lloyd, Brian Mawhinney, David Mellor, David Trippier and Gary Waller.

The Fawkes was neither as unified, nor as publicized, nor as much fun as the Blue Chip. Its membership included at least two Thatcherites in John Butcher and Peter Lloyd, and this guaranteed an argument. Though several Fawkesites agreed with Messrs Dorrell and Watson – arch-Wets – that Geoffrey Howe was making excessive sacrifices on the altar of a lower public sector borrowing requirement,

Mr Butcher and Mr Lloyd would always express a vigorous dissent-ing view. In those discussions, John Major was a floating voter. On any issue, he always sought to narrow the focus of the discussion to a specific issue which could be assessed pragmatically. Instead of the well-rehearsed sterilities of the Wet/Dry debate, John Major pre-ferred to examine detailed policy proposals.

Looking back on these early discussions, some of Mr Major's col-leagues say that they then thought of him as slightly Wet-of-Centre; others considered him a shade Dry-of-Centre. Nobody regarded him as an ideologue. This lack of ideological zeal owed nothing to any desire to keep in with all sides. Instead it stemmed from one of John Major's pronounced character traits – most unusual among politicians – an unwillingness to speak out when he is neither in possession of all the facts, nor responsible for the actions he is advocating. Mr Major was already well aware just how difficult it was to be Chancellor of the Exchequer. He knew that Geoffrey Howe would be in receipt of a mass of conflicting advice, cogently expressed, and that no amount of advice can relieve a Chancellor from the lonely burden of decision-making. He was not vain enough to think that the country would be better governed if he added his twopenceworth, so he abstained. He also felt strongly that politics was a team game; it was his duty to support his own side.

This is an impression confirmed by his maiden speech, delivered during the debate on Sir Geoffrey Howe's first Budget. It was a stylish performance, which followed the conventions of a maiden speech, paying – sincere – tribute to Sir David Renton and praising the Huntingdon constituency. Mr Major reminded the House that among Huntingdon's former Members was Oliver Cromwell, but added, 'He caused your predecessors, Mr Deputy Speaker, more trouble than I anticipate causing, at least in my early days.' Turning to economic poilicy, he said that public opinion required four things of the Government: to cut taxes, to curb inflation, to create new jobs, and 'as far as possible' to maintain satisfactory public services. He went on to argue, however, that: 'with the best will in the world the Chancellor and his colleagues cannot possibly achieve them all at the same time. In order to create jobs and to maintain public services, it is necessary first to cut taxes and to curb inflation.' He then addressed himself to the question of spending cuts. 'Whenever we talk about spending cuts there is bound to be a certain amount of uproar. It is never popular to cut services. But it seems that much of the uproar which is currently being engendered is to a large extent synthetic.' He therefore concluded: 'I think that the spending cuts are desirable.'[4]

This might seem a commonplace theme, but in the context of the time, both the content and the tone are interesting: they also express the basis of John Major's approach to government. In their enthusiasm for public spending, some of the Wets were perilously close to arguing that all public expenditure was *ipso facto* desirable. From his experiences in Brixton and Lambeth, John Major knew that this was untrue, and that a lot of public spending produced no public service. Many Thatcherites, however, were making an equal mistake. In their visceral hostility to the state and to its expenditure, they were in danger of overlooking the central importance of government spending in creating and maintaining the infrastructure of a modern society.

In 1979, public expenditure was out of control. The incoming Government inherited a spending programme which was based neither on a rational ordering of priorities nor on a realistic assessment of the burdens the economy could bear. As the Government – and John Major – realized, painful surgery was necessary. Reason and instinct both led Mr Major to a middle position; he neither shrank from nor revelled in the pain. He accepted that the planned level of public expenditure had to be reduced, partly in order to promote an economic recovery which would make it possible to finance higher public spending in the future. Unlike many backbenchers, John Major accepted the Government's arguments over the 1981 Budget. That Budget was framed in the depths of a recession. The Wets, the Keynesians and all other custodians of the conventional wisdom were calling for reflation; their advice was rejected. Geoffrey Howe – reinforced by Margaret Thatcher, Nigel Lawson and Alan Walters – decided to take four billion pounds out of the economy, while relaxing monetary policy. The Wets were in uproar; 364 economists wrote a letter to *The Times* predicting the end of the world – and the economy moved into the most rapid and sustained period of economic growth in modern history. At the Guy Fawkes's dinners, John Major was one of the minority who was prepared to argue in favour of Sir Geoffrey's decision, partly because he did not share his colleagues' willingness to criticize the Chancellor without being aware of all the arguments which had led him to make his decision.

For ambitious backbenchers, opposition is more fun than government.

---

4 *Hansard*, 13 June 1979, cols 520-2.

If one's party is in opposition, every question time provides an opportunity to unhorse a Minister. It only requires a couple of successes in parliamentary prime time for the backbencher in question to become a well-known figure, widely tipped as a coming man. But the loyal backbencher on the government side has many fewer opportunities to display his talents. That did not worry John Major. He was happy to progress in characteristic Major style, gradually and steadily. There was no dramatic breakthrough to fame, or notoriety – but by 1980/81 his name would crop up regularly in those endless Westminster conversations in which parliamentary reputations are traded like an active share on the Stock Exchange. I began to find that an increasing number of his colleagues would say: 'Have you met John Major?' Around this time, Lord Cranborne contacted Ladbrokes, the bookmakers, and said that he wanted to stake a bet on the first member of the 1979 intake to reach the Cabinet. 'You'll be thinking in terms of one of the Pattens, or William Waldegrave,' said Ladbrokes. 'No,' replied Robert Cranborne, 'John Major.' 'Who he?' enquired Ladbrokes – and quoted odds of 25–1. Lord Cranborne took them.

One reason for his growing reputation was the amount of time he spent in and around the Chamber; this meant that he got to know his colleagues – and they him. He enjoyed every aspect of life in the Commons, and was quickly recognized to be 'a good House of Commons man'. The new Member for Huntingdon soon caught the attention of the Whips. David Waddington (later Chief Whip), who served in Mrs Thatcher's first Whips' office, remembers that by the time he left the office to become a Parliamentary Secretary, in January 1981, John Major was already being discussed as a candidate for promotion; Lord Waddington is only surprised that it took Mr Major another two years to win his first Government appointment.

In early 1981, however, he did climb the first rung, and became Parliamentary Private Secretary to Patrick Mayhew, then Minister of State at the Home Office. In political terms, the Home Office is probably the most troublesome of all government departments, especially for a Tory Home Secretary. He and his advisers may conclude that the crime problem is insoluble, but many Tory backbenchers and Tory activists will disagree. They think there is an answer: the lash and the gallows. Late one night, during a long, hot Criminal Justice Bill debate, Willie Whitelaw – then Home Secretary – lay full length on the Front Bench, while the tooth-and-claw wing of the Tory Party expounded its views. In horizontal profile, the

Home Secretary needed only a covering of snow to resemble the Alps as seen from the Po Valley; there was also an expression of acute distaste on his features as he repeatedly muttered: 'God, I hate my party. God, I hate my party.'

The Home Secretary is also at the mercy of accidents. When an Irishman decided to drop in to the Queen's bedroom for a chat with Her Majesty, the press carried on as if Mr Whitelaw had given him a leg up over the Buckingham Palace wall. It is hardly surprising, therefore, that most Home Secretaries come to see their main task as damage limitation. Willie Whitelaw was a consummate House of Commons politician, and Paddy Mayhew is also a formidable operator. Even so, John Major managed to impress them both by his feel for the Parliamentary Party and his skill in predicting – and averting – danger. From then on, Mr Whitelaw regarded John Major as a protégé. A former Chief Whip himself, Willie thought he could see a future Chief Whip in the young PPS.

By 1981, the first members of the 1979 intake were joining the Government. In the early appointments, preference tended to be given to Scotsmen, other MPs with regional links, and some of the less rebellious Wets. This did not altogether please John Major. After the first four or five of his intake had been appointed, he told one of his friends at the Fawkes of his dissatisfaction at being passed over. But he had longer to wait: John Major was only the eleventh member of his year to win preferment. Ahead of him came: John Patten, Donald Thompson, David Mellor, Allan Stewart, William Waldegrave, Ian Lang, Peter Fraser, Tristan Garel-Jones, John Butcher and John Mackay. Finally, in the mini-reshuffle of January 1983 brought about by Sir John Nott's retirement, John Major was invited to become an Assistant Whip, the lowest form of ministerial life. But it was a happy appointment, and the beginning of two and a half successful years.

The Tory Whips combined the language of the hunting field and the practices of the adjutant's office. No one has written a serious study of the Tory Whips' office; nor would it be easy to do so. Like the Camorra or the Freemasons, the Whips guard their secrets, and pride themselves on running the last secure room in Western Europe. In essence, the Tory Whips are fourteen men[5] round a table, discussing problems. Individual Whips are selected on various criteria – but they also have to be acceptable to their fellow Whips. A black-balling system operates; any Whip can veto the appointment

---

5 There has never been a female Tory Whip in the Commons, though there have been several in the Lords. If Margaret Thatcher had served in the Whips' office, she might still be Prime Minister.

of any proposed Whip. Obviously, the black ball would not be used frivolously, and a strong Chief Whip should always be able to secure the appointment of a good candidate. But the black ball has been threatened on occasions. Some potential Whips are not even nominated, because it is known that certain members of the existing office would block them. Alan Clark was one such case, during the 1979 Parliament. Within the constraints of the black ball, the Chief Whip of the day always tries to ensure that all regions and social classes are represented. The Whips' office is also used as a staff college for bright youngsters, including members of the awkward squad.

The Whips' most important task is to ensure that whenever there is a vote in the House of Commons, the Government can be sure of a majority. But inasmuch as there is any man management in the Tory Party, the Whips do it. They have a decisive voice in junior ministerial appointments; they also spend much of their time reassuring those who have been passed over, but who still have prospects – and coping with those whose terminal lack of prospects is apparent to everyone but themselves.

John Major was an extremely good Whip. He was reckoned to be the best counter of heads in the Whips' office; his estimates of any likely dip in the Government's majority due to a backbench revolt were always the most reliable. His colleagues also came to respect his judgement when it came to personalities. In the words of Tristan Garel-Jones, one of his fellow Whips: 'The rest of us quickly realized that once John had expressed his views on a topic, there was not a lot more to be said.' Others came to share Lord Whitelaw's view that Mr Major had the makings of a future Chief Whip.

Apart from the most senior members of the office, each Whip is responsible for a region – in John Major's case, East Anglia – and for a government department. This involves liaising with the ministers concerned over the timetable of any Bills going through the House, and dealing with any difficulties that might arise. During this first eighteen months in the office, John Major covered the Home Office and Northern Ireland. For the parliamentary year 1984/85, he was made Treasury Whip. Of all government departments to which a Whip could be assigned, the Treasury is the most demanding. After each Budget, which generally occurs in March, a Finance Bill has to be passed through Parliament before the end of June. Such legislation is always complex, and likely to involve a difficult committee stage. That is where a good Treasury Whip can show his qualities –

for the Finance Bill also requires him to negotiate with the Opposition parties.

The Opposition knows that if the Government has a majority it will ensure that its Finance Bills reach the statute book virtually unamended. It is not the custom to filibuster finance bills to the point where the Government has to resort to a timetable – or 'guillotine' – motion to foreshorten the debate. The Opposition will still want to oppose, however; this is likely to mean a run of all-night committee sessions.

A skilful Treasury Whip starts out by establishing good personal relations with his Labour opponent. On that basis, he can do deals, which leave the Opposition's honour satisfied, but which also make life easier for his ministers. It would be unrealistic to try to avoid all-night sessions – but a good Treasury Whip can at least ensure that his ministers have advance warning as to which nights' sleep they can write off. Equally, an incompetent Whip is a Treasury Minister's nightmare; if the Whipping on a Finance Bill goes wrong, it could have a disruptive effect on the entire work of the Treasury.

Nigel Lawson, the then Chancellor of the Exchequer, was not a man to tolerate disruption, so he had never been noted for his patience. Like everyone else involved, Mr Lawson was greatly impressed by the Treasury Whip's efforts; he immediately marked down John Major as a future Treasury Minister. That decision had momentous consequences; John Major's performance on the 1985 Finance Bill won him the advancement which enabled him to become Prime Minister.

Back in 1985, however, his ambitions were less elevated: he was still looking forward to being a Parliamentary Under Secretary of State. By the summer of 1985, he had served as a Whip for two and a half years and won golden opinions. It was almost a certainty that he would be promoted in the reshuffle due in September – but John Major himself then took a gamble with his own prospects.

In July 1985, Mrs Thatcher gave a dinner in No. 10 for the Whips. In the course of the meal, she asked what the backbenchers were saying about the economy. John Major, as Treasury Whip, informed her that the Government's economic policy was widely misunderstood, and widely unpopular. She retorted that this was nonsense, and spoke to John Major as if *he* disagreed with her economic policy. Mr Major tried to point out that he was not speaking for himself, but merely giving an accurate account of the views of the Parliamentary Party. It is not easy, however, to point things out to Margaret Thatcher when she is in full flood. She persisted in treating him as if he was one of her Wet critics; he held his ground, and repeated his answer to her original question. Others tried to change the subject: she had no intention of changing the subject. The argument grew heated, before determined efforts by John Wakeham, the then Chief Whip, steered the evening away from the rocks.

As the dinner broke up, Denis Thatcher went up to John Major and said: 'She rather enjoyed that, you know.' This was intended as reassurance: it was unsuccessful. Mr Major was convinced that he had shot himself in the foot – and that the PM, who had hitherto been hardly aware of his existence, now had him marked down as a disciple of Ian Gilmour. He knew that what he had been telling her was true; he wished that in the run-up to a reshuffle, he had been less stubborn in defence of the truth. Mr Thatcher, however, seems to have assessed the situation correctly. Mr Major's argument with the PM did him no harm. In September, John Major was appointed Parliamentary Under Secretary for Social Security at the Department of Health and Social Security, arguably the most taxing of all Parliamentary Secretary posts. Our present system of social security was sired by the puritan rigour of Beveridge out of the political cunning of Lloyd George. Since the confident simplicities of the early days, however, there has been a downhill journey to the present morass of complexity, into which additional billions are poured annually – the current total is almost sixty billion – without having any noticeable effect in alleviating social problems. Today, social security is a vastly expensive intellectual mess, and a political minefield.

Newly-installed Parliamentary Secretaries at Social Security are quickly made aware of the problems facing them by the cases that land on their desk for adjudication. Generally speaking, the items sent up for ministerial decision would have defeated Solomon; they usually involve an irreconcilable contradiction between the claims of humanity on the one hand, and the legal position on the other. Hard cases make bad politics. The Minister can be certain that whenever a problem arises, the claimants' lobbies and their media spokesmen, the *Guardian* and the 'Today' programme, will attribute all the blame to his purblind meanness, insisting that by comparison with him, Scrooge sounds like Mother Theresa.

It is hardly surprising, therefore, that most sensible Tory ministers have concluded that when it comes to social security, the first priority is damage limitation. That was certainly the view taken by Norman Fowler, who had been Secretary of State at the DHSS since 1981; he adopted a similar attitude to health policy. Around the time of the 1987 election, it became fashionable in some circles to blame his supineness for the electoral difficulties which the health issue had caused. On election day itself, Lord Young opined that Mr Fowler should be sacked in the forthcoming reshuffle, as he had nearly caused the Government's downfall.

Four years on, David Young's strictures seem gravely unjust; in retrospect, Norman Fowler's looks better and better. Health will always cause the Tory Party problems in any election campaign (as the Government is now discovering), and Norman Fowler had kept his department largely under control for nearly six years; it destroyed his successor, John Moore, in about six months. The DHSS was subsequently split into two separate Cabinet departments – Health, and Social Security. Even with a lighter burden, however, none of Norman Fowler's successors has been able to improve on his record. Mr Fowler brought to his task a combination of old-fashioned Tory scepticism and political cunning. Over time, he recognized in his junior Minister a degree of political cunning equal to his own – but the scepticism coloured his initial reaction to John Major.

That was Mrs Thatcher's fault. She did not share Mr Fowler's pessimism, and was in favour of a more radical approach to social security. When she disagreed with the line one of her Secretaries of State was taking, it was often her practice to appoint Thatcherite junior ministers to his department. This did not make for an easy working environment. The Cabinet Minister in question sometimes concluded that his junior had been sent to report back on him to No. 10. Norman Fowler had entertained such suspicions of Rhodes Boyson and Ray Whitney, and he was also ready to regard John Major as a Downing Street mole. Mr Fowler's doubts quickly evaporated, however. Norman Fowler and John Major worked easily together, and shared a similar approach to the problems facing the department.

At that stage, the preparatory work was well in hand for the social security review of 1985/86 which was an attempt to control the rise in expenditure, while also deploying the social security budget more effectively, so as to help those in real need. Any changes in social security are bound to cause political trouble. In dealing with this, the department officials came to rely on John Major's parliamentary appraisals. All civil servants have an ambivalent approach to the political process. At certain moments in their career, faced with an incompetent minister or unreasonable backbenchers, most bright officials have been tempted to conclude that Westminster is merely a tiresome distraction from the real work of Whitehall. They are also aware, however, that despite all the frustrations, they cannot brush Parliament aside. Civil servants will certainly take decisions on behalf of an idle or useless minister, as well as doing most of his work. But there is one respect in which they cannot replace him: his parliamentary duties. Indeed, civil servants are prone to develop an exaggerated respect for a minister who can handle the Commons.

The officials who worked with John Major certainly formed a high opinion of him. He gained another reputation which he has never lost: of being a kindly and considerate boss. Some of the officials who saw a lot of him were aware of a certain reserve. One or two of the more perceptive ones realized that this was not just a matter of a new minister feeling his way in a strange environment. The insecurities caused by John Major's lack of education were coming into play: he still had to reassure himself that he could cope with a ministerial workload and command the respect of officials, almost all of whom had enjoyed a vastly more formal education than he had.

John Major encountered no difficulties, in either respect. From the moment of his arrival at the DHSS, he performed impressively. He had won Norman Fowler's confidence, while retaining the Prime Minister's approval. John Wakeham was pleased with his protégé's progress; John Major was very much on course to be Chief Whip in the new Parliament. However, the leap from Parliamentary Secretary to Chief Whip is too great to be accomplished in a single promotion; it was necessary for Mr Major to do a stint – albeit brief – as Minister of State. In the September 1986 reshuffle occasioned by Sir Keith Joseph's retirement, he was made Minister of State for Social Security; his predecessor, Tony Newton, moved across to Health.

Within a few weeks, he had to deal with the question of cold weather payments for the elderly. On the face of it, the Government should have had no difficulty in defending its record. Throughout the 1980s, there had been a steady increase in spending on heating allowances for pensioners receiving supplementary benefit. Whereas in the 1950s the mortality rate during the winter quarter had been 27 per cent higher than the average for the year as a whole, by the mid-1980s, that figure had fallen to around 14 per cent.

When emotions are aroused, however, and a supposedly compassionate issue dominates the headlines, facts, figures and a reasoned case are of little value. At the beginning of its term of office, the Thatcher Government had created a rod for its own back by introducing a system of 'exceptionally severe weather payments'. In the first place, this was inefficient; in 1985/86, £1.7 million had been paid out, at an administrative cost of £1 million. But the real cost was political. Every winter, a demand for such payments could always be used to create an outbreak of hypothermia hysteria. In 1986/87, that outbreak was particularly severe – no doubt fuelled by the imminence of a General Election. John Major deployed the obvious arguments, unsuccessfully. As a *Times* leader observed, ministers trying to defend their position inevitably sounded like Mr Gradgrind arguing with Mr Pickwick.[6] Mr Major decided that he had to give way. In order to do so, he had to confront the one powerful interest group in the country which had been quite unmoved by the cold weather panic: the Treasury. However, even Treasury ministers are influenced by General Elections. Mr Major secured additional millions, and the agitation subsided with the approach of Spring.

Mr Major went on to have a good election campaign. He appeared on the platform at several Central Office press conferences, and coped crisply with the questioning. Observers noted that Mrs Thatcher gave him at least his fair share of questions to deal with – and approved of his answers. As the election ended, John Major himself still hoped – and almost expected – to be made Chief Whip. It would have been a significant promotion, to a job he knew he would enjoy. Willie Whitelaw and John Wakeham both thought he ought to have the post, and there was every reason to expect that Mrs Thatcher would agree.

Suddenly, opposition arose, from an unexpected quarter. Chancellor Nigel Lawson had decided that *he* wanted John Major, as Chief Secretary to the Treasury: the minister in charge of public spending. Mr Lawson argued strongly that Mr Major was much the best qualified of all the available candidates, and was also able to point out that David Waddington, then Minister of State at the Home Office, would make an excellent Chief Whip. So indeed it proved: Mr Waddington got the job, and did it well. Mr Major became Chief Secretary, a post of Cabinet rank. Robert Cranborne had won his

---

6 *The Times*, 14 January 1987.

bet; John Major was the first of the 1979 intake to reach the Cabinet, a promotion which eventually enabled him to succeed Margaret Thatcher.

What would have happened if John Major had become Chief Whip is one of the most intriguing 'ifs' of modern political history. In Conservative governments, Chief Whips normally serve for an entire Parliament; it was only Nigel Lawson's resignation which led to the breach of precedent in 1989, with David Waddington becoming Home Secretary. The probability is that John Major would also have been promoted in 1989 – but not to the Foreign Office, or to the Treasury.

If Mr Major had been Chief Whip, however, there might not have been a change of premiership. Although it is hard to fault David Waddington's performance, it is also possible that had Chief Whip Major been promoted in November 1989, he would have acted even more strenuously to ensure that his successor was someone who enjoyed the PM's full confidence. It is also conceivable that if John Major had been Chief Whip, there would have been no reshuffle in November 1989. Mr Major would have understood Nigel Lawson better than David Waddington could; his intuition might have told him how Mr Lawson would react to the Walters affair. In retrospect, however – and this author certainly did not realize it at the time – by November 1989, Nigel Lawson's relationship with Margaret Thatcher had run its course. It was time for them to part. Although the manner of Mr Lawson's resignation caused some political damage, his remaining in office would also have been damaging.

On one point we can be reasonably certain. If John Major had become Chief Whip in 1987, he would not have been in a position to challenge for the Tory leadership in 1990. Nigel Lawson can claim some credit for helping John Major to become Prime Minister.

Chief Secretary

The Chief Secretary to the Treasury is the lowest-ranking Cabinet minister, and usually the least publicized. He has no department of his own, and is merely the Chancellor's deputy, in charge of the Government's public expenditure plans. That said, the Chief Secretary has one of the most vital – and arduous – jobs in Government.

For most of the past forty years, public spending has threatened to break out of control. As it already absorbs so much of the Gross Domestic Product, even a relatively small unplanned increase can lead to pressure on interest rates, panic in the markets, and an economic crisis. The rest of the economy cannot flourish unless the Government imposes tight limits on its spending. The price of public expenditure control is eternal vigilance, which cannot be exercised merely by rigidity. Though the word 'no' and its synonyms must feature largely in his vocabulary, a Chief Secretary would be unwise to refuse all requests. The public spending problem arises because of the pressures of democratic politics; a sensible Chief Secretary tries to find a way of accommodating those pressures. If the Chief Secretary is lax, the ensuing year is likely to be punctuated by a succession of public spending crises, as the markets and – under Labour Governments – the IMF force the Chancellor to claw back the cash his deputy should never have given away. But if the Chief Secretary is too unyielding, the result will be political crises. He must strike a balance. Doing so involves brutish hard work. For many months of the year, the Chief Secretary's life consists of meetings all day, and papers all night. During his hard-driven months, John Major regularly worked until midnight, and then started again at 5.30 a.m. When he faces his spending colleagues across the table, a Chief Secretary has to know their programmes and their arguments at least as well as they do – and they are many; he is one.

There are compensations for all the hard work, however. While many of his notionally more senior colleagues, closeted in their departments, cease to focus on the big picture, the Chief Secretary has to learn everything about the workings of government. It is a unique opportunity for a rising minister to complete his political education.

John Major approached his new task with enthusiasm, and with trepidation. Again due to his lack of university education, he was a little nervous as to how he would measure up in the Treasury. The Treasury, the most intellectually demanding of all government departments, is staffed by civil servants of the highest calibre. Treasury officials not only have to display ability, but intellectual self-confidence as well. From very early on in their careers, they are expected to contribute to the internal debate, which is not run on hierarchical lines. Junior officials are quite happy to contradict their seniors in public – and they are not much more deferential towards ministers.

The atmosphere in the Treasury has an excitement which even a visitor can detect. There is a sense of *esprit de corps* created over the years by very able people working hard in the engine room of government – and enjoying one another's company while doing so. Politicians who serve in the Treasury come to appreciate this; most Treasury ministers develop a great respect for their civil servants.

John Major started off with such a respect, tinged by wariness. On his first day as Chief Secretary, he confided to his private secretary, Jill Rutter, that he was not sure what all these characters with first-class degrees from Oxbridge would make of him. Then he paused: 'Er, where did you go to university?'

'Oxford.'

'I suppose you got a First?'

'Well, as a matter of fact, Chief Secretary, yes.'

Mr Major was very fortunate in Miss Rutter. She was the ideal private secretary for him, both in terms of assisting his work, and boosting his confidence. Jill Rutter is one of the ablest civil servants of her generation. Even in the Treasury, she is spoken of with awe, though it is alloyed with amusement. Miss Rutter is unconventional, and no respecter of persons. Two of her favourite expressions are 'dingbat' and 'brain-dead', which she applies liberally to unsound policy proposals, and to those who advocate them. The new Chief Secretary struck up an instant rapport with this engaging grammar-school meritocrat, whose formidable brain is reinforced by a caustic wit. Their partnership was solidified by a common love of cricket: Jill is also a Surrey supporter. During the summer of 1988, it was well known among Treasury cricket enthusiasts that around lunchtime and again towards close of play, the Test Match would be on in the Chief Secretary's office.

John Major has always enjoyed the company of intelligent women. In addition to the one he is married to, many of his closest friends and partners in politics and government have been women, including Emily Blatch, Judith Chaplin, Sarah Hogg, Jill Rutter, and Gill Shephard. Jill Rutter in particular alleviated what might otherwise have been a slightly lonely existence. The structure of the Chief Secretary's working hours reflected the fact that he had no home to go back to: only an empty flat. In the early evening, he would often go across to the House, and regularly ate in the Members' dining room. He would then return to the Treasury and do some more work.

In any private office, there is a convention that as long as the Minister is around, at least one civil servant will remain on duty. Miss Rutter was happy to put in late hours, as was her successor, Carys Evans. On some evenings, when pressure of work kept John Major at his desk, he would have a late dinner with Miss Rutter, Miss Evans or some of his other officials – frequently at an Indian restaurant. John Major always stoutly denies that he is addicted to curry; it all depends what is meant by addiction. On the evidence of everyone who has known John Major for the past twenty-five years, curries have constituted a substantial proportion of his food intake.

Letters to Santa Claus

Every summer, the Treasury draws up two sets of figures, and publishes one. This set becomes the official guideline: the target figure for public spending in the next financial year. But the second, unpublished, figure is the more important; it is the Treasury's realistic assessment of what will actually happen. The second figure is always the higher of the two.

While the Treasury does its sums, the other departments write their letters to Santa Claus. They work out what they would like to see in the way of increased spending and ask for it. Needless to say, those departmental bids always add up to ten billion or so more than the Treasury's planning total. The Chief Secretary then has to spend September and October shoehorning the government departments into their allotted space. He does this through 'bilaterals' – individual negotiations with spending ministers. If the two sides cannot agree, the dispute is then taken to 'Star Chamber', a committee of senior Cabinet Ministers formerly chaired by Lord Whitelaw, then by Cecil Parkinson, and more recently still by Sir Geoffrey Howe. Of later years, however, spending ministers have been increasingly reluctant to take their case to 'Star Chamber'. The original Star Chamber was a court used by the Tudors and early Stuarts to stamp their authority on recalcitrants; some ministers believe that the modern version has inherited much of the Henrican ethos. These days, even ministers whose departments had been telling the press that they were going all the way to Star Chamber tend to settle on the courtroom steps.

By any standards, John Major was a good Chief Secretary. He not only held public spending within the Treasury's published estimates; he hit the secret target as well. He achieved all this without recourse to Star Chamber, which was not required to sit during either of his years as Chief Secretary. Moreover, Mr Major's relations with individual colleagues were generally cordial. It is easy for a Chief Secretary to fall into the habit of adopting a peremptory tone in his notes to his colleagues. In his day, Leon Brittan was often accused of that – as is the current Chief Secretary, David Mellor. John Major never was; he tried to make it impossible for his colleagues to become angry with him, refusing their requests with almost Japanese subtlety.[7]

In his first year, there was a problem with the DHSS. John Moore asked for too little money; John Major eagerly acceded to his request – and within a few months, there had to be a supplementary provision. There were a number of reasons why the DHSS budget went awry. John Major did not want to be accused of doing favours for his old department; John Moore was under a similar constraint. He had been a Treasury minister until 1986, and wanted to prove that he still retained his Thatcherite orthodoxy. Mr Moore had a further temptation to demonstrate his toughness. At that stage, there were a number of newspaper articles suggesting that John Moore might ultimately succeed Margaret Thatcher. This may have induced hubris, leading to the fatal error of trying to demonstrate his political virility by a tough line on the DHSS budget. That mistake began the process which ended his ministerial career.

It became clear to the officials who witnessed the Major/Moore negotiations that beneath a veneer of civility, John Major thought little of the Health Secretary's abilities. This gave rise to speculation as to whether Mr Major was trying to do down a potential rival for the leadership. That, however, is far too fanciful and Machiavellian an intrepretation. Mr Major was not the only Cabinet colleague who found Mr Moore irritating, because of the disparity between pretension and performance. When he fell ill in 1988, John Moore received little sympathy from his colleagues, most of whom had often listened to him boasting about how fit he was. John Major may well have shared the irritation – though not over fitness – but there is no reason to suppose that it coloured his attitude during the spending round. There is a much more straightforward explanation. The Chief Secretary's task is to control spending. He cannot be expected to dispute a colleague's assessment, on the grounds that he is asking

---

7 The best recorded instance of a Chief Secretary's soft answer turning away wrath comes from 1974 or 1975, during Joel Barnett's period in that office. Reg Prentice, then Education Secretary, put up a paper asking for extra cash. Joel Barnett said to him: 'Terrific paper, Reg. Best one I've seen in this spending round. You make a watertight case; your arguments are unanswerable. And the answer's no.'

for too little money. Each Cabinet minister must be assumed to understand his own department's needs.

During his period at Education, in between rubber-stamping the GCSE, Sir Keith Joseph could often be heard bleating that 'we must help poor Nigel' (Lawson). In those days, 'poor Nigel' was perfectly capable of helping himself. The only result of Sir Keith's efforts on his behalf was to add to the Government's problems with the teachers. The experiences of Keith Joseph and John Moore ought to act as an awful warning to future generations of spending ministers. Even under a government committed to public expenditure restraint, public spending negotiations must be conducted adversarially, with individual ministers fighting their corner. Otherwise the whole exercise works as well as a tug-of-war contest would with only one team tugging.

However, John Major himself did not revel in this adversarialism. Once he had agreed an overall figure with a ministerial colleague, he tried to move the discussion into more creative areas. He always encouraged ministers to reassess their priorities, and whenever possible to switch resources from current spending to capital investment. He was also prepared to show flexibility – over small sums of money. Any spending minister who could make out a strong political argument for an inexpensive programme could be sure of a sympathetic hearing. On one occasion, towards the end of a negotiation with Chris Patten, then Minister for Overseas Development, John Major politely asked the officials present if they would mind leaving the room. They were surprised, as was Chris Patten; they all assumed that Mr Major was proposing to have a row with Mr Patten which he did not want officials to witness. Instead, John Major smiled sweetly at Chris Patten and said: 'This is the moment when you force my arm up my back and return in triumph to your department with an extra ten million pounds.' Mr Patten agreed on the spot; he was half way to his ministry before it occurred to him that he ought to have held out for £15 million.

In December 1988, after he had completed his second – and final – spending round, John Major outlined his philosophy of public expenditure in a speech to the National Association of Conservative Graduates. He made it clear that he stood for fiscal rigour. Public spending should continue to increase, but at a rate less rapid than the growth of national income, so that year by year, the state would consume a lower proportion of the nation's wealth. This would facilitate further tax cuts, thus stimulating the economy and creating a 'virtuous circle', in which increasing prosperity would finance spending increases, tax cuts, and reductions in the National Debt – leading to a fall in interest charges, and thus a further addition to the fiscal surplus.

Mr Major warned that if the economy were to slow down, the Government would have to take especial care to keep spending growth under control. He also made it clear, however, that he fully accepted the desirability of spending increases on worthwhile projects. The important point was to bring public expenditure under firm control, so that the Government could develop a strategy for public spending, rather than merely yielding to the pressure of events. Public expenditure would inevitably consist of a mixture of the unavoidable and the worthwhile, said Mr Major: 'The trick is to increase the latter and reduce the former.'

He was able to claim some successes: an extra £2 billion for health, an extra £1.4 billion for roads – plus attractive smaller items, such as an additional £5 million devoted to the Motability scheme for the disabled. He summarized his approach to the spending round: 'My job is to get behind the figures to separate what is really valuable from what is merely desirable.'

As her subsequent behaviour towards him showed, Margaret Thatcher was entirely satisfied with the way John Major performed his duties – so was Nigel Lawson. Until Mr Major became Prime Minister, it was hard to find anyone who disapproved of the way he had handled public spending. Since then, however, as part of the campaign of denigration conducted by two or three irredentist journalists, there has been some *sotto voce* disparagement.

The critics' case is as follows. John Major had a simple task as Chief Secretary. The Government's revenues were rising, while expenditures fell. Balancing the books was therefore a simple matter; John Major should have been far tougher and taken advantage of the boom to effect a substantial reduction in public spending as a proportion of GDP. However, for all its apparent subtlety, that is a nonsensical argument. Its premise is false: far from it being easier to cut public spending during a boom, the reverse is true. The key to spending cuts is not revenue, but politics. In a crisis, even Labour governments have been able to cut public spending – but when the economy is roaring ahead and the spending ministers know that the Treasury is piling up a sizeable budget surplus, they are much less inclined to take 'no' for an answer. As society becomes more affluent, the demand for certain public goods – health, education, the relief of poverty – increases even faster than the rate of economic growth. There were signs that Margaret Thatcher herself was prepared to recognize this, especially in the run-up to election campaigns. No wise Tory should seek to defy such a deep-rooted public mood; the challenge is not to cut public spending, but to convince the electorate that private provision can deliver better public goods than the state can.

The Chief Secretary's job is to achieve spending targets, not to decide what those targets should be. Throughout his time as Chief Secretary, Mr Major worked to a brief that had been approved by Margaret Thatcher. In 1987 and 1988, there were signs that John Major's virtuous circle had come to pass; the Government was simultaneously cutting taxes, increasing spending and repaying debt. In the event, this could not be sustained – but the reign of virtue was ended not by a lack of fiscal rigour, by by a defective monetary policy.

The Chief Secretary is also the Chancellor's deputy and, as such, entitled to involve himself in all aspects of economic policy; John Major did not make full use of his opportunities. Nigel Lawson was in the habit of holding meetings, attended by junior ministers, senior officials and political advisers, at which the discussion would range over monetary, fiscal and general economic policy. As one would expect from a meeting chaired by Nigel Lawson, these sessions were combative in character: contrasting views were expressed with absolute freedom and equal robustness. Chancellor Lawson enjoyed jousting with his Treasury knights, Sir Peter Middleton and Sir Terry Burns, and with other senior officials. He believed that policy should evolve out of the clash of arguments; he also liked to prove that he was the cleverest man in the room.

John Major did not relish these occasions. He obviously could not have been expected to attend them all: his own duties had to take priority. But he took any excuse to absent himself. Treasury officials were surprised by this, especially as it was well known that John Major saw himself as a future Chancellor; he seemed to be passing up the chance of some on-the-job training. This was widely attributed to a residual intellectual inferiority complex. John Major was not an economist: he could not have matched the debating skills of

Mr Lawson, Sir Peter and Sir Terry. It was assumed that where he could not hope to excel, Mr Major was reluctant to participate.

That was part of the explanation, but only a part. Questions of Chancellorial style were also involved. Nigel Lawson's way of conducting meetings was not to John Major's taste. He thought it produced more heat than light, with the participants encouraged to display their intellectual plumage rather than to concentrate on problem-solving. He was to organize matters very differently when he became Chancellor; there is no evidence that policy-making suffered as a result. Moreover, by 1988 and 1989, Mr Lawson's gatherings had more to do with theatricality than with policy-making. The latter function took place in much smaller meetings, attended only by Nigel Lawson, Peter Middleton and Terry Burns – sometimes indeed only by Mr Lawson and Sir Terry.

There was a further reason, however, why Mr Major absented himself from Mr Lawson's discussions. At that stage, John Major disagreed with a fundamental aspect of the Chancellor's policy. By 1987, Mr Lawson had decided that British membership of the Exchange Rate Mechanism ought to be the basis of counter-inflation policy. In the early 1980s, Mr Major had been in favour of British membership of the ERM. In those days he had shared the widespread belief that Britain needed international backing in the fight against inflation. By 1987, however, he had changed his mind for two reasons: a dislike of Euro-entanglement, and a belief that inflation could only be controlled by the right domestic monetary policy.

In private, Mr Major did express these views to Mr Lawson, but the Chancellor had made up his mind, and that was that. John Major took the view that it would be unwise to disagree with Nigel Lawson in public. First, there would be a danger of leaks; the fact that the Chancellor and the PM were in dispute was creating problems enough without other Treasury ministers joining in. Second, Mr Major felt that his motives might be misinterpreted; he would be accused of siding with the Prime Minister against the Chancellor in order to advance his own career. Later, Mr Major was to change his mind on the ERM; but between 1987 and 1989, he was right to conclude that there would be nothing to be gained from expressing his opinion.

Broad Horizons on a Narrow Boat

In 1987, John Major was still unknown outside Westminster. Even while he was Chief Secretary to the Treasury, he would often stroll out of the Treasury to have a hamburger at the Mc Donald's in Victoria, or a quick lunch at Tevere, a little Italian restaurant in Marsham Street which gives excellent value; he was never recognized. But his name was increasingly discussed in Conservative circles. It was generally acknowledged that he would be a force in the Party during the 1990s; there was increasing speculation that he might be Margaret Thatcher's ultimate successor, and that he might be her own nominee for the post. He had been the first member of his intake to reach the Cabinet, and was second youngest member; the youngest, Malcolm Rifkind, was a Scotsman and therefore a special case. John Major was popular in the House, and had a growing reputation as a departmental minister. Not long after the 1987 election, Norman Tebbit tipped him as Mrs Thatcher's successor; from then on, he was increasingly the subject of newspaper profiles and press speculation. Characteristically, he took little pleasure in this. He often had to be cajoled into co-operating with profile writers, partly because he disliked talking about his early years, and partly because he did not want to be seen to be pushing himself forward. Equally characteristically, he was already thinking hard about his future.

In August 1987, John and Norma Major took a narrow-boat on the Staffordshire canals with Robert and Dulcie Atkins. It was a perfect holiday for a busy Minister – ten days in which he could indulge the rare pleasure of idleness. Sitting in the sun with a pint of beer, listening to the Test match as the boat glided lazily on, and talking politics. One afternoon, he bluntly asked Robert Atkins the question that was exercising him: was there a realistic possibility of his becoming Prime Minister? Robert and he concluded that there was. They also decided on one step that he ought to take; to avoid being over-identified with any one wing of the Party. He had the Prime Minister's approval, and was therefore in good standing with the right of the Party. Through the Fawkes and more recently the Blue Chip, he had many friends on the left of the Party. As ever, he had no enemies. He should, therefore, continue to allow the largest possible number of his colleagues to conclude that his views were broadly in agreement with theirs.

This sounds like an exercise in cynical calculation. Calculated it certainly was; throughout his career, John Major has never stopped calculating. But it was much less cynical than it might appear. John Major had no intention of repudiating Thatcherism. On all the essentials of economic policy, he was in absolute agreement with the Prime Minister. At that stage, too, he shared, her views on Europe. He was also convinced, however, that the Tory Party would have to find a new agenda for the 1990s. Even during the 1987 Election, the voters had not seemed to warm to the Tory Party's attempts to refight the battles of the early 1980s. John Major was certain that a new decade would require a new programme, a new rhetoric and a new infusion of intellectual energy. It was not just self-interest which made him unwilling to align himself with any of the Party's existing factions. He thought that they were becoming increasingly out of date.

John Major showed no reluctance to contribute to the Party's intellectual debate. Throughout his time as Chief Secretary he would often raise the question of a new agenda, and wonder whether he should make a speech or two setting out his views. Two factors prevented him, however. First, he had no time; the demands of his job were such that he simply did not have the scope for leisured reflection. Second, if he had made an agenda-setting speech, it would undoubtedly have been interpreted as the first step in his campaign for the Leadership. He had no wish to encourage such comments, because they would have been entirely justified. John Major did not set out his stall; that would have to wait until he became Prime Minister.

The job of Chief Secretary is so unrelenting in its demands that at least under Tory Governments it is generally reckoned to be unfair to ask anyone to do it for more than a couple of years. By the summer of 1989, therefore, John Major had reason to expect a move; a double reason, indeed. At that stage, the expectation was that Nigel Lawson would serve as Chancellor until the next election, and that John Major would then succeed him. Before he became Chancellor, it would obviously be to his advantage to have run a department of his own. Mr Major himself had mixed feelings about this. It is rare for anyone to look forward to leaving the Treasury, and he was no exception. He was in the position of a bright officer on the General Staff who is aware that he will shortly be promoted, but also knows that the new job will be less interesting. John Major would have been quite happy if the promotion had been cancelled, and he had been asked to stay as Chief Secretary.

In the weeks before the reshuffle, there was growing speculation about John Major's next post; there seemed to be a number of alternatives. It had been predicted that John Moore and Paul Channon would leave the Government, thus creating vacancies at Social Security and Transport respectively. Nicholas Ridley would almost certainly hand over the Department of the Environment to a more voter-friendly colleague. It was also expected that Peter Brooke would hand over the chairmanship of the Party to a more senior figure, and that Tom King would move on from Northern Ireland.

None of these was an obvious vacancy for Mr Major. He had already served as a Social Security minister, so it seemed unlikely that he would return there, while the assumption was that the PM would move him to a higher-ranking Department than Transport. On occasions, John Major had expressed an interest in Northern Ireland, but over the years, Mrs Thatcher had shown a deplorable tendency to treat the Northern Ireland Office as a backwater. It was almost certain that she would want to deploy Mr Major in a post involved in the central thrust of Government economic policy.

John Major's name was canvassed as a possible Party Chairman, but that would not have given him the experience of running a department. There remained Environment, or some other slot in the jigsaw that might fall vacant. In the week before the reshuffle the position became even more confused; David Young and George Younger both announced their retirement from the Government. By reshuffle day – Monday 24 July – neither John Major nor anyone else had a clue as to his fate. At 4.30 that afternoon, he had heard nothing from No. 10, and he was beginning to wonder whether he would be moved. Cabinet Ministers involved in a reshuffle generally know their fate by late afternoon. Norman Lamont, who was hoping to succeed Mr Major as Chief Secretary, arrived in his office to enquire whether anything had been heard from No. 10, and was disappointed to be told that it looked as if there would not be a change of Chief Secretaries. John Major tried to sympathize with Mr Lamont's disappointment, and did not tell him that there was a bottle champagne in the fridge which would be opened regardless: either for a valedictory drink with his private office, or to celebrate the fact that he was staying on at the Treasury. Then the telephone rang; it was Charles Powell, inviting Mr Major to call on the Prime Minister at his earliest convenience.

The PM's decision to remove Geoffrey Howe from the Foreign Office meant that the reshuffle had turned out to be more extensive than anyone had expected. Indeed, it was the most controversial of all Margaret Thatcher's reshuffles – largely due to John Major's new appointment. Mr Major later described his meeting with the Prime Minister: 'She told me to sit down. She asked me how I was, and invited me to become Foreign Secretary . . . Yes, it was a somewhat memorable interview.'[8]

Foreign Secretary

John Major was a largely unknown figure. No one had expected him to become Foreign Secretary. Many commentators – and many Tory MPs – deeply disapproved of the decision to move Geoffrey Howe. Others argued that if there were to be a new Foreign Secretary, it ought to have been Douglas Hurd, whose qualifications were self-evident. John Major caught the backwash of surprise, resentment and scepticism. A number of articles appeared questioning the Prime Minister's judgement in appointing such an unqualified candidate with no knowledge of abroad, and concluding that she must have chosen him to be her poodle in the Foreign Office.

It did seem a curious appointment, but there were two obvious explanations for it. First, by promoting him to one of the great Offices of State, Mrs Thatcher was designating John Major as her heir apparent. If he were to serve as Foreign Secretary until the election and then move on to the Chancellorship, he would be a formidably well-qualified candidate for the premiership. Second, she wanted a Euro-sceptic at the Foreign Office: she regarded Douglas Hurd, himself a former diplomat, as too well-disposed towards the Community.

John Major approached his new responsibilities – and his new officials – in his customary wary manner. He was aware that he had much to learn; as Chief Secretary, he had barely had time to read the foreign news pages in the newspapers, let alone follow foreign affairs in depth. Mr Major had always liked to be sure of his ground before making decisions. Now, as Foreign Secretary, he found himself asked to ratify officials' decisions about issues he had not begun to study. These would be presented to him as purely routine matters: no doubt that was what they told Lord Carrington about the withdrawal of HMS Endurance from the Falklands.

---

8 *Sunday Telegraph*, 8 October 1989.

Parliament was about to rise, and Mr Major had made no holiday plans. He had always expected to spend August reading his way into a new department, so he retired to his garden in Huntingdon while an endless supply of red boxes full of briefing papers arrived from London. (Towards the end of the month, however, the Major family did escape for a few days to the Garel-Jones's country house in Spain, where they are still remembered with affection by the staff.) While in Huntingdon, he also had meetings with officials, happy to escape from London for the day to drink beer in the Foreign Secretary's garden.

Mr Major had entertained some doubts as to how he and the Foreign Office mandarins would take to one another, and whether he would find himself dealing with a group of supercilious characters who would sneer at his ignorance. He need not have worried. He inherited a distinguished collection of senior officials with whom he struck up an easy rapport. Those who reach the heights in the Foreign Office are generally men of the highest calibre, and that was certainly the case in the summer of 1990. Mr Major's suspicions were quickly replaced by admiration.

Apart from Charles Powell, he had most dealings with the officials concerned with European policy. There was Sir David Hannay, the ambassador to the EEC, a tough-minded Jewish Wykehamist whose *modus operandi* is a perfect blend of abrasiveness and finesse. He was reinforced by the then Under-Secretary for the EEC, John Kerr, a witty Scotsman who has one of the best minds in the Foreign Office and the cunning of Ulysses, as John Major recognized. His standard greeting to Mr Kerr was: 'Ah, how is Machiavelli today?' Mr Major took an immediate liking to Sir Ewen Fergusson, the ambassador to Paris. Sir Ewen, with the mien of a Highland Chief, is larger than life in personality as in physique. He played in the scrum for Scotland and only missed a British Lions' tour because of an attack of meningitis. His Bonn counterpart, Sir Christopher Mallaby, is a glittering Old Etonian, who looks like an archetypal mandarin; in any play based on the Bertie Wooster books, he would make a perfect Jeeves.

These formidable characters were reinforced by Stephen Wall, the Foreign Secretary's Principal Private Secretary. Ten years previously, Ewen Fergusson was coming to an end of his tour of duty as David Owen's Private Secretary; Mr Wall had been one of his juniors.

The question of a replacement for the then Mr Fergusson was raised with the Foreign Secretary. 'Why don't we just promote Stephen?' suggested Dr Owen. The Foreign Office had some difficulty in persuading David Owen that this would be an unacceptable disruption of hierarchy and career structures. Mr Wall continued to rise, at a more orthodox pace.

Mr Major had no problems with his officials, and he had also inherited an able team of junior ministers, among whom Francis Maude and William Waldegrave, both Ministers of State, were particularly highly regarded. With Mr Maude, John Major at once struck up an easy working relationship; with Mr Waldegrave, matters were more complicated. Perhaps because William Waldegrave won so many academic distinctions at such an early age, he seems to have difficulty in adjusting to the fact that some of his political contemporaries have surpassed him. Mr Waldegrave arrived at the House at the same time as John Major, and had been the first of the two to join the Government. He may have felt that the wrong man was Foreign Secretary, and the wrong man Minister of State. Some of those around Mr Major also suspected that indiscreet remarks by Mr Waldegrave had inspired press comments about the Foreign Secretary's inexperience.

As John Major worked through his boxes, two issues stood out at the head of the agenda. The first was Europe. On the EEC, John Major's instincts were similar to Margaret Thatcher's. He approved of the Common Market and of free trade, but was strongly opposed to any sort of federalism; he had been opposed to the British membership of the ERM. His ideal was de Gaulle's: a Europe of nation states (*l'Europe des patries*). Unlike Margaret Thatcher, however, John Major was ready to acknowledge that instinct was not enough, and that Gaullism no longer seemed to be on offer. He also began to conclude that Mrs Thatcher's Euro-diplomacy was ineffective. Mr Major's critics have a simple explanation for this change of mood: that not for the first time, an inexperienced politician had been nobbled by the Euro-fanatics of the Foreign Office. The truth is much more complex.

The diplomats did influence John Major's thinking, though neither David Hannay nor John Kerr could be described as Euro-fanatics. From them, he learned of the frustrations involved in being constantly one versus eleven, and of the diplomatic opportunities foregone because of the PM's insistence on fighting every last battle over every last syllable. They told the new Foreign Secretary that though Britain was winning a lot of ground over the Single Market, we could be even more successful if we adopted a more subtle approach. They also argued that although many Europeans were determined to make some progress towards Economic and Monetary Union and were reluctant to repudiate the Delors Report, the dangers of loss of economic independence had been much exaggerated. In reality, several other Governments secretly shared Margaret Thatcher's reservations – but they had been deterred from expressing their views openly because they did not want to appear to share her anti-Community stance – symbolized, in their view, by her refusal to join the ERM.

Mr Major arrived at three conclusions. The first was that the British economy and our hopes of prosperity were inextricably bound up with Europe. The second was that the Community would inevitably continue to evolve, at a pace that might be faster than we would like – but which would in no way realize the ambitions of the federalists. Finally, he decided that we ought to adopt a different diplomatic style. Needless to say, he shared none of these thoughts with Margaret Thatcher; had he done so, she would have been horrified and might instantly have lost faith in his judgement of foreign affairs, and in her own favourable assessment of his merits. It was not self-preservation, however, that inhibited him. He knew that he could only hope to achieve a gradual reorientation of British diplomacy if he retained the Prime Minister's confidence. In order to do that he would have to minimize the significance of what he was trying to do. So by the time John Major left the Foreign Office, he had his own agenda on Europe.

John Major had decided that he too wanted to be a good European. But his was not the little Europeanism of M Delors. His vision of Europe included not only the EFTA countries but also the emergent democracies of Eastern Europe. He wanted to see free markets and free trade across the entire continent, and he wanted Britain to play a leading role in shaping a new, wider Europe. His agenda also included British membership of the ERM. After Madrid, John Major had instantly grasped the point which Mrs Thatcher herself was still reluctant to admit: that her concessions had fatally undermined her capacity for continued resistance. This diplomatic assessment was reinforced by his political judgement. The ERM was dividing the Tory Party; it made the Government appear disunited and indecisive. In Mr Major's view, it was silly to suffer this degree of political damage from an issue which had in fact been resolved. During his period as Foreign Secretary, Mr Major regularly insisted that the question was no longer whether Britain would join the ERM, but when – and that the only remaining difficulty was the inflation rate.

The second item which demanded a lot of Mr Major's attention was South Africa. Here again, he had the benefit of outstanding diplomats. Sir Robin Renwick, the ambassador in Pretoria, has been much the most successful and influential foreign diplomat in the history of modern South Africa. During Mr Major's time as Foreign Secretary, the two men did not actually meet, but on the basis of the telegram traffic and frequent telephone conversations, John Major developed an affection and respect for Sir Robin, whom he referred to as 'the Governor-General'. On South Africa, the Foreign Secretary had no disagreements with the Prime Minister. He entirely shared her view – which was also Robin Renwick's – about the fatuity of economic sanctions. The Nationalist Government was irrevocably committed to reform, partly because apartheid could never have been reconciled with the needs of a modern economy. What South Africa needed was encouragement – and investment. That, however, was not the view of the Commonwealth – and there was due to be a CHOGM – Commonwealth Heads of Government Meeting – that October, in Malaysia. As Foreign Secretary, John Major had to join other foreign ministers to draft a communiqué, while the heads of Government enjoyed a more leisurely routine.

The Foreign Minister's meeting was chaired by the Canadian representative, Joe Clark. The English party regarded him as a good chairman. Throughout the session, the Australian Foreign Minister, Senator Gareth Evans, took a leading role, as if he was determined single-handedly to maintain his countrymen's reputation for blunt-spokenness. He had clearly been trained in the Sir Les Patterson school of diplomacy. At one stage during their seventeen-hour drafting session, the Zimbabwean Foreign Minister began to nitpick at some detail in the text. 'Geez,' expostulated Senator Evans; 'we're not here to draft the fucking Koran.' At that point the Malaysian Foreign Minister rolled his eyes and drew his finger across his windpipe.

By the end of the drafting meeting, Mr Major could feel proud of his handiwork. He had persuaded his fellow Foreign Ministers to restrain their enthusiasm for sanctions. Though this in no way reflected the British Government's policy, it did represent a significant shift by the Commonwealth. The new Foreign Secretary had performed well in his first attempt at detailed international negotiations. Margaret Thatcher, however, was too dismissive of the Commonwealth to give John Major the credit he deserved for nudging it in the direction of common sense. What struck her about the draft communiqué was not the extent to which the other Foreign Ministers had moved away from ignorance and prejudice, but the extent to which it still fell short of British Government policy. She set out to put that right. Charles Powell was asked to draft a supplementary communiqué, setting out HMG's views. John Major had no objection, either to the idea of a communiqué or to Mr Powell's text: it was issued.

Then the mayhem started. Encouraged by Senator Evans, the other Foreign Ministers and their Heads of Government were furious – and their reaction was understandable. The only purpose of the whole exercise had been to arrive at an agreed Commonwealth line, and in pursuit of this, the others had gone to considerable trouble to accommodate the British Government. Now Mrs Thatcher was treating them with contempt (they were right about that) and the British Government had been acting in bad faith (she had never had any faith in the Commonwealth). The British diplomatic correspondents seized on the whole issue. Some newspapers invented a rift between John Major and the Prime Minister: there had been no rift. Others claimed that the Foreign Secretary was simply acting as her lackey. That was also untrue. Mr Major had seen no reason to object to Mrs Thatcher issuing her statement; he had not realized that the others would be so upset.

Such an oversight did display a degree of *naïveté*. Then again, it was John Major's first CHOGM; he had not fully grasped the extent of the bad blood that had developed over the years between Mrs Thatcher and the other Commonwealth leaders. The real problem in Malaysia was created, not by Mr Major, nor by the other Foreign Ministers – nor even by Margaret Thatcher. It arose from the fatuity of the Commonwealth itself, 'the ghost of the deceased British Empire, sitting crowned upon the grave thereof' to paraphrase Hobbes. Any attempt to negotiate a joint foreign policy position between Britain and the rest was bound to be unsatisfactory, and unlike the EEC, there were no important British interests to safeguard.

While John Major was in Malaysia, events in London were moving to a crisis which would result in a premature end to his tenure of the Foreign Office. Once Nigel Lawson had resigned, Downing Street wasted little time in discussing his successor; Mr Major was the obvious choice. As he left the Prime Minister's study on his appointment as Chancellor of the Exchequer, he took Charles Powell's arm: 'Just when I had at last worked out where Mogadishu is.'

In his three months as Foreign Secretary, John Major had concentrated on mastering his brief, and had taken less interest than usual in British domestic politics. Before going to Malaysia, however, he had paid a visit to another Third World conference centre in Blackpool. There, he delivered a platform speech to the Tory Party Conference. In 1986, he had addressed the hall on the subject of social security, but in those days he had been only a junior minister in a peripheral debate. Now he was giving one of the most important speeches of the week, and was virtually obliged to earn himself a standing ovation. In advance, he was nervous, understandably enough.

John Major's anxieties were further increased by Nigel Lawson's performance. 1989 was the year of anti-communist revolutions. All over Eastern Europe, the puppet regimes were being swept from power, and all over the Winter Gardens, Blackpool, the triumph of democracy was being hailed by Tory ministers in need of an uplifting theme. No one had more need of uplift than Nigel Lawson; no one plundered Eastern Europe more ruthlessly. Listening to him, the poor Foreign Secretary complained bitterly that by the time it came to the one Conference speech in which Eastern Europe *had* to be discussed – his own – everyone would be fed up hearing about it. In the event, his speech went well, although it was not an inspiring text. But after a nervous beginning, in which some of his jokes fell flat, he recovered, imposed his authority on the audience, and won his standing ovation.

Despite the difficulties, John Major had enjoyed his time at the Foreign Office. He had been aware from the beginning that sections of the press would be determined to put an unfavourable construction on his relationship with Margaret Thatcher: 'There is a double jeopardy . . . If I take the same view as the Prime Minister, it will be said that I am just a placeman. But if I have differences with the PM and they become public knowledge, everyone says, "Ah! Splits." ' He saw no easy solution to this: 'Everyone will have to make their own judgement when I've done it for a while.' That judgement was aborted by events, but at the end of that *Sunday Telegraph* interview, I gave my provisional assessment of the Foreign Secretary's progress: 'John Major . . . is a cheerful man, in excellent spirits, relishing his job and increasingly confident of his own powers. This is a confidence many others will soon come to share.'[9]

Chancellor Of The Exchequer

It had been an extraordinary few months. Very few men have ever held three Cabinet posts in the same year.[10] In mid-summer, as Chief Secretary, John Major had conducted the opening negotiations with the Foreign Office on next year's spending round. In the early autumn, as Foreign Secretary, he had presented the FO's case. Now, as Chancellor, he would announce the results of the whole exercise in his Autumn Statement.

John Major had achieved one of his greatest political ambitions, but these were hardly the circumstances in which he would have chosen to inherit the Treasury. After ten years of Thatcherism, the inflation rate was once again surging towards 10 per cent. There is no painless way of dealing with inflation; it has to be squeezed out of the system by raising the price of credit and depressing the level of economic activity. Ministers had taken action accordingly, raising the interest rate to 15 per cent, the latest increase coming on the eve of the Tory Party Conference despite objections from the Party Chairman, Kenneth Baker. High interest rates were hurting businesses and mortgage-payers – but the pain was more evident than the cure. By November 1989, it was clear that the Government had tightened monetary policy sufficiently to make a recession inevitable. It was less clear when inflation would start falling.

From the first, Chancellor Major was aware of his dual responsibilities, political as well as economic. John Major hates inflation, and was determined to bring it down and keep it down. As regards high interest rates and the squeeze, he would often repeat the maxim: 'If it isn't hurting, it isn't working.' However, he was also aware of the need to ensure that an economic recovery was under way in time for the next Election. Those objectives were not easy to reconcile. In November 1989, the Parliament was passing its half-way stage, and the recession was only just beginning. It was becoming increasingly harder to harmonize the economic cycle and the electoral cycle.

---

9 *Sunday Telegraph*, 8 October 1989.

10 Tom King is one example, but a closer parallel is Harold Macmillan. He started 1955 as Minister of Defence, in April he became Foreign Secretary, and on 20 December he too moved to the Treasury. He became Prime Minister on 10 January 1957, thus beating John Major by about ten days on the final leg.

When John Major arrived at the Treasury, he found that a debate was taking place over the level of interest rates. There were those who thought that it would be better to raise them still higher in order to accelerate the recession. The quicker it occurred, the faster it would work, and the more time it would leave for a pre-election recovery. Some officials felt that Mr Major could use the markets' nervousness over Nigel Lawson's resignation as an excuse to put up interest rates by a further point. Over the next few weeks, Mr Major's successor as Chief Secretary, Norman Lamont, often advocated a 1 or even 2 per cent rise. John Major resisted their arguments.

He had concluded that 15 per cent ought to be high enough. Throughout his time as Chancellor, Mr Major always tried to keep in touch with the real economy beyond the statistics; on the basis of both his own travels around the country and of conversations with his colleagues, he believed that the squeeze was as tight as was necessary. In view of this, he felt able to take account of political arguments.

John Major wanted to protect Mrs Thatcher. If he had increased interest rates immediately on becoming Chancellor, the first beneficiary would have been Anthony Meyer. As we have seen, even after the defeat of Sir Anthony, the then PM's position remained precarious. A further hike in interest rates during the early months of 1990 would have guaranteed a disaster for the Tories in the May 1990 local elections; that could have finished off Margaret Thatcher.

In giving such weight to political considerations, Mr Major was not being irresponsible. He had first satisfied himself that his economic judgement was correct. The use of interest rates to manage the economy is not an exact science. It has been likened to using an elastic band to pull a brick along a table (a popular metaphor in the Treasury). First nothing happens, then you get a brick on the nose. John Major wished to avoid that fate; he felt that the downward pressure on the economy was already sufficiently great.

Once Mr Major had taken the decision to leave interest rates unaltered, counter-inflation policy became a matter of waiting, hoping and riding out market fluctuations. All Chancellors have to guard against the danger of becoming obsessed by the markets, whose short-term reactions can often seem perverse. Nigel Lawson, who himself possessed many of the instincts of a trader, found it impossible to restrain his annoyance when he thought that the actual traders had got it wrong. The Treasury was relieved to find that John Major found it easier to remain detached; officials were certain that this was the correct response, both for the stability of policy and for the Chancellor's peace of mind.

On inflation and monetary policy, John Major could do little to shape events. Policy had been set; his main task was to stick to the agreed course. Nor did he have much room for manoeuvre when it came to fiscal policy. As the Government was trying to depress demand, there was no scope for tax cuts, nor was the cash available. As the recession bit, revenues shrank, expenditures rose and budget surpluses evaporated. After the excitements of 1988, even Nigel Lawson had only managed a workmanlike Budget in 1989; John Major was condemned to another workmanlike Budget in 1990.

Within the strictly limited resources available to him, he tried to be as interesting and innovative as possible. He set out not only to devise a Budget for savings, but also to provide some assistance for businessmen. The Budget's main features were the introduction of TESSAs (tax exempt savings allowances) and the abolition of composite rate taxation, helping savers who did not pay income tax. Smaller businesses benefited from an increase in the VAT threshold and from the introduction of tax relief on bad debts.

The Budget received a cautiously favourable reception in the City, and there was a widespread view on the Tory benches that the Chancellor had done as well as could be expected given the economic situation. That was a judgement with which John Major was happy to concur: at that stage, he hoped that he would have the opportunity to frame a more memorable Budget, in easier circumstances.

There was one area of policy, however, where Mr Major could hope to shape events: Europe. Although Foreign Secretary Major had concentrated on the diplomatic aspects of Britain's relationship with the EEC, he had also become aware of the urgency of a positive response to the Delors proposals. Now, as Chancellor, it was his task to frame that response, subject of course to Margaret Thatcher's approval. He had a good ally in Douglas Hurd, his successor at the FO. The two men had already found a high regard for one another; this quickly developed into a firm friendship and an effective working partnership. They would often breakfast together. Political journalists became aware of this, and began referring to the 'Hurd/Major' axis, which, they claimed, had replaced the 'Howe/Lawson' axis and was equally hostile to Margaret Thatcher's vision of Europe. Again, the reality was more complex.

Douglas Hurd and John Major did work well together, and they also shared the view that Mrs Thatcher's Euro-diplomacy was inadequate. Equally, they had a strong hand; three Foreign Secretaries and two Chancellors in one year was quite enough; the PM was in no position to lose any more senior Ministers. Even so, they adopted an entirely different approach from Sir Geoffrey and Mr Lawson. Their aim was to encourage Margaret Thatcher to edge beyond her own negative instincts to a more constructive policy. In 1985, as Northern Ireland Secretary, Mr Hurd and the Cabinet Secretary Sir Robert Armstrong had been involved in a similar exercise over the Anglo-Irish Agreement (not an inspiring precedent). On Europe, as over Ulster, the aim was to persuade Margaret Thatcher, not to coerce her. In this, both men had an indispensable advantage which Geoffrey Howe never enjoyed and which Nigel Lawson had forfeited many months before he left office: good relations with Margaret Thatcher. That was hardly surprising in Mr Major's case; he was her protégé. Over the years, however, Douglas Hurd had proved most adept in handling his relations with Margaret Thatcher. He and she would never be bone of one another's bone, but he had always displayed a sure touch in his dealings with the PM. When he was Home Secretary, it had been his practice to keep her fully informed of any contentious issues that were likely to arise, so that he would be able to anticipate her reactions. As Foreign Secretary, he continued to handle his potentially most difficult bilateral diplomacy with aplomb.

Mr Hurd and Mr Major were in agreement on the ERM; they also had to devise a response to the Delors Report. In 1988, Chancellor Lawson had sought to counter it with a proposal for competing currencies, under which all citizens of EEC countries would have the right to use the currency of any member-state they chose. But Mr Lawson's proposal, which had never seemed more than a *jeu d'esprit*, was not taken seriously by the other eleven.

In January 1990, Mr Hurd and Mr Major were offered an alternative. Charles Powell had lunch with Sir Michael Butler, a former ambassador to the European Community who is now a director of Hambro's, and Sir Michael told him that another banker, Paul Richards of Samuel Montagu, had prepared a paper advocating a 'hard ecu'.[11] This would be a new European currency, which could

---

11 Ecu stands for European currency unit, whose value is linked to a basket of EEC currencies. The ecu was also a pre-revolutionary French coin, roughly equivalent to the English crown (or five shilling piece.) So yet again, the French have ensured that the Community's language and institutions defer to French traditions.

not depreciate. It would therefore be the hardest of all European currencies, and a means of imposing counter-inflationary discipline on all member states. Mr Powell was struck by the cogency of Mr Richards' plan. He transmitted it to the PM and to Messrs Hurd and Major, all three of whom shared his reaction. Within a few weeks, the hard ecu was Government policy; Mr Major made the announcement in a speech on 21 June.

In British eyes, the hard ecu had two decisive advantages over any single currency proposal likely to emerge from the Delors Report. The first was its anti-inflationary credentials; the second, its democratic ones. No one would be forced to use the hard ecu; its success of failure would depend on the free choice of the 330 million or so potential consumers of currency in the nations of the EEC. The hard ecu was popular in the Tory Party. The Europhiles welcomed the Government's constructive approach; the Euro-sceptics were reassured by its commitment to the free market. However, many of those who were congratulating Mr Major had not faced up to the full implications of the new plan; some of them seemed to believe that the hard ecu would amount to nothing more than a travellers' cheque for cosmopolitan sophisticates. That could turn out to be a gross underestimate. The hard ecu is far more appealing than the regulatory rigidities of the Delors plan; it could become a free marketeer's route to a single EEC currency. If it did circulate widely, the issuing authority would quickly evolve into a European central bank – another aspect of the Delors proposals which was repugnant to many Tories. It would be an irony if it were a Government headed by Margaret Thatcher which proved to have opened the road to European monetary union.

Initially, some of the other EEC states seemed determined to keep the hard ecu road closed. There were sceptical reactions from M Delors and the French – predictably. Less predictable was the apparent lack of support from the Germans. HMG had expected the Germans to welcome the hard ecu; after all, it alleviated the Bundesbank's anxieties about the consequences of monetary union. The Germans were particularly suspicious about calls for a democratic European monetary policy; they saw this as mere unscrupulous populism, and were convinced that 'democratic' was being employed as a euphemism for 'looser'. They had no wish to dissolve the Bundesbank into some Euro-mishmash of laxity and inflation. The hard ecu promised a monetary regimen at least as tough as the Bundesbank's: it could indeed end up as *Deutschmark über Alles*. But the Germans, perhaps because they are still uneasy about pursuing a Euro-diplomacy independently from the French, hung back. However, John Major reacted exactly as he was to react some months later over the question of a safe haven for the Kurds. He ignored rebuffs, and pressed ahead with his initiative. As of the middle of 1991, the hard ecu seems to have a secure place on the Euro-agenda.

The ERM

Chancellor Major may not have shared Chancellor Lawson's obsession with the markets, but in one respect, he did find their behaviour a source of growing irritation. By the spring of 1990, the pound had become ridiculously vulnerable to rumours about British membership of the ERM. No Chancellor can be happy with a situation in which a single newspaper article could produce a sterling crisis and its attendant political crisis. In his days as Chief Secretary, John Major had been inclined to agree with the argument that the ERM would not work because it was an attempt to buck the market. As Chancellor, he found that the markets in favour of British membership of the ERM. Staying out meant bucking them; the consequences were unpleasant.

The markets had concluded that as long as the British Government was hanging back from ERM membership, its commitment to counter-inflation could not be taken seriously. Though Mr Major thought this was an unfair conclusion, he found himself increasingly persuaded of a modified version of the markets' argument. He decided that no British Government committed to counter-inflation need fear membership of the ERM, which was bound to operate as a reinforcing discipline. By 1990, John Major was determined to expedite British membership of the ERM.

The PM's opposition was weakening, partly because she had been worn down by relentless pressure, and partly because she too is a politician, and could recognize the moment when it was no longer possible to defend a lost cause. The resignation of Nicholas Ridley on 14 July further undermined her political will, as well as removing an important anti-ERM voice from the Cabinet room. Inevitably, if unfairly, the absurd circumstances of Mr Ridley's resignation also served to discredit his views. Within a few days of Nick Ridley's departure, the PM had agreed in principle that Britain should join in the autumn. In so doing, she had also agreed to modify one of the Madrid conditions, and to accept that it would no longer be necessary to wait until inflation rates had converged, or even until the British inflation rate had started falling. The only requirement would be a guarantee that inflation was now under control. As to the timing of British membership, attention focused on a number of dates in early October.

Between July and October, the ERM issue was kept under review at a series of high-level secret meetings between the Prime Minister and the Chancellor. Every attempt was made – successfully – to avoid a leak of market-sensitive information. So tightly was the 'need-to-know' criterion drawn that the Foreign Secretary himself was not informed of the actual date until twenty-four hours before the decision was announced. Right until the last moment, some of the others feared that the Prime Minister would resile; she did not. The decision to join was announced after the markets closed on 5 October: technically, British membership took effect from Monday 8 October 1990. It was accompanied by a 1 per cent cut in interest rates – a *douceur* which had helped to assuage any final Prime Ministerial doubts. Slightly less than a year earlier, Nigel Lawson had resigned partly because he had despaired of ever being allowed to implement his strategy and join the ERM. Now John Major had succeeded. To judge by Mr Lawson's subsequent behaviour, his admiration for his erstwhile deputy's success may also have been tinged with resentment.

John Major had enjoyed his first year as Chancellor, and in the opinion of most of his colleagues, he had settled in well. From the start, no one had even pretended not to take him seriously; his suitability for the job had never been questioned. On his return to the Treasury, Mr Major experienced none of the self-doubt which had accompanied all his previous ministerial postings. His appointment was also welcomed by the senior officials in the Treasury. Though they had all found it immensely stimulating to work for Nigel Lawson, they had also become increasingly aware that the strained relations between No. 10 and No. 11 were making it harder to run a coherent economic policy.

From the beginning, John Major introduced his own distinctive working methods. There were no more large policy meetings run on adversarial lines. The new Chancellor preferred smaller groups, whose discussions were conducted in a much more measured manner. Indeed, some of those who took part have said that there was an almost Japanese atmosphere, with everyone searching for consensus. They came to realize, however, that despite his gentler tone, John Major was just as determined to have his own way as Nigel Lawson had been. It might appear consensual; it was Mr Major's consensus. Mr Lawson liked meetings that ended with corpses all over the stage; Mr Major preferred light banter and general agreement – on his terms.

The Chancellor also adopted a different attitude to speech-writing. Nigel Lawson had approached every major speech with at least one eye on posterity, as if he wanted each text to be a memorial more enduring than brass. He did much of the final drafting himself, but the preparatory stages consumed a great deal of Treasury manpower. Mr Major was less vaulting in his ambition. For any important occasion, he wanted a good speech, but when he was presented with one, he was happy. There was none of his predecessor's striving for literary immortality.

John Major's did have more immediate concerns. His parliamentary colleagues knew that he would have a crucial role in fighting the next election; it was his task to deliver an election-winning blend of economic recovery and counter-inflation. A growing number of Tory MPs also took it for granted that success might well deliver him the succession. Events turned out differently. Just over a year after becoming Chancellor, John Major received his second promotion within the Treasury. He became its First Lord, and also Prime Minister.

10 The Prime Minister

Thatcherism

John Major is the youngest Prime Minister of the twentieth century; at the time of his appointment he had served for the shortest period in the House of Commons than any of the previous Premiers. Whether he was also the least well-known figure to become Premier is debatable: it is almost impossible to compare the public standing of modern politicians with that of their predecessors before the age of saturation political coverage on television. It is indisputable, however, that he was the least well-known to the political classes.

Mr Major had followed the strategy he and Robert Atkins had devised on the canals of Staffordshire. He arrived in No. 10 with no ideological baggage train, beholden to no faction. The commentators who rushed to the archives to discover what manner of man had just become Prime Minister discovered very few major (in either sense of the word) speeches, containing no distinctive political philosophy. He had not begun the task of defining his agenda for the 1990s, which meant that at least he could start with a blank sheet of paper in No. 10. It would be hard for anyone to quote his own words against him. So, the commentators were forced to rely on the impressions that the new PM's colleagues had of him. These, too, were divergent. Right-wingers would insist that he was the Lady's anointed; Left-wingers would claim that he was not a Thatcherite. His campaign team had included those whose Thatcherite credentials were impeccable, such as David Davis, Michael Howard, Norman Lamont, Peter Lilley, Francis Maude and Richard Ryder. But two of his closest friends, Robert Atkins and David Mellor, were both Wets.

The new PM had inherited a Party in a state of considerable emotional turmoil. In some circles, the fact that he could claim to be a healer and a unifier was an asset; in others, it aroused suspicion and the fear of backsliding. From all sides, the same question was asked: where did he stand in relationship to Thatcherism?

Thatcherism has two aspects. In the first place, it is economic liberalism given political flesh. As such, its triumph in British politics is absolute. Incomes policy and a structural PSBR, those nostrums of the 1990s, are now consigned to the realm of economic archaeology. Even the Labour Party now claims that the market, the conquest of inflation and the control of public spending are at the heart of its economic thinking, and Labour politicians know that they must strive desperately to maintain that claim if they are to have any hope of being elected. John Smith, meanwhile, is formulating a set of tax proposals which, though they would be a foolish and damaging concession to the politics of envy, are still likely to be lower than the ones which prevailed Geoffrey Howe's first Budget. We are all Thatcherites now.

Thatcherite economic thinking is not only a British phenomenon: it is capturing the agenda in every continent. Never has a set of political ideas swept round the world so quickly. Obviously, this was not all achieved by one woman; in the late 1970s, the old economic order was collapsing, and Margaret Thatcher was only one of many figures proclaiming that collapse and advocating a free-market alternative. She was also the most charismatic of those advocates. Anyone who doubts her role as the demiurge of a new economic dispensation should visit Eastern Europe and see the eyes light up when her name is mentioned.

In Britain, however, Thatcherism was more than an economic creed. At its heart – at her heart – were patriotism and national revival. Margaret Thatcher could have said, paraphrasing de Gaulle, that she had always had a certain idea of Britain. Her economic views took on their urgency and stridency because she was convinced that they were best for Britain. She was equally convinced of their moral authority. Her belief in hard work and thrift, her abhorrence of borrowing and debt had nothing to do with economic theory, and would have had many professors of economics shifting uneasily in their seats. Her views derived from the Nonconformist conscience, as transmitted in a Tory version by Alderman Roberts. His daughter was the latest, greatest and possibly the final flowering of the Nonconformist conscience in British politics.

Any political creed evolved by such a personality from such sources will inevitably have more crusading zeal than intellectual coherence. To an economic Thatcherite, mortgage-interest tax relief ought to be an abomination. Margaret Thatcher would not even listen to the arguments against it. There were others who believed that the liberal economics of Thatcherism should form part of a libertarian approach to social questions; they were given equally short shrift. Greatly daring, a friend of hers once ventured to suggest that anyone who believed in freedom ought to favour a relaxation of the laws on the possession of marijuana. Again, there was no counter-argument, merely a horrified expression quickly culminating in a basilisk glare: 'That would be like legalizing theft,' snapped Mrs Thatcher. Margaret Thatcher believes that people should be free to do what they ought to do.

It is not possible to resolve all the paradoxes in Margaret Thatcher's creed. She believed in the conventional pieties; she also railed against the established order. She was once asked what she had changed, and replied 'everything'. That may not have been an accurate statement; it certainly expressed her desires. Just as reality fell short of desire, her actions and her rhetoric were often in contradiction. Anyone examining the Government's actual record might well have concluded that, in most respects, this was a pragma-tic Conservative administration, introducing change gradually and working with the grain of events. Anyone listening to Margaret Thatcher might find it incomprehensible that she had agreed to the Rhodesia/Zimbabwe settlement, the Anglo-Irish Agreement, the European Single Act and the decision to join the ERM, not to mention the steady increase in public expenditure.

Mrs Thatcher regularly exercised the privilege of her sex, refusing to reconcile the particular and the general. This was apparent in her view of the Civil Service. She generally appeared to regard civil servants *en masse* as second rate, on the grounds that if they were any good, they would have been in the private sector. But her attitude could not have been more different to the civil servants who worked for her; she often seemed to value them more highly than her ministers.

However long Margaret Thatcher had remained Prime Minister, there would have been paradoxes and contradictions. This was part of her political genius, but there were also costs. On certain areas of social policy, Thatcherism had nothing to say. Mrs Thatcher herself never developed a strategy for the public services, or for the under-class. The fact that she often gave the impression of gravely distrust-ing the former and slightly despising the latter enabled Opposition politicians to alarm the electorate by talk of 'cuts', when the Government was pouring additional billions into the public services every year.

Mrs Thatcher's approach was unsuccessful administratively as well as politically. There was little attempt to ensure value for money; new spending often reinforced bad old habits. This was particularly true of education, which remained, despite eleven and a half years of Thatcherism, the least Thatcherized area of British society. In far too many schools, the clock had stopped at the end of the 1960s. Towards the end of the 1980s, an increasing number of thoughtful Tories were aware of these problems, and wished that the Government would tackle them. There was a widespread feeling, however, that this would not happen as long as Mrs Thatcher was Leader. Once everything else went wrong for her, that was a contributory factor in her downfall. It also meant that Mr Major would be able to rely on extensive backbench support should he decide, not only to consolidate and extend Thatcherism, but also to remedy its deficiencies.

Majorism

In one respect, John Major is a stern and unbending Thatcherite. He rivals his predecessor in his dislike of inflation – 'First and foremost, I loathe inflation'[1] – and of public sector deficits. On both, he is determined that his Government will maintain her commitment – and improve on her record. However, he has also made clear his determination to move beyond the battles of the 1980s and to articulate a new vision for the 1990s.

Six days after becoming Prime Minister, Mr Major used his first important speech to begin the process of outlining his own philosophy. He declared that his primary purpose was 'to build a truly open society. Open because we believe that every man and woman should be able to go as far as their talent, ambition and effort take them.' He went on to link the drive for openness, not only to opportunity, but also to compassion and the public services: ' . . . amidst the inevitable competitive thrust of life, it should be a compassionate society . . . because some people do need a special helping hand to . . . enjoy a full life of choice and independence.'

In February, he went into more detail in a speech to the Young Conservative Conference – these days, a hard-line Thatcherite audience. He told them that education was 'at the top of my personal

---

1 Speech delivered at the Queen Elizabeth II Conference Centre, London, 4 December 1990.

agenda for the 1990s' and although he paid a pro forma tribute to some of the education reforms the Tory Party had introduced in the 1980s, he admitted that 'as a nation we cannot be proud of what has been done over the past thirty years for many of our children. Too many of them have been allowed to expect too little of themselves and too many other people have expected too little of them.' He broadened his theme to include all the public services: 'We must never accept the contention that limited Government means lower standards. That state services should be second best. I want to see an unending search for quality in all our public services.'[2]

In March, in the most important and comprehensive speech he has yet delivered, to the Conservative Party's Central Council, he again devoted his attention to the public services, committing himself to 'a citizen's charter to deliver quality in every part of [the] public service'[3] and went on to describe how this citizen's charter might work. There were three principles.

First, those who depend on public services must know where they stand and what they have a right to expect. Second, the quality of services provided will be enhanced by 'injecting competition, extending privatization and widening competitive tendering.'[4] Third, that there should be measures to ' . . . enforce accountability and achieve quality control . . . We will define clear and appropriate mechanisms for enforcing standards right across the public service. Sometimes an audit function. Sometimes an ombudsman. Sometimes simply the separation of powers between those who provide services and those who check on them . . . We will enforce publication of results by public services, make inspectorates truly independent and make properly accountable those who are in control of those services.'

It is easier to outline the principles governing such a programme than to implement it in detail. From the Southport speech, it was clear that Mr Major and his advisers have given thought to the topic. The Citizen's Charter is much more than a mere electioneering slogan; it is a commitment to several years' hard slog in Government. It will also involve remedying one of Thatcherism's principal deficiencies.

Through the privatization programme, Thatcherism did ensure that hitherto inefficient areas of the economy were subjected to the disciplines of the private sector. Beyond that, however, there was no attempt to transform the machinery of Government. This works well in two areas: the traditional Whitehall function of giving policy

---

2 Scarborough, 9 February 1991.

3 Southport, 23 March 1991.

4 Ibid.

advice to Ministers, and the armed forces. For the rest, nothing has happened in the 1980s to reverse the deterioration of the 1960s and 1970s. Bureaucratization, unionization and proletarianization have continued to encroach on institutions such as schools and hospitals, eradicating *esprit de corps*. Much of the lower reaches of the public sector has become demoralized. Privatization plus a machinery of audit and inspection would help to put this right, but it will take time. Nor are there are likely to be many set-piece engagements, such as the Miners' Strike, which destroyed the National Union of Mineworkers. The battles against NALGO, NUPE and the NUT will have to be fought as a war of attrition through a *bocage* of town halls and class-rooms.

It will be a campaign well worth winning, for success would help complete one of the great historic tasks of the Tory Party: the universalization of Conservative values. In the mid-nineteenth century, some of the Tory Party's most profound thinkers, including Salisbury, feared that the advent of democracy would inevitably lead to a coalition of the propertyless against the propertied, and that the social order itself could perish in the ensuing conflict. Since then, practitioners of Tory politics – including Salisbury as Prime Minister rather than pamphleteer – have set out to prove them wrong. The Second Reform Bill; Empire preference; the property-owning democracy; the era of 'you've never had it so good'[5]; the sale of council houses; the promotion of wider share-ownership – all were attempts by the Tory Party to break out of demographic limitations. The aim was to help consolidate Conservatism by creating the social preconditions for Conservatism. John Major proposes to capture more new territory.

Many Conservatives and most Labour politicians still think instinctively that certain policy issues – health, social services, *et al* – are Labour preserves, which certain population groups – principally municipal tenants and the poor – are Labour's people. John Major rejects both assumptions. Where Mrs Thatcher practised the dictatorship of the bourgeoisie, his aim is the universalization of the bourgeoisie. If he can transform this aspiration into a policy, Labour would have no ground left.

The Hundred Hour War

John Major may have inherited the premiership admirably unburdened by a philosophical past; he also inherited tasks more urgent

---

5 Macmillan actually said, 'Most of our people have never had it so good.'

than philosophy. When Mr Major took office, the forces of twenty-four nations were assembling in Saudi Arabia and the Gulf to strike at Saddam Hussein and to free Kuwait. Margaret Thatcher had been a talismanic figure in the mobilization of those forces; without her decisiveness and inspiration, there might well have been no Alliance, and she had continued to play a decisive role in its high councils. Britain's actual commitment of troops may have been dwarfed by that of the United States, but with Mrs Thatcher in charge, we still supplied a significant proportion of the Alliance's will.

Few of the Allies had expected Margaret Thatcher to fall; most of them knew nothing about John Major. Almost all reacted with dismay to events in Britain, and wondered what it would portend for the war effort. There was a voluminous signal traffic out of the Allied embassies in London, as all the information that could be mustered about Mr Major was relayed to the various capitals; inevitably, the telegrams were stronger on facts than on reassurance.

It was not only the Allies who had to be reassured. Out in the desert, British forces were preparing for combat. They all knew Margaret Thatcher, and the overwhelming majority of them regarded her with trust and devotion. For them, in a phrase that they would shortly help return with interest to its originator, she was the Mother of Battles. Now she had been replaced by a man many of them had not even heard of. Even some of Mr Major's Tory colleagues doubted whether he had sufficient experience to be a suitable war leader, and these anxieties were bound to be shared by the troops in the Gulf; it is important that fighting men about to go into action should have confidence in their political leaders.

Therefore, John Major, a civilian by temperament as by training, had to stamp his personality on an unfamiliar situation at a hazardous juncture. He succeeded. In terms of the Alliance, the key factor was his rapport with President Bush. Here, Prime Minister Major had the crucial asset of continuity in the person of (shortly to be Sir) Charles Powell, well known to all the leading figures in the Bush Administration. He had one further advantage. President Bush respected Margaret Thatcher. During his years in the limbo of the Vice-Presidency, she had treated him well and shown him a high regard. But their relationship was still an uneasy one.

George Bush found it easier to admire Margaret Thatcher from a distance than to work with her in close proximity. He had no desire to follow Ronald Reagan's example and play leading man to her leading lady, with the lady usually managing to secure top billing. As part of his attempt to establish an independent political identity, Mr Bush had sought to distance himself from Margaret Thatcher. Above all, he wanted to make it clear to her as to everybody else that he and not she was the Leader of the Western World. There was also a contrast of temperaments. The President did not relish her mode of discourse; his preference was for a much more relaxed, under-stated, laconic style. Their working method differed in another respect. Mr Bush enjoyed telephoning his fellow world statesmen, and would sometimes 'phone for little more than a chat. But Mrs Thatcher, though she was happy enough to talk when he called her, seemed to feel that as a mere head of government, she should not take the initiative in telephoning a head of state – a deferential reserve similar to the one which led Churchill to call Roosevelt 'Mr President'. Some of her staff felt that their dealings would have been easier if she had been more willing to pick up the 'phone.

The President found himself much more in tune with the new Prime Minister. From the start, it was 'John' and 'George', and Mr Major had a successful visit to Washington in late December. Because of time pressures, Mrs Thatcher had never spent a night at Camp David, the President's country residence in Maryland. But Mr Major did, even though the weather was too bad to permit a helicopter journey. The President and the Prime Minister made the two-hour drive in a stretched limousine, accompanied by Brent Scowcroft and Charles Powell, who had to take notes while sitting on flap seats. At Camp David, the talks continued in a casual atmosphere, inters-persed by family games. By the time the British party returned to London, a partnership had ripened into a friendship.

Mr Major also had a successful visit to the Gulf. He told a group of servicemen that there was only one solution to the conflict; Saddam Hussein had to leave Kuwait otherwise, he continued, in a tone of sombre authority: 'We shall ask you and your friends to remove him.' During the six-month phoney war from August until January, there had been a steady build-up of *matériel* in the Gulf, and also a steady build-up of doubt. Could the Alliance survive the strain of delay? Would the high-technology weaponry work in desert condi-tions? How would the Americans perform? After all, they had only managed to beat Grenada and Panama one–nil after extra time, and there were fears that the United States forces had still not emerged from the valley of the shadow of Vietnam. Once the fighting started, the doubts vanished. The weapons worked exactly as they was supposed to, and the Americans fought exactly as they were supposed to, with General Schwarzkopf proving himself a worthy successor to MacArthur and Patton. The war was an unqualified success; the problems began once the fighting ceased.

The Allies had never clarified their strategic objectives. This was not wholly President Bush's fault. Throughout the conflict, he had had to operate within constraints: the sensitivities of certain members of the Alliance; the terms of the UN resolution; and the fickleness of American domestic opinion. In most wars, heightened antagonism leads to enhanced war aims, and the winning side seizes the opportunities of victory to secure them. Not in the Gulf. From first to last, the Allies' goals never extended beyond the liberation of Kuwait and the dismantling of certain Iraqi weaponry. Although there was a powerful argument that no victory which left Saddam in place could properly be described as such, the Allies never committed themselves to his overthrow.

Since the war ended, there have been erroneous suggestions that General Schwarzkopf was reluctant to agree to a cease-fire, and had wanted to press on to Baghdad. In fact, Generals Schwarzkopf and Powell made a joint recommendation in favour of a cease-fire, on the grounds that it would be wrong to continue the fighting, as there were no military targets left. The British, who politely – and unavailingly – questioned this decision, found it hard to understand this display of chivalry. Some British officials even entertained the unworthy suspicion that the two Generals had seen an overwhelming public relations advantage in ending the ground war in exactly one hundred hours.

Mrs Thatcher has let it be known that she would have vigorously opposed any cease-fire, and that she wanted Saddam Hussein dead – or if alive, a prisoner to be put on trial. Given her standing with American public opinion, she would obviously have been in a strong position to put pressure on the President. Even so, it cannot be taken for granted that she would have had her way, especially against the American Generals' opposition.

There was never any possibility that Mr Major could have changed the Allies' rules of engagement. There was a tacit assumption among the Allied high command that Saddam could not survive an Iraqi defeat. It transpired, alas, that this was based on an underestimation of the machinery of terror which he and his Takriti associates could commanded. Saddam could still crush his own people, including the Kurds and the Southern Shias.

As President Bush later insisted, he had never encouraged the Kurds to rebel against Saddam, but the President looked defensive and uneasy when he was making that claim, and with good reason. He had expressed his hope that the Iraqi people would rid themselves of Saddam, and the Kurds could hardly be blamed for believing that if they rose in revolt, the Allies would grant them the status of co-belligerents. The Kurds did take the field, and were quickly defeated. Such was their terror of Saddam that millions of Kurds fled to inhospitable mountain regions, where there was neither food nor shelter. As the Allied world was greeting its returning heroes and preparing to celebrate a triumph, it learned via television that as a seeming consequence of our victory, millions of Kurds faced a choice: Saddam's torture chambers, or death from hunger and cold.

In the United States, the reaction was surprisingly muted; when it comes to the non-Jewish inhabitants of the Middle East, the American public's sympathy is not easily aroused. Apart from a few prohibitions on the use of warplanes, the Bush Administration did little, and seemed to be telling the Kurds to make their peace with Saddam Hussein. John Major decided that this was wholly unsatisfactory, and that the West had to respond.

There followed a remarkable initiative. The British Government pursued a bold policy, which involved military risks as well as diplomatic ones; it appears to have been a resounding success, largely due to the efforts of John Major, assisted by Douglas Hurd. Initially, Mr Major attempted to persuade the Americans of the need to act, but encountered considerable scepticism. He then decided that he would have to manoeuvre the Americans into changing their policy, and that to achieve this, he would need European help. After undertaking preliminary diplomacy, he used an EEC foreign-affairs council in Luxembourg on 15 and 16 April to float his plan for a 'safe haven' in Northern Iraq where the Kurds could live unmolested, under Allied protection. He received a wide measure of support from the Europeans, and in particular from the Germans.

In Washington, the initial reaction to safe havens was dismissive. The Administration declared its lack of interest in the scheme, and its extreme lack of enthusiasm for being bounced by the British and the Europeans. One Washington spokesman declared that the safe haven policy was 'dead'. He was wrong. It had only just been born.

The pressure from the UK and the EEC was applied at the right moment. Under the impact of television, American opinion was wavering. Within a few days the Administration had agreed to a modified version of the safe haven plan, which quickly became indistinguishable from the original safe haven policy. In military terms, this could have been a hazardous operation, for it involved a virtual invasion of Northern Iraq with only a fraction of the overwhelming strength which General Schwarzkopf had had available a few weeks earlier. The Iraqis, however, understood the consequences that would follow from any attack on Anglo-American forces; they had no stomach for a resumption of the war.

The safe haven policy has succeeded in its first objective: ensuring the survival of the Iraqi Kurds. There are obvious problems, however. As long as Saddam Hussein rules in Baghdad, no haven unprotected by Allied forces could possibly be safe. It would appear, therefore, that the British and Americans are committed to an indefinite deployment in Northern Iraq. However, by threatening Iraq with virtual dismemberment, it must also increase the pressure on Saddam: if the Kurds gain their safe haven, he may lose his.

The longer-term future of the safe haven policy is unclear. There are continuing risks, as in any open-ended military commitment. But the West had incurred a moral obligation to the Kurds, reinforced by the claims of humanity, and our own self-respect. We had to act. John Major saw this earlier and more clearly than any other Western statesman, and is entitled to great credit for doing so. The entire safe haven episode is a conclusive rebuttal of the charge of indecisiveness.

The Persona Problem

There was one irony about John Major's first weeks in office. Before he became Premier, there had been a general assumption that his two strongest attributes were his grasp of domestic policy, and his political skills. Meanwhile, he himself shared the doubts as to whether he was the right man to take over the premiership in the middle of a war. After a few weeks, those expectations had been virtually reversed.

He had handled the war well. Some Tories regretted the absence of Mrs Thatcher's triumphalist tone, but even most of them were prepared to acknowledge that Mr Major's style had been more in tune with the public mood. At the beginning of the war, Mr Major made a broadcast to the nation, which was generally adjudged to have been a great success, and to have captured the public mood. His tone was sombre, yet resolute. The new PM gave the impression that the decision to commit our hopes to battle weighed heavily upon him – but also that he was determined to see the matter through.

John Major had added the words 'God Bless' to the final draft of his address. One or two of his advisers protested: as one of them said 'I told him I thought that to say "God Bless" was naff, and would spoil the impact.' Mr Major courteously ignored the advice – and the official who had given it said that he found the words 'God Bless', as delivered, very moving.

The disappointments had come on the domestic front, both on policy and on politics. As regards policy, it would be unfair to blame Mr Major. He inherited two principal problems: inflation and the community charge. On inflation, there was little he could do. The counter-measures were in place; the PM – and everyone else – just had to wait for them to work. In the case of the community charge, a new policy was needed.

The community charge died with Margaret Thatcher. From the first moment, John Major was aware that there had to be a new policy – and that it would be difficult to minimize the embarrassment involved. The interval between his accession and the introduction of a replacement for the community charge could resemble the Retreat from Moscow. In the end, it turned out to be a surprisingly well-conducted and quickly-executed retreat. The early Cabinet committee discussions on a replacement were difficult. The Chief Whip, Richard Ryder, had warned that many backbenchers would be unhappy if the Government discarded the basic principle of the community charge – that all adults should pay something. Equally, there were widespread fears that if a property-based tax were reintroduced, many of the Party's supporters would suffer – and protest. The PM himself was briefly tempted to search for some hybrid solution, involving elements both of the community charge and of a property tax, but he quickly became convinced that such a scheme would maximize administrative complexity, and minimize political advantages. Michael Heseltine can claim most of the credit for devising the council tax, though the phrase itself came from Jeremy Sinclair of Saatchi and Saatchi.

The success of the council tax can best be judged by the speed with which the issue has ceased to be a political liability for the Government. The banding system has helped to minimize protests from Tory households, as has Labour's promise of a full-scale return to the rates. But even before the council tax was introduced, Mr Major had acted to alleviate the burden of local taxation.

Nigel Lawson and many Treasury officials had opposed the community charge because they feared that it would undermine the revenue-raising powers of local authorities, so leading to a shift in the tax burden from local to central government. Events had proved them right; John Major went even further. In the run-up to the Budget, he pressed for the introduction of a rebate to all community-charge payers, to be financed by an increase in VAT. Norman Lamont was deeply unenthusiastic about this, as any Chancellor would be. But the ex-Chancellor in No. 10 gently insisted. Reluctantly, Mr Lamont agreed. Although it was Mr Major's policy, No. 10 has never tried to take the credit for the £140 rebate.

During eleven and a half years in the House, John Major had earned a considerable reputation as a politician. However, this related to his powers of judgement and to his performance in small groups; he had never developed a command of the public art of politics. During his time as Chief Secretary, Robin Oakley of *The Times* had described how 'he commands the Commons without having to raise his voice.'[6] Within two years, however, Mr Major found himself in a job where it was much harder to command the Commons; he had still not learnt to raise his voice. The problem went deeper. Long before they reach high office, almost all politicians develop a public persona. This has the obvious danger of insincerity; with characters such as Harold Wilson, Denis Healey and Roy Hattersley it has often been impossible to tell which is the mask, and which the masquerade. But without such a persona, it is almost impossible to convey private strengths to a public audience.

John Major became Prime Minister with no public persona. He has therefore found the greatest difficulty in projecting himself to a larger audience. Those that have heard him speak to smallish audiences know that John Major is a relaxed, witty speaker with a good turn of phrase, who can move easily from humour to serious-

---

6 *The Times*, 14 December 1988.

ness. Over the years, many of those who have encountered him at such gatherings came away with the impression that this was a first-rate speaker. It is a quality which he finds hard to recapture in the Commons, or at a Party Conference. On such occasions, his voice seems to lose its resonance and his command of language goes. He tends to repeat phrases, and dissipate any forcefulness in his text by interpolating qualifying phrases and unnecessary adjectives or adverbs.

Equally, the private John Major comes across as a natural leader of men. He may have a gentle, affable manner, with absolutely no side or self-importance, but he speaks incisively and with natural author-ity. For the past twenty-five years, without overt self-assertion, he has generally emerged as the leader of any group in which he took part. That so many of his colleagues not only voted for him as Party Leader, but did so with such enthusiasm and confidence, is testimony enough to the leadership qualities as recognized by those who know him best.

Without ever seeking to do so, he also has the power to inspire those around him. When in a post-prandial mood, a surprising number of John Major's parliamentary colleagues can become quite misty-eyed in their enthusiasm for him. He will never arouse the same intensity of feeling as Margaret Thatcher did (for one thing, he is the wrong sex) but even pre-prandially, there are a large number of loyal and devoted Major partisans. Yet he has not begun to find a way of communicating the qualities which arouse that partisanship to the television audience. So the man who in large measure owed his election to his supposed political skills now has the task of developing a different set of political skills.

During Mr Major's first weeks in office, the absence of a persona had one other consequence: those around him noticed an excessively thin-skinned reaction to press criticism. Most politicians are much more wounded by hostile press notices than they admit, but the majority of them also learn to affect an air of insouciance, and to develop a leathery carapace. John Major was an exception, however. This was partly due to the fact that – his FO days excepted – he had received a favourable press over the years, and had never been exposed to the press's capacity for inaccuracy, unfairness and malice. For a time, his resentments grew, especially against some of the sillier critics in supposedly Conservative newspapers. He could not understand why, when there was so much going on in the world, the press seemed principally preoccupied with the number of 'O' levels he had acquired thirty years ago. He found it hard to come to terms with the media's interest in his private life, especially when that interest took the form of lies and calumny.

As soon as John Major became Prime Minister, rumours started spreading about his private life. He was credited with at least one mistress, who was variously described as a dressmaker, a cook, or a black Labour councillor in Lambeth. There was no truth in any of this, but it consumed almost as many Fleet St man-hours as the Gulf war had. For weeks, the tabloids camped outside the flat of one suspect. One senior figure in the BBC who, at that stage, had never met either of the Majors, would assert with absolute confidence at the dinner tables of London that the Majors' marriage was a shell. Similar rumours were even discussed at a *Times* leader conference. Norma Major reacted to all this with amusement. John Major did not. He was furious at these attempts to pollute his family life, and this unquestionably – and understandably – exacerbated the problem of thin-skinnedness. Ironically enough, it was *Private Eye*, a magazine which has never been noted for playing down scandal, which first gave the rumours extensive coverage – and dismissed them with contempt as utterly baseless.

It would be foolish, however, to overestimate the seriousness of the persona problem. It appears to affect his dealings with the political classes far more than his relationship with the wider public. When it comes to understanding public opinion, the political classes suffer from two defects. First, most of their social dealings are with fellow obsessives; they therefore find it hard to understand the mental processes of those for whom politics is a peripheral irrelevance. Second, the political classes are inveterate in their search for excitement. They resemble a gourmet who samples half-a-dozen cuisines in one week, and who is constantly searching for new sensations to titillate his palate. But most of the plain people of England still eat more or less the same plain food every day. They also distrust exciting politicians. As Disraeli said: 'The British people, being subject to fogs, and possessing a powerful middle calss require grave statesmen.'[7]

The public generally regarded Margaret Thatcher with much more respect than affection. She also enjoyed much more electoral success than electoral popularity. Her personality had never been such an overwhelming asset with the majority of voters as it was with her own

---

7 R Blake, *Disraeli*, (1965) p. 766

passionate supporters, and by 1990, Mrs Thatcher had become an electoral liability to her Party. Equally, the early opinion poll evidence suggests that John Major has one great asset with the voters: he is not Margaret Thatcher.

Epilogue

As of May 1991, John Major had good grounds for optimism about his own chances of re-election. Even in the depths of the recession, the Labour Party had only a slender lead in the opinion polls, and though Mr Major's Treasury team were unenthusiastic about the prospects for a 1991 Election, they were increasingly confident that they would be able to demonstrate clear signs of recovery by the spring of 1992.

However, the Tory Party's political position seemed more fragile than the opinion polls would suggest. The Monmouth by-election was lost to Labour with a twelve per cent swing, and the Conservatives also did badly in the local government elections. Labour were particularly effective at exploiting – and creating – the electorate's anxieties about the NHS. Nor had John Major himself succeeded in translating popularity into authority. The voters liked their new Prime Minister; many of them still did not feel that they knew him. That is something Mr Major intends to rectify over the next few months.

Here this provisional assessment of John Major must end with a provisional conclusion. In this author's opinion, John Major's beliefs, values and personality are in tune with the temper of the times, as is his Party's approach to Government. He now has the opportunity to stamp his imprint on the 1990s as decisively as – if less dramatically than – Margaret Thatcher stamped hers on the 1980s.

Appendix 1

According to the Major campaign's records, 41 MPs worked in John Major's campaign. Their names are as follows:

James Arbuthnot MP
Graham Bright MP
David Davis MP
Sir Anthony Grant MP
Robert Hayward MP
Michael Howard MP
Robert Jones MP
Peter Lilley MP
David Maclean MP
Francis Maude MP
Sir Gerry Neale MP
Cecil Parkinson MP
Michael Stern MP
David Waddington MP
Jacques Arnold MP
Sir William Clark MP
Eric Forth MP
John Gummer MP
Maureen Hicks MP
Robert G Hughes MP

Norman Lamont MP
Sir Nicholas Lyell MP
John Maples MP
David Mellor MP
Tony Newton MP
Richard Ryder MP
Norman Tebbit MP
David Wilshire MP
Nicholas Bennett MP
Anthony Coombs MP
Cecil Franks MP
William Hague MP
Terence Higgins MP
Michael Jack MP
Ian Lang MP
John MacGregor MP
David Martin MP
Andrew Mitchell MP
James Paice MP
Gillian Shephard MP
Donald Thompson MP

There is one further name which could also be added: Mrs Margaret Thatcher.

Epilogue

As of May 1991, John Major had good grounds for optimism about his own chances of re-election. Even in the depths of the recession, the Labour Party had only a slender lead in the opinion polls, and though Mr Major's Treasury team were unenthusiastic about the prospects for a 1991 Election, they were increasingly confident that they would be able to demonstrate clear signs of recovery by the spring of 1992.

However, the Tory Party's political position seemed more fragile than the opinion polls would suggest. The Monmouth by-election was lost to Labour with a twelve per cent swing, and the Conservatives also did badly in the local government elections. Labour were particularly effective at exploiting – and creating – the electorate's anxieties about the NHS. Nor had John Major himself succeeded in translating popularity into authority. The voters liked their new Prime Minister; many of them still did not feel that they knew him. That is something Mr Major intends to rectify over the next few months.

Here this provisional assessment of John Major must end with a provisional conclusion. In this author's opinion, John Major's beliefs, values and personality are in tune with the temper of the times, as is his Party's approach to Government. He now has the opportunity to stamp his imprint on the Nineties as decisively as – if less dramatically than – Margaret Thatcher stamped hers on the 1980s.

Index

L

Labour Party 1, 8, 11–13, 15, 18, 28, 31, 39, 48, 60, 86–7, 90, 91, 103, 114, 128, 155, 181, 184, 212, 214, 219, 228–9, 231, 233–4, 236, 240, 242, 259, 265, 292, 296, 303, 308
Laguerre, Barbara 216
Laker, Jim 210
Lambeth Borough Council 214, 227–36, 240, 255
  Ferndale Ward 227, 236
  Housing Committee 231–3, 235, 236
Lamont, Norman vii, viii, 35, 37, 74–5, 99–100, 119, 122, 126, 130–2, 136, 138, 141, 145, 150, 159–65, 168, 172, 177, 187, 193, 275, 284, 291, 303, 307
Lancaster, Burt 216
Lang, Ian 167, 177, 251, 257, 307
Larkhall Ward, Brixton 214
Law, Bonar 85, 185
Laud, Derek 175
Lawson, Dominic 88
Lawson, Nigel 4, 7, 8, 18, 27, 29, 31, 63, 64, 88, 99, 103, 104, 107, 128, 156–7, 184, 193, 255, 259, 263–4, 269, 271–2, 274, 281, 284–6, 288–90, 303
  and Thatcher 48–59, 60–2
  fall of 72–5, 78
Layfield, Sir Frank 14
Lee, John 253
Leigh, Edward 153–4, 181
Lennox-Boyd, Mark 72–3, 77–80, 83–6, 101, 105, 108, 185
Le Pen, Jean-Marie 20
Liberal Party 1–2, 86, 92, 218
Lilley, Peter 74, 115, 119, 122, 130–1, 145, 150, 162, 164, 167, 177, 245, 291, 307
Limehouse Declaration 1
Lipton, Colonel Marcus 212–13
Livingstone, Ken 234
Lloyd, Marie 199
Lloyd, Peter 253
Lloyd George, David 1, 57, 66, 260
London County Council (LCC) 213
Louis XIV 15, 20
Lucas, Jean 227, 235, 236–7, 244
Lyell, Sir Nicholas 252, 307

M

McAlpine, Lord Alastair 80, 107, 184
MacArthur, General Douglas 299
MacFarlane, Sir Neil 37
MacGregor, John 118–25, 138, 141, 177, 307
Mackay, John 257
Mackay, Lord James 118, 154
Maclean, David 168, 307
Macleod, Iain 67–9, 222–3
Macmillan, Harold, Earl of Stockton 4, 38–9, 60, 65–9, 94, 222, 248
Macmillan, Maurice 66
Madrid summit *see under* EEC
Mail on Sunday 189
Major, Elizabeth (JM's daughter) 231, 247